T0189409

Lecture Notes in Artificial Intelligence   13068

Subseries of Lecture Notes in Computer Science

More information about this subseries at http://www.springer.com/series/1244

Ildar Batyrshin · Alexander Gelbukh ·
Grigori Sidorov (Eds.)

Advances in
Soft Computing

20th Mexican International Conference
on Artificial Intelligence, MICAI 2021
Mexico City, Mexico, October 25–30, 2021
Proceedings, Part II

 Springer

Editors
Ildar Batyrshin 🆔
Instituto Politécnico Nacional
Centro de Investigación en Computación
Mexico City, Mexico

Alexander Gelbukh 🆔
Instituto Politécnico Nacional
Centro de Investigación en Computación
Mexico City, Mexico

Grigori Sidorov 🆔
Instituto Politécnico Nacional
Centro de Investigación en Computación
Mexico City, Mexico

ISSN 0302-9743   ISSN 1611-3349 (electronic)
Lecture Notes in Artificial Intelligence
ISBN 978-3-030-89819-9   ISBN 978-3-030-89820-5 (eBook)
https://doi.org/10.1007/978-3-030-89820-5

LNCS Sublibrary: SL7 – Artificial Intelligence

This Springer imprint is published by the registered company Springer Nature Switzerland AG
The registered company address is: Gewerbestrasse 11, 6330 Cham, Switzerland

Preface

The Mexican International Conference on Artificial Intelligence (MICAI) is a yearly international conference series that has been organized by the Mexican Society for Artificial Intelligence (SMIA) since 2000. MICAI is a major international artificial intelligence (AI) forum and the main event in the academic life of the country's growing AI community.

MICAI conferences publish high-quality papers in all areas of AI and its applications. The proceedings of the previous MICAI events have been published by Springer in its Lecture Notes in Artificial Intelligence (LNAI) series, vol. 1793, 2313, 2972, 3789, 4293, 4827, 5317, 5845, 6437, 6438, 7094, 7095, 7629, 7630, 8265, 8266, 8856, 8857, 9413, 9414, 10061, 10062, 10632, 10633, 11288, 11289, 11835, 12468 and 12469. Since its foundation in 2000, the conference has been growing in popularity and improving in quality.

The proceedings of MICAI 2021 are published in two volumes. The first volume, Advances in Computational Intelligence, contains 30 papers structured into three sections:

– Machine and Deep Learning
– Image Processing and Pattern Recognition
– Evolutionary and Metaheuristic Algorithms

The second volume, Advances in Soft Computing, contains 28 papers structured into two sections:

– Natural Language Processing
– Intelligent Applications and Robotics

The two-volume set will be of interest for researchers in all fields of artificial intelligence, students specializing in related topics, and for the public in general interested in recent developments in AI.

The conference received for evaluation 129 submissions from authors in 22 countries: Algeria, Argentina, Bangladesh, Belgium, Brazil, Canada, Colombia, Costa Rica, Croatia, Cuba, the Czech Republic, India, Japan, Kazakhstan, Mexico, the Netherlands, Peru, Portugal, Russia, Spain, Sweden, and the USA. From these submissions, 58 papers were selected for publication in these two volumes after a peer-review process carried out by the international Program Committee. The acceptance rate was 45%.

The international Program Committee consisted of 188 experts from 16 countries: Brazil, Colombia, France, Iran, Ireland, Japan, Kazakhstan, Malaysia, Mexico, Pakistan, Philippines, Portugal, Russia, Spain, the UK, and the USA.

MICAI 2021 was honored by the presence of renowned experts who gave excellent keynote lectures:

– Fabio A. González O., Universidad Nacional de Colombia, Colombia
– Eyke Hüllermeier, Paderborn University, Germany

- Piero P. Bonissone, Piero P. Bosissone Analytics, USA
- Marta R. Costa-Jussà, Universitat Politècnica de Catalunya, Spain
- Hugo Jair Escalante, National Institute of Astrophysics, Optics and Electronics, Mexico
- María Vanina Martínez, Consejo Nacional de Investigaciones Científicas y Técnicas, Argentina

Five workshops were held jointly with the conference:

- SC-AIS 2021: International Workshop on Soft Computing and Advances in Intelligent Systems
- WILE 2021: 14th Workshop on Intelligent Learning Environments
- HIS 2021: 14th Workshop of Hybrid Intelligent Systems
- CIAPP 2021: 3rd Workshop on New Trends in Computational Intelligence and Applications
- WIDSSI 2021: 7th International Workshop on Intelligent Decision Support Systems for Industry

The authors of the following papers received the Best Paper Awards based on the paper's overall quality, significance, and originality of the reported results:

- First place: "Multi-objective Release Plan Rescheduling in Agile Software Development," by Abel García Nájera, Saúl Zapotecas Martínez, Jesús Guillermo Falcón Cardona, and Humberto Cervantes, Mexico
- Second place: "Deep Learning Approach for Aspect-Based Sentiment Analysis of Restaurants Reviews in Spanish," by Bella-Citlali Martínez-Seis, Obdulia Pichardo-Lagunas, Sabino Miranda-Jiménez, Israel-Josafat Perez-Cazares, and Jorge-Armando Rodriguez-González, Mexico
- Second place: "Question Answering for Visual Navigation in Human-centered Environments," by Daniil Kirilenko, Alexey Kovalev, Evgeny Osipov, and Aleksandr Panov, Russia
- Third place: "Sign Language Translation using Multi Context Transformer," by M Badri Narayanan, Mahesh Bharadwaj K, Nithin G R, Dhiganth Rao Padamnoor, and Vineeth Vijayaraghavan, India
- Third place: "Comparing Machine Learning based Segmentation Models on Jet Fire Radiation Zones," by Carmina Pérez, Adriana Palacios, Gilberto Ochoa-Ruiz, Christian Mata, Miguel Gonzalez-Mendoza, and Luis Eduardo Falcón-Morales, Mexico/Spain

We want to thank all the people involved in the organization of this conference: the authors of the papers published in these two volumes – it is their research work that gives value to the proceedings – and the organizers for their work. We thank the reviewers for their great effort spent on reviewing the submissions, the Track Chairs for their hard work, and the Program and Organizing Committee members.

We are deeply grateful to the Center for Computing Research at the Instituto Politécnico Nacional (Mexico) for their warm hospitality to MICAI 2021. We would like to express our gratitude to the General Director, Arturo Reyes Sandoval, the Secretary of Research and Postgraduate Studies, Heberto Balmori Ramírez, the

Director of Research, Laura Arreola Mendoza, the Director of Postgraduate Studies, Luis Gil Cisneros, and the Director of the Center for Computing Research, Marco Antonio Moreno Ibarra.

The entire submission, reviewing, and selection process, as well as preparation of the proceedings, was supported by the EasyChair system (www.easychair.org). Last but not least, we are grateful to Springer for their patience and help in the preparation of these volumes.

October 2021

Ildar Batyrshin
Alexander Gelbukh
Grigori Sidorov

Conference Organization

MICAI 2021 was organized by the Mexican Society for Artificial Intelligence (SMIA, Sociedad Mexicana de Inteligencia Artificial) in collaboration with the Center for Computing Research, Instituto Politécnico Nacional.

The MICAI series website is www.MICAI.org. The website of the Mexican Society for Artificial Intelligence, SMIA, is www.SMIA.mx. Contact options and additional information can be found on these websites.

Conference Committee

General Chair

Félix A. Castro Espinoza   Universidad Autónoma del Estado de Hidalgo, Mexico

Program Chairs

Ildar Batyrshin	CIC-IPN, Mexico
Alexander Gelbukh	CIC-IPN, Mexico
Grigori Sidorov	CIC-IPN, Mexico

Workshop Chair

Hiram Ponce   Universidad Panamericana, Mexico

Tutorials Chair

Roberto Antonio Vázquez   Universidad La Salle, Mexico
Espinoza de los
Monteros

Doctoral Consortium Chairs

Miguel Gonzalez-Mendoza	Tecnológico de Monterrey, Mexico
Juan Martínez-Miranda	CICESE Research Center, Mexico

Keynote Talks Chair

Noé Alejandro   Centro Nacional de Investigación y Desarrollo
Castro-Sánchez   Tecnológico, Mexico

Publication Chair

Hiram Ponce   Universidad Panamericana, Mexico

Financial Chairs

Oscar Herrera-Alcántara   Universidad Autónoma Metropolitana, Mexico
Lourdes   Universidad Panamericana, Mexico
  Martínez-Villaseñor

Grant Chair

Félix A. Castro Espinoza   Universidad Autónoma del Estado de Hidalgo, Mexico

Local Organizing Committee

Marco Antonio Moreno   CIC-IPN, Mexico
  Ibarra
Eusebio Ricárdez Vazquez   CIC-IPN, Mexico
Elvia Cruz Morales   CIC-IPN, Mexico
Alejandra Ramos Porras   CIC-IPN, Mexico
Mauricio Sebastian Martín   CIC-IPN, Mexico
  Gascón
Jorge Benjamín Martell   CIC-IPN, Mexico
  Ponce de León
Cristian   CIC-IPN, Mexico
  Maldonado-Sifuentes
César Jesús Núñez-Prado   CIC-IPN, Mexico

Track Chairs

Natural Language Processing

Grigori Sidorov   CIC-IPN, Mexico

Machine Learning

Alexander Gelbukh   CIC-IPN, Mexico
Navonil Majumder   CIC-IPN, Mexico

Deep Learning

Hiram Ponce   Universidad Panamericana, Mexico

Evolutionary and Metaheuristic Algorithms

Roberto Antonio Vázquez   Universidad La Salle, Mexico
  Espinoza de los
  Monteros
Oscar Herrera-Alcántara   Universidad Autónoma Metropolitana, Mexico

Soft Computing

Miguel Gonzalez-Mendoza   Tecnológico de Monterrey, Mexico

Image Processing and Pattern Recognition

Lourdes Martínez-Villaseñor	Universidad Panamericana, Mexico

Robotics

Gilberto Ochoa-Ruiz	Tecnológico de Monterrey, Mexico

Intelligent Applications and Social Network Analysis

Iris Iddaly Méndez-Gurrola	Universidad Autónoma de Ciudad Juárez, Mexico

Other Artificial Intelligence Approaches

Nestor Velasco Bermeo	University College Dublin, Ireland
Gustavo Arroyo-Figueroa	Instituto Nacional de Electricidad y Energías Limpias, Mexico

Program Committee

Iskander Akhmetov	IICT, Kazakhstan
José David Alanís Urquieta	Carrera de Tecnologías de la Información y Comunicación Universidad Tecnológica de Puebla, Mexico
Giner Alor-Hernández	Instituto Tecnologico de Orizaba, Mexico
Joanna Alvarado-Uribe	Instituto Tecnologico y de Estudios Superiores de Monterrey, Mexico
Maaz Amjad	CIC IPN, Mexico
Jason Efraín Angel Gil	Instituto Politécnico Nacional, Mexico
Ignacio Arroyo-Fernández	Universidad Tecnológica de la Mixteca, Mexico
Gustavo Arroyo-Figueroa	Instituto Nacional de Electricidad y Energías Limpias, Mexico
Edgar Avalos-Gauna	Universidad Panamericana, Mexico
Fausto Antonio Balderas Jaramillo	Instituto Tecnológico de Ciudad Madero, Mexico
Alejandro Israel Barranco Gutiérrez	Instituto Tecnológico de Celaya, Mexico
Ramon Barraza	Universidad Autonoma de Ciudad Juarez, Mexico
Ari Yair Barrera-Animas	Tecnológico de Monterrey, Mexico
Ildar Batyrshin	Instituto Politecnico Nacional, Mexico
Gemma Bel-Enguix	UNAM, Mexico
Sara Besharati	Instituto Politécnico Nacional, Mexico
Rajesh Roshan Biswal	Tecnologico de Monterrey, Mexico
Vadim Borisov	National Research University "Moscow Power Engineering Institute", Smolensk, Russia
Monica Borunda	Instituto Nacional de Electricidad y Energías Limpias, Mexico

Alexander Bozhenyuk	Southern Federal University, Russia
Ramon F. Brena	Tecnologico de Monterrey, Mexico
Davide Buscaldi	LIPN, Université Paris 13, France
Sabur Butt	IPN Computing Research Center, Mexico
Hiram Calvo	Nara Institute of Science and Technology, Japan
Ruben Carino-Escobar	Instituto Nacional de Rehabilitación, Mexico
Felix Castro Espinoza	CITIS-UAEH, Mexico
Noé Alejandro Castro-Sánchez	Centro Nacional de Investigación y Desarrollo Tecnológico, Mexico
Hector Ceballos	Tecnologico de Monterrey, Mexico
Jaime Cerda Jacobo	Universidad Michoacana de San Nicolás de Hidalgo, Mexico
Ofelia Cervantes	Universidad de las Américas Puebla, Mexico
Haruna Chiroma	Federal College of Education Technical Gombe, Malaysia
Elisabetta Crescio	Instituto Tecnológico y de Estudios Superiores de Monterrey, Mexico
Laura Cruz	Instituto Tecnologico de Ciudad Madero, Mexico
Nareli Cruz Cortés	CIC-IPN, Mexico
Andre de Carvalho	University of São Paulo, Brazil
Jorge De La Calleja	Universidad Politécnica de Puebla, Mexico
Omar Arturo Domiguez Ramírez	UAEH, Mexico
Andrés Espinal	Universidad de Guanajuato, Mexico
Daniel Yacob Espinoza González	CIC-IPN, Mexico
Oscar Alejandro Esquivel Flores	UNAM, Mexico
Barbaro Ferro	BestS2S, Mexico
Karina Figueroa	Universidad Michoacana de San Nicolás de Hidalgo, Mexico
Denis Filatov	Sceptica Scientific Ltd, UK
Dora-Luz Flores	Universidad Autónoma de Baja California, Mexico
Juan Jose Flores	Universidad Michoacana, Mexico
Anilú Franco Árcega	UAEH, Mexico
Sofia N. Galicia-Haro	UNAM, Mexico
Vicente Garcia	Universidad Autónoma de Ciudad Juárez, Mexico
Leonardo Garrido	Tecnológico de Monterrey., Mexico
Alexander Gelbukh	Instituto Politécnico Nacional, Mexico
Claudia Gomez	Instituto Tecnolgico de Ciudad Madero, Mexico
Eduardo Gómez-Ramírez	Universidad La Salle, Mexico
Pedro Pablo Gonzalez	Universidad Autonoma Metropolitana, Mexico
Luis-Carlos González-Gurrola	Universidad Autonoma de Chihuahua, Mexico
Miguel Gonzalez-Mendoza	Tecnologico de Monterrey, Mexico
Gabriel Gonzalez-Serna	TecNM/CENIDET, Mexico

Fernando Gudiño	UNAM, Mexico
Rafael Guzman Cabrera	Universidad de Guanajuato, Mexico
Jorge Hermosillo	UAEM, Mexico
Yasmin Hernandez	Centro Nacional de Investigación y Desarrollo Tecnológico, Mexico
José Alberto Hernández	Universidad Autnoma del Estado de Morelos, Mexico
Betania Hernandez-Ocaña	Universidad Juárez Autónoma de Tabasco, Mexico
Oscar Herrera	UAM Azcapotzalco, Mexico
Laura Hervert-Escobar	Tecnologico de Monterrey, Mexico
Seyed Habib Hosseini Saravani	Instituto Politécnico Nacional, Mexico
Joel Ilao	De La Salle University, Philippines
Jorge Jaimes	Universidad Autónoma Metropolitana, Mexico
Olga Kolesnikova	Instituto Politécnico Nacional, Mexico
Nailya Kubysheva	Kazan Federal University, Russia
Angel Kuri-Morales	ITAM, Mexico
Carlos Lara-Alvarez	Centro de Investigación en Matemáticas, Mexico
José Antonio León-Borges	Universidad de Quintana Roo, Mexico
Victor Lomas-Barrie	UNAM, Mexico
Omar López Ortega	UAEH, Mexico
Gerardo Loreto	Instituto Tecnologico Superior de Uruapan, Mexico
Mykola Lukashchuk	Instituto Politécnico Nacional, Mexico
Yazmin Maldonado	Instituto Tecnológico de Tijuana, Mexico
Christian Efraín Maldonado Sifuentes	Tecnológico de Estudios Superiores de Cuautitlán Izcalli, Mexico
Jerusa Marchi	Federal University of Santa Catarina, Brazil
Aldo Márquez Grajales	Universidad Veracruzana, Mexico
Carolina Martín del Campo Rodríguez	CIC-IPN, Mexico
Lourdes Martínez	Universidad Panamericana, Mexico
Bella Citlali Martinez Seis	CINVESTAV-IPN, Mexico
Jose Martinez-Carranza	Instituto Nacional de Astrofísica, Óptica y Electrónica, Mexico
Juan Martínez-Miranda	Centro de Investigación Científica y de Educación Superior de Ensenada, Mexico
Iris Iddaly Méndez-Gurrola	Universidad Autónoma de Ciudad Juárez, Mexico
Efrén Mezura-Montes	University of Veracruz, Mexico
Sabino Miranda-Jiménez	INFOTEC, Mexico
Daniela Moctezuma	CONACYT - CentroGEO, Mexico
Saturnino Job Morales Escobar	Centro Universitario UAEM Valle de México, Mexico
Guillermo Morales-Luna	CINVESTAV-IPN, Mexico
Alicia Morales-Reyes	Instituto Nacional de Astrofisica, Optica y Electronica, Mexico
Masaki Murata	Tottori University, Japan
Antonio Neme	Universidad Nacional Autonoma de Mexico, Mexico

César Núñez	Centro de Investigación en Computación, Mexico
Gilberto Ochoa-Ruiz	ITESM, Guadalajara, Mexico
C. Alberto Ochoa-Zezatti	Universidad Autónoma de Ciudad Juárez, Mexico
Juan Carlos Olivares Rojas	Tecnológico Nacional de México/Instituto Tecnológico de Morelia, Mexico
José Luis Oliveira	University of Aveiro, Portugal
José Carlos Ortiz-Bayliss	Tecnológico de Monterrey, Mexico
Ismael Osuna-Galán	Universidad Politécnica de Chiapas, Mexico
Rushabh Patel	Children's Hospital of Philadelphia, USA
Karinaruby Perez Daniel	Universidad Panamericana, Mexico
Garibaldi Pineda García	University of Sussex, UK
Hiram Ponce	Universidad Panamericana, Mexico
Belem Priego-Sanchez	UAM Azcapotzalco, Mexico
Vicenc Puig	Universitat Politècnica de Catalunya, Mexico
José Federico Ramírez Cruz	Tecnológico Nacional de México/Instituto Tecnológico de Apizaco, Mexico
Tania Aglaé Ramírez Del Real	Universidad Politécnica de Aguascalientes, Mexico
Juan Ramirez-Quintana	Instituto Tecnológico de Chihuahua, Mexico
Jorge Reyes	Universidad Autónoma de Yucatán, Mexico
José A. Reyes-Ortiz	Universidad Autónoma Metropolitana, Mexico
Elva Lilia Reynoso Jardón	UACJ, Mexico
Gilberto Rivera	Universidad Autónoma de Ciudad Juárez, Mexico
Noel Enrique Rodriguez Maya	Instituto Tecnológico de Zitácuaro, Mexico
Katya Rodriguez-Vazquez	IIMAS-UNAM, Mexico
Ansel Y. Rodríquez González	Centro de Investigación Científica y de Educación Superior de Ensenada, Mexico
Alejandro Rosales	Tecnologico de Monterrey, Mexico
Alberto Rosales	National Politechnic Institute of Mexico, Mexico
Horacio Rostro Gonzalez	Universidad de Guanajuato, Mexico
Antonio Sanchez	Texas Christian University, USA
Angel Sanchez	University of Veracruz, Mexico
Luis Humberto Sánchez Medel	ITO, Mexico
Eddy Sánchez-Delacruz	Instituto Tecnológico Superior de Misantla, Mexico
Alejandro Santiago	Universidad Politécnica de Altamira, Mexico
Arsenii Shulikov	Instituto Politécnico Nacional, Mexico
Grigori Sidorov	CIC-IPN, Mexico
Rafaela Silva	UAM, Mexico
Efrain Solares	Autonomous University of Sinaloa, Mexico
Valery Solovyev	Kazan University, Russia
Juan Humberto Sossa Azuela	CIC-IPN, Mexico

Israel Tabarez	ITESM, Mexico
Antonio Jesús Tamayo Herrera	Universidad de Antioquia, Colombia
Eric S. Tellez	CONACyT - INFOTEC, Mexico
David Tinoco Varela	UNAM, Mexico
Nasim Tohidi	K. N. Toosi University of Technology, Iran
Aurora Torres	Universidad Autonoma de Aguascalientes, Mexico
Diego Uribe	Instituto Tecnologico de la Laguna, Mexico
José E. Valdés	CIC-IPN, Mexico
Jose Valdez	Instituto Politecnico Nacional, Mexico
Genoveva Vargas Solar	CNRS/LAFMIA, France
Nestor Velasco Bermeo	University College Dublin, Ireland
Juan Villegas-Cortez	UAM Azcapotzalco, Mexico
Yenny Villuendas-Rey	CIDETEC-IPN, Mexico
Saúl Zapotecas Martínez	UAM Cuajimalpa, Mexico
Alisa Zhila	NTENT, USA

Additional Reviewers

Ewin Cordoba
Raúl Dalí Cruz Morales
José Yaír Guzmán-Gaspar
Mukhtat Hamza
Nidiyare Hevia-Montiel
Andrey Labunets

Jesús-Adolfo Mejía-de-Dios
Erick Esteven Montelongo González
Alexandr Pak
Jose Fabian Paniagua Reyes
David Tinoco Varela
Gustavo Adolfo Vargas Hakim

Contents – Part II

Intelligent Applications and Robotics

Best Paper Award, Third Place

Contents – Part I

Best Paper Award, Third Place

Image Processing and Pattern Recognition

Evolutionary and Metaheuristic Algorithms

Best Paper Award, First Place

Natural Language Processing
Supervised

Supervised Machine Learning for Automatic Assessment of Free-Text Answers

Fabio Gomes Rocha[1,2] ⓘ, Guillermo Rodriguez[3(✉)] ⓘ,
Eli Emanuel F. Andrade[1,2], Adolfo Guimarães[1,2], Vitor Gonçalves[4] ⓘ,
and Rosimeri F. Sabino[5]

[1] Universidade Tiradentes, Aracaju, Sergipe, Brazil
eli.emanuel@souunit.com.br
[2] Instituto de Tecnologia e Pesquisa - ITP, Aracaju, Sergipe, Brazil
[3] ISISTAN (UNICEN-CONICET) Research Institute, Tandil, Bs. As., Argentina
guillermo.rodriguez@isistan.unicen.edu.ar
[4] CIEB, Instituto Politécnico de Bragança, Bragança, Portugal
vg@ipb.pt
[5] Universidade Federal de Sergipe, São Cristovão, Sergipe, Brazil
https://www.itp.org.br/pesquisa/laboratorios/LACIA

Abstract. The learning assessment seeks to collect data that allows for identifying learning gaps for teacher decision-making. Hence, teachers need to plan and select various assessment instruments that enable the verification of learning evolution. Considering that a more significant number of evaluation instruments and modalities increase the teachers' workload, the adoption of machine learning might support the assessing actions and amplify the potential of students' observation and follow-up. This article aims to analyze machine learning algorithms for automatic classification of free-text answers, i.e., evaluating descriptive questions written in Portuguese. We utilized a dataset of 9981 free-text answers for 17 questions. After pre-processing the data, we used eight classification algorithms. In conclusion, we highlight that the Logistic Regression, ExtraTrees, Random Forest, and Multi-layer Perceptron algorithms obtained results above 0.9 of F-score for both multi-class and binary classification.

Keywords: Learning assessment · Supervised machine learning · Multi-class classification · Free-text answers · Teacher decision making.

1 Introduction

Assessment in the learning process seeks to identify students' difficulties so that it is possible for the teacher to make adjustments as soon as possible. In this context, teachers need to plan and select various assessment instruments that allow for the verification of learning evolution, considering that a more significant number of assessment instruments and modalities increases the teacher's

I. Batyrshin et al. (Eds.): MICAI 2021, LNAI 13068, pp. 3–12, 2021.
https://doi.org/10.1007/978-3-030-89820-5_1

workload. Moreover, despite the importance of assessment, corrections are time-consuming to perform, especially when the answers are descriptive when the teacher must perform readings individually [1,2]. Thus, automated answer scoring emerged, which allows, based on various approaches, to carry out assessments in a practical and fast way by teachers.

With large-scale tests, the human effort requirement, which is utilized to evaluate students' replies to free-text questions, rose. They can score and analyze responses to free-text questions considerably more complete, pre-judged, and objective manner and in a much shorter time than human teachers, thanks to computer-aided automatic scoring systems. In the last few years, automated scoring systems for free-text questions have become significant and have developed dramatically [3].

Automated classification of responses for student assessment has been studied for decades. Proposed approaches include similarity-based answer grouping, clustering [4–6], rule-based classification or optimal answer models [7,8]. Similarity-based approaches manually define features that attempt to capture the similarity of responses at various levels [9–11].

Recently, deep learning has also been adapted for short answer classification, the difference being that the textual representation in space is learned by the [12] model itself. Thus, the adoption of machine learning might support the evaluative actions and provides an opportunity to expand the potential for student observation and monitoring.

In this sense, the objective of this work is to analyze potential algorithms that allow automatic classification of answers, i.e., evaluation of descriptive questions with a focus on content for the Portuguese language. To assess our goal, we used a dataset of 9981 free-text answers for 17 questions. After pre-processing the data, we obtained that the Logistic Regression, ExtraTrees, Random Forest, and Multi-layer Perceptron algorithms obtained results above 0.9 of F-score for both multi-class and binary classification.

The remainder of this paper is organized as follows. Section 2 presents the related works. Section 3 presents the methodology used in this work. Section 4 presents the results and discussion. Finally, in Sect. 5 we present our final considerations.

2   Related Work

Several research works have addressed the issue of automatic assessment of free-text answers. For instance, Galhardi, Barbosa, Souza and Brancher [13] developed an automatic classification system for short answer for Portuguese, they also elaborated a base, available in Kaggle, also adopted for the tests of this work. As a result, the authors obtained an accuracy of 69% in multi-class classification and 85% in binary classification.

Liu et al. [14] proposed a learning framework for automatic short answer scoring focusing on linguistic information extraction and accuracy modelling.

Already in the work of Lun et al. [15] the mDA-ASAS (Multiple Data Augmentation Strategies for improving performance on Automatic Short Answer

Scoring) was proposed, which seeks to learn the language representation combined with BERT (Bidirectional Encoder Representations of Transformers) that, according to the authors brings a significant gain to the evaluation process.

On the one hand, Tan et al. [16], automatic short answer scoring (ASAG) is a challenging task that aims to predict a score for a given student's answer. Thus, the authors adopted the two-layer graph network (GCN) to encode the undirected heterogeneous graph of all student responses.

On the other hand, Zhang, Lin, and Chi [17] exploited the deep belief networks (DBN) model for the response classification task. As a result, the exploitation of question models was identified, and deep learning models such as DBN can be productively applied to the ASAG task.

3 Our Methodology

One of the most significant aspects of the learning and teaching process is the evaluation of answers. Because the automatic evaluation of responses is critical, various systems have been developed in this digital era. Subjective responses are usually given in either short or extended form [18].

The research on automatic assessment frameworks is enormous, and various productions have recently been made available there. As a result, it is critical to accurately identify the type of question we are dealing with to move further. As a result, the goal of this section is to show our approach automatic grading long and descriptive answers to inqueries.

Figure 1 depicts our methodology for automated answers assessment. We have utilized the Python version 3.7.10 with the libraries NLTK for text processing and SKLearn for machine learning was used for this study. The data employed is from the Kaggle[1] database, consisting of 9,981 answers to 17 questions from the field of biology. The answers are categorized into four levels of correctness, with three parts with correct answers and one with errors or still deviations on the topic. Thus, 4,471 answers with a score of 0 (totally incorrect or with deviations), 2,332 answers with a score of 1, 1,884 answers with a score of 2, and 1,295 answers with a score of 3. When analyzing the binary classification (0 or 1), the dataset then becomes 5,511 positive answers and 4,471 negative answers.

For example, a question used to test Biology concepts is *"Qual a diferença entre a célula animal e a célula vegetal?"*, and the correct answer expected (reference) is *"A célula animal e vegetal apresentam formato diferenciado. A célula animal possui formato irregular, enquanto a célula vegetal apresenta uma forma fixa."*. Finally, a student' answer is *"A célula animal é composta por organelas iguais a da célula vegetal mas a célula vegetal tem diferentes mecanismos para sua sobrevivência vegetal"*.

For the pre-processing of the dataset responses, we used CountVectorizer (from Sckit-learn), accent removal, and a set of Portuguese stopwords provided by python's nltk package. For all models, SKLearn default values were used.

---

[1] https://www.kaggle.com/lucasbgalhardi/pt-asag-2018,ch1galhardi2018portuguese.

For the training of each question, Machine Learning classification models are used, as follows:

- Logistic Regression
- Support vector machine (SVC)
- AdaBoost
- ExtraTrees
- Random Forest
- Bernoulli Naive Bayes
- KNeighbors
- Multi-layer Perceptron.

For validation, the metrics collected are Precision, Accuracy, F1-score, and generating the ROC curve plot and the confusion matrix. The obtained results are then analyzed.

In particular, we investigated the following research questions (RQ):

- RQ1 Coverage: How many answers can be automatically assessed?
- RQ2 Accuracy: How accurate is the suggested assessment?

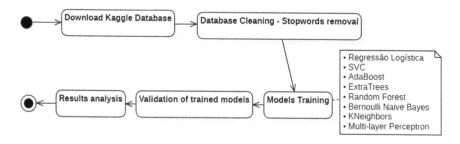

Fig. 1. Our methodology for automated answers assessment.

4   Experimental Results

This section aims to answer the above-mentioned research questions. The goal of our experiment was two-fold: first, to model assessment problem as a binary classification problem and second, to model assessment problem as a multi-class classification problem. As for the former, Table 2 shows the performance of the eight algorithms in terms of precision, accuracy and F1-score. Regarding the latter, Table 1 shows the performance of the eight algorithms in terms of the same set of metrics.

Table 1. Multi-class classification of grades (0 to 3).

Classification model	Precision	Accuracy	F1-score
Logistic Regression	0.92	0.686	0.919
SVC	0.873	0.685	0.869
Ada Boost	0.641	0.586	0.63
Extra Trees	0.981	0.686	0.981
Random Forest	0.981	0.688	0.981
BernoulliNB	0.768	0.653	0.751
KNeighbors	0.73	0.623	0.709
Multi-layer Perceptron	0.979	0.663	0.979

Table 2. Binary classification of grades.

Classification model	Precision	Accuracy	F1-score
Logistic Regression	0.957	0.884	0.957
SVC	0.949	0.877	0.948
Ada Boost	0.941	0.864	0.94
Extra Trees	0.993	0.883	0.993
Random Forest	0.993	0.883	0.993
BernoulliNB	0.916	0.87	0.915
KNeighbors	0.886	0.826	0.884
Multi-layer Perceptron	0.993	0.873	0.993

4.1 RQ1 Coverage: How Many Answers Can Be Automatically Assessed?

First, we collected the input data consisting of 9,981 answers to 17 questions from the field of Biology. The answers are categorized into four levels of correctness, with three parts with correct answers and one with errors or still deviations on the topic. Thus, 4,471 answers with a score of 0 (totally incorrect or with deviations), 2,332 answers with a score of 1, 1,884 answers with a score of 2, and 1,295 answers with a score of 3. When analyzing the binary classification (0 or 1), the dataset then becomes 5,511 positive answers and 4,471 negative answers. Our approach performed best in multi-class classification with Extra Trees, Random Forest and Multi-layer Perceptron, with 99.3% of precision. It is worth noting that all the algorithm received as input the same huge volume of data.

4.2 RQ2 Accuracy: How Accurate Is the Suggested Assessment?

We remarked that for multi-class scores, the algorithms Logistic Regression, ExtraTrees, RandomForest, and Multi-layer Perceptron obtained scores above

0.9. For binary classification, the exception is the KNeighbors algorithm, which had a score of 0.88. Thus, when analyzing the results, we can say that the algorithms that have better scores for multi-class classification also have similar results when applied to binary classification.

Next, we describe our findings from the algorithms' performance for binary classification. Figure 2 shows the confusion matrix and ROC curve for the AdaBoost algorithm (and the AUC = 0.92). Although the precision is moderate, the recall is considerably low (41%). As for BernoulliNB algorithm, Fig. 3 illustrates the confusion matrix and ROC curve (and the AUC = 0.92). Although the precision is slightly high, the recall is extremely low (35.6%). Figure 4 depicts the confusion matrix and ROC curve for the ExtraTrees algorithm (and the AUC = 1). Along the line of precision, the recall is considerably high (90.7%).

Regarding KNeighbors algorithm, Fig. 5 shows the confusion matrix and ROC curve (and the AUC = 0.97). Although the precision is moderate, the recall is considerably high (81.3%). Figure 6 depicts the confusion matrix and ROC curve for the Logistic Regression algorithm (and the AUC = 0.98). Although the precision is considerably high, the recall is moderate low (67.9%).

With regard to the Multi-Layer Perceptron algorithm, Fig. 7 shows the confusion matrix and ROC curve (and the AUC = 1). In the same line that precision, the recall is remarkably high (92.9%). Figure 8 illustrates the confusion matrix and ROC curve for the Random Forest algorithm (and the AUC = 1). In the same line that precision, the recall is considerably high (93.6%).

Finally, Fig. 9 shows the confusion matrix and ROC curve for the SVC algorithm (and the AUC = 0.98). Although the precision is extremely high, the recall is quite moderate (70.6%). To summarize, Random Forest outperformed the remaining algorithms in terms of Precision, Recall, F1-score, and accuracy.

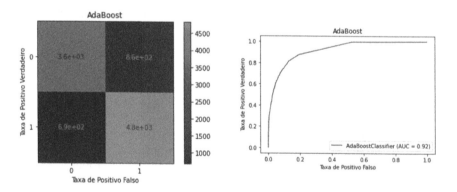

Fig. 2. Results of the AdaBoost algorithm (Confusion matrix and ROC curve).

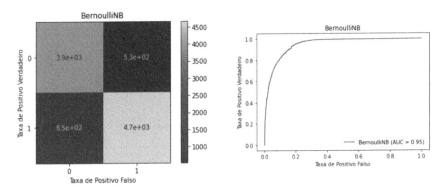

Fig. 3. Results of the BernoulliNB algorithm (Confusion matrix and ROC curve).

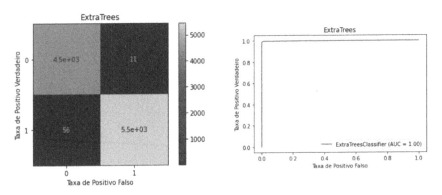

Fig. 4. Results of the ExtraTrees algorithm (Confusion matrix and ROC curve).

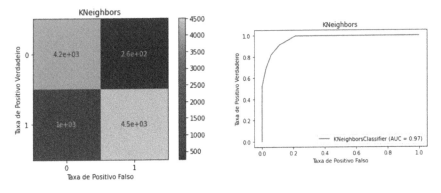

Fig. 5. Results of the KNeighbors algorithm (Confusion matrix and ROC curve).

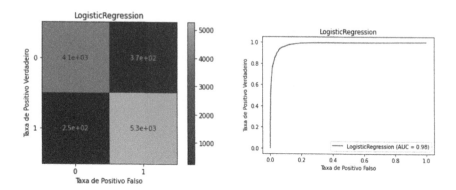

Fig. 6. Results of the Logistic Regression algorithm (Confusion matrix and ROC curve).

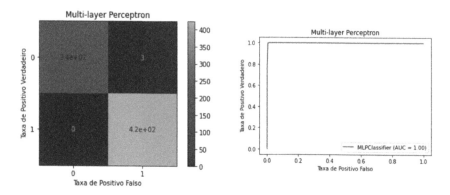

Fig. 7. Results of the Multi-layer Perceptron algorithm (Confusion matrix and ROC curve).

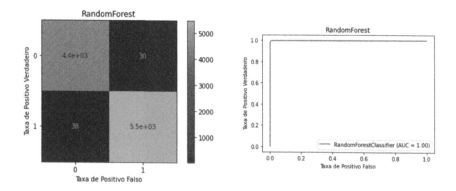

Fig. 8. Results of the Random Forest algorithm (Confusion matrix and ROC curve).

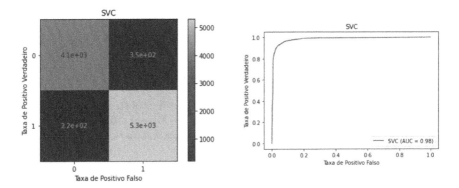

Fig. 9. Results of the SVC algorithm (Confusion matrix and ROC curve).

5   Conclusion and Future Work

We have explored the adoption of Machine Learning in the automatic classification of explanatory answers for the Portuguese language due to the sparse number of searches for this language. Thus, to identify the best algorithm for the task, the study was conducted for a Biology course in the Portuguese language. The tests were performed on the Sci-kit Learn library on the following algorithms: Logistic Regression, SVC, AdaBoost, ExtraTrees, Random Forest, Bernoulli Naive Bayes, KNeighbors, and Multi-layer Perceptron.

We noticed that for multi-class scores, the algorithms Logistic Regression, ExtraTrees, RandomForest, and Multi-layer Perceptron obtained scores above 0.9. For binary classification, the exception is the KNeighbors algorithm, which had a score of 0.88. Thus, when analyzing the results, we can say that the algorithms with better scores for multi-class classification also have similar results when applied to binary classification, and the same method can be used for both. To sum up, Random Forest is the optimal algorithm for automatic assessment of free-text answers in terms of Precision, Recall, F1-score, and accuracy.

As future work, we plan to apply our methodology in other domains and English and Spanish. Furthermore, we envision enriching our methodology with natural language processing and deep learning techniques to improve the effectiveness of the assessment.

References

1. dos Santos, J.C.A., Ribeiro, T., Favero, E., Queiroz, J.: Aplicação de um método lsa na avaliação automática de respostas discursivas. In: Anais do Workshop de Desafios da Computação Aplicada à Educação, pp. 10–19 (2012)
2. Passero, G., Haendchen Filho, A., Dazzi, R.: Avaliaçao do uso de métodos baseados em lsa e wordnet para correçao de questoes discursivas. In: Brazilian Symposium on Computers in Education (Simpósio Brasileiro de Informática na Educação-SBIE), vol. 27, p. 1136 (2016)

3. Çınar, A., Ince, E., Gezer, M., Yılmaz, Ö.: Machine learning algorithm for grading open-ended physics questions in Turkish. Educ. Inf. Technol. **25**(5), 3821–3844 (2020)
4. Basu, S., Jacobs, C., Vanderwende, L.: Powergrading: a clustering approach to amplify human effort for short answer grading. Trans. Assoc. Comput. Ling. **1**, 391–402 (2013)
5. Zehner, F., Sälzer, C., Goldhammer, F.: Automatic coding of short text responses via clustering in educational assessment. Educ. Psychol. Measur. **76**(2), 280–303 (2016)
6. Horbach, A., Pinkal, M.: Semi-supervised clustering for short answer scoring. In: Proceedings of the Eleventh International Conference on Language Resources and Evaluation (LREC 2018) (2018)
7. Leacock, C., Chodorow, M.: C-rater: automated scoring of short-answer questions. Comput. Humanit. **37**(4), 389–405 (2003)
8. Willis, A.: Using NLP to support scalable assessment of short free text responses. In: Proceedings of the Tenth Workshop on Innovative Use of NLP for Building Educational Applications, pp. 243–253 (2015)
9. Marvaniya, S., Saha, S., Dhamecha, T.I., Foltz, P., Sindhgatta, R., Sengupta, B.: Creating scoring rubric from representative student answers for improved short answer grading. In: Proceedings of the 27th ACM International Conference on Information and Knowledge Management, pp. 993–1002 (2018)
10. Sahu, A., Bhowmick, P.K.: Feature engineering and ensemble-based approach for improving automatic short-answer grading performance. IEEE Trans. Learn. Technol. **13**(1), 77–90 (2019)
11. Vij, S., Tayal, D., Jain, A.: A machine learning approach for automated evaluation of short answers using text similarity based on wordnet graphs. Wireless Pers. Commun. **111**(2), 1271–1282 (2020)
12. Filighera, A., Steuer, T., Rensing, C.: Fooling automatic short answer grading systems. In: Bittencourt, I.I., Cukurova, M., Muldner, K., Luckin, R., Millán, E. (eds.) AIED 2020. LNCS (LNAI), vol. 12163, pp. 177–190. Springer, Cham (2020). https://doi.org/10.1007/978-3-030-52237-7_15
13. Galhardi, L., Barbosa, C.R., de Souza, R.C.T., Brancher, J.D.: Portuguese automatic short answer grading. In: Brazilian Symposium on Computers in Education (Simpósio Brasileiro de Informática na Educação-SBIE), vol. 29, p. 1373 (2018)
14. Liu, T., Ding, W., Wang, Z., Tang, J., Huang, G.Y., Liu, Z.: Automatic short answer grading via multiway attention networks. In: Isotani, S., Millán, E., Ogan, A., Hastings, P., McLaren, B., Luckin, R. (eds.) AIED 2019. LNCS (LNAI), vol. 11626, pp. 169–173. Springer, Cham (2019). https://doi.org/10.1007/978-3-030-23207-8_32
15. Lun, J., Zhu, J., Tang, Y., Yang, M.: Multiple data augmentation strategies for improving performance on automatic short answer scoring. In: Proceedings of the AAAI Conference on Artificial Intelligence, vol. 34, pp. 13389–13396 (2020)
16. Tan, H., Wang, C., Duan, Q., Lu, Y., Zhang, H., Li, R.: Automatic short answer grading by encoding student responses via a graph convolutional network. In: Interactive Learning Environments, pp. 1–15 (2020)
17. Zhang, Y., Lin, C., Chi, M.: Going deeper: automatic short-answer grading by combining student and question models. User Model. User-Adap. Inter. **30**(1), 51–80 (2020)
18. Kapoor, B.S.J., Nagpure, S.M., Kolhatkar, S.S., Chanore, P.G., Vishwakarma, M.M., Kokate, R.B.: An analysis of automated answer evaluation systems based on machine learning. In: 2020 International Conference on Inventive Computation Technologies (ICICT), pp. 439–443. IEEE (2020)

Towards Multilingual Image Captioning Models that Can Read

Rafael Gallardo García[1(✉)] [iD], Beatriz Beltrán Martínez[1] [iD],
Carlos Hernández Gracidas[2] [iD], and Darnes Vilariño Ayala[1] [iD]

[1] Language and Knowledge Engineering Laboratory, Benemérita Universidad
Autónoma de Puebla, Puebla, Mexico
rafael.gallardo@alumno.buap.mx, {bbeltran,darnes}@cs.buap.mx
[2] Faculty of Physical and Mathematical Sciences, Benemérita Universidad Autónoma
de Puebla, Puebla, Mexico
cahernandezgr@conacyt.mx

Abstract. Few current image captioning systems are capable to read
and integrate read text into the generated descriptions, none of them was
developed to solve the problem from a bilingual approach. The design
of image captioning systems that can read, and, also work with different languages involves problems from a great variety of natures. In this
work, we propose *Multilingual M4C-Captioner*, a bilingual architecture
that can be easily trained with different languages with minor changes
in the configuration. Our architecture is a modified version of the M4C-
captioner, which mainly differs in the text embedding module and the
OCR's embedding module, our approach modifies the former in order
to use a pre-trained and multilingual version of BERT, and the last
by using the pre-trained FastText vectors for the target languages. This
paper presents results for the English and Spanish language, however, our
proposal can be easily extended to more than 100 languages. Additionally, we provide the first synthetically translated version of the TextCaps
dataset for image captioning with reading comprehension.

Keywords: Deep learning · Multi-modality · Optical character
recognition · TextCaps dataset · Vision and language

1 Introduction

The problem of generating a textual description of a given image is called image
captioning [8]. To solve this problem, models should be able to recognize important objects, their attributes and the relationships among the actors and objects
in the scene. Traditional image captioning systems can be used for automatic
image indexing, general purpose robot vision systems, and visual scene description for visually-impaired people, furthermore, the application areas include biomedicine, commerce, military, education, digital libraries, web searching and
robotics [1,8]. Additionally, humans are able to fully understand visual scenes
and frequently, it is critical to read associated text and comprehend it in the

© Springer Nature Switzerland AG 2021
I. Batyrshin et al. (Eds.): MICAI 2021, LNAI 13068, pp. 13–27, 2021.
https://doi.org/10.1007/978-3-030-89820-5_2

context of the visual scene [16], modern visual question answering and image captioning systems have the ability to read text and integrate it in their outputs, this kind of systems could strongly increase the capabilities and scope of traditional models, leading current vision systems to have a deeper and more complete understanding of their environment.

Traditional image captioning is considered an intellectually challenging problem [1], and even when in recent years these systems have seen steady increase of performance and quality, state-of-the-art image captioning methods fail to recognize and integrate or paraphrase the text in the scene [3,5,10,16], commonly because they focus only on the visual object while generating captions. In addition to the challenges of traditional image captioning, the addition of the ability to read and reason about text (henceforth, we will refer to this problem as *"image captioning with reading comprehension (RC)"*) raises new technical challenges. Figure 1 shows three examples of how traditional models lack the ability to integrate or comprehend the text in the visual scenes, while humans can easily enrich the caption by using the read text, an image captioning system with reading comprehension should be able to generate descriptions closer to the human-generated ones.

Traditional model: A box and a book are laying on a table.

Human: A book about CEOs is sitting on top of a box.

Traditional model: A group of birds in a sunset with the number 10 on it.

Human: The music book cover with Sibelius Symphonies from Minnesota Orchestra.

Traditional model: A big door at the entrance of the supermarket.

Human: A set of grey double doors are under a sign that says Motor Kars Tire & Auto Care.

Fig. 1. Comparison of descriptions generated by the visual attention model [25], and the captions generated by a human. Images and human captions were extracted from the TextCaps dataset.

As described in [16], an image captioning system with reading comprehension should be able to determine the relationships among different Optical Character Recognition (OCR) tokens and also the relationships between OCR tokens and the visual context, also, the system should be able to switch between the word from the model's vocabulary and the OCR tokens extracted from the image, moreover, the model may need to paraphrase or to infer meaning from previously never seen OCR tokens (which can be written in different languages).

As we saw above, image captioning with reading comprehension is shaping up to be a high impact research area, as it has a wide application range. All methods available in the literature focus on achieving state-of-the-art performance over the TextCaps challenge[1] [16], of which the test set is written in English, we are proposing the first bilingual approach (our experiments work for English and Spanish, but future work includes an extension to other languages) to have image captioning models that can read, without needing major changes in the architecture.

Our approach is based on the Multimodal Multi-Copy Mesh (M4C) architecture, proposed in [9]. Also, we are using the same modifications proposed in [16] to get a captioning model instead of a visual question answering (VQA) model, our implementation is built on top of the Multimodal Framework or MMF [17]. We also present a synthetically translated (by using a BART-based [11] pretrained model for machine translation [23]) version of the TextCaps dataset.

The main contributions of this work are listed below:

- We present the first bilingual approach to solve the image captioning with reading comprehension problem.
- Our architecture (Multilingual M4C-Captioner), can be easily adapted to more than 100 languages (the text-embedding module is pre-trained over the 102 languages with the largest Wikipedias) by modifying just one line in the configuration file,
- The multilingual M4C-captioner achieves near state-of-the-art performance for the English language, when using the multilingual text embedding approach.
- Our code, translation scripts, the translated version of TextCaps, and the pre-trained models are made publicly available in the GitHub repository of this paper.
- Thanks to the MMF framework design (our experiments are built on top of it) and documentation, the architecture is fully modular, and experiments are easy to reproduce.

In Sect. 2, we introduce the state-of-the-art for the image captioning with reading comprehension problem. Then, in Sect. 3 we present detailed information about the dataset, the translation procedure, all information related to our architectures and experiments. The Sect. 4 contains the results of the experiments, as well as the analysis of those results. Finally, the conclusions and future work are presented in Sect. 5. Information about our acknowledgments, data, materials and code can be found in Sect. 6.

2   State of the Art

To the best of our knowledge, there are six papers in the literature in which authors propose solutions to the *image captioning with reading comprehension*

---

[1] https://textvqa.org/textcaps/challenge.

problem, all of them obtain near state-of-the-art results or even surpass it on the TextCaps challenge. Due to the nature of the challenge, all literature methods focus on achieving high scores on the challenge's test set, which is written in English and unknown to the public, since the challenge consists of a server-side and blind evaluation of the outputs for the test set. This section will briefly describe each literature method, as well as their scores in the validation set of TextCaps, which is public and can be translated.

Multimodal Multi-copy Mesh Captioner (M4C-Captioner). This is the first approach to solve the problem, and was presented by the Facebook AI Research team as the baseline for the TextCaps challenge. The M4C-Captioner is based on the M4C model, which was state-of-the-art on the TextVQA challenge [9]. This model fuses different modalities by embedding them into a common semantic space, which is then processed by a multimodal transformer (MMT) [16], the caption generation head is performed by a pointer network, which allows the model to generate multi-word answers while mixing vocabulary and OCR tokens. The M4C-Captioner was taken as our baseline and will be detailed further in Sect. 3.

Multimodal Attention Captioner with OCR Spatial Relationship (MMA-SR). The MMA-SR architecture was proposed in [21]. This architecture first extracts feature representations from the image by using a pre-trained Faster R-CNN network, and extracts OCR information with external OCR systems. Then, the two modalities are fed into a multimodal attention network (the text generation is LSTM-based). In the last step, the caption is generated by using a dynamic pointer network, which selects candidates from the model's vocabulary or from the extracted OCR tokens.

Text-Aware Pre-training for Text-VQA and Text-Caption (TAP). Proposed in [26], the TAP model is in the first place of the TextCaps challenge. The main contribution of the TAP's paper is a novel way to help the model to learn better aligned representations among the text words, the visual objects and the scene text (OCR). The TAP team used a pre-training strategy, which consisted in three tasks: language modeling, image-text matching and relative position prediction. During the pre-training, the model learns useful representations for the three modalities, processed by a multimodal transformer (the fusion module). Once pre-trained, the fusion module is fine-tuned to perform specific tasks, such as VQA or image captioning.

Simple Is Not Easy (SBD). Authors of the Simple is not Easy paper [27] argument that sophisticated multimodal encoding frameworks are not strictly necessary to solve this problem. They proposed a "simple" attention mechanism, and argued that it was enough to perform at the same or even better level, when compared with more complex designs. The proposed architecture consists in the split of OCR tokens into visual and linguistic branches, which are then passed into vanilla attention blocks ant then to a fusion encoder (to combine the features of the different modalities). The captions are then generated with a transformer block that receives the multimodal combined representation of the inputs.

Confidence-Aware Non-repetitive Multimodal Transformers for Text-Caps (CNMT). CNMT [22] is an architecture built with three main components: a reading module, a reasoning module and a generation module. The reading module is better, when compared to previous systems, as authors claim to use better OCR systems and recognition confidence. The reasoning module (a multimodal transformer) fuses the OCR token features with object features, which are then passed to the generation module to predict captions iteratively. A pointer network is used to select tokens from the model's vocabulary or from the extracted OCR tokens. To avoid repetition, CNMT uses a repetition mask.

Anchor-Captioner (AnC). Anchor-captioner [24] is a graph-based approach to explore content diversity while captioning images. The architecture consists of four main components: a feature extractor (both for textual and visual information), a fusion module (self-attention layers), an anchor proposal module (AnPM), and an anchor captioning module (AnCM). Once the input features are fused in the self-attention layers, the AnPM constructs anchor-centered graphs to groups the relevant tokens, then, the AnCM uses a visual captioner to output a "global visual-specific caption", which is then used to generate several text-specific captions.

Human-Generated Captions. As described in paper [16], when collecting the annotations for the training and validation sets of the TextCaps dataset, the authors collected an additional 6th caption, in order to estimate human performance (see Table 1). Human estimated performance is not available for the validation set.

2.1 Summary of the State-of-the-Art

Overall, we have described six methods for image captioning with reading comprehension. In Table 2, we present a summary of the reported results for each architecture (only the best experimental scores are showed) over the evaluation set of TextCaps. As mentioned above, the TAP team achieved the highest scores both in evaluation and test sets. It is important to clarify that none of these works has been designed to solve the problem from a bilingual approach, which is the problem we tackle in this work.

Table 1. Evaluation of the human-generated captions for the TextCaps test set. These metrics are included just as a reference, as our work presents experiments and results over the validation set. Metrics in columns: BLEU-4 (B-4), METEOR (M), ROUGE L (R), SPICE (S), CIDEr (C).

TextCaps test set metrics				
Method B-4	M	R	S	C
Human 24.4	26.1	47.0	18.8	125.5

Table 2. Performance for image captioning with RC methods available in literature. The gray row indicates the baseline proposed by the authors of the TextCaps dataset, while bold numbers indicate the best scores. Metrics in columns: BLEU-4 (B-4), METEOR (M), ROUGE L (R), SPICE (S), CIDEr (C).

TextCaps validation set metrics				
Method	B-4	M	R	S	C
M4C-Captioner	23.3	22.0	46.2	15.6	89.60
MMA-SR	24.6	23.0	47.3	16.2	98.00
TAP	**25.8**	**23.8**	**47.9**	**17.1**	**109.2**
SBD	24.8	22.7	47.24	15.71	98.83
CNMT	24.8	23.0	47.1	16.3	101.7
AnC	24.7	22.5	47.1	15.9	95.50

3   Data and Methods

This section includes all necessary information to understand the architecture we propose, our experimental setup and the performed evaluations. The data is a fundamental component of the experiments, so, firstly, we present a brief description of the TextCaps dataset, as well as our approach to translate it. Then, the original M4C-Captioner architecture is described in detail, as well as our proposals of adaptations. The last subsection includes information related with the hardware, training, inference times, and hyperparameters of the experiments.

3.1   TextCaps Dataset

The TextCaps dataset was presented in 2020 by Oleksii Sidorov et al. from the Facebook AI Research team. The dataset follows the image splits of TextVQA, further information about the number of samples is detailed in Table 3. The training and validation sets include the images and its annotations, while the testing set just includes the images (the annotations are not publicly available). A very complete report of the dataset is available in the paper *TextCaps: a Dataset for Image Captioning with Reading Comprehension* [16]. The dataset is publicly available and can be easily downloaded[2].

---

[2] https://textvqa.org/textcaps.

The dataset consists of natural images, extracted from the Open Images dataset[3], all use the RGB color model. Each image could contain a wide variety of objects (8.4 objects per image on average), and may contain written text (OCR). Furthermore, every sample contains annotations that include 5 different captions (with an average length of 12.4 words per caption) and the OCR tokens (with its bounding boxes) detected with the Rosetta system [4].

Table 3. Summary of the number of samples in the TextCaps dataset.

Number of samples	Training	Evaluation	Testing
Images	21,953	3,166	3,289
Captions	109,756	15,830	16,445

3.2   Automatic Translation of TextCaps

In order to test the bilingual capabilities of our architecture, we decided to synthetically translate the TextCaps annotations. We found that the most practical approach to translate the dataset was to use the annotation files provided by the default configuration of TextCaps in MMF (which will be automatically downloaded when running our architecture).

The translation was performed by using the HuggingFace transformers library [23], and the *Helsinki-NLP/opus-mt-en-es* pre-trained model for machine translation. This model consists of a fine-tuned version of the BART architecture [11], trained over the Open Parallel Corpus[4] for English to Spanish translation. This model achieved a Bilingual Evaluation Understudy score of 54.9 in the Tatoeba Translation Challenge [19] (for BLEU, the closer a machine translation is to a professional human translation, the better it is.).

Our translation scripts and the translated annotation files are available in the GitHub repository of the paper.

3.3   M4C-Captioner

In Table 2, it is easy for the TAP method to outperform the others in all metrics. However, their pre-training and multitasking approach is much more resource-consuming than the challenge baseline. Furthermore, for the TAP and the MMA-SR architectures, there is no publicly available code yet. On the other hand, the SBD, CNMT, and AnC architectures are variations of the baseline architecture (M4C-Captioner), and are also built on top of MMF. We decided to use the M4C-Captioner as our baseline, as it is the best-documented alternative and with more derivative works that explore its potential.

---

[3] https://opensource.google/projects/open-images-dataset.
[4] https://opus.nlpl.eu/.

As mentioned before, the M4C architecture was first proposed to solve the TextVQA challenge, and then modified to establish the baseline for the TextCaps challenge, which originated the M4C-Captioner. To better explain the architecture, we present Fig. 2.

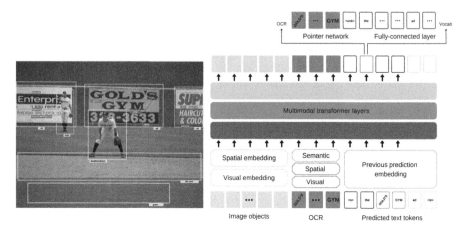

Fig. 2. M4C-Captioner architecture. This illustration was adapted from [16]. The yellow blocks and highlights indicate features that correspond to objects in the image, the red blocks correspond to textual and OCR features in the image. The green blocks are the modules that were originally developed to work with the English language. (Color figure online)

The M4C-Captioner encodes the visual information (both spatial and visual) by using a pre-trained Faster R-CNN [15] model (yellow blocks in Fig. 2), on the other hand, the textual features are encoded with a 3-layer BERT [7] model, pre-trained to solve a masked language modeling (MLM) task in English. As we can see in Fig. 2, the architecture encodes visual, spatial and semantic information of the OCR features; the visual features are extracted with the Faster R-CNN model, the character information is extracted with a Pyramidal Histogram of Characters network (PHOCNet) [18], and the semantic information is encoded with pre-trained FastText [13] vectors for English text. The spatial information (location features) are based on the OCR token's relative bounding box coordinates.

When all the modalities are embedded into a common semantic space, they are passed to the 4-layer multimodal transformer (gray long blocks in Fig. 2) to be processed. Finally, the output of the MMT is passed to a text generation head, which will be responsible for generating the caption. The generation head consists of two modules: a pointer network and a fully-connected (FC) layer, the pointer network will decide if an OCR token must be copied and introduced to the sequence, while the FC layer chooses tokens from the model's vocabulary.

3.4   Multilingual M4C-Captioner

In the last section, we described the M4C-Captioner architecture in detail. In this section, the Multilingual M4C-Captioner (ML M4C-Captioner) is introduced and described in detail. Our proposal mainly modifies the encoder of the original M4C-Captioner, trying to remove the language dependency of the OCR's semantic features and the text embedding (both highlighted in green in Fig. 2). In order to present a clearer explanation of our contribution, we introduce Fig. 3, with both versions of the encoder block, which belongs to both, the M4C-Captioner (left) and the ML M4C-Captioner (right).

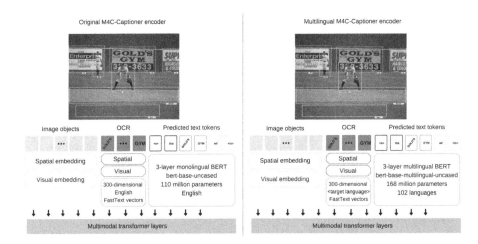

Fig. 3. A comparison of both encoders: the original M4C's encoder on the left and the ML M4C's encoder on the right. Modules highlighted in green indicates the principal difference between the two encoders. (Color figure online)

As mentioned before, the main differences between the encoders are highlighted in green in Figs. 2 and 3, which correspond to the OCR semantic features and the text embedding. While the original encoder is limited to the English language because of the usage of a monolingual pre-trained version of BERT, our proposal uses a multilingual pre-trained version of BERT, which was trained with the 102 languages[5] with the largest Wikipedias, and can be easily fine-tuned with each one of these languages. On the other hand, the OCR semantic features of our encoder can be selected from a total of 157 languages[6], nevertheless, the usable languages are limited to those also available on the multilingual BERT. The ML M4C-Captioner architecture is able to perform training and inference with all the languages that are available, both in the multilingual BERT embedding model and the FastText pre-trained vectors.

---

[5] https://github.com/google-research/bert/blob/master/multilingual.md.
[6] https://fasttext.cc/docs/en/crawl-vectors.html.

3.5 Experimental Setup

This section should work as a guideline to follow the experimental process. First, the software and hardware configurations are briefly described (full code and experimental information is available in the paper's repository). Then, we present a short list of the steps we followed to train and test the models. Finally, the architectures, its hyper-parameters and experimental details will be summarized.

Software and Hardware Setup. All code is written in Python, the deep learning framework is PyTorch, and all experiments are built on top of MMF [7]. Detailed requirements and instructions are available in the repository of the paper.

The translation tasks were accelerated with an NVIDIA Tesla V100 (16 GB of memory) graphic-processing unit (GPU). Nevertheless, the translation tasks can be easily executed in the majority of modern personal computers, however, to reduce running time, a CUDA capable GPU is recommended.

On the other hand, the training of all architectures was performed in an Azure Machine Learning Compute Instance (Standard-NC6), which has a 6-core processor, 56 GB of memory, and an NVIDIA K80 GPU with 11 GB of memory.

Experimental Process. The following list contains the general steps we followed in our experimental process:

1. Prepare software and hardware environments.
2. Evaluate the pre-trained version of the M4C-Captioner with original configurations.
3. Train and evaluate the M4C-Captioner with local configurations, in order to measure the impact of variations in hyper-parameters.
4. Design a version of M4C-Captioner that must be able to train with non-English languages (ML M4C-Captioner).
5. Train and evaluate the ML M4C-Captioner with local configurations, replacing just the monolingual BERT with the multilingual BERT.
6. Translate the TextCaps dataset as described in Sect. 3.
7. Train and evaluate the M4C-Captioner with local configurations, using the translated TextCaps dataset and replacing the monolingual BERT with the multilingual BERT as well as the FastText vectors.

The performance of all models was measured by 5 metrics: BLEU-4 [14], METEOR [6], ROUGE-L [12], SPICE [2] and CIDEr [20].

Architectures and Configurations. We found that the clearest way to present each architecture and its configuration is with a table, therefore, we present the Table 4.

All architectures were trained with the English version of TextCaps using the same hyper-parameters, all training information is available on the project's

---

[7] https://mmf.sh/.

Table 4. All trained and evaluated architectures. Full configuration files and logs are available on the repository of the paper.

Model	TextCaps language	FastText	Text BERT	BERT vocab size	M4C vocab size	Total parameters
m4c-captioner-zoo (Baseline)	English	English: wiki.en.bin	bert-base-uncased	30522	6736	92,185,168
m4c-captioner-local	English	English: wiki.en.bin	bert-base-uncased	30522	6736	92,185,168
en_ml-m4c-captioner	English	English: wiki.en.bin	bert-base-multilingual-uncased	105879	6736	150,059,344
es_ml-m4c-captioner	Spanish	Spanish: cc.es.300.bin	bert-base-multilingual-uncased	105879	7207	150,421,543

configuration files (see the paper's repository). The training of the es-ml-m4c-captioner architecture was slightly different, this one was trained with a *batch_size* = 8 and an *update_frequency* = 8, in order to accumulate the gradients until a total of 64 samples were processed. The first row of the table corresponds to the pre-trained model of the M4C-Captioner, provided by the original authors through the MMF framework.

4   Results

As we can see in Table 5, the best model so far was that provided by the authors of the M4C-Captioner (m4c-capioner-zoo). However, the locally-trained model (m4c-captioner-local) performed good and achieved similar scores when training with local configurations (i.e. smaller batch size, no gradient accumulation, more updates), even surpassing the pre-trained model by 1.3 points on the CIDEr score. Overall, the local configuration's impact can be summarized as follows: a reduction of 0.3 points on BLEU-4, an increase of 0.5 points on METEOR, an increase of 0.1 points on ROUGE-L, an increase of 0.7 points on SPICE, and the aforementioned improvement over CIDEr. The locally-trained model achieved better scores in 4 of the 5 metrics, which means that the local configuration does not have a negative impact on the model's performance.

Once the possible negative impact of a local configuration during training is discarded, we can proceed to analyze the results of the Multilingual M4C-Captioner, trained with the English version of TextCaps (en-ml-m4c-captioner). This architecture uses the multilingual version of BERT to embed the textual data and uses the same FastText vectors and dataset as the first two architectures, which help us to see that the impact on the performance and the variations in the metrics are due to the text-embedding module. The impact (measured in % of relative improvement) of the monolingual BERT replacement can be summarized as follows (when comparing against m4c-captioner-local): -3%, -0.44%, -0.21%, -0.6%, and -1.8% on the BLEU-4, METEOR, ROUGE-L,

Table 5. Performance of each model over the validation set of TextCaps, both English and Spanish sets, are included. The best results are highlighted with bold numbers (not applicable for Spanish since there is just one model). Metrics in columns: BLEU-4 (B-4), METEOR (M), ROUGE L (R), SPICE (S), CIDEr (C).

Model	FastText	Text BERT	English TextCaps validation set metrics				
			B-4	M	R	S	C
TAP	English: wiki.en.bin	bert-base-uncased	**25.8**	**23.8**	**47.9**	**17.1**	**109.2**
m4c-captioner-zoo (Baseline)	English: wiki.en.bin	bert-base-uncased	23.4	21.8	46.0	15.0	89.1
m4c-captioner-local	English: wiki.en.bin	bert-base-uncased	23.1	22.3	46.1	15.7	90.4
en-ml-m4c-captioner	English: wiki.en.bin	bert-base-multilingual-uncased	22.4	22.2	46.0	15.6	88.7
Model	FastText	Text BERT	Spanish TextCaps validation set metrics				
			B-4	M	R	S	C
es-ml-m4c-captioner	Spanish: cc.es.300.bin	bert-base-multilingual-uncased	21.0	21.6	41.6	6.1	63.2

SPICE and CIDEr metrics, respectively. Nevertheless, a slight decrease on the performance was an expected behavior, since the capacity of the text-embedding escalated from 1 to 102 languages, while just using 52% more parameters than the monolingual version (our TextBERT's parameters went from 110 million to 168 million).

The experiments over the translated version of TextCaps are a proof-of-concept of the Multilingual M4C-Captioner architecture (see Fig. 4 for graphical examples), the scores reported in Table 5 are slightly worse than those in the

Human: A banner for the <u>Igreja Adventista Do 7 Dia</u> is hung on a balcony railing.

English model: a sign that says <u>igreja adventista do do do dia</u>.

Spanish model: una señal que dice que <u>igreja adventista</u> está en una pared de ladrillo.

Human: A blue <u>Intel Pentium</u> inside box sitting on a white table

English model: a blue box with the word <u>desktop</u> on it.

Spanish model: una caja azul con la palabra <u>pentium</u> en ella.

Human: One of the jets parked show the letters <u>AF</u> and number <u>711</u> on the tail.

English model: a small plane with the number <u>711</u> on the tail.

Spanish model: un avión con el número <u>711</u> en la cola.

Fig. 4. Three examples of the captions generated by our bilingual model. The first caption is the ground truth description, annotated by a human; the second caption is the one generated by the en-ml-m4c-captioner model, and the last caption corresponds to the output of the es-ml-m4c-captioner model. The underlined words are those taken from the extracted OCR tokens, the remaining comes from the model's vocabulary.

English-based experiments, which was also an expected behavior since the synthetically translated TextCaps may have inherited the biases and mistakes of the BART model for machine translation. Furthermore, the OCR tokens in the dataset can be written in different languages, which adds a level of complexity to the bilingual approach. However, the scores obtained by the Spanish-based model are not so far from those in the state-of-the-art in English, and further experimentation or fine-tuning could strongly improve the results.

5   Conclusions and Future Work

So far, we have proposed a bilingual image captioning architecture, which is called *Multilingual M4C-Captioner*. This architecture has demonstrated to achieve near state-of-the-art performance when working with English data, even when the text-embedding module increased its capacity from 1 to 102 different languages. Furthermore, all the experiments here presented are easily repeatable by using the MMF framework and the publicly available repository of our work.

When trying to solve the problem from a bilingual approach, data availability is one of the big issues to solve, mainly because most of the research is English-focused. Our architecture inherits the problems of the machine translation system, and these problems can lead to grammarly-incorrect captions, incorrect or weird words or sentences, and unnatural image descriptions. However, most of the generated captions are useful and informative, also, the measured metrics indicate a good overall performance, which suggests that we are on the right path, but more research is needed to improve the quality of these systems.

On the other hand, both models, English-based and Spanish-based, kept the capacity to read and integrate text in their descriptions, even when the read text could be in different languages. While the Multilingual M4C-Captioner almost doubled the number of parameters of the original M4C-Captioner, all architectures were trained without problem with less than 15 GB of memory and just one NVIDIA K80 GPU (we avoided complex training strategies such as multi-GPU training). All models were trained on the same hardware, and none used more than 25 GPU hours.

As the first bilingual approach to solve the problem, this can be considered as a success, since the models achieved good scores in both languages, and the models were easily trained with different languages by modifying just one line of code. More advanced and accurate machine-translation systems in conjunction with strong research in this area will lead to better systems and results.

Future work and derived work could include the addition of more pre-trained models (for several languages) and the adaptation of better image captioning systems to solve the problem from a bilingual or multilingual approach. Also, the improvement of the ML M4C-Captioner is an interesting research area; better OCR systems, more advanced language-reasoning modules and a better generation head could increase the system's performance.

6 Declarations

Acknowledgments. We thank Microsoft Corporation, who kindly provided an Azure sponsorship with enough credits to perform all experiments.

Code Availability. The software requirements, Python code and scripts, the translated dataset and detailed instructions to reproduce our experiments are available on the following GitHub repository: https://github.com/gallardorafael/multilingual-mmf

References

1. Amirian, S., Rasheed, K., Taha, T.R., Arabnia, H.R.: A short review on image caption generation with deep learning. In: Proceedings of the International Conference on Image Processing, Computer Vision, and Pattern Recognition (IPCV), pp. 10–18. The Steering Committee of The World Congress in Computer Science (2019)
2. Anderson, P., Fernando, B., Johnson, M., Gould, S.: SPICE: semantic propositional image caption evaluation. In: Leibe, B., Matas, J., Sebe, N., Welling, M. (eds.) ECCV 2016. LNCS, vol. 9909, pp. 382–398. Springer, Cham (2016). https://doi.org/10.1007/978-3-319-46454-1_24
3. Anderson, P., et al.: Bottom-up and top-down attention for image captioning and visual question answering. In: Proceedings of the IEEE Conference on Computer Vision and Pattern Recognition, pp. 6077–6086 (2018)
4. Borisyuk, F., Gordo, A., Sivakumar, V.: Rosetta: large scale system for text detection and recognition in images. In: Proceedings of the 24th ACM SIGKDD International Conference on Knowledge Discovery & Data Mining, pp. 71–79 (2018)
5. Chen, Y.C., et al.: UNITER: learning universal image-text representations (2019)
6. Denkowski, M., Lavie, A.: Meteor universal: language specific translation evaluation for any target language. In: Proceedings of the Ninth Workshop on Statistical Machine Translation, pp. 376–380 (2014)
7. Devlin, J., Chang, M.W., Lee, K., Toutanova, K.: BERT: pre-training of deep bidirectional transformers for language understanding. arXiv preprint arXiv:1810.04805 (2018)
8. Hossain, M.Z., Sohel, F., Shiratuddin, M.F., Laga, H.: A comprehensive survey of deep learning for image captioning. ACM Comput. Surv. (CsUR) **51**(6), 1–36 (2019)
9. Hu, R., Singh, A., Darrell, T., Rohrbach, M.: Iterative answer prediction with pointer-augmented multimodal transformers for textVQA. In: Proceedings of the IEEE/CVF Conference on Computer Vision and Pattern Recognition, pp. 9992–10002 (2020)
10. Huang, L., Wang, W., Chen, J., Wei, X.Y.: Attention on attention for image captioning. In: Proceedings of the IEEE/CVF International Conference on Computer Vision, pp. 4634–4643 (2019)
11. Lewis, M., et al.: BART: denoising sequence-to-sequence pre-training for natural language generation, translation, and comprehension. arXiv preprint arXiv:1910.13461 (2019)

12. Lin, C.Y.: ROUGE: a package for automatic evaluation of summaries. In: Text Summarization Branches Out, pp. 74–81 (2004)
13. Mikolov, T., Grave, E., Bojanowski, P., Puhrsch, C., Joulin, A.: Advances in pre-training distributed word representations. In: Proceedings of the International Conference on Language Resources and Evaluation (LREC 2018) (2018)
14. Papineni, K., Roukos, S., Ward, T., Zhu, W.J.: BLEU: a method for automatic evaluation of machine translation. In: Proceedings of the 40th Annual Meeting of the Association for Computational Linguistics, pp. 311–318 (2002)
15. Ren, S., He, K., Girshick, R., Sun, J.: Faster R-CNN: towards real-time object detection with region proposal networks. arXiv preprint arXiv:1506.01497 (2015)
16. Sidorov, O., Hu, R., Rohrbach, M., Singh, A.: TextCaps: a dataset for image captioning with reading comprehension. In: Vedaldi, A., Bischof, H., Brox, T., Frahm, J.-M. (eds.) ECCV 2020. LNCS, vol. 12347, pp. 742–758. Springer, Cham (2020). https://doi.org/10.1007/978-3-030-58536-5_44
17. Singh, A., et al.: MMF: a multimodal framework for vision and language research (2020). https://github.com/facebookresearch/mmf
18. Sudholt, S., Fink, G.A.: PHOCNet: a deep convolutional neural network for word spotting in handwritten documents. In: 2016 15th International Conference on Frontiers in Handwriting Recognition (ICFHR), pp. 277–282. IEEE (2016)
19. Tiedemann, J.: The Tatoeba translation challenge - realistic data sets for low resource and multilingual MT. In: Proceedings of the Fifth Conference on Machine Translation, pp. 1174–1182. Association for Computational Linguistics, Online, November 2020. https://www.aclweb.org/anthology/2020.wmt-1.139
20. Vedantam, R., Lawrence Zitnick, C., Parikh, D.: CIDEr: consensus-based image description evaluation. In: Proceedings of the IEEE Conference on Computer Vision and Pattern Recognition, pp. 4566–4575 (2015)
21. Wang, J., Tang, J., Luo, J.: Multimodal attention with image text spatial relationship for OCR-based image captioning. In: Proceedings of the 28th ACM International Conference on Multimedia, pp. 4337–4345 (2020)
22. Wang, Z., Bao, R., Wu, Q., Liu, S.: Confidence-aware non-repetitive multimodal transformers for textcaps. arXiv preprint arXiv:2012.03662 (2020)
23. Wolf, T., et al.: Huggingface's transformers: state-of-the-art natural language processing. arXiv preprint arXiv:1910.03771 (2019)
24. Xu, G., Niu, S., Tan, M., Luo, Y., Du, Q., Wu, Q.: Towards accurate text-based image captioning with content diversity exploration. arXiv preprint arXiv:2105.03236 (2021)
25. Xu, K., et al.: Show, attend and tell: neural image caption generation with visual attention. In: International Conference on Machine Learning, pp. 2048–2057. PMLR (2015)
26. Yang, Z., et al.: TAP: text-aware pre-training for text-VQA and text-caption. arXiv preprint arXiv:2012.04638 (2020)
27. Zhu, Q., Gao, C., Wang, P., Wu, Q.: Simple is not easy: a simple strong baseline for TextVQA and TextCaps. arXiv preprint arXiv:2012.05153 (2020)

Best Paper Award, Second Place

Question Answering for Visual Navigation in Human-Centered Environments

Daniil E. Kirilenko[1], Alexey K. Kovalev[2,3]($\boxtimes$), Evgeny Osipov[4], and Aleksandr I. Panov[1,3]

[1] Moscow Institute of Physics and Technology, Moscow, Russia
panov.ai@mipt.ru
[2] HSE University, Moscow, Russia
akkovalev@hse.ru
[3] Artificial Intelligence Research Institute FRC CSC RAS, Moscow, Russia
[4] Lulea University of Technology, Lulea, Sweden
evgeny.osipov@ltu.se

Abstract. In this paper, we propose an HISNav VQA dataset – a challenging dataset for a Visual Question Answering task that is aimed at the needs of Visual Navigation in human-centered environments. The dataset consists of images of various room scenes that were captured using the Habitat virtual environment and of questions important for navigation tasks using only visual information. We also propose a baseline for a HISNav VQA dataset, a Vector Semiotic Architecture, and demonstrate its performance. The Vector Semiotic Architecture is a combination of a Sign-Based World Model and Vector Symbolic Architectures. The Sign-Based World Model allows representing various aspects of an agent's knowledge, and Vector Symbolic Architectures serve on a low computational level. The Vector Semiotic Architecture addresses the symbol grounding problem that plays an important role in the Visual Question Answering Task.

Keywords: Visual question answering · Semiotic approach · Vector symbolic architecture · Habitat · Visual Navigation

1 Introduction

In recent years, models that work with unimodal data have achieved significant results in computer vision (CV) and natural language processing (NLP). And nowadays, researchers have started paying attention to multimodal tasks especially at the intersection of CV and NLP: Image Captioning [19], Visual Question Answering (VQA) [6], Visual Dialog [4], Visual Commonsense Reasoning [32], and Vision-and-Language Navigation (VLN) [2,18].

The advance in virtual assistants requires further development within the framework of embodied Artificial Intelligence (AI). Embodied AI is the study of intelligent systems with a physical or virtual embodiment (robots and egocentric personal assistants). The embodiment hypothesis is the idea that "intelligence

© Springer Nature Switzerland AG 2021
I. Batyrshin et al. (Eds.): MICAI 2021, LNAI 13068, pp. 31–45, 2021.
https://doi.org/10.1007/978-3-030-89820-5_3

emerges in the interaction of an agent with an environment and as a result of sensorimotor activity" [20]. As a testbed, the task of Visual Navigation in human-centered environments might be used as it is possible to supplement it with an ability to interact with humans in the natural language. In VLN, the agent has to navigate the environment following instructions in the natural language, and in VQA, the system has to answer questions about the content of a given image. The combination of VLN and VQA gives an agent that can answer (and, potentially, ask) questions about the environment an opportunity to replenish its scene understanding and clarify instructions.

When an agent faces such tasks, the symbol grounding problem (how symbols get their meanings) [9] arises. We approach this problem from the semiotic point of view by applying Vector Semiotic Architecture, which is a combination of the Sign-Based World Model [22,26] and Vector Symbolic Architecture [12].

The goal of our work is to take one more step toward creating an embodied AI assistant system that will improve human-machine interaction by using a natural language question, which, in the future, can help to set tasks or refine them for AI agents in the simplest way.

The contribution of this paper is twofold: first, a challenging dataset for a Visual Question Answering task that aims to address the needs of Visual Navigation in human-centered environments is proposed. The HISNav VQA dataset is simpler than VQA [6], but more complex than CLEVR [11], and focuses on questions about positions and relations of objects. It also does not suffer from disembodiedness, as images are taken from the robot's camera, and unsituatedness, as scenes resemble environments a robot is supposed to operate in. Second, the Vector Semiotic Architecture baseline is proposed, and its performance is demonstrated on the HISNav VQA dataset. The advantages of Vector Semiotic Architecture are the interpretability of an answering process and the grounding of semiotic representation of objects in robot sensory inputs.

2   Related Works

The research interest in multimodal tasks in the intersection of CV and NLP leads to the emergence of VQA datasets that cover commonsense knowledge and are general-purpose [6], that use synthetic image-question pairs [11], and that are based on questions asked by vision-impaired people [8]. Despite that fact, the area of Visual Navigation in human-centered environments is not covered by VQA datasets, although the ability of an intelligent agent to answer questions about the environment it operates in and, by that, adjust its action is very promising.

These needs are partially satisfied by VLN works [2,18]. But the features of the problem formulation (the agent has to follow linguistic instruction to navigate across the environment based on visual information) do not imply that the agent asks or answers questions to clarify these instructions. That said, this ability is important in situations where the environment can change dynamically and the agent has to re-plan to complete the task.

Most VQA models reduce the task to the classification problem and use neural networks to solve it [1]. Other research directions include the use of external knowledge [31] and neural-symbolic approach [30]. The latter is of particular interest as it combines the advantages of connectionism and symbolism while compensating for their drawbacks. The approach allows obtaining interpretable answering procedures and using rich and efficient tools of deep neural networks. In this work, we use [30] as a starting point. In [30], the scene is represented in the form of the data frame listing objects and their attributes. The process of answering a question is performed by applying a deterministic program that filters the scene data frame and outputs the result as the answer. The disadvantage of representing a scene as a table (data frame) is the loss of structure. We address that problem by applying the scene representation proposed in [17]. In [17], a model that combines a Sign-Based World Model [23, 24] and Vector Symbolic Architectures [12] was proposed. Binary Spatter Codes [12] were used to represent causal matrices as vectors. In this work, we applied Spatial Semantic Pointers [15] that provide a convenient way to work with continuous coordinates.

The Sign-Based World Model (SBWM) is a cognitive architecture that allows representing different aspects of agent knowledge. The main information unit in this architecture is a sign – a four-component structure. The meaning component represents the agent's experience of interaction with a concept related to a sign. Knowledge shared across the group of agents is represented by the significance component. The image component serves to distinguish one concept from another. The fourth component is a name that serves a nominative function. SBWM was used for various applications, such as goal setting [25], reasoning [13, 16], and hierarchical planning [14]. Each sign component is represented by a binary matrix of a special form, where columns are events and rows are the appearance of a particular feature in the particular event. These matrices are called causal matrices. In [17], causal matrices are encoded using Vector Symbolic Architectures.

Vector Symbolic Architectures (VSA), or hyperdimensional computing [12], is a family of methods that use vectors of high dimensionality to encode concepts and use vector operations to manipulate them. The concept representation is holistic, which means that no particular position in a vector is interpretable. That representation allows reducing symbolic manipulation to vector operations. VSA is instantiated by many variations [5, 12, 27] that differ in vector space and operations but follow the same computational properties.

3   HISNav VQA Dataset

We present a challenging dataset that consists of images of various room scenes (captured using the Habitat virtual environment [21]) and questions to these images. Our dataset tests the ability of VQA systems to answer questions important for navigation tasks using only visual information. Among the tasks that need to be solved to correctly answer the questions are recognition of objects, the correct determination of their properties, and counting. To answer spatial questions, it is necessary to determine the position of objects relative both to the observation point and to each other. Thus, a model that can accurately answer such questions can be effectively used to solve navigation problems for robotic platforms, and our dataset is a way to check the necessary visual reasoning abilities. Various samples of image-question pairs from the proposed dataset are demonstrated in Fig. 1. Our HISNav VQA dataset is publicly available.[1]

question: what is in the upper right corner?
answers: painting, picture

question: how many windows are on the wall?
answers: 3, 3

question: what is wall color?
answers: white, beige

question: what is opposite the door?
answers: hallway, wall

Fig. 1. Examples of image-question pairs from the HISNav VQA dataset

3.1   Images

We used the HISNav dataset [28] as a source of images, which was assembled in the virtual environment Habitat [21]. Habitat is a highly efficient photorealistic 3D simulation for research in embodied AI, that is a great platform for our purposes. For more closeness of synthetic images to images from real cameras, Gaussian noise was added to some of them. All HISNav dataset includes 135,962 images, each RGB image has a resolution 640 × 320, and ground truth instance labels of 40 classes (wall, floor, chair, door, table, sofa, etc.) correspond to each image. The original dataset includes pictures of 49 unique scenes that present different rooms with various content.

In HISNav, each subsequent image is too close to the previous one, which is undesirable for the dataset purposes. We want the images to be so different from each other that the answers to the same question differ in most cases (or the reason for the answer should be different in the case of the same answer). For this reason, we used only one in thirty image from the initial data. In addition,

---

[1] https://bit.ly/2XR5OUc.

images with a small amount of content on them (less than five objects on the image) were removed. Images that had strong visual artifacts are also discarded.

3.2 Human-Asked Questions

The crowdsourcing service Yandex.Toloka[2] was used to collect questions and answers to them. The collection of questions and answers had two stages, which were performed by different groups of participants.

First, we asked performers to ask questions about the images (Appendix A). We limited the types of asked questions to the following four main ones: questions about mutual arrangement of objects, quantity, properties of objects, and questions about relative to the observer location. The resulting questions were rigorously assessed following the given instruction. Also, during this stage, performers were asked to give an answer to their question and mark the type of question. This part of the work was not evaluated strictly since the main task of this stage is to collect questions. The total number of workers who participated in this stage was 1,172, with an overall task acceptance rate of 0.63.

The second stage is collecting answers. This time, performers had to answer questions about the images that were collected in the previous step. The instructions for this task were written to bring all answers to the same form and to reduce the number of unique answers in the resulting data. For each image-question pair two answers were collected to reduce the likelihood of erroneous markup. The total number of workers who participated in this stage was 787, with an agreement rate of 0.37.

3.3 Synthetic Questions

For question generation a modular algorithm was written, it generates seven types of questions based on the tabular representation of each scene, which was obtained from the results of the instance segmentation of the corresponding image (Fig. 2). The following question templates were used:

– What color is the nearest object to the [single obj]?
– What color is the [single obj] to the [single obj]?
– What is the nearest object to the [single obj]?
– In which part of the image is the [single obj]?
– How many [multiple obj] are there?
– How many [multiple obj] are to the left/right of the [single obj]?
– Is there a [object] to the left/right of the [single obj]?

Here [single obj] is any object type that is represented in the image in a single instance, [multiple obj] is the type of object that is represented in the image by more than one instance, and [object] is a placeholder for any type of object that may not even be represented.

---

[2] https://toloka.yandex.com.

Q: What color is the nearest object to the column?   A: Beige
Q: What color is the door to the right of the chair?   A: Grey
Q: What is the nearest object to the chair?   A: Column
Q: In which part of the image is the column?   A: Up-left
Q: Is there a sofa to the right of the chair?   A: No

Fig. 2. Examples of generated questions

3.4 Dataset Analysis

Our dataset is different from other VQA datasets like CLEVR [11] and VQA v2.0 [6]. VQA v2.0 is a very large and diverse dataset full of common-sense questions. This is good in the case of creating a universal VQA model that can answer a broad variety of questions. CLEVR is much less diverse and, like our dataset, consists of synthetic images. At the same time, it has a weak variety of objects and scenes represented on them, which is why the number of unique words in questions and answers is extremely small. Also, the structure of questions is extremely complex and dissimilar to what people use. Both datasets suffer from disembodiedness, as images are taken from different shoot points (an agent position is not considered), and unsituatedness, as scenes do not resemble the actual environment in which an agent is supposed to operate. That limits the application of these datasets for Visual Navigation in human-centered environments. By the latter, we mean ordinary rooms with furniture and elements of everyday life in which we are all used to living. On the other hand, the proposed dataset is focused on important navigation questions such as the location of various objects, uses images that resemble the operating environment, and are taken from an agent viewpoint. This is what distinguishes it from other VQA datasets.

The HISNav VQA dataset includes 3,500 images with one human-asked question per image and two answers per question. There are 712 unique answers and all questions contain 868 unique words. This is about an order of magnitude more than the CLEVR dataset has and at the same time an order of magnitude less than the VQA dataset (Table 1).

Figure 3(a) shows the distribution of collected human-asked questions by their first four words. The ordering of the words starts toward the center and radiates outward. The arc length is proportional to the number of questions containing the word. White areas are words with contributions too small to show. This figure demonstrates the complexity and variety of human questions,

Table 1. Quantitative comparison of VQA datasets' complexity

Dataset	Unique words	Unique answers
VQA v2.0 [6]	14576	162496
CLEVR [11]	80	28
HISNav VQA (ours)	868	712

synthetic questions are built on seven structural templates of fixed length, while all possible structures of human questions do not fit in this figure, and their length varies from three to 13 words.

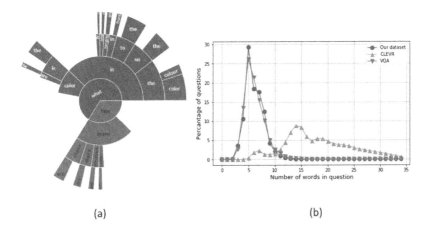

(a)   (b)

Fig. 3. Comparison of question lengths for different VQA datasets

Figure 3b shows the distribution of question lengths for three datasets: ours, VQA v2.0, and CLEVR. Our dataset and VQA v2.0 turned out to be close since both consist of questions asked by people, and for CLEVR, the distribution turned out to be significantly shifted due to the artificial syntactic complexity of synthetic questions. This fact additionally shows that this dataset is poorly suited for training an assistant who would answer people's questions.

Figure 4 shows various quantitative statistics for our dataset: (a) is the distribution of question types given by Yandex.Toloka workers; (b) is the distribution of answers to questions about color. Due to the specifics of the scenes used, the number of possible colors is also small, but this number is sufficient to test the ability of the model to distinguish the colors of objects, which is important both for the task of navigation and for assistants; (c) is the distribution of answers to count-questions, all the number-answers are in the range from 0 to 9, this is not a large range, but sufficient for room scenes, because there are rare cases when it is needed to count so many objects in rooms; (d) is the distribution of answers to what-containing questions, which are the most common and important for our purposes.

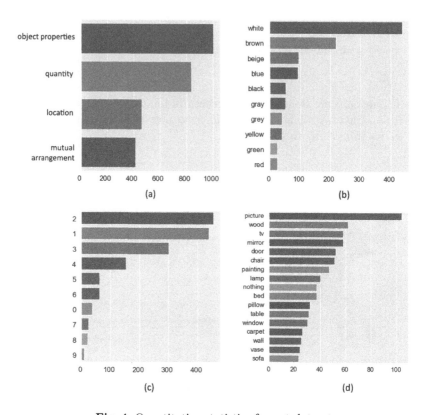

Fig. 4. Quantitative statistics for out dataset

4   Vector Semiotic Architecture Baseline

In this section, we propose a Vector Semiotic Architecture Baseline that addresses the symbol grounding problem and provides an interpretable answering procedure. The Vector Semiotic Architecture model is inspired by NS-VQA [30] and uses the scene representation from [17]. The model consists of three main parts: a scene parser, a question parser, and a program executor. The scene parser uses an instance segmentation model to extract attributes, such as coordinates and color, for each object. The question parser is an attention-based sequence to sequence model [3] that receives a sequence of words in a natural language as input and outputs a sequence of programs for execution. Both the encoder and the decoder have two hidden layers with a 256-dim hidden vector, and the dimension of word vectors is 300. The executor is a collection of functional modules that are sequentially applied to the scene representation to get the answer to a question. The dimension of HD vectors is set to 1,000.

Compared to the work in [17], we use a variance of the Semantic Pointer Architecture (SPA) [5] – Spatial Semantic Pointers [15] – to represent causal matrices and work efficiently with continuous values such as coordinates. Here we use real random vectors with a unit norm. The unique feature of this approach is using special algebraic operations: circular convolution and convolutive power, which is defined as follows

$$\mathbf{u} \otimes \mathbf{w} := IDFT(DFT(\mathbf{u}) \odot DFT(\mathbf{w}))$$

$$\mathbf{u}^p := \Re(IDFT((DFT(\mathbf{u})^p)_{j=0}^{D-1}))$$

where $\mathbf{u}, \mathbf{w}$ are two random vectors, $\Re$ denotes taking the real part of a number, $\odot$ denotes element-wise multiplication, and DFT and IDFT denote the Discrete Fourier Transform and Inverse Discrete Fourier Transform respectively. With these operations, we can encode two numerical values corresponding to the coordinates x, y by generating two random unitary vectors corresponding to the coordinate axes $\mathbf{X}, \mathbf{Y}$ (vector $\mathbf{u}$ is called unitary if $\forall \mathbf{v} : \|\mathbf{v}\| = \|\mathbf{v} \otimes \mathbf{u}\|$):

$$\mathbf{V} = \mathbf{X}^x \otimes \mathbf{Y}^y.$$

Thus, to answer the question "What is the object to the left of the chair?" we have to encode coordinates of a chair into a vector $\mathbf{V}_{chair}$, construct a vector that represents a region left to the chair $\mathbf{V}_{left}$ [15], and compute the similarity between this vector and vectors of other objects coordinates.

5 Experiments

In this section, we test the performance of two baseline models on the HIS-Nav VQA dataset. For human-asked questions, the model's answer is considered correct if it matches at least one of the two ground-truth answers.

5.1 Neural Network Baseline

We implemented a simple neural network baseline for the VQA task. A bag-of-words representation of questions is used as 300-dim vectors. Resnet18 [10] is used to obtain embedding of an image as a vector of dimension 512. Question and image embeddings are concatenated and then passed to a multi-layer perceptron classifier with two layers of 512 hidden units. We used ReLU activation in hidden layers and a softmax for an output layer. The accuracy of this model on synthetic questions is 0.57, and on human questions 0.43. The model was trained using SGD with standard parameters and a batch size of 64. The main problem with this model is that it is sensitive to the bias in our data: the model learns to predict only the most frequent answers to questions.

5.2   Vector Semiotic Architecture

We first trained the VSemA model in a supervised manner on a subsample of synthetic questions (32 questions of each type, 224 in total). This model achieved an accuracy of 0.82 on the validation part of synthetic questions. Further, this model was trained using the REINFORCE [29] algorithm on human questions. The reward was given only for the correct answer, and, as a result, it reached an accuracy of 0.20 on the corresponding validation set.

To obtain the best performance on synthetic data, we used a larger subsample, and, as a result, we got a nearly perfect accuracy of 0.98 (Table 2).

Table 2. Baselines performance (accuracy)

Model	Synthetic questions	Human-asked questions
Our approach	0.98	0.20
Simple NN	0.57	0.43

On human-asked questions, our model demonstrates moderate performance compare to a neural network baseline. Error analysis reveals two main causes. First, our model relies on an instance segmentation mask, and therefore it fails to answer questions about instances that are not segmented. The left half of Fig. 5 depicts a stair with a corresponding question "How many steps are shown on the image?". Our model does not distinguish individual stair steps – it sees them as a whole and, thus, predicts a wrong answer. The second cause also affects the neural network baseline – the ambiguity of questions. In the right half of Fig. 5, both models give wrong answers in terms of ground truth, though predictions are generally correct (both the door and the chair are in the room). This is since there are more than two objects in the room that leads to ambiguity. Other examples of predicted answers are shown in Appendix B.

Question: how many steps are shown on the image?
Answers: 2, 2
Our approach: 0
NN baseline: 2

Question: what is in the room?
Answers: cart, armchair
Our approach: chair
NN baseline: door

Fig. 5. Examples of Vector Semiotic Architecture model mispredictions

6   Discussion

The proposed HISNav VQA dataset aims to address the needs of Visual Navigation in human-centered environments. The dataset also does not suffer from disembodiedness and unsituatedness and might be used to advance research in the field of assistance robotics or for VLN.

We demonstrated the performance of Vector Semiotic Architecture on a challenging dataset HISNav VQA and achieved nearly perfect performance on synthetic questions. The performance on human-asked questions demonstrates the limitations of our model due to reliance on the instance segmentation mask. This limitation may be addressed by pretraining on a dataset with a large number of classes [7]. On the other hand, our approach provides an interpretable answering procedure compare to a neural network baseline. Also, nearly perfect performance on synthetic questions gives us the ability to construct the domain- and task-specific questions with a high probability of getting the right answer that is crucial for application purposes.

For future work, we plan to increase the performance of Vector Semiotic Architecture on human-asked questions by using datasets with a large number of segmentation classes and exploiting the questions' syntactic structure. We also plan to use HISNav VQA and the proposed model to build a prototype agent that can first operate in a virtual and then in a real-world environment. We hope our work draws researchers' attention to this task, as there are still unresolved problems and challenges.

7   Conclusion

In this work, we propose HISNav VQA – a challenging dataset for a Visual Question Answering task that is based on the Habitat dataset and concentrates on questions about spatial arrangements of the scene objects. The dataset may be used in the scenario of the Vision-and-Language Navigation task in human-centered environments where a robot asks and answers questions to clarify instructions. We also demonstrate the performance of the Vector Semiotic Architecture on the proposed dataset and compare it to a simple neural network baseline.

Acknowledgements. The reported study was supported by RFBR, research Project No. 19-37-90164.

A   Appendix: Data Labeling

Ask the question to this image.

🔢 [   ]

Answer your question with a short phrase.

🔠 [   ]

What is your question about?

2️⃣ ☐ Mutual arrangement

3️⃣ ☐ Quantity

4️⃣ ☐ Properties of objects

5️⃣ ☐ Location relative to the observer

Mark this if it is impossible to ask the question.

6️⃣ ☐ impossible to ask a question

Fig. 6. The user interface for data labeling in Yandex.Toloka

B   Appendix: Examples

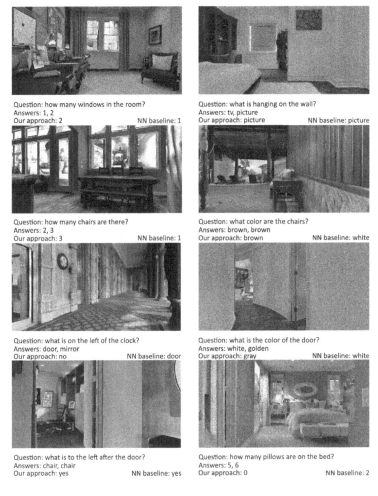

Fig. 7. Examples of predicted answers given by Vector Semiotic Architecture and NN baseline. First row: both models give the right answer. Second row: NN baseline fails. Third row: Vector Semiotic Architecture fails. Last row: both models fail.

References

1. Anderson, P., et al.: Bottom-up and top-down attention for image captioning and visual question answering. arXiv e-prints arXiv:1707.07998, July 2017
2. Anderson, P., et al.: Vision-and-language navigation: interpreting visually-grounded navigation instructions in real environments (2018)
3. Bahdanau, D., Cho, K.H., Bengio, Y.: Neural machine translation by jointly learning to align and translate. In: 3rd International Conference on Learning Representations, ICLR 2015 - Conference Track Proceedings, pp. 1–15 (2015)
4. Das, A., et al.: Visual dialog. In: Proceedings of the IEEE Conference on Computer Vision and Pattern Recognition (CVPR) (2017)

5. Eliasmith, C.: How to Build a Brain: A Neural Architecture for Biological Cognition. Oxford University Press, New York (2013)
6. Goyal, Y., Khot, T., Summers-Stay, D., Batra, D., Parikh, D.: Making the V in VQA matter: elevating the role of image understanding in Visual Question Answering. In: Conference on Computer Vision and Pattern Recognition (CVPR) (2017)
7. Gupta, A., Dollar, P., Girshick, R.: LVIS: a dataset for large vocabulary instance segmentation. In: Proceedings of the IEEE Computer Society Conference on Computer Vision and Pattern Recognition, June 2019, pp. 5351–5359 (2019)
8. Gurari, D., et al.: VizWiz grand challenge: answering visual questions from blind people. In: 2018 IEEE/CVF Conference on Computer Vision and Pattern Recognition, pp. 3608–3617 (2018)
9. Harnad, S.: The symbol grounding problem. Physica D **42**(1), 335–346 (1990)
10. He, K., Zhang, X., Ren, S., Sun, J.: Deep residual learning for image recognition. In: 2016 IEEE Conference on Computer Vision and Pattern Recognition (CVPR), pp. 770–778 (2016). https://doi.org/10.1109/CVPR.2016.90
11. Johnson, J., Hariharan, B., van der Maaten, L., Fei-Fei, L., Zitnick, C.L., Girshick, R.: CLEVR: a diagnostic dataset for compositional language and elementary visual reasoning. In: CVPR (2017)
12. Kanerva, P.: Hyperdimensional computing: an introduction to computing in distributed representation with high-dimensional random vectors. Cogn. Comput. **1**(2), 139–159 (2009)
13. Kiselev, G., Kovalev, A., Panov, A.I.: Spatial reasoning and planning in sign-based world model. In: Kuznetsov, S.O., Osipov, G.S., Stefanuk, V.L. (eds.) RCAI 2018. CCIS, vol. 934, pp. 1–10. Springer, Cham (2018). https://doi.org/10.1007/978-3-030-00617-4_1
14. Kiselev, G., Panov, A.: Hierarchical psychologically inspired planning for human-robot interaction tasks. In: Ronzhin, A., Rigoll, G., Meshcheryakov, R. (eds.) ICR 2019. LNCS (LNAI), vol. 11659, pp. 150–160. Springer, Cham (2019). https://doi.org/10.1007/978-3-030-26118-4_15
15. Komer, B., Stewart, T.C., Voelker, A.R., Eliasmith, C.: A neural representation of continuous space using fractional binding. In: 41st Annual Meeting of the Cognitive Science Society. Cognitive Science Society, QC (2019)
16. Kovalev, A.K., Panov, A.I.: Mental actions and modelling of reasoning in semiotic approach to AGI. In: Hammer, P., Agrawal, P., Goertzel, B., Iklé, M. (eds.) AGI 2019. LNCS (LNAI), vol. 11654, pp. 121–131. Springer, Cham (2019). https://doi.org/10.1007/978-3-030-27005-6_12
17. Kovalev, A.K., Panov, A.I., Osipov, E.: Hyperdimensional representations in semiotic approach to AGI. In: Goertzel, B., Panov, A.I., Potapov, A., Yampolskiy, R. (eds.) AGI 2020. LNCS (LNAI), vol. 12177, pp. 231–241. Springer, Cham (2020). https://doi.org/10.1007/978-3-030-52152-3_24
18. Ku, A., Anderson, P., Patel, R., Ie, E., Baldridge, J.: Room-across-room: multilingual vision-and-language navigation with dense spatiotemporal grounding. In: Proceedings of the 2020 Conference on Empirical Methods in Natural Language Processing (EMNLP), pp. 4392–4412, November 2020
19. Lin, T.-Y., et al.: Microsoft COCO: common objects in context. In: Fleet, D., Pajdla, T., Schiele, B., Tuytelaars, T. (eds.) ECCV 2014. LNCS, vol. 8693, pp. 740–755. Springer, Cham (2014). https://doi.org/10.1007/978-3-319-10602-1_48
20. Linda Smith, M.G.: The development of embodied cognition: six lessons from babies. Artif. Life **11**, 13–29 (2005)
21. Savva, M., et al.: Habitat: a platform for embodied AI research. In: Proceedings of the IEEE/CVF International Conference on Computer Vision (ICCV) (2019)

22. Osipov, G.S., Panov, A.I., Chudova, N.V.: Behavior control as a function of consciousness. I. world model and goal setting. J. Comput. Syst. Sci. Int. **53**(4), 517–529 (2014)
23. Osipov, G.S., Panov, A.I.: Relationships and operations in a sign-based world model of the actor. Sci. Tech. Inf. Process. **45**(5), 317–330 (2018). https://doi.org/10.3103/S0147688218050040
24. Osipov, G.S., Panov, A.I.: Rational behaviour planning of cognitive semiotic agent in dynamic environment. Sci. Tech. Inf. Process. **48**(6) (2021)
25. Panov, A.I.: Goal setting and behavior planning for cognitive agents. Sci. Tech. Inf. Process. **46**(6), 404–415 (2019)
26. Panov, A.I.: Behavior planning of intelligent agent with sign world model. Biol. Inspired Cogn. Archit. **19**, 21–31 (2017)
27. Plate, T.A.: Holographic reduced representations. IEEE Trans. Neural Networks **6**(3), 623–641 (1995). https://doi.org/10.1109/72.377968
28. Staroverov, A., Yudin, D.A., Belkin, I., Adeshkin, V., Solomentsev, Y.K., Panov, A.I.: Real-time object navigation with deep neural networks and hierarchical reinforcement learning. IEEE Access **8**, 195608–195621 (2020)
29. Williams, R.J.: Simple statistical gradient-following algorithms for connectionist reinforcement learning. Mach. Learn. **8**, 229–256 (2004)
30. Yi, K., Wu, J., Gan, C., Torralba, A., Kohli, P., Tenenbaum, J.B.: Neural-symbolic VQA: disentangling reasoning from vision and language understanding. arXiv e-prints arXiv:1810.02338, October 2018
31. Yu, J., Zhu, Z., Wang, Y., Zhang, W., Hu, Y., Tan, J.: Cross-modal knowledge reasoning for knowledge-based visual question answering. Pattern Recogn. **108**, 107563 (2020)
32. Zellers, R., Bisk, Y., Farhadi, A., Choi, Y.: From recognition to cognition: visual commonsense reasoning. CoRR abs/1811.10830 (2018)

Improving a Conversational Speech Recognition System Using Phonetic and Neural Transcript Correction

Mario Campos-Soberanis⬤, Diego Campos-Sobrino$^{(\boxtimes)}$⬤, and Rafael Viana-Cámara⬤

SoldAI Research, Mérida, Yucatán, Mexico
{mcampos,dcampos,rviana}@soldai.com

Abstract. This article describes the successful implementation of a conversational speech recognition system applied to telephonic sales performed by an autonomous agent. Our implementation uses a postprocessing corrector based on phonetic representations of text and subsequent neural network classifier. The classifier assesses the proposed correction's relevance to reduce the errors in the transcript sent to a downstream Natural Language Understanding engine. The experiments were carried on correcting transcripts from real audios of orders placed by customers of a large bottling company. We measured the Word Error Rate of the corrected transcripts against human-annotated ground-truth to verify the improvement produced by the system. To evaluate the corrections' impact on the entities detected by the Natural Language Understanding engine, we used Jaccard distance, Precision, Recall, and F_1. Results show that the implemented system and architecture enhance the transcript relative Word Error Rate on a 39% and Jaccard distance on 13% in comparison to the Automatic Speech Recognition baseline, making them suitable for real-time telephonic sales systems implementation.

Keywords: Automatic speech recognition · Phonetic correction · Neural networks · Named entity recognition

1 Introduction

Nowadays, voice-enabled systems are gaining popularity, and virtual assistants, such as Amazon Alexa, Apple Siri, or Google Home, are becoming part of our daily life. Voice driven assistants have been used to access contents on the Web, control smart devices, and manage calendars through different applications, e.g., voice search engine [24] and voice shopping [14]. In such systems, the Spoken Language Understanding (SLU) is usually performed in two steps: first, an Automatic Speech Recognition (ASR) is used to transcribe human speech; then Natural Language Understanding (NLU) models are applied on ASR transcripts to interpret users' requests. Different from traditional approaches, where NLU is applied on the original text, applying it on ASR transcripts poses new challenges,

I. Batyrshin et al. (Eds.): MICAI 2021, LNAI 13068, pp. 46–58, 2021.
https://doi.org/10.1007/978-3-030-89820-5_4

as ASR systems often generate transcripts with errors [9, 16]. These ASR errors can cause failures in virtual assistants' downstream tasks and applications, such as intent classification or slot filling [18], affecting the end-user experience. Similarly, several other end-to-end learning methods have been proposed for spoken language understanding (SLU) task [8, 12, 15, 17] without requiring intermediate text and show promising results on multiple tasks. However, their success heavily depends on a large amount of labeled training data. Such data is usually scarce and thus limiting the performance.

Despite the extensive investigation on the components of conversational systems as separated subjects, there is relatively scarce research on the implementation of such systems in industry settings. Particularly when addressing Out-Of-Vocabulary (OOV) words which is an important requirement for conversational systems adoption.

In a conversational system, there usually exist a set of components that work together to interact with users [2]. An STT component converts speech to text and sends it to an NLU component responsible for extracting user intents and relevant entities. These elements are passed to a control unit to decide proper actions. After that, a Natural Language Generation (NLG) component generates text output, and then a text-to-speech (TTS) component synthesizes voice to answer the user.

There exist some variations adding or integrating more components, but the general architecture is the same.

In this work, we present a Telephonic Sales System (TSS) implementation that models the products as named entities. The ASR component of the system correct transcripts using a post-processing phonetic correction component and sends them to an NLU engine that extracts entities mentioned by the user and determines the system behavior.

The results of this work give insights about baselines and implementation of integrated TSS in industrial scenarios where OOV words recognition is a functional requirement of the application. The ASR post-processing module uses a phonetic correction strategy and a DNN classifier to perform transcript correction to help the NLU engine recognize as many entities as possible.

The paper presents related work in Sect. 2, with Sect. 3 describing the system implementation. Section 4 shows the NLU pre-processing module. The experiments performed to measure the pre-processing module performance are described in Sect. 5, and the results are discussed in Sect. 6. Finally, conclusions and future work are presented in Sect. 7.

2   Background

There are different approaches regarding the ASR component in conversational systems. End-to-end training has attracted much attention recently and has improved the ASR performance in many cases; however, errors still exist in transcripts, mainly when the speech contains many OOV words, as in Telephonic Sales Systems (TSS).

One of the first breakthroughs in end-to-end ASR came from the Connectionist Temporal Classification (CTC) loss [11], which has been extended to train models that predict grapheme sequences [9] in conjunction with a language model (LM) based on recurrent neural networks (RNNs). This architecture is referred to as the RNN-transducer [10]. More recently, the attention-based encoder-decoder model has been applied to ASR [4,5].

One of the approaches to deal with OOV words in ASR is to correct transcription mistakes using post-correction techniques. A significant number of these initiatives involve user feedback mechanisms to learn error patterns. One such strategy to learn the error patterns has been reducing the ASR post-correction problem to a spelling correction problem [1], transforming the transcript to its correctly spelled form.

A model of ASR as a noisy transformation channel is presented by Shivakumar et al. [19] where a correction system is proposed capable of learning from the aggregated errors of all the ASR's independent modules. The proposed system uses the long-term context employing a neural network LM and can better choose between the possible transcriptions generated by the ASR and reintroduce previously pruned or unseen phrases. The system discussed in the article provides consistent improvements over 1.9% of the baseline ASR.

A novel Natural Language Processing (NLP) task called ASR post-processing for readability (APR) is proposed [13], that aims to transform the noisy ASR output into a readable text for humans and downstream tasks while maintaining the semantic meaning of the speaker. Also, it describes a method to address the lack of task-specific data by synthesizing examples for the APR task using the datasets collected for Grammatical Error Correction (GEC) followed by TTS and ASR. The article compare fine-tuned models based on several open-sourced and adapted pre-trained models with the traditional pipeline method. The results show that fine-tuned models improve the APR task's performance significantly, hinting at the potential benefits of using APR systems.

The paper [20] proposes some new ideas. Named entities are used to establish the context, leading the speech recognition pronunciation element into the post-treatment of speech recognition. Speech recognition results are represented with pronunciation primitive characters. Based on the improved dynamic edit distance, authors find the appropriate entity context, and then according to the context, they try to optimize the recognition results.

A versatile post-processing technique based on phonetic distance is presented in [21]. This article integrates domain knowledge with open-domain ASR results, leading to better performance. In particular, the presented technique can use domain restrictions using various degrees of domain knowledge, ranging from pure vocabulary restrictions through grammars or n-grams to restrictions on acceptable expressions.

Phonetic matching is used in applications such as name retrieval, where the spelling of a name is used to identify other strings that are likely to be of similar pronunciation. In their work [25], the authors explain the parallels between information retrieval and phonetic matching and describe the new phonetic matching techniques. Experimental comparison with existing techniques such as Soundex and edit distances based on precision and recall, demonstrates that the new techniques are superior. Also, reasoning from the similarity of phonetic matching and information retrieval, a combination of evidence to phonetic matching is applied.

In [3] phonetic correction strategies are used to correct errors generated by an ASR system. The cited work converts the ASR transcript to its International Phonetic Alphabet (IPA) representation to compare phonetic similarities between candidates and phrases in a domain-specific context. The authors use a sliding window algorithm to select candidate sentences for correction and edit distance between their phonetic representations to select the correction. Authors report improvement in 30% of the phrases recognized by Google's ASR service. This work is extended in [22] adding a neural component to prevent overly aggresive corrections reporting a 43.9% on relative WER improvement.

When constructing conversational systems, an NLU component is usually needed to map user intents to system actions. Still, depending on the robustness of the NLU component, it can be sensitive to transcripts mistakes. To make NLU models more robust to phonetic confusion between similar-sounding expressions, the novel phonetic-aware text representations were proposed [7]. Specifically, the representation of ASR transcripts at the phoneme level, aiming to capture pronunciation similarities, which are typically neglected in word-level representations (e.g., word embeddings). To train and evaluate the phoneme representations, noisy ASR transcripts of four existing datasets are generated: Stanford Sentiment Treebank, SQuAD, TREC Question Classification, and Subjectivity Analysis. The results show that common neural network architectures exploiting the proposed phoneme representations can effectively handle noisy transcripts and significantly outperform state-of-the-art baselines. This was tested on actual utterances spoken to the Alexa virtual assistant.

3   Approach and Implementation

The system is implemented using a PBX framework to make and receive phone calls; it communicates with other components using a REST interface and web services. The system, as shown in Fig. 1 is comprised of the following components: a Phone call controller (PBX); an ASR to transform the call recording to text transcript; a Correction Algorithm (CA) that corrects the ASR output according to the application context; a Correction decider (CD), which decides if the NLU engine should process the CA suggestion or the ASR transcript; an NLU engine to classify natural language intents and recognize entities; a Conversation Controller (CC) to perform problem-specific actions for the user's goal fulfillment; and a TTS to synthesize the text response produced by the CC into a sound file that can be played in the user's call.

A single interaction of the user with the system executes the following steps:

1. A customer calls the system.
2. The system uses the PBX REST interface to record the user's voice.

3. The system sends the recorded audio to a general-purpose ASR system and gets a transcription.
4. The system sends the ASR transcription to the CA.
5. The CA generates a correction suggestion for the transcript.
6. The CA sends the ASR output along with the suggestion and correction hyperparameters to the CD to evaluate the proposed correction.
7. The CA uses the CD output to send the appropriate input to the NLU engine.
8. The NLU engine process the input and return intents and entities found to the CC.
9. The CC selects an action based on the NLU engine's answer and a state machine.
10. The CC synthesizes the text using a Text To Speech (TTS) service.
11. The CC sends the audio response to the user through the PBX.

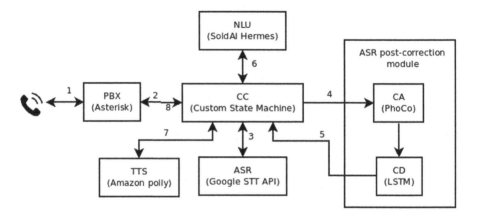

Fig. 1. System components

The presented mechanism is general and can be applied to a wide range of applications involving natural spoken communications between humans and machines. Currently, this approach is being used in a beverage order system for a large company in Mexico.

In this particular implementation, we used the following components: Asterisk as PBX; Google Speech-to-Text as the ASR; PhoCo as the CA; an LSTM neural network as CD; a custom deterministic state machine as CC; the NLU used was Hermes by SoldAI; and Amazon's Polly for TTS. However, the proposed technique can be implemented with alternative components to those mentioned above as long as they perform an equivalent functionality.

The used NLU engine performs intent and named entity recognition on short utterances trained with few-shot examples regarding the intents and entities relevant to the specific domain. In this particular case, the NLU is provided with examples of place orders and named entities of bottling company products.

Since the NLU engine uses a few-shot learning approach, it is sensitive to input noise, especially in settings where the Knowledge DataBase is relatively small. In those scenarios, transcription errors can harm the NLU performance, therefore preprocessing techniques, such as PhoCo, can help get a more precise recognition of intents and entities.

The system has an internal state machine developed to use the output of NLU to complete an order from the user. It uses a dynamic slot filling strategy to ask for clarification until it gets order completion. This strategy asks the customer relevant questions to identify particular items from a product list with various characteristics and specifications.

Finally, the system places an order in the company's delivery system using an API call, and a follow-up link for the order is sent to the customer.

4   NLU Preprocessing Module

This section presents the NLU preprocessing module's general architecture comprising the Phonetic corrector module and Neural classification module. This module is designed to work with few examples and short utterances, which is the case of the implemented TSS application. It needs fewer examples than those end-to-end deep learning systems often used in the state of the art research. It also applies a fast correction strategy using the PhoCo algorithm that allows the system to process information in near real-time and shortens the overall application response time.

4.1   Phonetic Correction

PhoCo algorithm [3] uses a string alignment approach to suggest corrections concerning a context. The context consists of words and phrases common in a specific domain but uncommon or not existent in general language, a string similarity threshold, a phonetic representation scheme, and a candidate generation algorithm, which are the algorithm's hyperparameters. The algorithm takes a hypothetical transcript from the ASR and outputs a corrected version of the transcript. The boost provided by the algorithm to context-specific words makes it suitable to work in systems that require product-specific recognition, particularly for TTS. This algorithm has been applied to TTS systems specialized to recognize products in business selling pizzas, wines, and beers.

4.2   Neural Classification Module

A neural classification module was implemented to evaluate PhoCo output. The network takes as inputs the ASR transcription, the PhoCo correction, and the PhoCo hyperparameters and outputs a binary number indicating if the proposed correction should be done. This module uses an RNN with the following layers in sequence, as shown in Fig. 2: an Embedding layer of size 128; an LSTM layer

of 64 hidden units; a 1D Max Pooling layer; a dense layer; and a single output
layer using a sigmoid activation function.

The topology was designed to be robust for text processing. The first layer
takes as input an indexed representation of the word ASR hypothesis and the correction suggestion generated by the PhoCo algorithm, as well as the parameters
used by PhoCo to generate the correction suggestion. Those inputs are passed
through an embedding layer, which learns a dense representation of the input,
including useful syntactic and semantic properties. Afterward, learned representations are passed to an LSTM layer with useful properties to track long and
short-term memory dependencies. The next layer applies a Max Pooling operation, which has been reported to be useful for the tracking of important features
on the text and makes the networks robust to feature translation. Finally, a
dense layer is applied and passed to a single neuron using a sigmoid activation
to perform the binary classification. The network was trained using an Adam
optimizer with a learning rate of 0.001. The last layer's output is then used to
decide if the correction suggested by PhoCo should be applied or if it is better
to use the ASR original hypothesis.

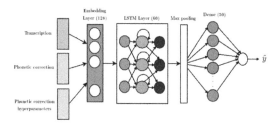

Fig. 2. Classification topology

5   Experiments

The experiments were performed using real audio from the telesales system. We
used 640 real audio transcriptions split in 80% for training, 10% for validation,
and 10% for testing. Those hypothetic transcripts were passed to the PhoCo
algorithm using different candidate selection algorithms, phonetic representation, and different thresholds computed using a grid search strategy from 0.05
to 0.6 with a 0.05 step size. This augmentation produced 72 variants for each
transcript, getting 36,864 examples for training and 9,216 divided evenly for validation and testing. The datasets were preprocessed doing text normalization
and noise removal and then used to train the network presented in Sect. 4.2 iter-
ating over different variations of the model and topologies. The validation set
was used to test different regularization hyperparameters changing the Dropout
rate. Once the best model in the validation set was found, we evaluated the
test set computing Precision, recall, and F_1 metrics. The network was trained
using an Nvidia GPU GTX 10880 TI running TensorFlow 2.0 and Keras API in

a Debian 10 GNU/Linux system. Afterward, the PhoCo algorithm is executed, including the neural corrector module to get the ASR correction to its final version. Then we calculate the Word Error Rate (WER) of the corrected transcript regarding the ground-truth and compare it with the WER obtained using the ASR hypothesis and the ground-truth.

We choose WER as a metric since it is well known and used for ASR evaluation [6]. The WER is computed counting the edit operations needed to transform the ASR hypothesis string h into the ground-truth target string t and dividing by the number of words in the target phrase as followed:

$$WER_{h,t} = \frac{S + I + D}{N} \tag{1}$$

In Eq. (1) S is the number of substitutions, I is the number of insertions and D is the number of deletions needed to transform h in t.

To measure the algorithm's impact on the NLU system and by extension on the conversational agent, the NLU engine was fed with different ASR outputs, PhoCo corrections, classifier corrections, and real transcripts ground-truth. The obtained entities were recorded, then the three sets of hypothesized entities were compared using Jaccard distance with the ground-truth.

Jaccard distance [23] is useful for comparing how similar a set of entities found by the NLU engine from one evaluated phrase is, to the set of entities found in the ground-truth. More traditional metrics such as precision, recall, and F_1 score were calculated to examine the correction's effect on entity recognition's task at specific threshold configurations of the correction system.

Notice that our gold standard for the recognized entities is not necessarily the actual entities present in the text but those found by the specific NLU engine when fed with the ground-truth text as input. That is because we are not evaluating the accuracy of the NLU in the detection of entities, but rather how effective is the correction of the ASR in our specific application setting. However, we expect our results to be useful independent of the NLU system to be used.

6   Results and Discussion

The trained Neural classification module results are presented in Table 1, and shows a high F_1 score of 0.98, indicating good performance. Results obtained indicate a good fit of the network to generalize to the test set.

Table 1. Evaluation metrics computed over the test dataset.

Class	Precision	Recall	F_1 score	Support
0	0.99	0.99	0.99	3302
1	0.96	0.97	0.97	1305
Macro average	**0.98**	**0.98**	**0.98**	**4607**

To compare the experimentation results we considered three output transcripts produced for each example: the original transcript returned by the ASR T_a; the transcript corrected by the PhoCo T_p and the one selected by the classifier T_c. Notice that T_c is always either one of T_a or T_p, since the classifier doesn't modify the transcriptions only decide if the correction produced by the PhoCo is recommended or not.

We used WER as a general measure of concordance between the different transcripts and the ground-truth. Then, we use Jaccard distance, precision, recall, and F_1 score to measure the agreement between the set of entities found by the NLU when fed with the transcripts T_p, T_a and T_c and the set of entities produced by the ground-truth. The global WER computed with all transcripts from the test set obtained directly from the ASR was **0.298**. The corrected transcripts produced by the PhoCo reduced the global WER to **0.207** whereas the classifier reduced the global WER on the test set to **0.181**. Those results represent improvements on relative WER to the ASR in the order of 30% and 39%, respectively. The Table 2 summarize those results.

Table 2. WER between transcriptions groundtruth and transcriptions from ASR, PHOCO and classifier.

WER	ASR	PHOCO	Classifier
Global	0.298	0.207	0.181
Relative	-	30%	39%

The WER metric shows that using the PhoCo improves the transcript's accuracy, and furthermore, when the neural classifier is used, the results are even better. Those results are encouraging; however, we are interested not only in the transcripts accuracy improvement but also in enhancing the user experience when interacting with the system. In that regard, one of the key elements is to correctly recognize the maximum possible number of entities contained in the phrase uttered by the user, since unrecognized entities provoke additional interactions between user and agent, in which the former is inquired to provide information for the slot filling process completion.

Considering as the objective the set of entities found in the ground-truth phrase when processed by the NLU system, we use Jaccard, precision, recall, and F_1 to measure the performance of the different hypothesized transcripts.

As shown in Table 3 the ASR has a good precision but low recall; that is expected since the ASR lacks the knowledge of the specific entities used on the application domain and is unable to recognize OOV words correctly.

Table 3. Average metrics for entity recognition with respect to NLU groundtruth output.

Metric	ASR	PHOCO	Classifier
Jaccard	0.28	0.19	0.15
Precision	0.98	0.87	0.97
Recall	0.76	0.85	0.85
F_1	0.85	0.86	0.91

The main task of the PhoCo is to transform the transcription in such a way that it contains as many domain-specific terms as possible. That behavior is expected to improve recall on the entity recognition task but comes with the cost of reduced average precision. In general, the F_1 score improves marginally with the PhoCo transcripts. However, those results vary according to the threshold parameter. We performed metric computation grouped by threshold level used in the experiments to visualize that dependency.

Regarding the classifier, the results show that it is able to determine when the correction proposed by the PhoCo should be used and when to keep the original transcript from the ASR. As can be seen in Table 3, the classifier reaches the same level of recall as the PhoCo, but without paying a significant price on precision, which produces a higher F_1 overall.

Precision and recall on NER task are shown on Fig. 3. The baseline precision obtained with the ASR is maintained, even improved a bit, by the PhoCo and the classifier up to a threshold of around 0.4, then the precision starts to degrade dramatically due to the aggressive correction policy, but kept at very good levels when the classifier is used. The recall presents an improvement both with the PhoCo and the classifier against the ASR baseline.

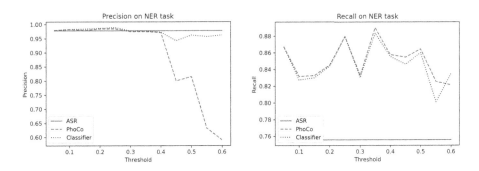

Fig. 3. Precision and Recall by threshold level

Figure 4 exhibits the performance measured by F_1 for the PhoCo with and without the classifier adjustment, compared with the ASR baseline. As shown, the PhoCo produces better results than the ASR on the entity recognition task up to a 0.4 threshold; then its performance starts to decay up to the point of being worse than the ASR.

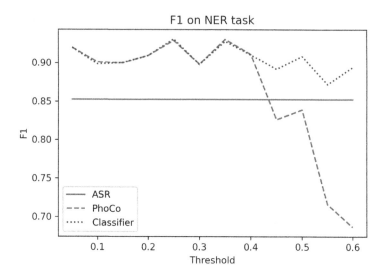

Fig. 4. F_1 by threshold level

7   Conclusions and Future Work

A method was presented to improve the transcripts produced by an ASR system as a preprocessing step for NLU tasks in the context of automatic conversational agents. In particular, the method was tested on an agent currently in production, which takes orders via phone for a bottling company. The experimentation was carried out with audio recordings from real customers placing orders to the system. The method comprises two stages, the PhoCo and a neural classifier that validates the PhoCo output against the ASR proposed transcription. The PhoCo algorithm has shown good results but lacked flexibility. In general, it helps the system to recognize OOV words but degrades the precision due to correction mistakes, lowering its performance for higher levels of the threshold parameter ($t > 0.4$). The neural classifier serves as a PhoCo regularizer in the sense that avoids overly aggressive corrections that do not generalize well while maintaining those that could be useful for the task at hand, achieving a better F_1 score. WER metrics were computed for the different outputs produced by the ASR, the PhoCo, and the classifier compared to the ground-truth transcript. The 0.298 ASR baseline was reduced to 0.207 by the PhoCo and to 0.181 when including the classification stage. Those results represent a significant relative WER improvement of 30% and 39%, respectively. The method also proves its worth when measured for the entity recognition task, as shown by the improvement on F_1 score from 0.85 to 0.91.

The results are relevant, considering the application is currently in production. An improvement in recognizing named entities and the audio transcript is vital to enhance the user experience while reducing time and resources consumed in the sales ordering process. On the other hand, given the independence of the developed method concerning the ASR system and the NLU engine used, it could be utilized within a pipeline as an intermediate step between both components for other applications and independently of the ASR and NLU specifics. In the future, we pretend to solidify our experimentation with more data and from different application domains and compare the method against end-to-end correction approaches.

References

1. Bassil, Y., Alwani, M.: Post-editing ERRO correction algorithm for speech recognition using bing spelling suggestion. Int. J. Adv. Comput. Sci. Appl. **3** (2012). https://doi.org/10.14569/IJACSA.2012.030217
2. Berg, M.: Modelling of natural dialogues in the context of speech-based information and control systems. Ph.D. thesis, July 2014
3. Campos-Sobrino, D., Campos-Soberanis, M., Martínez-Chin, I., Uc-Cetina, V.: Corrección de errores del reconocedor de voz de google usando métricas de distancia fonética. Res. Comput. Sci. **148**(1), 57–70 (2019)
4. Chan, W., Jaitly, N., Le, Q.V., Vinyals, O.: Listen, attend and spell: A neural network for large vocabulary conversational speech recognition. In: ICASSP (2016). http://williamchan.ca/papers/wchan-icassp-2016.pdf
5. Chorowski, J., Bahdanau, D., Cho, K., Bengio, Y.: End-to-end continuous speech recognition using attention-based recurrent NN: first results. In: NIPS 2014 Workshop on Deep Learning, December 2014 (2014)
6. Errattahi, R., Hannani, A.E., Ouahmane, H.: Automatic speech recognition errors detection and correction: a review. Procedia Comput. Sci. **128**, 32–37 (2018). https://doi.org/10.1016/j.procs.2018.03.005, http://www.sciencedirect.com/science/article/pii/S1877050918302187, 1st International Conference on Natural Language and Speech Processing
7. Fang, A., Filice, S., Limsopatham, N., Rokhlenko, O.: Using Phoneme Representations to Build Predictive Models Robust to ASR Errors, pp. 699–708. ACM, July 2020. https://doi.org/10.1145/3397271.3401050
8. Ghannay, S., Caubrière, A., Estève, Y., Laurent, A., Morin, E.: End-to-end named entity extraction from speech. In: EEE Spoken Language Technology Workshop (2018)
9. Graves, A., Jaitly, N.: Towards end-to-end speech recognition with recurrent neural networks. In: 31st International Conference on Machine Learning (ICML 2014), vol. 5, pp. 1764–1772, January 2014
10. Graves, A.: Sequence transduction with recurrent neural networks (2012)
11. Graves, A., Fernández, S., Gomez, F., Schmidhuber, J.: Connectionist temporal classification: labelling unsegmented sequence data with recurrent neural 'networks. In: Proceedings of the 23rd International Con-ference on Machine Learning, vol. 2006, pp. 369–376, January 2006. https://doi.org/10.1145/1143844.1143891
12. Haghani, P., et al.: From audio to semantics: approaches to end-to-end spoken language understanding. In: Spoken Language Technology Workshop (2018)

13. Liao, J., et al.: Improving readability for automatic speech recognition transcription (2020)
14. Limsopatham, N., Rokhlenko, O., Carmel, D.: Research challenges in building a voice-based artificial personal shopper - position paper. In: Proceedings of the 2018 EMNLP Workshop SCAI: The 2nd International Workshop on Search-Oriented Conversational AIpp, 40–45, January 2018. https://doi.org/10.18653/v1/W18-5706
15. Lugosch, L., Ravanelli, M., Ignoto, P., Tomar, V.S., Bengio, Y.: Speech model pre-training for end-to-end spoken language understanding (2019)
16. Ogawa, A., Hori, T.: Error detection and accuracy estimation in automatic speech recognition using deep bidirectional recurrent neural networks. Speech Commun. **89** (2017).https://doi.org/10.1016/j.specom.2017.02.009
17. Qian, Y., et al.: Exploring ASR-free end-to-end modeling to improve spoken language understanding in a cloud-based dialog system. In: 2017 IEEE Automatic Speech Recognition and Understanding Workshop (ASRU), pp. 569–576 (2017). https://doi.org/10.1109/ASRU.2017.8268987
18. Schumann, R., Angkititrakul, P.: Incorporating asr errors with attention-based, jointly trained RNN for intent detection and slot filling. In: 2018 IEEE International Conference on Acoustics, Speech and Signal Processing (ICASSP), pp. 6059–6063, April 2018. https://doi.org/10.1109/ICASSP.2018.8461598
19. Shivakumar, P.G., Li, H., Knight, K., Georgiou, P.G.: Learning from past mistakes: improving automatic speech recognition output via noisy-clean phrase context modeling. CoRR abs/1802.02607 (2018), http://arxiv.org/abs/1802.02607
20. Song, S., Zhang, N., Huang, H.: Named entity recognition based on conditional random fields. Clust. Comput. **22**, 1–12 (2019). https://doi.org/10.1007/s10586-017-1146-3
21. Twiefel, J., Baumann, T., Heinrich, S., Wermter, S.: Improving domain-independent cloud-based speech recognition with domain-dependent phonetic post-processing. In: Proceedings of the Twenty-Eighth AAAI Conference on Artificial Intelligencevol. vol. 2, pp. 1529–1535, July 2014
22. Viana-Cámara, R., Campos-Soberanis, M., Campos-Sobrino, D.: Modelo híbrido fonético-neural para corrección en sistemas de reconocimiento del habla. Res. Comput. Sci. **149**(8), 1163–1177 (2020)
23. Vorontsov, I., Kulakovskiy, I., Makeev, V.: Jaccard index based similarity measure to compare transcription factor binding site models. Algorith. Mol. Biol. AMB **8**, 23 (2013). https://doi.org/10.1186/1748-7188-8-23
24. Vtyurina, A., Fourney, A., Morris, M., Findlater, L., White, R.: Bridging screen readers and voice assistants for enhanced eyes-free web search. In: he World Wide Web Conference, pp. 3590–3594, May 2019). https://doi.org/10.1145/3308558.3314136
25. Zobel, J., Dart, P.: Phonetic string matching: lessons from information retrieval, July 2002. https://doi.org/10.1145/243199.243258

Estimation of Imageability Ratings of English Words Using Neural Networks

Vladimir V. Bochkarev$^{(\boxtimes)}$ ⓘ, Andrey V. Savinkov ⓘ, and Anna V. Shevlyakova ⓘ

Kazan Federal University, Kremlyovskaya 18, Kazan 420008, Russia

Abstract. The article considers the problem of imageability ratings estimation of English words using artificial neural networks. To train and test the models, we use data of several freely available psycholinguistic databases. We compared two approaches based on different vector representations of words. The first approach uses pre-trained fastText vectors. The second one utilizes explicit word vectors built on the basis of co-occurrence statistics with the most frequent words extracted from the Google Books Ngram corpus. We employed the MRC Psycholinguistic Database to obtain the value of Spearman's correlation coefficient between imageability ratings and their estimations. The highest resulting value equaled 0.882. This significantly improves the results obtained in previous works. The approach proposed in this paper can be used to create large dictionaries with imageability ratings, which is important for many practical problems.

Keywords: Imageability · Word co-occurrence · Neural networks · fastText · Google Books Ngram

1 Introduction

The notion of imageability of words has been traditionally the focus of attention in psycholinguistics and psychology for several decades. To obtain values for estimation of imageability, researchers conducted experiments. They informed the participants about the experimental procedures and asked them to score words using a numeric scale. As a result, several databases of words with imageability ratings appeared.

The largest one is the MRC Psycholinguistic Database that includes syntactic information and psychological data for the entries. It contains 150837 words [1] with only 9240 words that possess imageability ratings. The other bases relevant for our work are a database presented in [2] (hereinafter, PYM), the Toronto Word Pool (TWP) by Friendly et al. [3], and two datasets described by Clark and Paivio (CP) [4]. PYM provides the set of 925 nouns with imageability ratings; TWP consists of 1080 rated words. CP consists of two datasets that include 925 and 2311 words with imageability ratings.

MRC is a database that collected imageability ratings on largest set of words. The number of the rated words seems to be relatively small because it is time- and labour-consuming to obtain data experimentally.

Therefore, due to significant complicacy of manual data collection, imageability prediction is gaining attention and significance in natural language processing. Computational methods can contribute much to imageability studies and related tasks [5]. There

© Springer Nature Switzerland AG 2021
I. Batyrshin et al. (Eds.): MICAI 2021, LNAI 13068, pp. 59–69, 2021.
https://doi.org/10.1007/978-3-030-89820-5_5

are recent articles that have touched upon the problem of imageability by using automated processing. Charbonnier and Wartena use a regression model to predict concreteness and imagery of words [6]. Nikola Ljubesic et al. [7] investigate the predictability of imageability via supervised learning, using word embeddings as explanatory variables. To reveal metaphors, Tsvetkov et al. [8] use a logistic regression classifier to propagate imageability scores from MRC ratings to all words for which they have vector space representations.

The work objective is to create an estimator that predicts imageability based on distribution of words as we assume that contexts of use of words with high imageability ratings differ from those with low imageability ratings. To do it, use vector representations of words are used.

There are different approaches to word vector representations [9–11]. Currently, the most widely used methods are based on neural network vector models (word embeddings) [12, 13]. However, less complicated explicit word representations are also commonly used [14]. In our paper, we compare testing of these two approaches to estimate imageability ratings. Firstly, we use pre-trained fastText word vectors [15]. The authors showed in [15] that using a combination of several modifications of the standard word2vec training pipeline significantly improves the quality of the resulting word vectors. Some data pre-processing strategies were also tested in this paper. An important result of [15] was high-quality vector representations of words obtained by training on large sets of texts (with a total size of about 600 billion words). These sets of vectors pre-trained using the fastText algorithm are available for free use.

In the above-mentioned papers [6, 7], the fastText vectors are used as input data for the model. To estimate imageability rating, the regression by the SVM method was used in [6] and two approaches were tested in [7] using SVM and the feedforward neural network.

Secondly, we use the method of explicit word representation based on bigram frequencies [16]. We also perform semantic analysis of contexts that contribute most to changes in imageability rating estimations.

2   Data and Method

The study was performed using several online resources. The MRC, PYM, CP and TWP databases were employed as sources of imageability ratings. We used the MRC data to train and test the model; and to compare our results with the previously obtained ones, we tested the model on PYM, CP, and TWP.

We built models based on both explicit word vectors and word embeddings. The first method requires data on frequencies of bigrams that we borrowed from the English subcorpus of Google Books Ngram [17]. It is the largest database of electronic texts that provides data on frequencies of individual words, as well as n-grams and syntactic bigrams. N-grams are contiguous sequences of words. Syntactic bigrams are basic units of syntactic structure, non-linear bigrams that reflect syntactic relations where one word is the head and another one is its dependent [18]. The GBN offers data on frequencies of n-grams that include up to 5 words.

The GBN corpora have been updated three times. The present study uses data of the third version of the GBN English subcorpus, namely on frequencies of bigrams and syntactic bigrams. We obtained explicit word vector representations using the method of co-occurrence with the most frequent word (CFW). The CFW method is described in several papers [19–21]. According to this method, the word W is represented by vectors of bigram frequencies Wx and xW, where W is the target word and x is the context word. Most frequent words in the corpus are regarded as context words. Our paper uses 20,000 context words. Thus, the dimension of the vectors was 40,000.

Pre-trained vectors trained using fastText were also employed to build the models. We used vectors trained without subword information following recommendations described in [6]. Thus, two sets of pre-trained vectors were utilized, namely word vectors trained on Wikipedia 2017 and word vectors trained on Common Crawl [15].

If fastText vectors can be directly fed to the input of a neural network, the use of CFW method requires preprocessing of input data. Based on previous works [22], we use three ways of preprocessing of the input data. The first way was a simple normalization of the input data matrix by rows (each row of the input data is the bigram frequencies for the selected target word) so that the sum of the elements of the row equaled one. One more way is to determine the vector components for each target word by calculating the Pointwise Mutual Information for each bigram [16]:

$$PMI(c, t) = \log_2 \frac{p(c|t)}{p(c)} = \log_2 \frac{p(c, t)}{p(c)p(t)} \tag{1}$$

where p(c) and p(t) are individual probabilities (relative frequencies) of the target and context words, respectively, p(c,t) is probability (relative frequency) of a bigram in the Google Books Ngram texts. Negative values PMI(c,t) indicate that this bigram occurs less frequently in the texts than it would occur in a random text. Obviously, frequencies of such bigrams are not very informative; however, their negative values of PMI can significantly affect training of the neural network. To reduce the influence of such low-frequency bigrams, we used another modification of expression (1) by adding one to the expression under the logarithm:

$$\tilde{PMI}(c, t) = \log_2 \left(\frac{p(c|t)}{p(c)} + 1 \right) = \log_2 \left(\frac{p(c, t)}{p(c)p(t)} + 1 \right) \tag{2}$$

Then, using the expression (2), the vectors of the bigram frequencies were transformed into vectors of the PMI values; and the probabilities of the bigrams p (c, t) and the individual probabilities of the target and context words p(t) and p(c) were determined by normalizing corresponding frequencies to the corpus size.

The last way of representing the input data was to take the logarithm of frequencies of all bigrams following the expression: $\log_2(F(c,t) + 1)$. In this expression, one is added to the logarithm to avoid the incorrect operation of taking the logarithm of zero bigram frequencies.

To solve the problem of imageability prediction of the target words, the direct distribution neural network (multilayer perceptron) was chosen. The neural network contained 40000 neurons in an input layer, 64, 128, and 128 neurons in three hidden layers, respectively, and one neuron in an output layer. The output neuron predicted the imageability factor of the target words. The rectifier activation function (RELU) [23] was used as the activation function for the input layer and all hidden layers. The output layer was activated by the linear activation function. We used the batch normalization [24] for the input layer and all three hidden layers since it speeds up the training of the neural network and it gives some regularization effect. This results in decreasing overfitting of the model and eliminating the need in dropout in our case. Other methods of regularization have also been tried to improve the quality of neural network training such as L2-regularization and the dropout layer. However, these methods did not significantly improve the training results.

The model was trained using the backpropagation method applying the Adaptive Moment Estimation ("Adam") [25] algorithm; the mean absolute error (L1-Loss) function was used as the loss function. Spearman's correlation coefficient between image-ability ratings and their estimations was used as a criterion for the quality of network training.

The model was trained at various initial values of the learning rate parameter to determine the optimal value that provides maximum of the Spearman correlation. The network training procedure was performed for each parameter value five times; the learning rate parameter, weight coefficients of the network and other fitting parameters of the recognizer were stored for the selection of best training result.

The neural network was created and trained in the PyTorch framework [26] for machine learning.

A neural network of similar architecture was also used for the case of using pre-trained fastText vectors as input data, but the dimension of the input vectors in this network was only 300. For this case, we also used the same optimization algorithm, loss function, and selection technique of the network parameters as in the previous one.

3   Result

To test the trained models, 20% of words with imageability ratings were selected from the MRC database. The selection was carried out at random so that frequency distributions of words in the training and test samples were approximately the same. The selected 20% of words were not used at the stage of training the neural network but were utilized to test the quality of the resulting model. Thus, 960 words were selected for the test sample from 4802 words that have pre-trained fastText vectors and are presented in the MRC database. The values of Pearson's, Spearman's, and Kendall's correlation coefficients between the values of imageability ratings and their estimates are shown in Table 1.

Table 1. Pearson's, Spearman's, and Kendall's correlation coefficients between the values of imageability ratings and their estimates using the fastText vectors for the MRC dataset

Set of vectors	Pearson (r)	Spearman (ρ)	Kendall (τ)
CommonCrawl	0.853	0.854	0.666
Wikipedia	0.841	0.842	0.649

Better results were obtained using vectors trained on the CommonCrawl corpus (that coincides with the findings by Wartena [6]). Similarly, 964 words were selected for the test sample from 4824 words that and are presented both in the GBN corpus and the MRC database. The testing results of the CFW method using various types of input data and methods of their normalization are shown in Table 2.

Table 2. Pearson's, Spearman's, and Kendall's correlation coefficients between the values of imageability ratings and their estimates using the CFW method for the MRC dataset

Set of vectors		Normalization to 1	PMI	$Log_2(1 + x)$
Ordinary bigrams	r	0.747	0.861	0.864
	ρ	0.764	0.869	0.868
	τ	0.573	0.685	0.684
Syntactic bigrams	r	0.770	0.859	0.874
	ρ	0.776	0.862	0.882
	τ	0.587	0.678	0.694

As one can see from the table, the use of ordinary and syntactic bigrams provides comparable accuracy. In this case, the best results (the value of Spearman's correlation coefficient equals 0.882) are obtained using the logarithmic frequencies of the bigrams. However, this method has a drawback that the resulting estimates may change when applied to data obtained from a corpus of a different size. As for the other two ways of preprocessing normalized values are fed to the input of the model that do not depend on the size of the utilized corpus. Therefore, to conduct further comparisons, we choose the method with PMI vectors for ordinary bigrams which provides slightly lower accuracy (the value of Spearman's correlation coefficient is 0.869).

Comparing the values given in Tables 1 and 2, one can see that the use of explicit vector representation gives higher accuracy for this task. Figure 1 shows bidimensional distribution of the values of imageability ratings and their estimates. Figure 1, A shows the results obtained using the CFW (ordinary bigrams, PMI) method, and Fig. 1, B shows the results obtained using fastText (CommonCrawl). Comparing these figures, one can conclude that the CFW method has a slight advantage over fastText.

Now we consider how the accuracy of imageability estimation depends on word frequency. It is a complicated task to carry out detailed analysis of the dependence of accuracy on frequency since the size of the test sample is small. We used the following approach. Having sorted the words in the test sample by frequency, Spearman's correlation coefficient was calculated in a sliding window (the window length was 225). The geometric mean of frequency of words that fell into the sliding window was calculated for each position of the window. The calculation results are shown in Fig. 2. The results for explicit word vectors (ordinary bigrams, PMI) are shown by black dots, the results for fastText are shown by circles (a set of CommonCrawl vectors). The advantage of CFW is most significant for high-frequency words. The accuracy of both methods begins to decrease with frequency decrease and the gap between them also decreases. Nevertheless, the CWF method retains a slight advantage for the least frequently occurring words in the test sample.

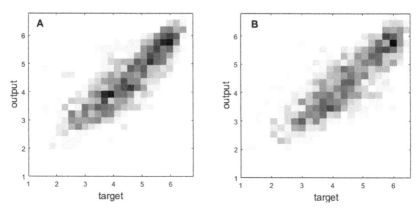

Fig. 1. Bidimensional distribution the values of imageability ratings and their estimates. A – explicit word vectors (ordinary bigrams, PMI); B – fastText (CommonCrawl set of vectors)

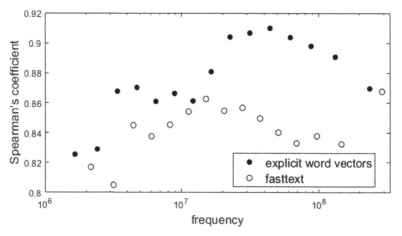

Fig. 2. Dependence of imageability rating estimation accuracy on word frequency

Now we compare the achieved level of accuracy of imageability estimation with the results obtained in earlier studies. The above-mentioned study [7] also uses fastText vectors (CommonCrawl) as input data. The authors perform comparative testing of regression on MRC data using SVM and feedforward neural network (FNN) and obtain Spearman's correlation coefficients between the imageability rating values and their estimates of 0.803 and 0.787, respectively, for the two methods they used. It is noteworthy that the second method (fastText + FNN) corresponds to what we have done; however, the value of Spearman's coefficient (it equals 0.852, see Table 1) that we obtained for a similar case is significantly higher. It can be assumed that this difference relates to differences in the regularization methods used in our study and in [7].

Data on testing the model on the TWP, CP and PYM datasets are presented in [6]. To compare our results with the data given in [6], we selected words from the TWP and PYM datasets that were not included in the training set and found imageability estimates for them. Table 3 shows the values of the correlation coefficients between the values of imageability ratings and their estimation. It should be emphasized that, in this case, we compare the estimation obtained by the neural network with the rating values extracted from PYM, TWP and CP; we do not use the ratings from the MRC database on which the network was trained. For comparison, we present the results obtained using the CFW (ordinary bigrams, PMI) method and those obtained using the fastText vectors (a set of CommonCrawl vectors). The values of the correlation coefficients obtained in [6] are shown in the last row of the table. We chose the best values from those given in [6] that were obtained also using the fastText vectors trained on the CommonCrawl dataset by utilizing the SVM method.

Table 3. Pearson's, Spearman's, and Kendall's correlation coefficients between the values of imageability ratings and their estimates for the TWP, PYM and CP datasets

Method		TWP	PYM	CP_A	CP_E
CFW	r	0.867	0.874	0.771	0.880
	ρ	0.879	0.881	0.794	0.871
	τ	0.720	0.693	0.594	0.688
fastText	r	0.838	0.827	0.809	0.863
	ρ	0.821	0.827	0.808	0.845
	τ	0.638	0.629	0.604	0.657
fastText + SVM [6]	r	0.774	0.813	0.676	0.796
	ρ	–	–	–	–
	τ	0.559	0.618	0.499	0.569

As you can see, our models give noticeably higher accuracy even when using the same input data (fastText vectors). This seems to be result from the fact that neural networks are a more efficient approximation method than SVMs.

4 Result Interpretation

Our task is to reveal the context words that have the greatest impact on the accuracy of imageability estimation and perform their semantic analysis. We have 20 thousand context words, and we consider bigrams of the Wx and xW types. Thus, the neural network has 40 thousand inputs. We zero out each of these inputs in succession and calculate the imageability rating for all words from the test sample. When the i-th output is disabled, there is less information at the input of the neural network and the correlation coefficient between the values of the imageability rating and its estimate $\rho^{(i)}$ will usually be less than the correlation coefficient ρ obtained using the full vector of input data. Then, we determine the change in the correlation coefficient for each of the i-th inputs $\Delta\rho^{(i)} = \rho^{(i)} - \rho$. The greater the drop in the correlation coefficient with the disabled i-th input, the more information on imageability is contained in the frequency values of the corresponding bigram pattern that include the context word. After sorting the bigrams in ascending order $\Delta\rho^{(i)}$, we find word combinations at the top of the resulting list that being included to the sample can contribute most to the accuracy of imageability estimation.

Thus, we analysed contexts the studied words appear in and determined the context words which contribute most to the accuracy of imageability estimation. Our aim was to reveal such words without detailed analysis; however, in some cases, we provide interpretation of the described contexts.

We divided the above-mentioned context words into groups. The largest and most "influential" one is represented by words describing physical features of an object (or used in figurative sense):

1. Form (shaped, symmetrical, shapes, asymmetric, uneven, spherical, squared, deformed).
2. Size and height (biggest, enormous, gigantic, tall, huge).
3. Temperature (warm, warmed)
4. Spatial orientation (vertical, horizontal, outside, inside, inner, diagonal, beneath, below)
5. Colour (dusky, yellow, blue)
6. Material (plastic, nylon, leather)
7. Physical state (healthy, drunken, swollen)

We suppose that these words contribute much to imageability ratings as they contain relevant semantic information for description of highly imageable words or used in figurative sense with scarcely imageable ones. If we, for example, use the word *spherical*, we most likely think of some perceptible object that possesses such form. This word is unlikely to combine with words with low imageability ratings such as *love* or *imagination*. The words from the second subgroup describe size and height that basically refer to highly imageable objects though can be used as intensifiers with scarcely imageable words (like *enormous influence*). The words from the third subgroup such as *warm* can be interpreted as having high temperature that can be felt by the skin. We suppose that it often refers to words with high imageability ratings that can be in contact with human skin. However, it is also used in figurative sense like in *warm feelings* or *warm welcome*. The words forming the fourth subgroup denote how objects "interact" with the world around them, show their orientation in the space. We suspect that they most often combine with words that have visual image, i.e., with high imageability ratings. Colour terms represent the fifth subgroup and can be used either in set expressions (*black hole, yellow press*) or collocate with objects whose colour can change and this change is relevant [27]. We suppose that these words are more often used with highly imageable objects since differentiation by colour is not relevant for words with low imageability ratings. Objects that are made of some material like plastic or nylon are usually artefacts, things made by people. Therefore, they are highly imageable. The words from the last subgroup describe physical state of some objects that are likely to be highly imageable, in our opinion.

The second large group of context words that we determined includes words (*roasted, fried, perforated, skinned, wrinkled*) that describe physical changes of something. They also contribute much to the accuracy of imageability ratings as they most likely describe objects with high imageability ratings.

One more group consists of such words as *invisible, perceptible, imaginary, disappeared, stolen* that denote whether we can percept or feel something. They denote presence or absence of something and can be used with both low and highly imageable words.

The words *real, genuine, fake, artificial* form one more group of "influential" words.

The other group includes words that describe behaviour or effects produced by something (*annoying, roaring, teasing*).

Among the context words that contribute most to imageability ratings are words (nouns) that form a valent structure, i.e. describe some stable semantic relations with other nouns (like *skin, holiday*), opinion adjectives (*friendly, luxurious*), some verbs (*switches, lasts, palms, prevents*).

If we analyse the structure of the top list bigrams, we can see that the largest group of context words is presented by adjectives, participle two and -ing forms. Nouns and verbs co-occur with the target words less often; and functional words is the rarest group to occur in the whole sample (as the number of functional words itself is not that large).

5 Conclusion

The paper considers a method for imageability ratings estimation of English words using data on the distribution of these words. To train and test the models, we use data of several freely available psycholinguistic databases. We tested two approaches to word vector representations. The first one used pre-trained fastText vectors as input data for the model. The second one utilized explicit word vectors based on co-occurrence statistics with the most frequent words (CFW) extracted from the Google Books Ngram corpus.

We employed the MRC Psycholinguistic Database to obtain the value of Spearman's correlation coefficient between imageability ratings and their estimations. The highest resulting value equaled 0.882. Even though the model was trained only on the MRC database data, the testing showed a high level of correlation between the estimates obtained by the neural network and the values of imageability ratings given in [2–4] (see Table 3). The comparative analysis showed that we managed to significantly improve the accuracy of predicting imageability ratings obtained in earlier works, for example, in [6].

Comparison of the two algorithms unexpectedly showed a slight advantage of the CFW method over the method that uses pre-trained fastText vectors. However, both approaches have obvious advantages. As follows from the presented results (see Fig. 2), if we use pre-trained fastText vectors, the estimation accuracy decreases more slowly with decreasing word frequency. This makes it possible to best extrapolate imageability ratings to the widest range of words using synchronous data. In turn, the CFW method can be easily adapted to diachronic data, for example, extracted from the Google Books Ngram corpus. Another advantage of this approach is the ease of interpretation of the obtained results. We tried to reveal and perform semantic interpretation of the most informative context words that contribute much to imageability ratings estimation.

The results of the study can be used to create large dictionaries with imageability ratings, which is important for many practical problems.

Acknowledgements. This research was financially supported by RFBR, grant № 19–07-00807.

References

1. Coltheart, M.: The MRC psycholinguistic database. Quart. J. Exp. Psychol. Sect. A **33**(4), 497–505 (1981). https://doi.org/10.1080/14640748108400805
2. Paivio, A., Yuille, J., Madigan, S.: Concreteness, imagery, and meaningfulness values for 925 nouns. J. Exp. Psychol. **76**(1), 1–25 (1968). https://doi.org/10.1037/h0025327
3. Friendly, M., Franklin, P., Hoffman, D., Rubin, D.: The Toronto word pool: norms for imagery, concreteness, orthographic variables, and grammatical usage for 1,080 words. Behav. Res. Method Instrument. **14**, 375–399 (1982)
4. Clark, J., Paivio, A.: Extensions of the Paivio, Yuille, and Madigan (1968) norms. Behav. Res. Method Instrument Comput. **36**, 371–383 (2004)
5. Solovyev, V.D., Ivanov, V.V., Akhtiamov, R.B.: Dictionary of abstract and concrete words of the Russian language: a methodology for creation and application. J. Res. Appl. Linguist. **10**, 215–227 (2019)
6. Charbonnier, J., Wartena, C.: Predicting word concreteness and imagery. In: Proceedings of the 13th International Conference on Computational Semantics - Long Papers, pp. 176–187. Association for Computational Linguistics, Gothenburg, Sweden (2019). doi:https://doi.org/10.18653/v1/W19-041
7. Ljubešić, N., Fišer, D., Peti-Stantić, A.: Predicting concreteness and imageability of words within and across languages via word embeddings. In: Proceedings of The Third Workshop on Representation Learning for NLP, pp. 217–222. Association for Computational Linguistics, Melbourne, Australia (2018). doi:https://doi.org/10.18653/v1/W18-3028
8. Tsvetkov, Y., Mukomel, E., Gershman, A.: Cross-lingual metaphor detection using common semantic features. In: Proceedings of the First Workshop on Metaphor in NLP, pp. 45–51. Association for Computational Linguistics, Atlanta, Georgia (2013)
9. Weeds, J., Weir, D., McCarthy, D.: Characterising measures of lexical distributional similarity. In: Proceedings of the 20th International Conference on Computational Linguistics, pp. 1015–1021. COLING, Geneva, Switzerland (2004)
10. Pantel, P.: Inducing ontological co-occurrence vectors. In: Proceedings of the 43rd Conference of the Association for Computational Linguistics, pp. 125–132. Association for Computational Linguistics, USA (2005)
11. Mikolov, T., Sutskever, I., Chen, K., Corrado, G., Dean, J.: Distributed representations of words and phrases and their compositionality. In: Advances in Neural Information Processing Systems. vol. 26, pp. 3111–3119. Curran Associates, Inc. (2013)
12. Mikolov, T., Corrado, G.S., Chen, K., Dean, J.: Efficient estimation of word representations in vector space. In: Proceedings of the International Conference on Learning Representations, pp. 1–12. (2013)
13. Kutuzov, A., Øvrelid, L., Szymanski, T., Velldal, E.: Diachronic word embeddings and semantic shifts: a survey. In: Proceedings of the 27th international conference on computational linguistics, pp. 1384–1397. Association for Computational Linguistics, Santa Fe, New Mexico, USA (2018)
14. Tang, X.: A state-of-the-art of semantic change computation. arXiv preprint arXiv:1801. 09872 (2018). doi:https://doi.org/10.1017/S1351324918000220
15. Mikolov, T., Grave, E., Bojanowski, P., Puhrsch C., Joulin, A.: Advances in pre-training distributed word representations. In: Proceedings of the International Conference on Language Resources and Evaluation, LREC 2018, pp. 52–55. European Language Resources Association, Miyazaki, Japan (2018)

16. Bullinaria, J., Levy, J.: Extracting semantic representations from word co-occurrence statistics: a computational study. Behav. Res. Method **39**, 510–526 (2007). https://doi.org/10.3758/BF03193020

17. Lin, Y., Michel, J.-B., Aiden, E.L., Orwant, J., Brockman, W., Petrov, S.: Syntactic annotations for the Google Books Ngram corpus. In: Li, H., Lin, C.-Y., Osborne, M., Lee, G.G., Park, J.C. (eds.) 50th Annual Meeting of the Association for Computational Linguistics 2012, Proceedings of the Conference, vol. 2, pp. 238–242. Association for Computational Linguistics, Jeju Island, Korea (2012)

18. Sidorov, G., Velasquez, F., Stamatatos, E., Gelbukh, A., Chanona-Hernández, L.: Syntactic Dependency-Based N-grams as Classification Features. In: Batyrshin, I., Mendoza, M.G. (eds.) MICAI 2012. LNCS (LNAI), vol. 7630, pp. 1–11. Springer, Heidelberg (2013). https://doi.org/10.1007/978-3-642-37798-3_1

19. Xu, Y., Kemp, C.: A Computational Evaluation of Two Laws of Semantic Change. In: Proceedings of the 37th Annual Meeting of the Cognitive Science Society, CogSci 2015, Pasadena, California, USA (2015).

20. Khristoforov, S., Bochkarev, V., Shevlyakova, A.: Recognition of Parts of Speech Using the Vector of Bigram Frequencies. In: van der Aalst, W.M.P., et al. (eds.) AIST 2019. CCIS, vol. 1086, pp. 132–142. Springer, Cham (2020). https://doi.org/10.1007/978-3-030-39575-9_13

21. Solovyev, V., Bochkarev, V., Khristoforov, S.: Generation of a dictionary of abstract/concrete words by a multilayer neural network. J. Phys: Conf. Ser. **1680**, 012046 (2020). https://doi.org/10.1088/1742-6596/1680/1/012046

22. Savinkov, A., Bochkarev, V., Shevlyakova, A., Khristoforov, S.: Neural Network Recognition of Russian Noun and Adjective Cases in the Google Books Ngram Corpus. In: Karpov, A., Potapova, R. (eds.) Speech and Computer, SPECOM 2021, LNCS, vol. 12997, pp. 626–637. Springer, Cham (2021). https://doi.org/10.1007/978-3-030-87802-3_56

23. Glorot, X., Bordes, A., Bengio, Y.: Deep sparse rectifier neural networks. In: Gordon, G., Dunson, D., Dudik, M. (eds.) Proceedings of the Fourteenth International Conference on Artificial Intelligence and Statistics, vol. 15, pp. 315–323. PMLR, Fort Lauderdale, FL, USA (2011).

24. Ioffe, S., Szegedy, Ch.: Batch Normalization: Accelerating Deep Network Training by Reducing Internal Covariate Shift. arXiv preprint arXiv:1502.03167v3 (2015).

25. Kingma, D., Ba, J.: Adam: A method for stochastic optimization. arXiv preprint arXiv:141 26980 (2014).

26. Paszke, A., Gross, S., Massa, F., Lerer, A., Bradbury, J., et al.: PyTorch: An Imperative Style, High-Performance Deep Learning Library. In: Advances in Neural Information Processing Systems, vol. 32, pp. 8024–8035. Curran Associates, Inc. (2019).

27. Rakhilina, Ye.V.: Kognitivnyy analiz predmetnykh imen: semantika i sochetayemost'. 2nd edn. Russkiye slovari, Moscow (2008).

Hypernyms-Based Topic Discovery Using LDA

Ana Laura Lezama Sánchez[1]([⊠]) [iD], Mireya Tovar Vidal[1] [iD],
and José A. Reyes-Ortiz[2] [iD]

[1] Facultad de Ciencias de la Computación, Benemérita Universidad Autónoma de
Puebla, 72590 Puebla, Mexico
ana.lezama@alumno.buap.mx, mireya.tovar@correo.buap.mx
[2] Departamento de Sistemas, Universidad Autónoma Metropolitana,
Ciudad de México, Azcapotzalco 02200, Mexico
jaro@azc.uam.mx

Abstract. Information Technologies have created many documents,
which are the basis of information systems, capable of speeding up the
process for which they were developed. These processes provide results
trying to imitate human knowledge, but it is still essential to generate
techniques that support each other to provide even more precise results.
It is essential to incorporate techniques in the automatic extraction of
topics to reflect results with greater coherence according to the topic
in question. In this work, the behavior of the Latent Dirichlet Analysis (LDA) algorithm is studied by incorporating the hypernymy-type
semantic relationship extracted from WordNet in order to improve the
results obtained when applying LDA on a set of documents without the
use of an external source of knowledge. The experimental results showed
an improvement when incorporating hypernyms providing a 1.23 topic
coherence for GoogleNews corpus.

Keywords: Topic discovery · Hypernyms · Latent dirichlet analysis

1 Introduction

The constant growth of information technologies has generated large amounts
of digital texts. Therefore, the need has arisen for tools capable of search, organize and understand large amounts of text in short periods. Topic discovery is
a technique used to understand, summarize and organize large amounts of textual data. Topic discovery is a Natural Language Processing (NLP) technique
that allows automatic extraction of meaning from texts by identifying recurring
topics. The goal of topic discovery is to extract information from texts to find
the central topic. The purpose is that specific topics appear more in relevant
documents and not so much in irrelevant documents. Topic discovery automatically analyzes texts to determine grouped words for a set of documents, known
as unsupervised machine learning, because it does not require a predefined list

I. Batyrshin et al. (Eds.): MICAI 2021, LNAI 13068, pp. 70–80, 2021.
https://doi.org/10.1007/978-3-030-89820-5_6

of tags or training data that humans have previously classified. For the development of this task in the literature, there are techniques for the discovery of topics, such as latent semantic analysis (LSA), latent Dirichlet analysis (LDA), and probabilistic semantic analysis (PLSA) [6].

In this paper, we present a method to discover the topics present in nine data sets, with the difference that the hypernyms of each word that conforms to each data set were incorporated. The proposed work aims to provide LDA with external knowledge extracted from the WordNet lexical database [8]. The aim of the work is for LDA to generate coherent topics for each text analyzed. The automatic discovery of topics is based on different systems, such as knowing the topics in a set of news or tweets analyzed.

The rest of this paper is structured as follows: in Sects. 2.1 to 2.4 the general information about some of the traditional methods for discovery of topics are described, in Sect. 3 some proposals are presented by various authors for the discovery of topics, in Sect. 4 the proposed method is displayed, in Sect. 5 the experiments and the data set are presented and finally in Sect. 6 the conclusions are described and future works.

2   Preliminaries

In this section, the theory that will support the method proposed.

2.1   Latent Dirichlet Allocation

Latent Dirichlet Analysis (LDA) is a probabilistic model that obtains all possible results for a specific task in a data set. This model was developed in 2003 by [2], they showed the faults of *TF-IDF* because they can't understand the semantic of words. The LDA is a probabilistic generative model because it gets all possible results for a given phenomenon, for data collections. It is a hierarchical bayesian model of three levels, document, word, and topic, that considers a topic distribution over a fixed vocabulary. The model takes several predefined topics for all collections previously and is defined than words that belong to those topics. The processing of the model consists of recognizing in than level the topics present in the documents choosing a distribution on the topics, i.e., the set of predefined topics with its most probable words. Later in each word of a document is assigned a topic and is select the words for the related topic [1].

2.2   Latent Semantic Analysis

Latent semantic analysis (LSA) calculates how often words appear in documents in all the corpus and assumes that similar documents will contain approximately the same word frequency distribution for certain words [1]. Syntactic information (word order) and semantic information are ignored, and each document is treated as a bag of words [1].

LSA originates in LSI (Latent Semantic Indexing), an automatic method of information retrieval that incorporates singular value decomposition (SVD) to overcome semantic difficulties generated by synonymy and polysemy. LSA is exclusively used to determine the semantic similarity between the elements analyzed from the co-occurrence with which it is used in specific verbal contexts [5].

The main idea of the LSA is that a piece of text can be represented as a linear equation whose meaning corresponds to the sum of the meanings of the words that compose it and the meaning of the words, i.e., the frequency it co-occurs in that fragment [5].

2.3   Probabilistic Latent Semantic Analysis

Probabilistic Latent Semantic Analysis (PLSA), also named Probabilistic Latent Semantic Indexing (PLSI), is a statistical technique for analyzing co-occurrence data. From this technique, a low-dimensional representation of the observed variables can be derived regarding their affinity with certain hidden variables. The model has applications in information retrieval, natural language processing, machine learning, among others.

2.4   WordNet

WordNet is a lexical database in English structured in the form of a graph. It is a compound of lexical units and relationships between them, and it also incorporates psycholinguistic information, organized based on meanings (*thesaurus*) [8].

In this lexical database, nouns, verbs, and adjectives are organized into sets of synonyms, each representing an underlying lexical concept. It was created at Princenton University [11].

- WordNet provides:
  - Semantic descriptions (gloss).
  - Lettering.
  - Pronunciation.
  - Derived forms.
  - Etymology.
  - Grammar information.
  - Synonyms and antonyms.
  - Concept-based descriptions.
  - Psycholinguistic relationships between concepts.

3   Related Work

Some authors have used several techniques of topic discovery. Below, we expose some research related to this work.

In [18], a method of semantic discovery topics based on the degree of conditional co-occurrence is proposed. The method divides each document into multiple subdocuments; according to the semantic structure, the words with solid semantic relevance are extracted depending on the degree of co-occurrence of each document. The experiments reflected results are superior to the existing. The authors tested with four Chinese corpora compiled and classified by the Fudan University and Sougou Lab. The corpus has 20 categories divided into 20 thousand documents. Also, they use three corpora, two in English and one in Chinese, with a large set of movie review data and Reuters-21578. The authors evaluated their results using the measures precision, recall, and F-score.

In [3], an alternative representation that is referred to as deep latent Dirichlet (DLDA) is proposed. The authors included changing the parameters of the simplex method, deriving a Fisher information matrix, and calculating the inverse of the information matrix generating a stochastic gradient algorithm. The proposed representation learned parameters of different layers with adaptive step sizes of the theme layer. For the experiments, the authors used the data sets 20-newsgroup, Reuters, and Wikipedia in English.

In [19], an analysis of Twitter news posts in the two most important Spanish newspapers during the COVID-19 pandemic crisis, through the topic discovery and a network analysis method is proposed. The authors found that center-left media focused more on family life and life issues (livelihoods), while center-right media focused on news from the Spanish capital (Madrid). The distribution and proportion of the information frames concluded that the country newspaper focused more on public health professionals and alarming information in real-time (update of the pandemic) during the first two periods. The coverage of the world on Twitter focused on information related to the state of alarm and lockdown (Lockdown). During the recovery period, the proportion of general political news (Politics) increased significantly, being the third most prominent informational framework at this stage.

In [9], is present an analysis to evaluate the distinctiveness topics, the terms and features essential, the speed of diffusion of information, and the and network behaviors for COVID-19 tweets. The authors propose pattern matching and topic discovery through latent Dirichlet analysis (LDA) to generate twenty topics discussing case spread, healthcare workers, and personal protected equipment. The proposed analysis contributes to machine learning methods not previously reported in the literature of COVID-19 Twitter. The analysis identifies the unique grouping behavior of different topics to improve understanding of the topics present and helped to assess the quality of the generated topics. The authors provide an estimate of retweet times to understand how quickly information about COVID-19 spreads on Twitter. Also, highlight that median COVID-19 retweet time for a sample corpus in march 2020 was 2.87 h, approximately 50 min faster than Chinese social media posts on H7N9 in march 2013.

A method is proposed in [13] for the detection of topics in collections of documents based on the contextual information of the documents. The method starts by automatically obtaining a graph-based representation model from each of the documents in the collection, which are integrated back into a single graph. The PageRank and HITS algorithms were used to determine the relevance of the topics and based on this relevance. They identified the relevant topics of the document collection. For the validation of the method, two study cases were conducted focused on demonstrating the applicability of the method in the analysis of textual sources. Measurements of accuracy, precision, and F_1score are used to compare ordered lists obtained due to the relevance calculation phase of the proposed method and the keywords identified manually by the authors (topics obtained). The bodies used for experiments are the domain of Ebola and New York news.

A novel unsupervised topic modeling for short texts is present in [12] that uses distributed representations of words and phrases. Its model is in the low-dimensional semantic vector space represented by the dense word vectors using Gaussian mixture models. The authors found that by learning representations in long enough context windows, it is possible to learn robust embeddings of words that can be exploited to learn the semantics of entire short messages. The data sets used were tweets in English, Spanish, French, Portuguese, and Russian.

In [4], an automated model of topic extraction, categorization, and relevance ranking for multilingual surveys and questions that exploit machine learning algorithms such as topic modeling and fuzzy grouping are described. The authors describe different pre-processing steps they consider to eliminate noise in the multilingual text of the survey. The authors subsequently describe different methods for grouping questions into survey categories according to their relevance. They also describe their experimental results on a large group of survey data sets in the German, Spanish, French, and Portuguese languages.

An analysis is proposed in [7], of existing methods through the discovery of the topic with LDA. The analysis presents various schemes on clustering in tweets, using three twitter data sets divided into generic, specific, and event data sets. The authors performed automatic hashtag tagging, which improved hashtag grouping results for a subset of metrics. This method is evaluated with the metric topic coherence and topic coherence normalized.

In [10], an exhaustive review of various short text topic modeling techniques proposed in the literature is proposed. The authors presented the development of the first comprehensive open-source library, STTM, for Java that integrates all the algorithms surveyed within a unified interface. The methods were tested with various real-world data sets and performance compared with each other and with the long-text topic modeling algorithm. The datasets used are in English and specific domains such as technology, biomedicine, and others. The evaluation of this work involving the discovery of topics, grouping, and classification was done with metrics topic coherence, purity, precision, and accuracy.

In [15], a proposal for evaluating relationships in artificial intelligence and SCORM domain ontologies is proposed. The authors use syntactic, lexical patterns, and dependency analysis to evaluate class-inclusion and ontological relationships. The evaluation validated such relationships using an associated reference corpus and syntactic, lexical patterns in domain ontologies. The evaluation focuses on a reference corpus to find the validated relationships. The experiments showed the existence of a high memory in the frequency of occurrence of the patterns. To evaluate the quality of the proposed approach, the authors carried out a validation by human experts and by the use of a baseline.

An approach for evaluating taxonomic relations of restricted domain ontologies to find evidence of relationships to evaluate in a reference corpus is present in [14]. The approach employs lexical-syntactic patterns to evaluate taxonomic relationships in which the concepts are entirely different. It uses a particular technique based on subsumption for those relationships in which one concept is fully included in the other, is to say if one of the two concepts of a given taxonomic relationship is part of the other concept. The authors propose using a technique of subsumption to search for evidence of a hyponym in the reference corpus. The syntactic and lexical patterns are transformed into regular expressions used to discover evidence of taxonomic relationships in the reference corpus. The approach is evaluated with the accuracy metric and by human experts. The authors detail that if two concepts of a taxonomic relationship are entirely different, they use lexical-syntactic patterns to find evidence of relationship validity in the reference corpus. The language English is used, and the domains are artificial intelligence and SCORM.

In [16], an approach for automatically identifying taxonomic relationships (hypernyms/hyponyms) and non-taxonomic relationships in restricted domain ontologies is exhibited. The authors used formal concept analysis, a method used for data analysis, but in this case, It is used to discover relationships in a restricted domain corpus. The approach uses two variants to fill the incidence matrix. The formal concepts are used to evaluate the ontological relationships of two ontologies. The authors used a typed dependency analyzer to determine the verb of a given sentence, which is associated with the ontological concepts of a triplet, of which the relationship component was validated employing an information retrieval system. The approach is evaluated using the accuracy metric and by human experts.

An approach to the automatic evaluation of relationships in restricted domain ontologies is introduced in [17]. The authors use the evidence found in a corpus associated with the same ontology domain to determine the validity of ontological relationships. The approach employs latent semantic analysis, a technique based on the principle that words in the same context have semantic relationships. The authors evaluated concepts and semantic relations of three domain ontologies through latent semantic analysis, presenting two variants, the first based on cosine similarity and the second based on committee grouping. The approach was evaluated with the precision metric. The work is focused on English, and the domain is artificial intelligence, OIL, and SCORM.

4   The Proposed Method

This section presents a method for topic discovery using LDA incorporating the hypernym extracted from WordNet.

- Corpora preprocessing: this point includes converting uppercase to lowercase, removing punctuation marks such as .,:; / & among others.
- Sentence segmentation: Lists are generated, divided into unigrams, and assigned to each one.
- Hypernyms extraction: With the lists obtained in the previous step, the hypernym of the first sense of each word is extracted and stored for later processing.
- Adding hypernyms: After the hypernyms are extracted and each new list obtained is processed to obtain only the first hyperonym of the first sense, it is added to the original sentence.
- Applying simple LDA: The method LDA is applied in the original corpus without hypernyms.
- Applying LDA: at this point, the hypernyms were added to the corpus, which will be the entry to LDA; that is to say, on these new lists, the existing topics will be extracted, including the added hypernyms.
- Evaluation: in this case, the evaluation of the results obtained was done with metric topic coherence as seen in the state of the art that uses the Eq. 1 to measure how coherent the recovered topics are and, in our case, how coherent it was to add the hypernyms.

$$PMI(w_i, w_j) = \frac{2}{T(T-1)} \sum_{1 \le i < j \le T} \log \frac{p(w_i, w_j)}{p(w_i)p(w_j)} \tag{1}$$

where T are the main words $p(w_i)$ (resp. $p(w_j)$) is the probability that the word w_i (resp. $p(w_j)$) appear in a text window of a given size, while $p(w_i, w_j)$ shows the probability that w_i and w_j co-occur in the same window.

4.1   Datasets

To analyze the effects and differences of applying the LDA model with and without hypernyms, we selected 9 data sets. First, a preprocessing was made that included removing spelling signs and stop words. The information for the 9 data sets is shown in Table 1 where N represents the number of documents in each data set.

5   Results

In this section, the results obtained in the experiments made (see Table 2), also in Table 3 some of the topics found by each data set.

Table 2 shows the results obtained by applying LDA on the 9 data sets (LDA column) and the results obtained by first extracting the hypernyms and then applying LDA *(LDA + H)*.

Table 1. Description of the datasets

Dataset	D	Description
Technology	12,295	Description of technological device failures.
SearchSnippets	12,295	Results of web search transaction
StackOverflow	16,407	The dataset randomly selects 20,000 question titles from 20 different tags
Biomedicine	19,448	Abstract to papers in biomedical literature
Tweet	2,472	Microblog tracks at Text Retrieval Conference (TREC)
GoogleNews	11,109	News extracted from google
PascalFlickr	4,834	Dataset of captions of pascalflickr
20newsgroup	20,000	Comprises around 18000 newsgroups posts
Reuters	18,456	Documents from the reuters financial

5.1 Experimental Results

This subsection presents the results obtained by applying LDA on a corpus enriched with their respective hypernyms.

Table 2. Results obtained with topic coherence of proposed method.

Dataset	LDA	$LDA+H$
Technology	0.78	1.34
SearchSnippets	1.39	1.84
StackOverflow	1.23	1.51
Biomedicine	2.13	2.40
Tweet	0.78	1.29
GoogleNews	0.80	1.23
PascalFlickr	1.26	1.87
20newsgroup	1.52	1.59
Reuters	1.31	1.79

In Table 2 shows the results of the topic coherence without adding hypernyms (LDA column) and adding hypernyms ($LDA+H$ column). It is observed that the level of topic coherence increases when the hypernyms of the words that compose the corpus are added. Applying hypernyms provides LDA with more information because it interprets the corpus as a bag of words regardless of their place in the document. The best result obtained is the one shown in the column $LDA + H$, that is, the results provided by LDA when the hypernyms of each unigram obtained are added because more meaning is being provided for each word, thus enriching the corpus LDA can obtain topics with more representative words by having the corpus and hypernyms of this.

Table 3. The words that compose the topics for each data set.

Dataset	$T+LDA$	$T+LDA+H$
Corpus	Time, Emotion, Property, Period...	Bad, Web, Home, Countenance....
SearchSnippets	People, Talk, Boston, Nursing...	Aspect, Features, Fairytale, Cast...
StackOverflow	Problem, External, Using, List	Catch, Object, Objects, Allusion...
Biomedicine	Mice, Salmonella, Resistance, Experimental	Fundamental, Factor, Factors, Monkey...
Tweet	Edu, Science, School, University	Giffords, Date, Road, Gabrielle...
GoogleNews	China, Air, Zone, Defense	Face, Seahawks, Countenance, Year...
PascalFlickr	White, Sitting, Black, Floor...	National, Capital, City, Date...
20newsgroup	Phone, Call, Fax, Modem...	Age, Accept, System, Block
Reuters	Capital, Cash, Markets, Investment,	Bargaining, Talks, Adrenarche, Beam

The Table 3 presents 4 of 10 topics extracted only with LDA ($T+LDA$ column) and with hypernyms and LDA ($T+LDA+H$) for each of data sets. More related words were observed when adding hypernyms compared to when working with the original corpus without additional information.

6   Conclusions

In this paper, an approach was proposed to enrich a traditional LDA model by extracting the hypernyms of each word that compose a sentence using WordNet. In order to contrast with a simple LDA, it considers that the documents are analyzed as monosemic; that is, they only have one meaning, and given that a word may have vital information for the analysis. It was considered essential to include a hypernym for each word composing the data sets' documents. Based on the results obtained, it can be observed that the behavior of LDA with hypernyms provides higher results in comparison when only the data sets are provided with traditional pre-processing. In general, the results obtained by adding hypernyms a greater efficiency compared to those reported in the literature. As future work, the extraction of hyponyms is proposed to compare to what extent it benefits to provide other relationships to LDA, to analyze the behavior of LDA with a semantic relationship different from the one presented in this work, and develop a topic discovery method that incorporates information that is currently not taken into account when working with LDA.

Acknowledgements. The authors would like to thank Universidad Autónoma Metropolitana, Azcapotzalco. The present work has been funded by the research project SI001-20 at UAM Azcapotzalco, partly supported by project VIEP 2021 at BUAP and by the Consejo Nacional de Ciencia y Tecnología (CONACYT) with the scholarship number 788155.

References

1. Alfaro-Flores, R.: Evaluación del efecto en el algoritmo de análisis semántico latente al utilizar colecciones de datos cada vez más grandes para la detección y extracción de sinónimos y su independencia respecto al lenguaje, por medio de su implementación distribuida. Tesis de maestría, Instituto Tecnológico de Costa Rica (2014)
2. Blei, D.M., Ng, A.Y., Jordan, M.I.: Latent dirichlet allocation. J. Mach. Learn. Res. **3**, 993–1022 (2003)
3. Cong, Y., Chen, B., Liu, H., Zhou, M.: Deep latent dirichlet allocation with topic-layer-adaptive stochastic gradient riemannian mcmc. In: International Conference on Machine Learning, pp. 864–873. PMLR (2017)
4. George, C.P., Wang, D.Z., Wilson, J.N., Epstein, L.M., Garland, P., Suh, A.: A machine learning based topic exploration and categorization on surveys. In: 2012 11th International Conference on Machine Learning and Applications, vol. 2, pp. 7–12. IEEE (2012)
5. Gutiérrez, R.M.: Análisis semántico latente:¿teoría psicológica del significado? Revista signos **38**(59), 303–323 (2005)
6. Li, C., Duan, Y., Wang, H., Zhang, Z., Sun, A., Ma, Z.: Enhancing topic modeling for short texts with auxiliary word embeddings. ACM Trans. Inf. Syst. (TOIS) **36**(2), 1–30 (2017)
7. Mehrotra, R., Sanner, S., Buntine, W., Xie, L.: Improving LDA topic models for microblogs via tweet pooling and automatic labeling. In: Proceedings of the 36th International ACM SIGIR Conference on Research and Development in Information Retrieval, pp. 889–892 (2013)
8. Miller, G.A.: Wordnet: a lexical database for english. Commun. ACM **38**(11), 39–41 (1995)
9. Ordun, C., Purushotham, S., Raff, E.: Exploratory analysis of Covid-19 tweets using topic modeling, UMAP, and DIGraphs (2020)
10. Qiang, J., Qian, Z., Li, Y., Yuan, Y., Wu, X.: Short text topic modeling techniques, applications, and performance: a survey. IEEE Transactions on Knowledge and Data Engineering, p. 1 (2020)
11. R., G.: Recuperación y acceso a la información. Addison-Wesley, Harlow (2000)
12. Sridhar, V.K.R.: Unsupervised topic modeling for short texts using distributed representations of words. In: Proceedings of the 1st Workshop on Vector Space Modeling for Natural Language Processing, pp. 192–200 (2015)
13. Torres-Rondón, A., Hojas-Mazo, W., Simón-Cuevas, A.J.: Método de detección de tópicos en documentos basado en análisis contextual del contenido. Informática (2018)

14. Tovar, M., Pinto, D., Montes, A., González, G., Vilariño, D., Beltrán, B.: Use of Lexico-syntactic patterns for the evaluation of taxonomic relations. In: Martínez-Trinidad, J.F., Carrasco-Ochoa, J.A., Olvera-Lopez, J.A., Salas-Rodríguez, J., Suen, C.Y. (eds.) MCPR 2014. LNCS, vol. 8495, pp. 331–340. Springer, Cham (2014). https://doi.org/10.1007/978-3-319-07491-7_34

15. Tovar, M., et al.: Evaluación de relaciones ontológicas en corpora de dominio restringido. Computacion y sistemas **19**(1), 135–149 (2015)

16. Tovar, M., Pinto, D., Montes, A., Serna, G., Vilariño, D.: Patterns used to identify relations in corpus using formal concept analysis. In: Carrasco-Ochoa, J.A., Martínez-Trinidad, J.F., Sossa-Azuela, J.H., Olvera López, J.A., Famili, F. (eds.) MCPR 2015. LNCS, vol. 9116, pp. 236–245. Springer, Cham (2015). https://doi.org/10.1007/978-3-319-19264-2_23

17. Tovar, M., Pinto, D., Montes, A., González, G.: An approach based in LSA for evaluation of ontological relations on domain corpora. In: Carrasco-Ochoa, J.A., Martínez-Trinidad, J.F., Olvera-López, J.A. (eds.) MCPR 2017. LNCS, vol. 10267, pp. 225–233. Springer, Cham (2017). https://doi.org/10.1007/978-3-319-59226-8_22

18. Wei, W., Guo, C.: A text semantic topic discovery method based on the conditional co-occurrence degree. Neurocomputing **368**, 11–24 (2019)

19. Yu, J., Lu, Y., Muñoz-Justicia, J.: Analyzing Spanish news frames on twitter during Covid-19–a network study of el país and el Mundo. International journal of environmental research and public health **17**(15), 5414 (2020)

Virality Prediction for News Tweets Using RoBERTa

Christian E. Maldonado-Sifuentes$^{(\boxtimes)}$ ⓘ, Jason Angel, Grigori Sidorov ⓘ,
Olga Kolesnikova ⓘ, and Alexander Gelbukh ⓘ

Instituto Politécnico Nacional, IPN, Centro de Investigación en Computación, CIC,
Ciudad de México, Mexico
{cmaldonados2018,sidorov}@cic.ipn.mx
https://www.gelbukh.com/

Abstract. The virality of a tweet is essential to convey its message to a broader audience and, eventually, to generate influence. This is especially important for news outlets as they struggle to transition from traditional media to online formats. As their usual readers will not migrate directly to digital news outlets need to gather new audiences from the spaces where real-time information and discussions are happening; this is Social Media and in particular Twitter. Since the news websites and Twitter languages differ greatly news outlets need to write their tweets properly to maximize their impact on Twitter. We propose a method to predict if a tweet will be influential or not influential based on its text using a variant of Google BERT named RoBERTa, and a corpus of 5000 high-quality and automatically labeled highly-influential and non-influential tweets to train and classify tweets in these categories. Our method reaches an F1 of 0.873, improving 4 and 9 over approaches using LSTMs and n-grams respectively.

Keywords: Twitter influence · Twitter virality · Twitter popularity · Applied deep learning · Social media · BERT · RoBERTa

1 Introduction

Social Media content virality has been a subject of interest for several disciplines almost since the advent of Online Social Networks in the first decade of the 21st century, when technologists, marketers and the public in general noticed the influence of traditional social networks was surpassed by their online counterparts.

In July of 2006 the social *microblogging* service Twttr was born. Soon it would be renamed as Twitter and it would create, inadvertently, an Online

This work was supported by the CONACYT, Mexico, under Grant A1-S-47854 and by the Secretaría de Investigación y Posgrado of the Instituto Politécnico Nacional under Grants 20200859, 20211784, 20211884, and 20211178.

© Springer Nature Switzerland AG 2021
I. Batyrshin et al. (Eds.): MICAI 2021, LNAI 13068, pp. 81–95, 2021.
https://doi.org/10.1007/978-3-030-89820-5_7

Social Network space where brands, celebrities, insitutions and the public in general to coexist, in a more horizontal field [1], but specially fertile for news [2].

The demise of traditional newspapers, treated as mere myth and hype several years into the extended usage of the World Wide Web [3] soon became an undeniable and evident fact with the explosion of Twitter. Previously some already renowned journalists has started their blogs, gaining some traction [4]. But the accelerated demise of traditional journals started with the extended adoption of social media and citizen journalism [5].

As of today, it is undeniable that the war between traditional newspapers and online journalism is decided in favor of the latter. The huge and expensive machinery of traditional media has had to lean-down and decisively move online in order to survive [6]. The late adoption of online schemes and the ever-changing language of Twitter has created a gap between the expressions of news that become viral —and have more chances of being influential— in the social media and those that are merely listed.

While virality depends largely on network dynamics [7] some news pieces shared on twitter by the same accounts and in similar time-frames become more viral than others. This information suggests that the style and linguistic features of a tweet have an influence on their performance and virality [8]. Finding out if the text of a tweet conforms to the current style and wording before *tweeting* it, will prove a valuable task for news outlets to stay relevant in the current competitive environment.

We propose a method to classify tweets as influential or not influential based on their text. For this, we collect a number of tweets, select the highest quality examples of influential and not influential tweets and proceed to train a Machine Learning algorithm which we then use for classification. The focus of this method is on usability and speed of implementation, thus, manual labelling of the corpus is out of the question.

Contributions. Our main contribution is an automated end-to-end method for virality prediction that can be run continuously due to low computational costs. We claim that these characteristics make it viable for real-world applications.

We also contribute our approach to the under-explored task of *tweet virality prediction using the text of the tweet*. In our view this work also contributes more evidence towards the argument that the text of the tweet (not only the network of the account) is relevant for its virality. In this respect we contribute an open and labelled corpus of Mexican news tweets available for scrutiny and other works.

2 Related Works

While Twitter virality, popularity, engagement and influence are topics of interest for various research communities across disciplines, and given the fact that tweets are mainly composed of text, it is noteworthy that very few works have been done using the text of the tweet as the main input to predict virality. This is specially troubling since many other tasks (i.e. sentiment analysis or hate-speech detection) are done this way.

In this section we will, thus, provide a reference for tasks similar to ours even if done by different methods and towards the end, works that resemble ours more closely.

In their 2018 article "To Retweet or Not to Retweet: Understanding What Features of Cardiovascular Tweets Influence Their Retransmission"; Tufts, Ungar, Guntuku and Merchant manually labelled 1251 tweets on the topic of cardiovascular disease tweets with the attributes: novelty, utility, theme and source. They found a correlation between messages with higher utility and medical sources and a larger number of retweets. While their scope, topic and methods are vastly different from ours it can be inferred that textual information has relevance for the dissemination of information [9].

Also in 2018 Keib, Himelboim and Han produced the domain-specific work "Important tweets matter: Predicting retweets in the #BlackLivesMatter talk on twitter". In which they use sentiment analysis to show that tweets that show emotions (positive or negative) are more likely to be retweeted than neutral or *emotionless* tweets. Again this is support for the idea that textual features of a tweet are contributors to their virality [10].

Another topic-specific research entitled "The Impact of Language on Retweeting during Acute Crises: Uncertainty Reduction and Language Expectancy Perspectives" the authors Lee and Yu use a NLP approach, checking for linguistic style and linguistic content. The 2019 study applies Uncertainty Reduction Theory, Linguistic Inquiry, and Word Count (LIWC) to determine style and content cues. Their findings include that the usage of concrete language promotes the virality of tweets during disaster situations [11].

Closer to our task, for their relatedness to news tweets and machine learning textual approach are Bandari, Asur and Huberman with their 2012 work "The Pulse of News in Social Media: Forecasting Popularity" in which they use the text of tweets (as well as the text of their corresponding full article texts) to predict the *retwittabiliy* of items that contained specific news. They achieve an accuracy of 86.93 with their best configuration using traditional Machine Learning algorithms (Naive Bayes, SVM, J48 Tree and Bagging). Sadly, they do not provide a corpus so it is difficult to test our method on their data, thus comparison has to be done in less specific terms [12].

Another noteworthy development is the industrial-grade and large-scale system developed in a collaboration between Microsoft Research and the Technological University of Denmark (DTU). It is explained in "Scalable Privacy-Compliant Virality Prediction on Twitter" where the authors Kowalczyk and Larsen present it as consisting of several proprietary technologies including the Azure solutions and APIs and the Twitter Enterprise API Firehose. It is the only work —to our knowledge— that includes the Twitter Privacy Compliance Firehose API. It is significant that the authors—at a great computational and monetary cost— attempt to predict the exact number of retweets (not categories). We mention the work for its resemblance to the task we intend to attack but, too many proprietary, and high-cost technologies are used in their work to be subject of comparison [13].

Finally, in 2020 Xiao, Liu, Ma, Li and Luo present the work we consider closer to ours: "Time sensitivity-based popularity prediction for online promotion on Twitter" with considerable differences we find their work to be similar in scope and intent. To analyze their results, they do not use the standard F1 metric, but the Geometric Mean from of sensitivity and specificity, sometimes referred to as G-Mean2, achieving 0.6972. In their repository the corpus is preprocessed and does not show the original text. In spite of the differences in methodology and result metrics, these researchers use linguistic features and time bins to predict the virality of a tweet. Since these inputs are the same as our inputs and the output is also similar to ours, we can say our method and theirs are comparable we use or own data and compare with them by calculating the G-mean2 [14].

3   Our Method

Regarding the virality prediction task we propose a classification task on automatically labelled data. This is both similar to a distant supervision a supervised approach, a hybrid method of sorts, since the data are tweets obtained through the basic Twitter Search API, from which we receive some data about each tweet.

Amongst other datum we get the number of tweets and retweets and also the number of followers and followed people from the emitter user account, also referred to as tweep.

Since the straightforward retweet number is not enough to establish a fair comparison and because the characteristics of the tweep are related to the amount of interactions such as likes and retweets (i.e. a twitter account with more followers will have a larger audience) we propose a formula to account for these factors and then label the tweets with the result of said metric.

When each tweet has been given an influence value according to our metric we proceed to select the higher quality examples for influential and non-influential tweets. With these we then train the modern RoBERTa algorithm for classification and proceed to evaluate its performance.

For research purposes we use a standardized corpus collected in 2020 through this we can compare current performance with previous iterations of our method, but the purpose of the method is to be applicable in real-world situations. In particular since we focus on news outlets Twitter accounts of Mexico we have found that training the algorithm with current data is necessary at least every two days in order to preserve its predictive power in reality.

Thus, our method is designed such it can be applied from top to bottom within a couple of hours and with little or no human intervention. For this to be viable the method required to include the collection and labelling script. It can also rely on external tweet corpora provided that it contains enough information to calculate the tweet influence.

3.1   Corpus

As far as we know ours is the only corpus of Spanish news tweets of Mexico that has preserved the measures for number of followers of the user account, number of accounts the user follows, and the retweets, and favorites (akin to likes in other social media and iconographically represented by a read heart as of 2021) of the individual tweet. The lack of Mexican news tweets corpus in Spanish is notorious as almost any person looking for these type of tweets has to collect the tweets themselves (Aguilar 2018).

Our corpus was collected and labelled automatically via a script of our own authorship. This script connects to the Standard Twitter Search API, and requires a Developer OAuth Consumer Key. The script uses the LAMP architecture and is provided alongside the corpus in the Corpus Archive, the users will have to provide their own Developer OAuth Consumer Key.

Corpus Composition. Our corpus before data processing was composed by 133,877 tweets downloaded on May 15, 2020, collection of tweets started at 14:23 hrs and ended at 15:55 hrs the tweets were given an Influence value using our Tweet Influence Formula (described in Subsect. 3.2.) at the time of downloading and in batches of 100 tweets.

After download completion the items were sorted in descending order, discarding repeated tweets and retweets. Of the final selection we took the top 2,500 tweets and labelled them as *hinf* for *highly-influential* and the bottom 2,500 tweets and labelled them as *ninf* for *non-influential* obtaining a balanced corpus of 5000 tweets with high-quality examples for both categories.

In the archive we provide we present both the full 133,877 tweet corpus in two columns with the result of the influence ponderation in one and the preprocessed text in the other, and the 5000 high-quality tweet corpus with two columns one with the *hinf* or *ninf* labels and the other with the preprocessed tweet text.

Complete Corpus Preservation and Twitter Privacy Policies. For the purpose of compliance with the privacy policy of Twitter we do not provide the whole information of the emitter accounts, only, as stated before, the ponderation or the label and the tweet text. For archival and forensic purposes we keep a copy of the "complete" file with 11 columns: Username, Tweet ID, Time of Post, Original Tweet, Processed Tweet, Followers, Followed, Retweet, Favorited, Listed, and Ponderation.

This corpus can be provided to the interested academic parties upon specific request via institutional email to the authors and with a signed affidavit of understanding and compliance with the Twitter privacy policies, which include, but are not limited to, prevent the dissemination of the user information of tweets that have been marked as private or deleted by the user.

Corpus Sources and Source Selection. Using the specialized online directories Socialbakers and Prensa Escrita, as well as the authors' journalism background we gathered the most representative Mexican news outlets tweet accounts.

While there are tweet accounts for over 300 news outlets of Mexico, and 900 journalists and news anchors many of them are not used regularly, or are used for advertising purposes. TV channels and radio stations also present more listings of their programs and promotional content than news. In the case of journalists and news anchors their account are often used for mixtures of personal opinions, comments on other accounts and some news.

Because of these limitations over the course of the years we have handpicked the accounts that produce mostly news tweets and little or no tweets of other types. Our final list includes yet another criteria which is that news tweets should be mainly nation-wide as opposed to localized.

The 46 selected accounts are: reforma, larazon_mx, lacronicadehoy, milenio, unomasunomx, lajornadaonline, capitalmexico, elgmx, el_universal_mx, laprensaoem, impactomx, elsolde_mexico, ddmexico, contrareplicamx, sdpnoticias, eleconomista, heraldodemexico, diariobasta, noticiasmiled, excelsior, maspormas, publimetromx, proceso, forbes_mexico, elarsenalmx, 20mmexico, huellasmx, diario24horas, lasillarota, sinembargomx, cnnee, lpomx, notimex, soycarlosmota, _vicenteserrano, carlosloret, cirogomezl, nachorgz, lopezdoriga, aristeguionline, julioastillero, lordmolecula, reporte_indigo, ntelevisa_com, laoctavadigital and elfinanciero_mx.

Corpus Preprocessing. For preprocessing of the text we preserve links whilst converting them to 'words' by taking away hyphens, underscores, forward slashes, question marks and colons. We preserve stop words and named entities. We then convert all the text to lowercase, eliminating multiple spaces and all remaining punctuation. Text is converted to UTF-8 to preserve emojis.

While it is common to eliminate links we preserve then as they gain significance as words in the news context where it is common practice to publish different tweets pointing to the same news item (same URL).

3.2 Tweet Influence Formula

To label our corpus automatically we produced this simple formula which uses the measures provided by the Twitter API and combines them to create a ponderation of the measures that allows for comparison on similar terms of tweets produced by accounts with different audience sizes and compositions.

Formula Rationale. In this formula we present, basically a way to grossly estimate the influence of the user account (tweep) and the influence (reach, engagement or popularity) of the tweet and ponder them using a simple ratio.

For the influence of the account we take into account both the number of followers (accounts that follow the tweep) and the followed (number of accounts followed by the tweep). We deem negative the common and fraudulent practices of "follow for follow" or "follow back" where an account follows others with the expectation of being followed back, this usually occurs on specific days or through explicit hashtags and "bios".

Of course if an account obtains followers through these means the followers will be following a lot of other accounts and thus, be low-quality, low influence and will also have saturated timelines, having little to no chance of being read by these followers, no matter how abundant. We intend to reflect the detrimental effect of this practice by subtracting a percentage of the followers if this ratio is negative and adding a percentage if the ratio is positive.

For the tweet itself we intend to reflect the nature of the tweet influence subtracting a percentage of the interactions if the tweet is more retweeted than liked, and vice versa, given that tweets are usually more liked than retweeted, the opposite ratio would imply that the tweet is disliked but re-posted for purposes of mockery or derision.

Formula. We will define the number of *followers* as w, the *followed* accounts as d, the *retweets* as r and finally the number of tweet *favorites* as f. We will label the influence of the tweet as inf_t, the influence of the account as inf_a and the ratio of both as inf_{twt}. We have set the impact of the proposed metric to add or subtract 10% of the original values but this can change according to the criterion of whom applies it so we set the constant $A = 10$. Additionally for simplicity we will define two extra variables $g = r + f$ and $h = w - d$. Given these:

$$inf_t = g + \frac{g \cdot \left(\frac{f}{r}\right)}{A} \tag{1}$$

$$inf_a = w + \frac{h \cdot \left(\frac{w}{d}\right)}{A} \tag{2}$$

$$inf_{twt} = \frac{inf_t}{inf_a} \tag{3}$$

$$inf_{twt} = \frac{g + \frac{g \cdot \left(\frac{f}{r}\right)}{A}}{w + \frac{h \cdot \left(\frac{w}{d}\right)}{A}} \tag{4}$$

To avoid nested fractions we multiply by $\frac{A}{A}$:

$$inf_{twt} = \frac{Ag + g \cdot \left(\frac{f}{r}\right)}{Aw + h \cdot \left(\frac{w}{d}\right)} \tag{5}$$

After further algebraic simplification we get:

$$inf_{twt} = \frac{gd \cdot (Ar + f)}{wr \cdot (Ad + h)} \tag{6}$$

3.3   Method Overview

This subsection intends to provide a sense of our method at a glance, if this is all you need feel free to skip the next title. We start by obtaining the data, succinctly, this consists of downloading all the available tweets of all selected users, proceeding then to discard all retweets and repeated tweets and saving the main corpus.

For the data processing, we calculate the pondered influence of each tweet using our formula. We then sort the tweets by influence in descending order and use the top and bottom 2500 tweets and label them as *hinf* and *ninf* respectively. Proceeding to preprocess the text removing punctuation and converting to lowercase.

Finally we move to use this high-quality samples corpus to test several algorithms looking to improve our results from previous works, comparing the models. This abbreviated version is presented in Fig. 1.

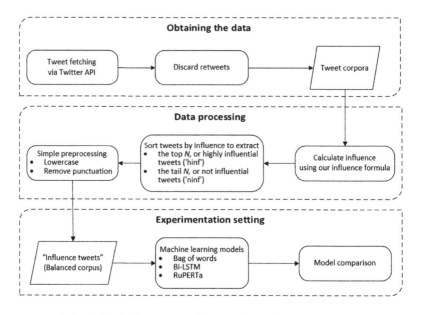

Fig. 1. Method overview. Source: Created by the authors.

3.4   Method Description

In the following subsections we aim to describe our method in better detail, this section might help those who want to reproduce our method or intend to use parts of our method in different ways. We go to some detail specially in the fetching subsection in the hopes to help others looking to download multi-user Twitter corpora, since it can easily lead to the blocking of the OAuth key and even the banning of the account used for the API Calls. A workflow diagram can be found in 1.

Data Fetching. We developed a downloading/labelling script in PHP for server to server connection and run the script in an external web-server for easy access and sharing purposes. The Search API allows only for 100-tweet batches at a time, and a maximum of the latest 3,200 tweets of each user. This is 32 API calls per user and can quickly block an account considering the 180 calls per 15-min limit imposed by the Search API.

Attempting to download the allowed tweet limit for more than 5 users at a time will most certainly trigger the Twitter restriction alert. The API response once the limit is reached varies greatly and it is not properly documented on the Twitter API corresponding documentation. It can vary from simply refusing to connect, or taking a long time, to sending a "limit reached" response, to outright disabling the OAuth token without prior notice. If the OAuth token is disabled there is also not a defined time when resuming download is acceptable. In our experience, it is best to wait for at least an hour before trying again.

To avoid these issues two approaches were attempted. The first was to download only 5 users at a time waiting 15 min before downloading the next batch, but this required a long time to download the whole 46 users we had selected and prompted failures such as the random stopping of the script after idling for long.

We then implemented our second approach which was to set a 2 s delay between each individual call, applying the preprocessing and our formula to each 100-tweet batch as soon as they're downloaded, consuming an extra 2 s and since each call takes between 2 and 4 s to download the response this ensured no more than 180 calls were made on a 15-min time span, eliminating the need for lengthy waits and possible interruptions, while preserving the token and account.

Using the second method also eliminates the need to apply the pre-processing and pre-labelling to the whole corpus after the fetching completed, thus reducing a few more minutes from the whole process.

Data Labelling. Once the tweet influence formula is applied to all the items of the corpus the tweets are sorted by influence. Attention is paid to eliminate retweets since the retweets preserve the interactions information (favorites and retweets) from the original tweet, thus creating a distortion in the influence formula as the user account that emitted the original tweet has different stats. If the tweet is repeated but it is not a retweet it is preserved, as even if it has a different influence score this discrepancy will either lead to a duplicity of category if it had similar number of interactions or a to it being discarded on the next step of the difference in score was higher. The preprocessing script then proceeds to label the top 2,500 tweets as *hinf* or highly influential and the bottom 2,500 as *ninf* or not influential. This number was selected after trying several sizes for the categories as it provides the highest quality examples for the final corpus and creates a balanced corpus.

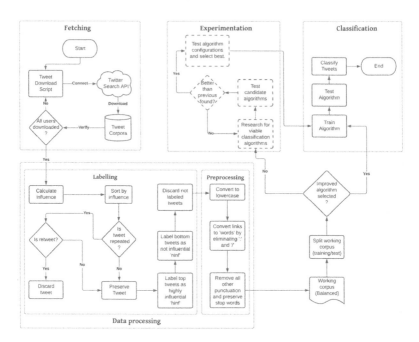

Fig. 2. Method workflow. Source: Created by the authors.

Data Preprocessing. As mentioned before the preprocessing was very simple, we preserved stop words and avoided any stemming, as this proved to be more effective. We preserved the links and converted them to 'words' by eliminating special characters, colons and dashes. The test of the tweet was converted to lowercase and all punctuation eliminated, as well as extra spaces.

Classification. For the classification we used the best algorithm on the high-quality tweet corpus, using a training-test split of 80%/20% with balanced classes both for the training and the test sets. We use the best algorithm we found after experimentation which was RuPERTa the Spanish version of RoBERTa, as found in the Hugging Face repository.

Experimentation. For the experimentation we studied the literature and our previous results on similar tasks and found that for tweet classification tasks using text there were several approaches using traditional machine learning algorithms such as Naive Bayes, J48 Tree, SGD and Voted Perceptron. Also deep learning algorithms such as LSTM, Bi-LSTM, and BERT (Transformers) variants. As noted in the workflow diagram 2 experimentation is only needed if looking for a better algorithm and our proposed automated method only.

For the tests with traditional ML algorithms we applied linguistic feature extraction and selection with the algorithm selection in TagHelper [15] and the resulting feature-optimized corpus in ARFF format was fed to the WEKA [16] framework applying the AutoWEKA [17] plugin for faster search space exploration. For LSTMs and Bi-LSTMs we wrote a bash script to test several configurations using the Uber Ludwig [18] pipelines.

We tested several algorithms and configurations ending with the BERT variants, RuPERTa [19], the Spanish version of the *Robustly optimized BERT pretraining approach* (RoBERTa) showed promise as the Bi-directional Transformer models surpassed previous deep learning and machine learning models on diverse text classification tasks. To train and classify with RuPERTa we used the pipeline provided via Huggingface [20]. Due to time constraints only the default configuration was tested.

4   Results and Discussion

Our work produced a method susceptible to end-to-end automation for the task of *tweet virality prediction using the text of the tweet*. It attained a Macro F1 measure of 0.873.

4.1   Results

Best Configurations. Here we present the results for the best configuration of the tested algorithms Table 1. ZeroR algorithm [21] lacks predictive power is just used as baseline for random selection. As stated before in Sect. 3.4 algorithms were selected from experience, bibliographic research and our own previous work on the task. Class sizes for traditional Machine Learning algorithms are slightly larger as previous experiences showed this class size improved the results significantly in these algorithms.

Table 1. Best algorithm configurations. Ordered ascending.

Algorithm	Class size	Corr. Class. Inst	Corr. Class. Inst.%	Prec	Recall	F1
ZeroR (baseline)	3,000	3,000	50.00%	N/A	0.500	N/A
J48	3,000	4,427	73.77%	0.741	0.733	0.737
SGD	3,000	4,454	74.22%	0.744	0.742	0.743
Naive Bayes	3,000	4,616	76.92%	0.741	0.747	0.744
Voted perceptron	3,000	4,692	78.19%	0.782	0.782	0.782
LSTM	2,500	4,048	80.96%	0.825	0.791	0.808
Bi-LSTM	2,500	4,224	84.50%	0.816	0.877	0.845
RuPERTa	**2,500**	**4,364**	**87.28%**	**0.861**	**0.885**	**0.873**

As we can see in the previous table the best algorithm was RuPERTa even with its base configuration proved to be significantly better than the next competitor the Bi-LSTM. Configuration files for Bi-LSTM are provided in the file repository, alongside the full 133k and the high-quality 5k corpus. The 6k corpus used for traditional ML algorithms was not included but they can be extracted easily from the 133k corpus using the method described in the Sect. 3.4 subsection. Configuration files were not provided for the RuPERTa algorithm as it is used with the base configuration found in Huggingface.

Comparison with Similar Works. As mentioned in the Sect. 2 the task of *tweet virality prediction using the text of the tweet* has been largely ignored as the belief that virality is network-related as opposed to content-related has led to the vast majority of works on virality prediction falling under the task *tweet virality prediction using the network information of the emitter account.* Another subset of works has taken on the task of *tweet virality prediction using the initial cascading interactions.* Using vastly different approaches, Bandari et al. and Xiao et al. have taken on the same (or a very similar) task that we have nevertheless they use different metrics to the area-standard F1 metric. While Bandari used Accuracy, Xiao used G-mean2 (the geometric mean of sensitivity and specificity).

Since the confusion matrices aren't provided in their works it is impossible to derive the F1 metric and it is also impossible to convert between Accuracy and G-mean2 thus in the next table we will present the Accuracy and G-mean2 metrics for our present work and compare in those terms with the other two. A highly noteworthy caveat needs to be applied though, the dataset that Xiao provides is incompatible with our method since it is exploded into linguistic features and, thus, it is impossible to rebuild the original tweets from their text, Xiao's method can be applied on our corpus but it is out of the scope of this work to reproduce their method this way since the scripts provided in their repositories do not have the functionalities to do so. Even more dire is the situation with the work of Bandari since no dataset is provided at all, they describe, in turn how to collect it, but some of the tools used in their work have gone offline, making it impossible to reproduce.

With these caveats in mind lets proceed to compare the results shown in the Table 2.

Table 2. Comparison with similar works.

Author	Corpus size	Labelling	G-mean2	Accuracy
Maldonado et al.	133k	Automatic	**0.862**	**0.873**
Bandari et al.	44k	Manual	N/A	0.837
Xiao et al.	323k	Automatic	0.707	N/A

Since the tasks were similar but the classification categories were amply different it is also not plausible to establish a fair comparison between the methods, still this approximation gives us some idea of the power of our method. Also providing our full corpus will enable others to apply different methods on the same dataset.

4.2   Findings

In this subsection we will discuss some of our findings and realizations during the progress of this work. These include main and side findings, amongst the main findings we found the following.

About Our Results. We can say with confidence that our results (even the weakest performing algorithms) are far above the baseline and its statistically significant margin of error. With a range of 23.77% and 37.30% above the ZeroR baseline. Our result is even stronger considering we have balanced categories in our high-quality example corpus. We also show that traditional and modern ML algorithms can work well with small corpora —thousands as opposed to millions of items—.

We also found that it is easier for most algorithms to correctly classify non-influential tweet by a slight margin. This is probably due to the homogeneous nature of this category, with all the tweets receiving a twt_{inf} score of 0.000, while the highly-influential category is more diverse in scores, for this specific corpus going from 0.0014 to 0.2763, rounded to 4 decimal digits.

Implications for Research on Virality. The results obtained show that to a high extent the text of the tweet can be a good predictor of virality, in our method we attempt to discount the influence of the account (network-approach) with our inf_{twt} formula (described in Subsect. 3.2). This allows for a more accurate comparison between tweets of disparate influence accounts and focus more on the content.

Our results suggest that further work on the role of the textual content of a tweet in virality is in order and should have a higher presence within the *Twitter virality research area* also important is to note that the inclusion of more open methods and corpora is in order to further the research on this topic. To this end we make our labelled corpus open.

Twitter Basic API Limits - a Word of Caution. Due to the recently hardened usage limits of the basic Twitter Search API this download has to be done in batches of 100 tweets and with carefully staged pauses otherwise is easy to get the account OAuth token temporarily or permanently blocked. Since obtaining the tokens again includes the creation of a new account and to apply for it in a human-in-the-loop process this might take from 5 to 12 days, potentially halting a research process.

Multiple accounts are not a simple solution either, since the 2018 restrictions which require a working mobile number to get a confirmation code and using multiple accounts to use the same API endpoint from within the same IP Address might lead to the banning of all the OAuth tokens including those of unsuspecting colleagues or coworkers sharing the IP Address.

While it is possible to appeal Twitter's preemptive action, it can take as many as 4 weeks to get an answer with no guarantee that it will be favorable.

In our earlier (pre-2018) works we found that the restrictions were enforced more consistently and less astringently. Also the *punishments* were limited to a few minutes of "Limit-exceeded" response that allowed for API call attempts until the restriction was lifted. Doing this in the present can lead to permanent banning of the account.

5 Conclusion

In this work we developed a method to classify tweets as highly influential or not influential using the textual content of the tweets. Moreover the method does not require manual annotation of the data since we create categories by rating the influence of the tweet with a formula that attempts to discount the influence of the emitter account. We achieved a high level of confidence as the top algorithm managed to score an F1-measure of 0.873, 37.3% above the 50% baseline in a balanced corpus.

This method has enough confidence for commercial applications and can be implemented in a fully automated fashion, thus, providing the foundation for an innovation product which can serve several markets including Public Relations and Marketing firms, News outlets, political and commercial campaigns and other similar possible customers. This process can be executed end-to-end in hours rather than days making it suitable for continuous training with up-to-date data that reflects the ever-changing environment of social media in general, but the specially rapid changes in topics, narratives and styles on the Mexican News environment.

Future work includes transdisciplinary collaborations to use our method for analysis in areas such as anthropology, marketing, sociology and others. Also we plan to explore more configurations of RuPERTa and other transformer algorithms.

References

1. Jansen, B.J., Zhang, M., Sobel, K., Chowdury, A.: Twitter power: tweets as electronic word of mouth. J. Am. Soc. Inf. Sci. Technol. **60**(11), 2169–2188 (2009)
2. Kwak, H., Lee, C., Park, H., Moon, S.: What is twitter, a social network or a news media? In: Proceedings of the 19th International Conference on World Wide Web, pp. 591–600 (2010)
3. Hendriks, P.: Epilogue the myth of the death of newspapers. In: Newspapers: A Lost Cause?, pp. 195–201. Springer, Cham (1999)
4. Johnson, T.J., Kaye, B.K.: Blog day afternoon: are blogs stealing audiences away from traditional media sources? In: CYBERMEDIA, p. 320 (2006)
5. Minuti, D.: Journalism and ethics-ethics in journalism in the era of prolific sources. Academicus Int. Sci. J. 109–119 (2010)
6. Liu, Y., Chen, W., Li, J.: Transformation and development of traditional media in new media environment. In: Xie, Y. (ed.) New Media and China's Social Development. RSCDCP, pp. 25–46. Springer, Singapore (2017). https://doi.org/10.1007/978-981-10-3994-2_3

7. Goel, S., Anderson, A., Hofman, J., Watts, D.J.: The structural virality of online diffusion. Manag. Sci. **62**(1), 180–196 (2016)
8. Maldonado, C.E.: How to improve the reach and impact of social media content. Res. Comput. Sci. **127**, 59–68 (2016)
9. Yang, Q., Tufts, C., Ungar, L., Guntuku, S., Merchant, R.: To retweet or not to retweet: understanding what features of cardiovascular tweets influence their retransmission. J. Health Commun. **23**(12), 1026–1035 (2018)
10. Keib, K., Himelboim, I., Han, J.Y.: Important tweets matter: predicting retweets in the# blacklivesmatter talk on twitter. Comput. Hum. Behav. **85**, 106–115 (2018)
11. Lee, C.H., Yu, H.: The impact of language on retweeting during acute crises: uncertainty reduction and language expectancy perspectives. Ind. Manag. Data Syst. Forthcoming (2019)
12. Bandari, R., Asur, S., Huberman, B.: The pulse of news in social media: forecasting popularity. In: Proceedings of the International AAAI Conference on Web and Social Media, vol. 6 (2012)
13. Kowalczyk, D.K., Larsen, J.: Scalable privacy-compliant virality prediction on twitter. arXiv preprint arXiv:1812.06034 (2018)
14. Xiao, C., Liu, C., Ma, Y., Li, Z., Luo, X.: Time sensitivity-based popularity prediction for online promotion on twitter. Inf. Sci. **525**, 82–92 (2020)
15. Rosé, C., et al.: Analyzing collaborative learning processes automatically: exploiting the advances of computational linguistics in computer-supported collaborative learning. Int. J. Comput.-Supp. Collab. Learn. **3**(3), 237–271 (2008)
16. Witten, I.H., Frank, E., Hall, M.A., Pal, C., Data, M.: Practical machine learning tools and techniques. In: DATA MINING. vol. 2, p. 4 (2005)
17. Thornton, C., Hutter, F., Hoos, H.H., Leyton-Brown, K.: Auto-WEKA: Combined selection and hyperparameter optimization of classification algorithms. In: Proceedings of KDD-2013, pp. 847–855 (2013)
18. Molino, P., Dudin, Y., Miryala, S.S.: Ludwig: a type-based declarative deep learning toolbox. arXiv preprint arXiv:1909.07930 (2019)
19. Pachón, V., Vázquez, J.M., Olmedo, J.L.D.: Identification of profession & occupation in health-related social media using tweets in spanish. In: Proceedings of the Sixth Social Media Mining for Health (# SMM4H) Workshop and Shared Task, pp. 105–107 (2021)
20. Wolf, T., et al.: Huggingface's transformers: State-of-the-art natural language processing. arXiv preprint arXiv:1910.03771 (2019)
21. Desai, A., Sunil, R.: Analysis of machine learning algorithms using Weka. Int. J. Comput. Appl. **975**, 8887 (2012)

Sentiment Analysis on Twitter About COVID-19 Vaccination in Mexico

Claudia Bernal, Miguel Bernal, Andrei Noguera$^{(\boxtimes)}$, Hiram Ponce, and Edgar Avalos-Gauna

Facultad de Ingeniería, Universidad Panamericana, Augusto Rodin 498, 03920 Mexico City, Mexico
{0242244,0244740,0187940,hponce,eavalos}@up.edu.mx

Abstract. This paper conducts a sentiment analysis of Twitter's posts, between late October 2020 and late April 2021, regarding COVID-19 vaccination campaign in Mexico through several machine learning models such as Logistic Regression, Neuronal Network, Naive Bayes and Support Vector Machine. To prepare data, Natural Language Processing techniques were used such as tokenization, stemming, n-grams and stopwords. The best performance was achieved by Logistic Regression with an accuracy score of 83.42% while classifying tweets according to a positive or negative sense. This work suggests that sentiment analysis with Twitter information allows to witness a relevant part of the public discussion around specific topics. For this study, the tweets analyzed showed a similar behavior to other search and reference electronic tools, such as Google Trends regarding conversation around COVID. In addition, the present analysis allows the classification and tendency of public opinion. Furthermore, this study shows that measuring people's opinion through machine learning and natural language processing techniques can generate significant benefits for institutions and businesses given that obtaining information on Twitter is less expensive and can be processed and analyzed faster than other opinion analysis techniques such as surveys or focus groups.

Keywords: Sentiment analysis · Twitter · COVID-19 · Vaccine strategy · Python

1 Introduction

In 2020, the history of human society changed radically. The emergence of the SARS-Cov-2 virus [3] and its rapid expansion across almost the entire globe led the world's governments to implement actions aimed at stopping the number of contagions and deaths, collaterally affecting jobs, social and economic activities.

Instantaneously, COVID-19 pandemic became the world's top searched topic in Google and the most important issue in the news [4]. Moreover, millions of publications have been made in social media, such as Twitter, about the

© Springer Nature Switzerland AG 2021
I. Batyrshin et al. (Eds.): MICAI 2021, LNAI 13068, pp. 96–107, 2021.
https://doi.org/10.1007/978-3-030-89820-5_8

response of Global and National Leaders regarding the measures aimed to stop the pandemic such as lockdown, testing and vaccination campaigns.

In today's data-driven world, social media is an important way for opinion research and, in some cases, is far more effective than other traditional techniques, for instance, surveys or focus groups [12]. Twitter is a convenient source of data to deploy opinion studies because information can be obtained, processed and analyzed in a faster way. At the same time, data is available for free and people's points of view can be analyzed from a variety of perspectives, without recruiting a huge team [6].

To understand the opinion in tweets related to the vaccination campaign in Mexico, an assessment of machine learning techniques for sentiment analysis was carried out. Logistic Regression, Neuronal Network, Naive Bayes and Support Vector Machine were the algorithms used in combination with natural language processing techniques. Data was collected from Twitter, using the "Snscrape" software and searching for tweets concerning the COVID-19 vaccination process in Mexico. The time span for the tweets collection ranged between October 2020 and April 2021. The reason for starting in October 2020 has to do with the announcement by Mexico's government about the possible arrival of vaccines in the following months to the country. The end date is related to the beginning of the vaccination campaign for older adults. The time span covers key stages during the vaccination process such as planning, acquisition, preparation and vaccinating people. As a result 1,000,023 tweets were scraped.

The contribution of this study is to detect polarities and patterns in Twitter user opinions, related to COVID-19 vaccine and its process, to find key insights which will eventually allow government institutions and pharmaceutical companies to define improvements in communication.

2 Related Work

The following papers were selected due their relevance and relation to the object of study; on the one hand, the importance of analyzing COVID-19 conversation's evolution and on the other hand the application of Machine Learning techniques which provides benefits for deeper and faster analysis. The research [7] is focused on the mesoscopic scale of online clusters on interested-base communities among the internet (not necessarily twitter). This study took previously defined communities, and even other information sources. A relation between universes of information and the magnitude of fast spread of hate conversation around COVID-19 was observed. It also shows that once information was released into the internet, it doesn't matter if it is erased from the source platform, information becomes viral and it can trespass its original sharing platform. It was concluded that misinformation is a high risk that affects the health sector amongst countries. COVID-19's conversation evolves rapidly in the internet. Thus, the need of an analysis with the same swift characteristics. An assessment [11] of machine learning techniques for sentiment analysis on twitter was carried out. Their results showed that Tweets can be polarized over specific topics. One important remark is that classification algorithms can also be used to identify the fidelity of text. It was concluded that having great access to large sources of information in the cloud, the usage of artificial intelligence will provide the chance to recognize whenever the information is real or was created for some malicious purpose. Finally, [2] Python's NLTK library was implemented on Tweets referring to COVID-19 to measure the importance of social networks as informative channels. The focus group considered for this paper was Arabia. From their results, a clusterization considering the information available and the awareness of population was created. It was discovered the importance of the information released on Twitter and how accordingly to the quality of the post the conversation evolves in distinct levels, making significant a previous study before the release of information.

3   Methodology

This section describes the workflow used to generate a sentiment analysis model to classify tweets about COVID-19 vaccination campaign in Mexico. First, the data were extracted from twitter and saved in a file. Then a descriptive analysis was carried out to evaluate the vaccination strategy used. From the cloud-word analysis, the most important terms from the data were selected, cleaned and labeled accordingly. Natural language processing and an assessment of a machine learning algorithms for sentiment analysis was done with all tweets tagged manually. Finally, an analysis of the results were implemented using word-cloud, plots and a comparison with google trends. The overall workflow process used for this study is shown in Fig. 1:

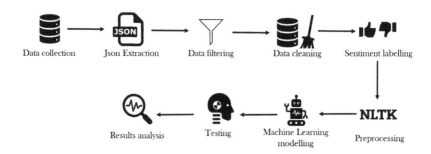

Fig. 1. Sentiment analysis on Twitter workflow used.

3.1   Data Extraction

To extract the tweets for classification, we used *"Snscrape"* [13], an open source software that allows users to get tweets without twitter's API key. Snscrape has neither limitation in the number of tweets nor in the period of time to extract. To cover only Mexico and the vaccination process as main topics, three filters were used: The first is a geographic fence that allows extracting only tweets from Mexico. The second is a list of health institutions such as: the Federal Government's Ministry of Health and the Ministry of Health of the Government of Mexico City and the Federal Government. The third filter extracted only tweets in Spanish. Hashtaged tweets were neglected as they would be related to nearby countries and it is difficult to filter them since the location is not accurate. The resulting dataset consists of 1,000,023 tweets. Each observation contained user's fields and tweet's information. The search period was determined between late October 2020 and late April 2021.

3.2 Data Transformation and Export Resulting Dataset

Further text pre-processing was carried out in order to retain vaccination process tweets only. Python's re library (for regular expressions) was used to identify related words within the tweet text. The tweet fields extracted were: id, tweet url, date of publication, tweet text, content shared, url of application source and application source. The user fields extracted were: id, username, displayname, users verification, creation date, number of followers, number of status, number of friends, number of favourites, location and profile url. In addition, the application source was processed to obtain the source where the tweet was published, i.e., Android, IOS/iOS, Web and Ipad/iPad, to name a few. Finally, the 1,000,023 tweets were filtered to 128,605 as the result of the previous process and were saved as the final data set.

3.3 Data Labeling

Given that supervised machine learning algorithms were used, it is necessary to have a target attribute and some *training* data in which the value for the target attribute is known [9]. This target attribute is commonly recognised as the label and in a sentiment analysis refers to the value that evaluates (or classifies) the text according to its sentiment (e.g. positive or negative). In order to generate the labels, a collaborative solution was developed to classify the sentiment in two options: positive or negative. A random data sample was selected and the dataset partition was hosted on a web page, a web interface was generated to choose between positive and negative-sense publications as shown in Fig. 2. The labelling step was performed by the authors of the study. For this purpose, the following criteria was used to tagging the tweets:

- Positive: Tweets which showed a positive reaction to vaccination strategy, from people who agree with the sanity measurements and also are thankful with the government due to the progress in numbers and communications.
- Negative: Tweets which reflect lack of information, regarding dates, numbers and progress of vaccination. Also, contains opinions about something that can be improved or disagreed.

Fig. 2. Web interface for labelling sentiment.

3.4 Text Processing and Feature Extraction

The text must be processed with natural language processing techniques in order to be able to perform a sentiment analysis. The data cleaning consisted in the following steps:

- Remove the html tags and content.
- Lower the text and convert to unicode string.
- Remove the mentions, tweet url, emoticons and the special characters.

Different methods and configuration were used to extract the features from the text. Some of them consisted in tokenize the words and leaving the stopwords, removing the stopwords or removing the stopwords except "no". It was also applied stemming, transform the words to its roots, in some cases. This allows us to have variants for the classification process and alternating with the Machine Learning algorithms to obtain the best model for the project. The must be converted to vectors so that the Machine Learning algorithm can interpret it correctly. The Two methods were used for word-vector implementation: TF-IDF and CountVectorizer.

3.5 Machine Learning Models

To explore the use of machine learning models as the first attempt to classify, the best known and easiest to implement models were used. The following Machine Learning algorithms were used to make the classification: Support Vector Machine (SVM) with Gaussian kernel, Logistic Regression, Multilayered Perceptron Neural Networks (MLPClassifier) and Naive Bayes. To evaluate the distinct algorithms varying internal parameters were used as well as different text processors and vectorization methods in order to get the most accurate model.

Logistic Regression: Logistic regression allows to estimate probability from a quantitative variable belonging to a qualitative variable [14]. Logistic Regression is an algorithm to model the probability to belong to a given group. As a result, the final assignation is done by the resulting number of probability and it is classified into a group. One of the main uses for this model is to classify into groups according to the value that the forecast takes.

It is possible to take the binary decision as belonging to category 0 or 1. Logistic Regression uses the return value and passes through a sigmoidal function allowing a better categorization approach.

Neuronal Network: Neuronal network is based on the biological interaction of neurons. By setting that analogy, it is possible to establish that given a number of perceptions a reaction is settled. Once the model is trained, it gets a number of entries and return the answers to the perception that defines the classification probability, in which the largest number is the classification label or group [1].

Naive Bayes: Naive Bayes is based on applying Bayes' theorem with the "naive" assumption of conditional Independence between all pairs of features. This probabilistic model is based on conditional probability [5]. Bayes' theorem is that the posteriory probability states the likelihood probability multiplied by the prior probability between the marginal probability (probability of evidence).

$$P(A|B) = \frac{P(B|A) * P(A)}{P(B)}$$

Support Vector Machine: SVM allows using variation kernel functions. The main difference is that these functions are not necessarily linear. This model transforms the data into a hyperplane with a linear solution and then gets areas to classify the data [8].

3.6 Experiments

To select the best model, each classifier ran different configurations. The variations were: training and testing size, text processing for tokenization, hyperparameter tuning for creating the vectors and for the model initialization. The objective was to find the best hyper-parameters and model configurations.

Training and Testing Size

- 70% training and 30% testing.
- 80% training and 20% testing.

Text Processing Variation

- Tokenization: Consisted to separate the word by space without additional filters.
- Tokenization without stopwords: Consisted to separate the word by space and removing the stopwords.

- Stemming: Consisted to separate the word by space, removing the stopwords and transforming the word into its root.
- Negation tokenization: Consisted to separate the word by space, removing the stopwords and adding the "no" word using regex to know if the text contained it.

Vector Generator and Model Variations

Table 1 shows the algorithms and configuration used during text pre-processing and classification process for the current study.

Table 1. Algorithms and configuration of hyperparameters for text pre-processing and classification.

Algorithm	Type	Hyperparameters	Description
TF-IDF	Vector generator	Default	The default internal text tokenizer and any previous text processing were used
TF-IDF	Vector generator	N-grams	The configuration used for grouping words were: (1, 1), (1, 2) and (2, 2)
CountVectorizer	Vector generator	Default	The default internal text tokenizer and any previous text processing were used
CountVectorizer	Vector generator	Binary	Instead of returning the frequency, it returns to 0 if the word was not repeated or to 1 when had two or more repetitions.
Neural Network	Classification model	Neurons and layers values	50–50, 100–70 and 100–100. Layers-neurons respectively
Neural Network	Classification model	Standardization	Consists in making homogeneous values
SVM	Classification model	Standardization	Consists in making homogeneous values
Naives Bayes	Classification model	Dense	Returns a matrix of the vectors

Metrics

In this work, the accuracy metric is used for model evaluation as expressed in (1) [10]:

$$a = \frac{TP + TN}{TP + TN + FP + FN} \tag{1}$$

where TP represents the true positives (those records correctly labeled), TN are the true negatives (Those records who were not labeled correctly), FP are the false positives (Those records who were labeled but they were not supposed to be labeled), and finally FN are the false negatives (Those records who were not labeled but they were supposed to be labeled). These classification categories come from the confusion matrix model. Accuracy is expected to have a value close to 1 for an optimum classifier performance. Yet, a value equals to 1 will mean overfitting.

3.7   Machine Learning Model Selection

For a best algorithm selection, all combinations were saved in a list and all processes were run sequentially to train the models. Then it went through the validation test to obtain the metrics that will define the best model to perform the classification.

4   Results and Discussion

Table 2 shows the top ten models with their word-vector technique, text configuration, and accuracy. The default training and testing used were 70%–30% respectively. Table 2 was sorted by the highest accuracy. Amongst all model combinations, Logistic Regression and Support Vector Machine (SVM) exhibited the highest accuracy values. The difference between scores were minimal, yet, the first model was selected as main classifier due to the following reasons: The logistic regression requires less effort to implement, consumes less computational resources, is less complex, and has a better accuracy score than all the other models. One interesting remark is that even though eight out of ten models used CountVectorizer, TF-IDF achieved the top result.

Table 2. Top 10 machine learning algorithms.

	Model	Vectorizer	Configuration	Accuracy
1	Logistic Regression	TF-IDF	Stopwords included	0.8342
2	Logistic Regression	CountVectorizer	Stopwords included	0.8309
3	Support Vector Machine	CountVectorizer	Stopwords removed	0.8227
4	Logistic Regression	CountVectorizer	Stopwords removed	0.8223
5	Logistic Regression	CountVectorizer	Stopwords removed	0.8223
6	Logistic Regression	CountVectorizer	Stopwords removed and add "No"	0.8211
7	Support Vector Machine	CountVectorizer	Stopwords removed and text stemmed	0.8211
8	Logistic Regression	CountVectorizer	Stopwords removed and binary parameter	0.8169
9	Support Vector Machine	CountVectorizer	Stopwords removed and text stemmed	0.8158
10	Logistic Regression	TF-IDF	Stemmed text	0.8147

Figure 3 shows the confusion matrix from the best model in Table 2. As the classification is binary the matrix contains two values: positive and negative. The model detected the positive class rather than the negative.

A comparison between the four model's accuracy in Logistic Regression and SVM was significant, however, both models got higher results than Neural Networks and Naive Bayes. Table 3 shows the best score and configuration by model.

Table 3. Best model accuracy results by machine learning algorithm type.

	Model	Vectorizer	Configuration	Accuracy
1	Logistic Regression	TF-IDF	Stopwords included	0.8342
2	Support Vector Machine	CountVectorizer	Stopwords removed and text stemmed	0.8309
3	Neural Network	TF-IDF	Stopwords included	0.7681
4	Naive Bayes	TF-IDF	Stopwords included	0.7356

The 128,605 tweets were classified by the model. The result was 108,667 negative and 19,938 positive tweets. The positive tweets represent 15.5% and the negative tweets 84.5% of the tweets.

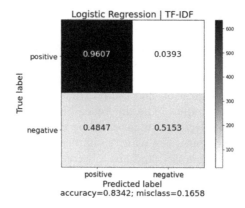

Fig. 3. Confusion matrix of the best model result.

Figure 4 shows the search frequencies for the term "vaccination" between October 30, 2020 and the first week of April 2021. As can be seen, there are spikes that match with specific events related to the vaccination campaign such as Spike 1. Arrival of vaccines (December 24, 2020); Spike 2. Start of registration for older adults (February 02, 2021); Spike 3. Initiation of vaccination of older adults (March 15, 2021).

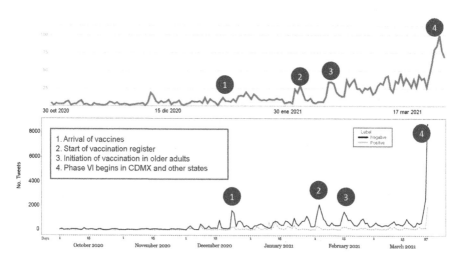

Fig. 4. Top chart is vaccination term frequencies in Google Search (Google trends) and bottom chart is Tweets analyzed.

These same spikes in frequencies are observable in the tweets analyzed, from which it is possible to listen to the real world through a sentiment analysis performed from a machine learning model.

In addition, the results show the trend of opinion over the time analyzed: as noted in Fig. 5, negative publications maintain steady growth that, as mentioned in previous paragraphs, correlates with vaccination strategy milestones such as the arrival of vaccines, the start of registration for older adults through a website and the start of vaccination.

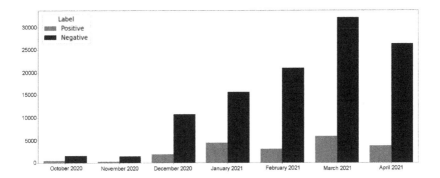

Fig. 5. Positive and negative tweets per month.

The patterns identified through the word cloud in Fig. 6, regarding negative tweets, allow observing the topics of concern for the population about the vaccination process such as: ability to vaccinate the entire population, registration through the website, political use of vaccination, attention time, brand of the vaccine, transparency and sufficient information.

Fig. 6. Word-cloud negative classification result

5   Conclusions

The conclusions of this work can be summarized in two lines of action: the first is with respect to the machine learning model, where we can say that Logistic Regression was the most effective model due to the simplicity of its implementation and its performance, with an accuracy of 83.42%, compared to other more sophisticated models that showed less accuracy.

A possible improvement in the performance of this model could include strengthening the training set by using a larger sample, as well as adjustments to the manual categorization task, which could include a double check in the sentiment labelling.

It is important to note that sentiment analysis with Twitter information allows observing a relevant part of the public discussion around specific topics. In the case of this study, the tweets analyzed showed a similar behavior to other search and reference electronic tools, such as Google Trends.

While it is true that these results show the behavior of past events, the approach of this study suggests the desirability of using Twitter to know people's opinions in real time by obtaining results more effectively, cheaply, and quickly, compared to other public opinion analysis techniques such as surveys or focus groups.

The second line of action highlights the improvements that are advisable to the Mexican Government's communication campaign on the vaccination process. After rating the sentiment of 128,605 records, using the best performing machine learning model, it is noted that 84.5% of tweets were negative.

In this regard, areas of opportunity are noted in official government communication such as: ensuring dose adequacy for health personnel and vulnerable groups for i.e., elderly people, highlighting the clarity of the implementation stages and consideration of the second dose; proper operation of the registration system; the effectiveness of acquired vaccines; transparency and access to procurement and contract information; as well as the possible opening of the process so that private instances can apply vaccines.

References

1. Albawi, S., Mohammed, T.A., Al-Zawi, S.: Understanding of a convolutional neural network. In: 2017 International Conference on Engineering and Technology (ICET), pp. 1–6 (2017). https://doi.org/10.1109/ICEngTechnol.2017.8308186
2. Aljameel, S.S., et al.: A sentiment analysis approach to predict an individual's awareness of the precautionary procedures to prevent COVID-19 outbreaks in Saudi Arabia. Int. J. Environ. Res. Public Health **18**(1), 218 (2020)
3. GOBMX: Covid-19 preguntas frecuentes. https://bit.ly/3cJEUBy
4. Google: Google trends. https://bit.ly/3s2e0ex
5. Lewis, D.D.: Naive (Bayes) at forty: the independence assumption in information retrieval. In: Nédellec, C., Rouveirol, C. (eds.) ECML 1998. LNCS, vol. 1398, pp. 4–15. Springer, Heidelberg (1998). https://doi.org/10.1007/BFb0026666
6. Murphy, J.: Social media in public opinion research. American Association of Public Opinion Research, May 2014

7. Velásquez, N., et al.: Hate multiverse spreads malicious COVID-19 content online beyond individual platform control. https://arxiv.org/ftp/arxiv/papers/2004/2004.00673.pdf
8. Pisner, D.A., Schnyer, D.M.: Support vector machine. In: Mechelli, A., Vieira, S. (eds.) Machine Learning, pp. 101–121. Academic Press (2020). https://doi.org/10.1016/B978-0-12-815739-8.00006-7. https://www.sciencedirect.com/science/article/pii/B9780128157398000067
9. Provost, F., Fawcett, T.: Data Science for Business, 1st edn. O'Reilly Media, Sebastopol (2013)
10. Raschka, S.: Python Machine Learning. Packt Publishing Ltd., Birmingham (2015)
11. Sande, J.: Analisis de sentimientos en Twitter. http://openaccess.uoc.edu/webapps/o2/bitstream/10609/81435/6/jsobrinosTFM0618memoria.pdf
12. Shadpour, D.: How social media can serve as the new focus group for your brand. https://bit.ly/3r2ur9p
13. Snscrape. https://pypi.org/project/snscrape/
14. Wright, R.E.: Logistic regression. In: Grimm, L.G., Yarnold, P.R. (eds.) Reading and Understanding Multivariate Statistics, pp. 217–244. American Psychological Association, Washington, DC (1995)

Text-Independent Speaker Identification Using Formants and Convolutional Neural Networks

Antonio Camarena-Ibarrola[1]([✉])(ID), Miguel Reynoso[1], and Karina Figueroa[2](ID)

[1] Facultad de Ingeniera Eléctrica, División de Estudios de Postgrado, Universidad Michoacana de San Nicolás de Hidalgo, 58000 Morelia, Mich, Mexico
{antonio.camarena,0850750b}@umich.mx
[2] Facultad de Ciencias Fisico-Matemáticas, Universidad Michoacana de San Nicolás de Hidalgo, 58000 Morelia, Mich, Mexico
karina.figueroa@umich.mx
http://dep.fie.umich.mx/~camarena
http://fismat.umich.mx/~karina

Abstract. Text-Independent Speaker Identification consists in finding out the identity of an individual using his/her voice independently of the content of the speech signal, that is, regardless the words uttered by the speaker. This problem is harder than Text-dependent speaker recognition where the speaker has to utter some specific word or phrase so he/she can be recognized. However, Text-Independent Speaker Identification is what we have to solve when the speaker has to be recognized without his/her collaboration as is frequently the case in many practical situations. Our proposal consists in searching within the speech signal for voiced speech content, which is the kind of speech produced when the vocal cords are vibrating. Once these segments of speech are identified, the formants are determined, formants are the resonance frequencies of the vocal tract. We use these formants to produce images which we believe should be different from one speaker to another, the way such images are built is original. Each image represent a specific speaker and so the problem of identifying speakers is turned into a problem of image recognition and we know how useful convolutional neural networks are for that purpose. For our experiments we used a collection of recordings from 21 individuals and achieved an accuracy of 92% outperforming the best results for text-independent identification published in recent works that used the same collection for testing.

Keywords: Speaker identification · Formants · Convolutional neural network

© Springer Nature Switzerland AG 2021
I. Batyrshin et al. (Eds.): MICAI 2021, LNAI 13068, pp. 108–119, 2021.
https://doi.org/10.1007/978-3-030-89820-5_9

1   Introduction

Two related but separate problems are Text-Dependent Speaker Identification (TD-SI) and Text-Independent Speaker Identification (TI-SI). When somebody claims to be the owner of some credentials or having the attributes to perform some action, he would be willing to utter any specific phrase he is asked to, such recognition task belongs to the field of TD-SI or more specifically to Text-Dependent Speaker Verification (TD-SV). However, in a number of situations a speaker has to be recognized in a speech recording where none of the words uttered there are the same as those present in another recording of his/her voice that is being used as reference for identification purposes. Such would be an example of Text-Independent Speaker Verification (TI-SV). When no individual is claiming to own an identity that just needs to be verified and still his/her identity needs to be discovered using his/her voice to that effect, and also the content of his speech is different from any known speech content (i.e. uttered words or phrases) from such individual, then we are dealing with the TI-SI problem which is the one addressed in this paper and is the hardest of them.

2   Previous Work

Speaker recognition has been a subject of research since 1976 when pitch and Linear Prediction Coefficients (LPC) where used to characterize speakers, and Dynamic Time Warping was used to establish similarity between them for TD-SV [12]. Atal in 1976, also extracted LPC coefficients to characterize the voice of the speakers but used gaussian mixtures to determine the probability that such voice was uttered by specific speakers in the TD-SI problem [2]. In 1975, Lieberman and Blumstein published physiology studies regarding sensibility of the human auditory [9]; they showed how we perceive lower frequencies better than higher ones. From then on, most works in speech or speaker recognition use some logarithmic scale such as the Bark or the Mel scales. In 1995, Thvenaz and Hügli studied the usefulness of the LPC residual for the TI-SV problem [15]. The LPC residual is really the error signal or the difference between the original speech signal and the signal synthesized with the LPC coefficients. The envelope of that signal is similar to the glottal flow which characterizes the speaker. In 1999, Plumbe et al. used the glottal flow for speaker identification as well, they estimated the shape of the glottal pulses more carefully using inverse filters to estimate the shape of the pulses at the glottal valve before they are reshaped by the vocal tract [11]. To understand this, consider that the speech is captured after it has been shaped by the vocal tract, the vocal tract is modeled as a filter whose parameters are the LPC coefficients. In order to find out the shape of the signal before the filter, the speech signal needs to be inverse-filtered. In 2000 Besacier and Bonastre computed the energy per band in base-2 logarithm to identify speakers, they used subband coding for fast characterization [3]. Back in 1990, Hermansky had used the Perceptual Linear Prediction (PLP) coefficients to characterize speakers because he found out them to be more adequate than LPC coefficients for speaker identification [8]. Nevertheless, in 2009, Yu and Zhang found that the Mel-Frequency Cepstral Coefficients (MFCC) were more robust than the Linear Prediction Cepstral Coefficients (LPCC) for speaker recognition, they did not compared with PLP coefficients because LPCC coefficients were found to be less correlated than PLP [16]. Since then, MFCC coefficients have been perhaps the most used feature for speaker recognition. However in 2017, spectral entropy determined for each critical band as defined in the Bark scale was found to be more robust than MFCC for noisy speech signals in the TI-SI problem. In 2019, Bunrit *et al.* determined the spectrogram from each 2 s of the speech signal, the spectrogram is an image that shows the amount of energy both in frequency and time, the spectrogram is fed to a Convolutional Neural Network (CNN) for TI-SI showing results that outperformed MFCC based recognizers [4]. In 2020, instead of spectrograms, entropygrams were used as images for using CNN for TD-SI, entropygrams are images that show how the amount of information (i.e. entropy) content distributes both in time and frequency, it was determined that entropygrams work better than spectrograms for low resolution images and much better when the speech signals are noisy [6].

3   Proposal

Text-Dependent Speaker Recognizers deal with speech signals with the same content in terms of the sequence of words or phonemes uttered, therefore they have to deal with rhythm, the speed at which sounds are emitted from the vocal tract, the way in which energy evolves in time in those speech signals. The key point is that time is important and the characterization of the speakers have that implicit. Examples of such characterizations are time series, sequences of feature vectors, spectrograms, and entropygrams whose horizontal axis is time. There are a number of techniques to deal with timing, such as dynamic time warping, hidden Markov models, and neural networks. On the other hand, Text-Independent Speaker recognizers deal with speech signals whose content may be quite different and characterization disregards time, examples of characterization for Text-Independent speaker recognition are clouds of points [5,10], the shape of the glottal pulse [14], and vowel formants [1].

   We still want to take advantage of the ability of convolutional neural networks to recognize images so we need to convert speech signals into images in order to use them to identify speakers. However, we cannot use spectrograms or entropygrams since they are both time dependent, the spectrograms of the utterances of two different words of phrases would not look alike. Then we came out with an original way to convert speech signals into images that we believe would look similar if the speaker is the same even if the word or phrase uttered is different.

3.1   Converting Speech Signals into Images Disregarding Time

The speech signal is framed, our frames are short segments of 30 ms overlapped by 2/3, so we end up with a frame for every 10 ms of the speech signal, to each frame the Hamming window is applied avoiding phony frequencies due to sudden changes at the beginning and end of the frame. The Hamming window function is given in Eq. 1

$$hamming(n) = 0.54 + 0.46cos(2\pi n/N) \tag{1}$$

where N is the size of the frame in samples

Speech frames can be classified as voiced or unvoiced. Voiced speech signals are pseudoperiodic while unvoiced speech signals are rather chaotic. Periodicity in voiced speech is due to vibration of the vocal cords and vowels are good examples of voiced speech. When a signal is periodic or pseudoperiodic the autocorrelation function has a peak located at the period of the signal. Equation 2 is used to determine the short-time autocorrelation function of a frame of speech signal s. We use a center-clipping spectral flattener before computing the autocorrelation function. This way we keep only the frames with voiced speech, discarding frames with unvoiced speech or with no speech at all.

$$R(k) = \sum_{m=0}^{N-k-1} s(m)s(m+k) \quad \forall \ 0 \leq k \leq N-1 \tag{2}$$

For each frame with voiced speech we determine the formant frequencies which are the resonant frequencies of the vocal tract. The vocal tract acts like a multi-band pass filter. For each band there is a bandwidth and a center frequency which is called "formant" since it contributes to shape the speech. To determine the formant frequencies and their bandwidths we use the following procedure:

1. Determine the LPC coefficients α_k of the speech signal inside the frame using the autocorrelation method and solving the following system of equations with the Levinson-Durbin procedure.

$$\sum_{k=1}^{p} \alpha_k R(|i-k|) = R(i) \ i = 1, 2, ..., p \tag{3}$$

2. Since $\alpha_1, \alpha_2, ..., \alpha_p$ are the LPC coefficients of an all pole filter that models the vocal tract, we need to find the roots of $A(z) = 0$, where $A(z)$ is shown in Eq. 4, these roots are the poles of the filter

$$A(z) = 1 - \sum_{k=1}^{p} \alpha_k z^{-k} \tag{4}$$

3. The roots of $A(z) = 0$ that correspond to formants occur in complex conjugate pairs, for each conjugate pair we keep only the root with the positive imaginary part, then we compute for each root z_k its angle as

$$\theta(z_k) = tg^{-1}(Imag(z_k)/Real(z_k)) \tag{5}$$

4. The frequency of each formant is related to the angle of the corresponding pole, then we use Eq. 6 which just converts the frequencies from radians/sample to Hertz.

$$freq(z_k) = \frac{F_s \theta(z_k)}{2\pi} \tag{6}$$

where F_s is the sample frequency

5. The Bandwidth of each pole is related to its distance to the origin of the complex plane Z [13], and it is determined as

$$bw(z_k) = -\frac{F_s}{\pi} ln(\sqrt{Real(z_k)^2 + Imag(z_k)^2}) \tag{7}$$

6. Some roots of $A(z) = 0$ are indeed formants but some are just spectral shaping poles. It is known that poles that do not correspond to formants have large bandwidths, so for each pole z_k, we compute the ratio: $bw(z_k)/freq(z_k)$ and if this ratio is greater than 0.5 we discard it.
7. The remaining poles are considered formants, sort them by their frequency in ascendent order.

Once the central frequency and bandwidths of the formants from frames with voiced speech have been determined we proposed two models to generate images from the speech signal to represent speakers.

Model I. In this model the frequency of the first two formants are used to determine the center (x, y) of a circle whose radius r is proportional to the frequency of the third formant, the circle is painted in a color that depends on the bandwidth of the same first three formants, the amount of red, green and blue is proportional to the bandwidth of formants 1, 2, and 3 respectively. In Fig. 1 four of these images are shown, the ones at the top were extracted from two audios belonging to the same speaker (Aaron), the ones at the bottom were extracted from audios from another speaker (Erendira). Observe how similar the images are when are extracted from the same speaker regardless of the order in which voiced sounds are emitted or if some of those sounds are absent which is the case for Text-Independent speaker recognition. Also observe how the images differ when extracted from different speakers

Model II. In this model the frequency of the first two formants are used to determine the center (x, y) of a circle whose radius r is fixed, the circle is painted in a color that depends of the bandwidth of the same first three formants, the amount of red, green and blue is proportional to the bandwidth of formants 1, 2, and 3 respectively In Fig. 2 four of these images are shown, the ones at the top were extracted from two audios belonging to the same speaker (Aaron), the ones at the bottom were extracted from audios from another speaker (Erendira). As in the case of Model I, using Model II the produced images are very similar when extracted from the same speaker and how the images differ when extracted from different speakers, that is what we need for implementing a speaker identification system, low intraclass distances and high interclass distances.

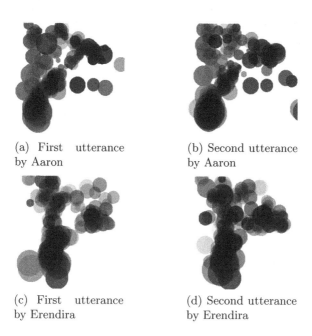

(a) First   utterance
by Aaron

(b) Second utterance
by Aaron

(c) First   utterance
by Erendira

(d) Second utterance
by Erendira

Fig. 1. Four Images produced using Model I after 4 utterances by two different speakers (Aaron and Erendira)

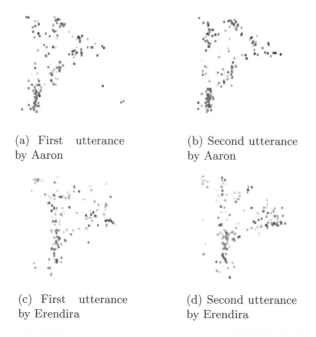

(a) First   utterance
by Aaron

(b) Second utterance
by Aaron

(c) First   utterance
by Erendira

(d) Second utterance
by Erendira

Fig. 2. Four images produced using Model II after 4 utterances by two different speakers (Aaron and Erendira)

3.2 Convolutional Neural Network (CNN)

In image processing, filters are used to manipulate images, the filters may be designed to emphasize borders, reduce noise, smooth the image, etc., it really depends on the coefficients of the filter. The basic operation between the coefficients of the filter and the pixels of the image is convolution. A convolutional neural network implements filters in its convolutional layers using coefficients (i.e. parameters) that instead of being obtained from the work of a designer, are learned in an optimization process during training such as back propagation. The purpose of the filters in the first convolutional layer is to recognize primitive shapes, subsequent convolutional layers recognize more complex shapes since they are formed by the simpler shapes recognized in the previous layers

Our CNN is rather conventional, it has four convolutional layers, and three dense layers, the first convolutional layer has 16 filters with a window size of 3×3, the second one has 32 filters with the same window size of 3×3, the third convolutional layer has 32 filters with windows of 2×2, and the last one has 64 filters with windows of 2×2. All convolutional layers use padding and the *ReLU* activation function, also between convolutional layers there are *maxpooling* layers with 2×2 windows that reduce the image size for subsequent layers. After the four convolutional layers we added three dense layers, the first two of them with 128 neurons, and using the *ReLU* activation function while the last dense layer has 21 neurons and uses the *SoftMax* activation function. Table 1 shows the specifics of the CNN.

Table 1. Specifics for the CNN used

Layer	Shape	Number of parameters
Conv2d_1	256,256,16	448
Maxpooling2d_1	128,128,16	0
Conv2d_2	128,128,32	4,640
Maxpooling2d_2	64,64,32	0
Conv2d_3	64,64,32	4128
Maxpooling2d_3	32,32,32	0
Conv2d_4	32,32,64	8,256
Maxpooling2d_4	16,16,64	0
Flatten_1	16384	0
Dense	128	2,097,280
Dense_1	128	16,512
Dense_2	21	2,709
		Total 2,133,973

4 Experiments

For assessing the performance of our proposed method for TI-SI we used a collection of speech recordings in wave format, sampled at 8,000 Hz, monoaural, and with a precision of 16 bits per sample. The collection include the voice from 21 individuals, all of them Mexicans, with ages between 18 and 30, 9 of them are women and 12 men. Each individual uttered 34 words, four times each word. The whole collection has 2,856 wav files organized in 21 folders, the collection can be downloaded from: http://dep.fie.umich.mx/~camarena/dsp/elocuciones21.tar.gz.

The speech signals, which in these tests are read from wav files, are first divided into short frames of 30 ms overlapped by 2/3, so we have one frame for every 10 ms of audio and we discard the frames with unvoiced speech or with no speech as explained before since only the frames with voiced speech actually have formants. Since we are assessing a Text-Independent Speaker Identification system, we randomly select M frames among those with formants (i.e. frames with voiced speech). Remember that the central frequencies along with the bandwidths of the formants are used to decide the location and color of a single circle, and in the case of Model I also the size of the circle. Therefore, parameter M controls the number of colored circles of the generated images. If M is too small we would get images not rich enough to represent a speaker and If M is too high we would get images overcrowded with colored circles, we don't really know the optimum number of circles so we expect the tests would let us discover that.

The process of randomly selecting M frames is repeated 50 times for each speaker, using the first and the third utterances of the words, so we ended up with 1050 images that were used for training. Then, using the second and forth utterances of the words we repeated the process and obtain another set of 1050 images that were used for testing. From the training set we used 20% (210 images) to conform the validation set.

The Convolutional Neural Network described before was trained using the *Adam* optimizer, for 20 epochs with a *batch_size* of 10. The loss function was *categorial_crossentropy* as defined by Eq. 8

$$\text{Loss} = -\sum_{i=1}^{c} t_i \log f(s_i) \tag{8}$$

where $f(s_i)$ is the output at the ith class, being f the activation function and t_i is the target value at the same class

Since the target value for all negative classes is zero and for the positive class is 1, after replacing the *softmax* value function, the resulting equation for computing the loss function is:

$$\text{Loss} = -\log \left(\frac{e^{s_p}}{\sum_{j=1}^{c} e^{s_j}} \right) \tag{9}$$

where s_j is the weighted sum at the input of the jth neuron of the output layer and s_p is the weighted sum at the input of the positive class neuron in the output layer.

For dealing with overfitting we use the *early-stopping* technique which monitors the loss function with validation data and if it starts increasing, training is halted. However, such increment of the loss with the validation data might be just a fluctuation, so to prevent *early-stopping* from halting training prematurely a lapse called *patience* is used, if the loss keeps increasing for more epochs than the patience, then training stops. We use a patience of 6.

The tests were run in a computer with an Intel core i5 10400F processor and RTX 2060 graphics card. The training took about 40 s since each epoch takes about 2 s although early stopping sometimes stops training before 20 epochs.

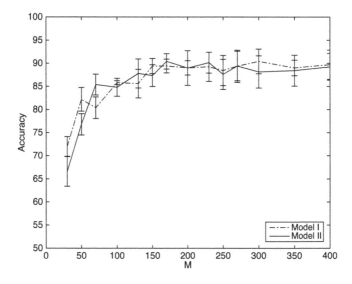

Fig. 3. Results: Mean accuracies vs M (number of random frames) for both models.

Since the training starts with random values for the parameters (i.e. weights) of the convolutional neural network and the optimizer is known to adjust the parameters to a local rather than the global minimum loss, then we repeated both training and tests 30 times starting every time with random parameters. The accuracies reported in Fig. 3 are actually the means of the accuracies obtained with both models for generating images using a number of randomly selected frames of the speech signal (i.e. circles in the images) that vary from M = 30 up to M = 400. The standard deviations are shown as vertical bars.

Before our experiments we did not know the minimum number of frames (i.e. M) that would serve the purpose of modeling speakers, but we could see in Fig. 3 that both models need at least $M = 170$ frames (i.e. circles) to achieve an accuracy above 90%. Model I achieves a mean accuracy of 92% for M = 300, but Model II achieved that same accuracy for $M = 170$. Model I works slightly better for $M \geq 270$ frames.

It seems like increasing the number of frames above 300 is of no use for the purpose of increasing accuracy. We did not increased M further than 400 because we thought the images might be getting overcrowded with too many colored circles and would no more serve the purpose of modeling speakers.

Regarding sensibility, the accuracies obtained with the proposed method outperform those obtained with other approaches using the same collection [5,7], this can be seen in Table 2.

Table 2. Accuracy obtained

	Proposed Model I (M = 230)	Proposed Model II (M = 170)	Cloud point matching/KD-Tree [7]	K-NN classifier/polygon matching [5]
Accuracy	**92%**	**92%**	89%	90%

Figure 4 shows the confusion matrix for Model I for M = 200 for the run where it achieved its best accuracy which was 93.2%. For a multi-class recognizer accuracy is computed as:

$$accuracy = \frac{\sum_{i=1}^{c} M_{i,i}}{\sum_{i=1}^{c} \sum_{j=1}^{c} M_{i,j}} \tag{10}$$

where M is the confusion matrix and c is the number of classes

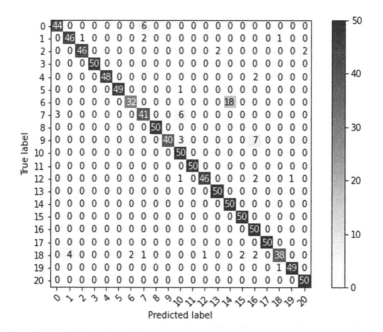

Fig. 4. Confusion matrix for Model I, M = 200 for the run of best accuracy (93.2%)

5   Conclusions and Future Work

We have shown that automatic text-independent speaker identification can indeed be accomplished by producing images that depend on the formant frequencies and their bandwidths extracted from voiced speech segments disregarding time, using those images as models for the speakers and classifying them with a convolutional neural network, both proposed models I, and II work for this purpose. We did not know before the experiments the minimum number of frames (i.e. M) that would be adequate, but now we know we need at least $M = 170$ frames. As a future work, there are many other ways to produce the images, for example, using the second and third formant frequencies to determine the coordinates of the center of the circles while the first formant frequency might define the size of the corresponding circle. Also a fourth and even fifth formant might be estimated and use this information as well to produce the images for representing speakers.

References

1. Almaadeed, N., Aggoun, A., Amira, A.: Text-independent speaker identification using vowel formants. J. Sig. Process. Syst. **82**(3), 345–356 (2016). https://doi.org/10.1007/s11265-015-1005-5
2. Atal, B.: Automatic recognition of speakers from their voices. Proc. IEEE **64**(4), 460–475 (1976). https://doi.org/10.1109/PROC.1976.10155
3. Besacier, L., Bonastre, J.F.: Subband architecture for automatic speaker recognition. Sig. Process. **80**(7), 1245–1259 (2000)
4. Bunrit, S., Inkian, T., Kerdprasop, N., Kerdprasop, K.: Text-independent speaker identification using deep learning model of convolution neural network. Int. J. Mach. Learn. Comput. **9**, 143–148 (2019). https://doi.org/10.18178/ijmlc.2019.9.2.778
5. Camarena-Ibarrola, A., Castro-Coria, M., Figueroa, K.: Cloud point matching for text-independent speaker identification. In: 2018 IEEE International Autumn Meeting on Power, Electronics and Computing (ROPEC), pp. 1–6 (2018). https://doi.org/10.1109/ROPEC.2018.8661454
6. Camarena-Ibarrola, A., Figueroa, K., García, J.: Speaker identification using entropygrams and convolutional neural networks. In: Martínez-Villaseñor, L., Herrera-Alcántara, O., Ponce, H., Castro-Espinoza, F.A. (eds.) MICAI 2020. LNCS (LNAI), vol. 12468, pp. 23–34. Springer, Cham (2020). https://doi.org/10.1007/978-3-030-60884-2_2
7. Camarena-Ibarrola, A., Luque, F., Chavez, E.: Speaker identification through spectral entropy analysis. In: 2017 IEEE International Autumn Meeting on Power, Electronics and Computing (ROPEC), pp. 1–6 (2017). https://doi.org/10.1109/ROPEC.2017.8261607
8. Hermansky, H.: Perceptual linear predictive (PLP) analysis of speech. J. Acoust. Soc. Am. **87**(4), 1738–1752 (1990)
9. Lieberman, P., Blumstein, S.E.: Speech Physiology, Speech Perception, and Acoustic Phonetics. Cambridge University Press, Cambridge (1988)
10. Luque-Suárez, F., Camarena-Ibarrola, A., Chávez, E.: Efficient speaker identification using spectral entropy. Multimed. Tools Appl. **78**(12), 16803–16815 (2019). https://doi.org/10.1007/s11042-018-7035-9

11. Plumpe, M.D., Quatieri, T.F., Reynolds, D.A.: Modeling of the glottal flow derivative waveform with application to speaker identification. IEEE Trans. Speech Audio Process. **7**(5), 569–586 (1999)
12. Rosenberg, A.: Automatic speaker verification: a review. Proc. IEEE **64**(4), 475–487 (1976). https://doi.org/10.1109/PROC.1976.10156
13. Snell, R., Milinazzo, F.: Formant location from LPC analysis data. IEEE Trans. Speech Audio Process. **1**(2), 129–134 (1993). https://doi.org/10.1109/89.222882
14. Taseer, S.K.: Speaker identification for speakers with deliberately disguised voices using glottal pulse information. In: 2005 Pakistan Section Multitopic Conference, pp. 1–5 (2005). https://doi.org/10.1109/INMIC.2005.334384
15. Thévenaz, P., Hügli, H.: Usefulness of the LPC-residue in text-independent speaker verification. Speech Commun. **17**(1–2), 145–157 (1995)
16. Yu, J.C., Zhang, R.L.: Speaker recognition method using MFCC and LPCC features. Comput. Eng. Des. **30**(5), 1189–1191 (2009)

Nahuatl Neural Machine Translation Using Attention Based Architectures: A Comparative Analysis for RNNs and Transformers as a Mobile Application Service

Sergio Khalil Bello García$^{(\boxtimes)}$ (D), Eduardo Sánchez Lucero$^{(\boxtimes)}$ (D),
Edmundo Bonilla Huerta(D), José Crispín Hernández Hernández(D),
José Federico Ramírez Cruz(D), and Blanca Estela Pedroza Méndez(D)

Tecnológico Nacional de México/Instituto Tecnológico de Apizaco,
90300 Tzompantepec, Tlaxcala, Mexico
{m19371364,eduardo.sl,edmundo.bh,crispin.hh,federico.rc,
blanca.pm}@apizaco.tecnm.mx

Abstract. Machine Translation is a problem that consists of automating the task of translating a sentence into another target language done by a computer, and is still in research, especially with low-resource languages. The neoteric introduction of attention techniques inside the Natural Language Processing (NLP) field in coalescence with a broader disposal of word-segmentation and Web Scrapping techniques; including the lack of a proper online tool translation for Nahuatl dialect, inspired this work in an effort to produce such a tool. Once availability of suitable corpus via Web Scrapping is searched for with scrutiny, therefore, doubling the state of the art in parallel phrases; several vocabulary files were produced using two sorts of word segmentation tools in order to extract the morphemes and break down the agglutination Nahuatl contains. By performing a comparative analysis between Recurrent Neural Networks (RNNs) and Transformers, incorporating two segmentation techniques and two different corpus, it is possible to improve the state of the art regarding Nahuatl by more than four times the BLEU score (66.45) with second validation by using a Fuzzy similarity library. Such experiments confirmed the hypothesis that by increasing the corpus size by double, using transformers and sub-word segmentation, a translation from Spanish to Nahuatl is the best approach that can be accomplished so far with the current tools; outperforming many times Statistical Machine Translation (SMT) and RNNs which do not contain attention, plus the deployment of an application that serves as a platform for the language.

Keywords: Neural Machine Translation · Nahuatl · Transformers · Recurrent Neural Networks · Mobile application

© Springer Nature Switzerland AG 2021
I. Batyrshin et al. (Eds.): MICAI 2021, LNAI 13068, pp. 120–139, 2021.
https://doi.org/10.1007/978-3-030-89820-5_10

1 Introduction

The task of translating a sentence from one language to another has been one of the most challenging ones within the field of Artificial Intelligence, specifically inside NLP. This is because languages are complex structures created by a society based on traditions, culture and events; this gives the languages many ways of being interpreted that, for a machine, cannot be easily expressed via hard-coded programming. However as the techniques and processing power of machines has evolved, this task has nowadays become ubiquitous for several users around the globe that use online translators for all mainstream languages such as French, English or Spanish right in their hands. Online translators like Google Translate or Bing are services that can take a text input of a user and digest it using Neural Machine Translation (NMT) which is a set of tools and models that processes the requested text and transform it into a suitable translation, using cutting edge technology where RNNs and Transformers are involved. Aforesaid success of these tools is achieved not only because of sophisticated models, but also because of the ease of use and reach that mobile applications provide. For the time being, mobile applications are the main way for millions of people to interact with the digital world and said complicated technology, in the form of a service; where communities are build-up around them and fed back with several amounts of data every day. This is the reason why this work was encouraged into creating a Nahuatl translation tool, given the fact that all major platforms lack the language even in beta versions. Although Bing has already introduced a couple of native Mexican languages, it still lacks Nahuatl. Nahuatl is a low-resource polysynthetic language (tending to agglutinate prefixes and suffixes) in terms of digital literature compared to Spanish or English, and the trend is accentuated in terms of parallel phrases, however there are two main sources of said resource that this work takes advantage of, Axolotl and JW (The most translated web page of the world). Using these two corpus plus two ways of sub-wording and two distinct NMT attention-based architectures, it is possible now to conduct an analysis of how much Nahuatl can be improved to be a suitable candidate for an online translation tool backed up by metrics like BLEU, and thus, creating a community that nourishes the models creating a self-improving tool.

2 State of the Art

Machine Translation is a field that has perceived a steady growth with Example Based Machine Translation introduced in 1999 by Somers [29] and then an improvement over Rule Base Machine Translation in 2002 by Charoenpornsawat [5], however no approaches for Nahuatl were published using said techniques. Since the introduction of SMT by Koehn [16] in 2009, Nahuatl began to be translated using Machine Translation as shown by Mager [23]. Nonetheless the biggest leap forward for Machine Translation was made when Neural Networks started to take over the scene of NLP with novel architectures brought from the field of Artificial Vision, this is known as NMT. Regarding Nahuatl, NMT entered the scene in 2019 where Ríos Dolores *et al.* [28] performed experiments using an RNN plus attention supported by the framework OpenNMT [14].

2.1   How Big is Nahuatl?

Nahuatl is a polysynthetic macro-language from the Yuto-nahua family spoken in Mexico and it contains more than 20 variants according to the norm ISO 639-3 [19] with over 1.5 million native speakers, making it the most spoken native tongue in Mexico [23].

2.2   NMT Related Works

There are remarkable online translation tools that use cutting-edge technologies to obtain the best results. Despite this, Nahuatl is left behind by these tools.

Google NMT: For quite some time the golden standard has been Google Translate. In 2016 a paper describing a detailed implementation of the production service was published; showcasing the use of RNNs and an attention mechanism called Google Neural Machine Translation (GNMT) [37] scoring **41.16** BLEU at its best, however a revised evaluation in 2019 [1] showed a range from **60** to **91** BLEU score in different languages that Google Translate currently supports. The detailed architecture used by GNMT is a Sequence to Sequence (Seq2Seq) bi directional RNN (BiRNN) that uses cells of Long-Short Term Memory (LSTM), containing 8 layers inside the encoder and 8 layers in the decoder with residual connections featuring an attention mechanism.

GPT-3: Recently in 2020 the paper *Language Models are Few-Shot Learners* [26] specified a language model called Generative Pre-trained Transformer (GPT) in its third iteration. The model can perform several task including translation which was an emerging behavior. Trained with 175 billions parameters and more than a trillion words from Common Crawl's [27] and Wikipedia, making GPT-3 the largest language model at the time. The architecture is composed by 96 stacked encoder-decoder layers, 96 multi-head attention layers and a batch size of 3.2 million. The translation behavior emerged because there was about 93% English content, with French, German and Romanian being the rest; triggered by the following clever notation: "Translate from English to French: sea otter = loutre de mer, peppermint = menthe poivrée, cheese = "; the notation provides the description of the task to do, a series of examples on how to perform said task and a prompt that the model has to auto-complete. The best BLEU result was around **41.8** approaching earlier state of the art results which gave an insight about the future of this architecture.

2.3 NLP Nahuatl Related Works

In 2018 the paper *Challenges of language technologies for the indigenous languages of the Americas* [22] presented a research review about the digital resources available for NLP for indigenous American languages, making emphasis on the struggle of the problems while working with such languages given their low profile and presence on digital media. For the purpose on this work, several projects are presented concerning Nahuatl only.

Morphological Analysis: Lemmatization and steamming are broadly used techniques on NLP, despite this, Nahuatl did not present rules or techniques that could help on this subject. However in 2009 the tool *chachalaca* was created specifically for Nahuatl [11] performing morphological analysis focusing on the classical variant. Besides Gutierrez-vasques *et al.* [8] performed automated segmentation using Rnns for Nahuatl and Mexicanero through Morfessor [34].

Corpus and Digital Resources: The paper [22] is correct in saying that most of the digital resources are strongly flooded with political and religious content. It identifies two principal sources for Nahuatl, *El gran diccionario Náhuatl* [31] and the great advancement that Axolotl [4] represented providing the first parallel corpus of Spanish-Nahuatl.

Translation: The first approach made to automate the translation of Nahuatl was performed using SMT by Mager *et al.* [23] obtaining a BLEU score of **10.14** for Nahuatl at best using 985 parallel phrases. Finally a more recent thesis work introduced RNN with attention to Nahuatl in 2019 [28] using the framework OpenNMT [14] obtaining a BLEU score of **8.36** for NMT but a score of **14.28** for SMT, both with 7,293 parallel phrases.

Additionally in 2020 [38] introduced the use of Transformers in a low-resource language with Cherokee and English using a parallel corpus of 13,639 parallel sentences, where three architectures were tested, SMT, RNNs and Transformers. The publication points out that the Transformers performed worst because of the low number of parallel phrases used and obtained RNN at its best with a BLEU of **15.8**. These results are interesting for this work because Transformers are a trend that improves most of the mainstream languages.

2.4 Related Nahuatl and Translation Services

Google Translate: A broadly popular service of automatic translation. It incorporates text translation, text to speech, speech recognition, text recognition inside images and drawn text as well as offline models; all of this for over 100 languages. Additionally it provides an API for developers.

Bing Translator: Microsoft provides a translation tool that supports over 70 languages with a similar approach to Google's. However this service stands out with the integration of Maya Yucateco and Otomí de Querétaro [13].

AULEX Dictionary: AULEX is a proposed dictionary [33] to be used in the academical environment because many words were incorporated by academics and are rarely or never used by native people. This dictionary aims to teach better how formal and informal Nahuatl is used as well as encourage its classical grammar. The dictionary executes a simple search that matches both sides of the spectrum in the translations.

Axolotl Web Corpus: Axolotl web [10] is a digital corpus that serves as a compendium of translations for Nahuatl-Spanish pairs. The service contains over 18,000 pairs and performs advanced search using special queries *Lucene/Solr* [9].

3   Models Description

Next both RNN and Transformer architectures are described as well as the technologies used to build the platform. First of all, We explain why Nahuatl is such an unique language compared to Spanish given its polysynthetic nature.

3.1   Nahuatl

Nahuatl translations can present some challenges. Most of its sentences present agglutination of adjectives, adverbs and components such as radical and verbal nominators. This allows Nahuatl to code a huge variety of functions that Spanish only expresses through its syntax.

Nahuatl: Nosiua uan na ipan tochaj. Istakcihuatl.
Spanish: Mi esposa y yo en nuestra casa. Mujer blanca.

3.2   Bi-directional Recurrent Neural Network Plus Attention

An RNN is a natural generalization of a Sequenced Feed Forward neural network [30]. Mainly used for mapping the non fixed-size inputs, like the source sentences, Sequence to Sequence (Seq2Seq) no matter if the alignment of inputs or outputs are known beforehand. Each layer contains multiple nodes where each node acts as a memory cell, in this case, a Gated Recurrent Unit (GRU); then it forwards the gradient and corrects it in the back propagation stage.

The RNN is able to learn the distribution over said sequence, therefore each output, in each time step, is the conditional distribution $p(x_t|x_{t-1}, \ldots, x_t)$ and by combining those probabilities, the total probability of a given sequence is defined by the Eq. 1 and the output is activated by a softmax function.

$$p(x) = \prod_{t=1}^{T} p(x_t|x_{t-1}, \ldots, x_1) \tag{1}$$

As an Encoder-Decoder architecture, the model uses two networks, the first has the task of reading and transforming the input sequence x into a fixed size vector called "context vector" c and the second, to generate the last output sequence y. Therefore the distribution of two networks has to be calculated as in Eq. 2 [37].

$$p(y|x) = \prod_{t=1}^{T} p(y_t|y_{t-1}, \ldots, y_1; x_{t-1}, \ldots, x_1, c) \tag{2}$$

Teacher Forcing: To improve the learning further of the RNN during the early stages of learning, a Teacher Forcing [35] module is introduced in the model, which introduces a programmed sampling [3] that inserts the correct outputs from the ground truth dataset in order to mitigate the early wrong predictions that the model performs; then gradually decrease the probability of correction made in the learning process using the total number of epochs to train; until the network starts to learn better by itself. The decay of probability T given the current epoch e_t is calculated based on the difference of 1 with e_t over the total of epochs F_e as in Eq. 3.

$$p(T|e_t) = 1 - \frac{e_t}{F_e} \tag{3}$$

Finally the decision of applying such behavior given the current epoch e_t is determined by Eq. 4, where R_n stands for a random generated number between 0 and 1.

$$ApplyTF = R_n < p(T|e_t) \tag{4}$$

Attention Mechanism: Introduced by Luong *et al.* [21] and Bahdanau *et al.* [2], is based on a basic brain function over filtering what is important and discarding what is not. This mechanism is responsible for managing and quantifying the interdependence of the sequences. Because of this, the attention mechanism serves as a bypass over the bottle neck that the final hidden state represents on a traditional RNN.

As seen in Fig. 1, instead of only propagating to the decoder the last hidden h_i state, the attention mechanism transmits all the hidden state vectors h_j outputting a "context vector" c_i, calculated by Eq. 5, c_i contains all vectors with a score a_{ij}.

$$c_i = \sum_{j=1}^{n} a_{ij} h_j \tag{5}$$

The score a_{ij} represents the attention weights learned by a network denoted by a *tanh* function and is calculated by Eq. 6.

$$a_{ij} = \frac{e^{f_{ij}}}{\sum_{k=1}^{n} e^{f_{ij}}} \tag{6}$$

where f_{ij} is Eq. 7.

$$f_{ij} = tahn(h_j + s_{i-1}) \qquad (7)$$

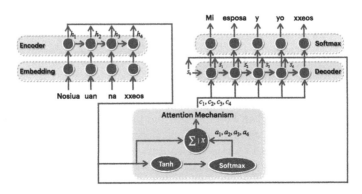

Fig. 1. Graphical representation of an RNN with an attention mechanism. The encoder passes all its hidden states to the attention mechanism and the decoder passes its last hidden state, then the mechanism processes the scores and creates a sequence of attention vectors.

3.3   Transformer

As attention presented a trend of improving NLP in general, introduced by the paper *Attention is all you need* [32], Transformers mostly implemented attention dropping the concurrence; making it faster and more parallelizable to train thanks to the addition of "Multi-head Attention" and thus, modules that can be stacked several times. First the encoder accepts a pre-processed vector of inputs with positional encoding using *sin* and *cos* functions to determine the relations between inputs because the model lacks recurrence; the inputs pass over a multi-headed attention module, this module applies self-attention, this form of attention allows the model to associate each input word with the rest of them, allowing it to learn characteristics of the input such as grammar, structure and morphemes. This process is done by a scaled attention product, using three input vectors, Q, K, V, named query, key and value respectively; these values are operated by the module as in Fig. 2.

Q and K are passed through a matrix multiplication then scaled to avoid exploding values and then softmaxed to obtain probabilities similar of what the simple mechanism does. However the result is matrix-multiplied by V, concatenated and passed through a linear layer. Self-attention can be described by Eq. 8 where $\sqrt{d_k}$ represents a scale factor.

$$Att(Q, K, V) = softamax\left(\frac{QK^T}{\sqrt{d_k}}\right) \qquad (8)$$

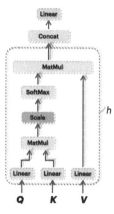

Fig. 2. The multi-headed attention mechanism is in charge of giving a better context among sequences by being stacked h times, each layer should be able to learn a specific aspect of the sequence.

Following with the decoder it has three key differences, first this module slightly changes its input given the fact that if the model can see future matches at first glance, this will be considered as cheating; for this reason before the calculating of the softmax, the words after this step are filled with $-\infty$; therefore, once the softmax function is applied they will be turned into zeros, this process is known as masking. The model uses then a second multi-headed attention mechanism to pair the encoder outputs and the decoder attention outputs.

Finally the third difference is that a final linear layer with a softmax function gives the final probability over an output of the same size as the vocabulary; the position with the higher probability is the correspondent token on the output, then this process is repeated again with the new predicted output until the "end of string" token is outputted. The whole transformer model can be seen in the Fig. 3.

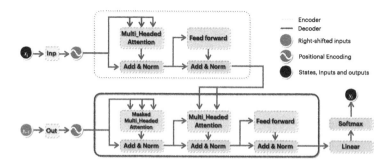

Fig. 3. Encoder-decoder transformer model with three multi-headed attention modules and positional encoding.

3.4   Bilingual Evaluation Understudy and FuzzyWuzzy

BLEU: Is a measure technique introduced by Papineni *et al.* [24] broadly used by the NLP community, the score varies from 0 to 1 although a newer notation %BLEU [15] uses its percentage form.

BLEU uses the geometric average of n-grams multiplied by a length penalty BP where longer predictions are severely punished whereas short ones are tolerated. Equation 9 represents such penalty.

$$BP = \begin{cases} 1 & \text{if } c > r \\ e^{1-r/c} & \text{if } c \leq r \end{cases} \tag{9}$$

Then Eq. 9 is multiply by the geometric average to calculate the final score at Eq. 10.

$$BLEU = BP * e^{\sum_{n=1}^{N} w_n log p_n} \tag{10}$$

FuzzyWuzzy: In order to obtain a second metric to calculate the similarity between the validation dataset and the results the models produce, FuzzyWuzzy [1] was used as a string matching library for Python that uses the *Levenshtein* distance to calculate the similarity between them. All sentences of the validation set were compared using `process.extractOne` which uses `fuzz.WRatio` as a weighted scorer that uses multiple results.

3.5   Axolotl

Axolotl is the first serious parallel corpus of Spanish-Nahuatl phrases [9], containing over 18,000 pairs from different variants. The file was processed using Python and Pandas in order to normalize the text and discard unexpected symbols. The final yield consisted of 46,144 unique words for Nahuatl and 24,808 for Spanish.

3.6   JW

Using Web Scrapping techniques, a parallel corpus was obtained from the JW web page, the most translated web site [25] thanks to its enormous network of editors around the world [36]. With more than 750 languages, the web site offers 5 Nahuatl variants, however based on the data from Ethnologue [7], the Huasteca variant was used because it reaches almost 410,000 native speakers. After processing the corpus to align the sentences manually and discarding arabic numbers and undesired symbols, the text suffered an extra step to strip the religious bias replacing expressions and words to a more generalized vocabulary. After the process the resulting size is 35,069 pairs, 17,848 Nahuatl unique words and 19,320 Spanish words. Table 1 shows a brief comparative between the state of the art corpus and the obtained in this work.

---

[1] GitHub repository https://github.com/seatgeek/fuzzywuzzy.

Table 1. Comparative of features between JW and Axolotl corpus

Feature	JW	Axolotl
Size	6.6 MB	4.8 MB
Number of phrases	35,069	17,895
Spanish words	19,320	24,808
Nahuatl words	17,848	46,144
Characters	37	37
Variant	De la huasteca	Several

3.7 SentencePiece Tokenization

Besides the traditional tokenization word by word directed by the frequency of appearance inside the documents (TF-IDF) [20] described by the Eq. 11 and implemented with Spacy, another sub-wording technique is introduced using the tool SentencePiece [18].

$$TF - IDF = \left(\frac{t_n}{n}\right) * \left(log\left(\frac{N}{n}\right)\right) \tag{11}$$

Using Unigram Language Model (ULM) [17] the tool scans the corpus matching the most frequent n-grams replacing the space with an underscore trying to obtain the morphemes from Nahuatl. Figure 4 shows both tokenization techniques.

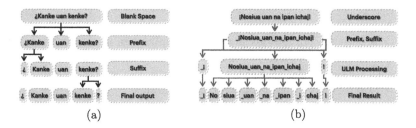

(a)   (b)

Fig. 4. Comparative of each tokenizer (a) Spacy performing simple segmentation. (b) SentencePiece trying to obtain morphemes.

3.8 Main Technologies

To better support such a platform, several technologies backup the development of the system. Table 2 presents a list of tools categorized in three principal stages.

4 Implementation and Experiments

This work aims to deliver a functional application for academic and public use, and to satisfy such requirements the architecture shown in Fig. 5 is used.

Table 2. List of technologies used to develop the Nahuatl translation platform categorized by stages

Machine learning	Server	Client
FastAI	Debian	Objective-C
SentencePiece	Docker	Swift/SwftUI
Jupyter Notebooks	NGINX	Catalyst
JavaScript	MariaDB	Xcode
	Python	jSON
	Django	

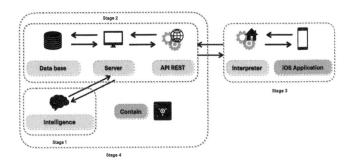

Fig. 5. General project architecture divided into 4 development stages. Stage 1: Model training. Stage 2: Back-end development. Stage 3: Mobile application development. Stage 4: Deployment.

The platform can not only serve translations, but can also collect corrections from mistaken translations or even new ways of translation from the several variants it supports based on the ISO 639-3 norm [19]; as well as group folders of translation in order to improve language teaching.

4.1 RNN

Implementation: Using the framework and implementation of FastAI [12]. The built RNN has 512 GRU nodes, all using the Rectified Liner Unit (ReLU) activation function, followed by linear layers and the decoder implementing the attention mechanism with 512 in features. To reduce over-fitting, a dropout layer was added with a value of 0.15 for the encoder and 0.35 for the decoder. Finally the last stage of the Feed forward function implements Teacher Forcing. The metric used was BLEU and the loss function CrossEntropy.

Training: By combining Axolotl and JW, Spacy and SentencePiece and direction of translation, the RNNs were trained with a learning rate of 9.12^{-04} from 25 to 40 epochs before plateau and optimized with AdamW.

4.2   Transformer

Implementation: FastAI also offers a Transformer implementation that has 6 stacked encoders and decoders, 8 multi-headed attention with a d-head size of 32 and a model size of 256 dimensions. As the paper [32] mentions the loss function was LabelSmoothingCrossEntropy to yield a better BLEU score.

Training: Also combining Axolotl and JW, Spacy and SentencePiece (this time with both Spanish and Nahuatl) and direction of translation, the Transformers were trained with a learning rate of 2.71^{-04} from 40 to 50 epochs before plateau and optimized with AdamW.

4.3   The Application

Using a secured REST API created with Django, the main application developed for iOS and macOS systems with Swift and SwiftUI, presented a client where registered and unregistered users can request translations with a simple UI (Fig. 6) that aims to use, in most of its elements, icons to avoid the use of text given the fact that most native people do not know how to read. Despite that, the applications have been translated to English, Spanish and Nahuatl. There is a light weight version written in Objective-C to focus the translation use among people.

Fig. 6. Main translation UI on iOS.

4.4   Model Evaluation and Comparative

With 20 models from datasets of 18k and 35k pairs of size using different tokenization techniques, a comparative analysis was run with validation batches from 10% to 20%. Results of Table 3 show that there is a difference between the direction of the languages, JW tends to favor Spanish to Nahuatl while Axolotl tends to favor Nahuatl to Spanish, this could be because Axolotl has some mixed variants on it. Therefore, many words can be mapped over one Spanish word while one Spanish word can be mapped to several others. However the Fuzzy similarity shows that even though the JW (Spacy) from Spanish to Nahuatl BLEU score is worse, a slightly better similarity between validated and output sentences was achieved. Another observation is that SentencePiece improves to some degree the BLEU score; also, the size of the corpus on a low resource language has little effect over the results using RNN.

Table 3. BLEU and Fuzzy results for the different models run by an RNN with attention.

Dataset	Tokenization	From	To	BLEU	Fuzzy similarity	$\sigma\%\pm1$	$\sigma\%\pm1.96$	$\sigma\%\pm2.58$
JW (35k)	Sentence	NAH	SPA	37.6264	68.02	70.96	98.64	99.62
JW (35k)	**Sentence**	**SPA**	**NAH**	**43.8582**	70.13	71.48	98.80	99.43
JW (35k)	Spacy	NAH	SPA	35.7084	67.27	73.20	98.82	99.62
JW (35k)	Spacy	SPA	NAH	37.8644	**70.19**	71.39	98.27	99.25
Axolotl (18k)	Sentence	NAH	SPA	41.2468	69.58	67.92	97.80	99.19
Axolotl (18k)	Sentence	SPA	NAH	34.6288	62.45	57.53	99.42	99.79
Axolotl (18k)	Spacy	NAH	SPA	40.0839	66.46	71.74	97.42	98.71
Axolotl (18k)	Spacy	SPA	NAH	32.2177	67.58	64.30	98.14	99.54

Transformers (Table 4) showed a significant improvement over RNN contrary to the result presented by [38] where a low resource language performed worse with transformers than with RNN, they theorized that the reason was the low-resource dataset, in an architecture based on BERT [6], their best performance yielded using 5 layers and 2 heads and thus the less complexity in the architecture, the better it fitted less data; however we used 6 layers and 8 heads. A deeper reading revealed that their corpus size was about 14K whereas Axolotl was 18K, although it is not a significant difference taking into account that most mainstream languages vary from 100K to 1M+ pairs; the improvement seen by Nahuatl using transformers was substantial and in line with the trend seen in [32], one reason could have been that Nahuatl can relate better with Spanish given the past combination they had and relative simplicity compared to Cherokee.

Second, the trend presented by the datasets was maintained with JW. Supporting Spanish better and Axolotl supporting Nahuatl better as well as the trend of SentencePiece improving BLEU score, furthermore it was a greater

Table 4. BLEU and Fuzzy results for the different models run by Transformers. Sentencex2 refers to SentencePiece used in both Nahuatl and Spanish.

Dataset	Tokenization	From	To	BLEU	Fuzzy similarity	$\sigma\%\pm1$	$\sigma\%\pm1.96$	$\sigma\%\pm2.58$
JW (35k)	Sentence	NAH	SPA	62.5145	67.50	54.18	99.24	99.85
JW (35k)	**Sentence**	**SPA**	**NAH**	**66.4544**	**74.68**	64.78	98.72	99.79
JW (35k)	Spacy	NCH	SPA	56.4513	69.05	67.98	99.24	99.91
JW (35k)	Spacy	SPA	NCH	60.9273	73.47	67.29	98.87	99.76
JW (35k)	Sentencex2	NCH	SPA	60.1455	67.52	54.73	99.27	99.97
JW (35k)	Sentencex2	SPA	NCH	65.1669	74.42	65.35	98.61	99.79
Axolotl (18k)	Sentence	NCH	SPA	55.4888	71.00	64.83	98.09	99.13
Axolotl (18k)	Sentence	SPA	NCH	50.3683	66.18	56.78	99.10	99.79
Axolotl (18k)	Spacy	NCH	SPA	54.7046	68.64	69.16	97.77	99.50
Axolotl (18k)	Spacy	SPA	NCH	47.8439	62.38	64.54	98.15	99.74
Axolotl (18k)	Sentencex2	NCH	SPA	56.5424	62.56	70.75	96.62	97.08
Axolotl (18k)	Sentencex2	SPA	NCH	55.1322	67.50	54.18	99.24	99.85

improvement over Spacy this time. This could be possible taking into account that Transformers indeed benefit over more data with JW. Third the trend of BLEU scores held better with Fuzzy similarity, showing how transformers tend to be more consistent overall. Finally as transformers proved to be better by a significant amount, a tokenization using SentencePiece for both languages was performed revealing a close match between only Nahuatl SentencePiece and both, for Axolotl, it was a better run than for JW, again the noisy data that Axolotl introduced can explain why this is the case because there are some Nahuatl words infiltrated somewhere in the Spanish side seen after training.

4.5   Comparatives Among and with Another Models

Current scores well outperformed the state of the art results for Nahuatl machine translation presented by [23] using SMT and [28] with RNNs plus attention. As seen in Fig. 7, there is a trend over RNNs and Transformers results given a dataset and a tokenization technique; with Transformers outperforming RNNs in all results not only for BLEU but also for Fuzzy similarity; showing a much closer match but still better with transformers overall as well as validating the best BLEU score yielded.

Results also outperformed the Cherokee scores [38], in both RNN and Transformers. Finally taking into account the multi-diversity of GPT-3 [26] compared well for most results even though it has the largest data source of all. However GNMT really excels as the gold standard with an 88 BLEU score [1] translating English to French. Table 5 compares the BLEU score as well as the size of corpus used to train the model while Fig. 8 shows how close Nahuatl can get to a production tool compared with past attempts.

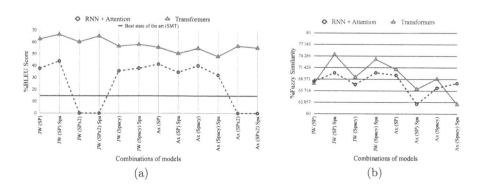

(a)   (b)

Fig. 7. Comparative charts of RNN and transformers. SP represents SentencePiece. SPx2 means the SP was used in both languages. (a) BLEU comparative with the state of the art [28] (14.28). (b) Fuzzy similarity follows the same trend with better performance in transformers.

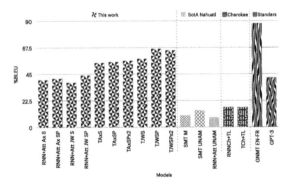

Fig. 8. Model names are a reduced version of the names on Table 5. This chart compares BLEU scores with the state of the art.

4.6 Emerging Behaviors

As common now for Transformers, there are two principal emerging behaviors [32] present in those models that were unexpected to find during experiments.

Mexican Spanish: Experiments conducted with transformers pointed to the emergence of a modern Mexican Spanish pleonasm found mostly in rural environments, linking it with Nahuatl origins.

As shown in Table 6, there are two sentences in Spanish, the second introducing the pleonasm, either way, the Nahuatl model synthesizes both of them to their correct translation despite one of the inputs being wrong. This could be caused because of the prefix "i" to indicate belonging and being valid in Spanish for "su" and "de él".

Table 5. Comparative analysis of relevant models over BLEU score and corpus size.

Model	%BLEU	Corpus size
RNN + Att Ax Spacy	40.08	18,000+
RNN + Att Ax Sentence	41.24	18,000+
RNN + Att JW Spacy	37.86	35,000+
RNN + Att JW Sentence	43.85	35,000+
Transformer Ax Spacy	54.70	18,000+
Transformer Ax Sentence	55.48	18,000+
Transformer Ax Sentencex2	56.54	18,000+
Transformer JW Spacy	57.97	35,000+
Transformer JW Sentence	**66.45**	35,000+
Transformer JW Sentencex2	65.16	35,000+

(continued)

Table 5. (*continued*)

Model	%BLEU	Corpus size
SMT Mager	10.14	985
SMT UNAM	14.28	7,200+
RNN + Att UNAM	08.36	7,200+
RNN Cherokee + Transfer Learning	16.9	14,100+
Transformer Cherokee + Transfer Learning	16.8	14,100+
GNMT Fre-Eng	88.00	36,000,000
GPT-3	41.80	1,000,000,000,000+

Table 6. Example of a pleonasm introduced in Spanish, Nahuatl language maps correctly to its meaning, having two correct ways of translation in Nahuatl but only one in Spanish.

Language	Sentence	Correctness
Spanish (input)	¿De quién es el hijo?	Yes
Nahuatl (output)	¿Ajkia eli ikone?	Yes
Spanish (input)	¿De quién es su hijo?	No
Nahuatl (output)	¿Ajkia eli ikone?	Yes

Base 20 Numbers: The Transformer model using SentencePiece was not only able to translate simply numbers from one language to another, but it also learned how to transform those numbers from base 10 to base 20.

Numbers in Spanish are expressed in base 10 whereas in Nahuatl, they are expressed in base 20 just like in the Mayan system (see Fig. 9).

The JW dataset contained about 60% of numbers from 1 to 100 besides other larger numbers.

Table 7 shows the predicted numbers by the transformer, most of them were correct, however when the direction of translation changed to Spanish, the model is only able to translate half of the number correctly, but no literal meaning is detected, showing that the model does try to convert from base 20 to base 10. A final note,

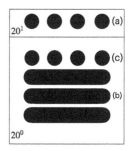

Fig. 9. Number ninety nine in the Maya system related to Nahuatl, (a) naupoali, (b) onkaxtoli, (c) on-nahui.

when asked to translate said numbers using Spacy the transformer obtained the base 10 name of the numbers but in Nahuatl, one example is 99 that was expressed as "naupoalomatlaktli uan chikome".

Table 7. Out of corpus numbers translated from base 10 to base 20 and vice versa. (x) denotes a wrong translation.

Direction	Input	Output
SPA-NHC	Ochenta y tres	Naupoali-om-eyi
SPA-NHC	Noventa y dos	Naupoal-om-matlaktli-om-ome
SPA-NHC	Noventa y siete	Naupoal-on-kaxtoli-ome
SPA-NHC	Noventa y nueve	Naupoal-on-kaxtoli-on-naui
SPA-NHC	Ciento diez	Chikompa matlaktli
NHC-SPA	Naupoali-om-eyi	Ochenta y siete (x)
NHC-SPA	Naupoal-on-kaxtoli-ome	Cincuenta y siete (x)

5   Conclusions

This work hypothesized that attention based architectures and word segmentation could improve Nahuatl NMT and, as a result, a service could be built around it to create a community to support further development on the models. The experiments confirmed that by increasing the corpus the state of the art provided by doubled and the use of attention mechanism inside RNNs; and moreover the use of Transformers (declaring that such a technique has not been used in Nahuatl), can indeed improve Nahuatl NMT translation. Transformers not only outperformed previous Nahuatl works but also other low-resource languages like Cherokee. The models also uncovered some emerging behaviors that could help to comprehend a tighter relation between Nahuatl and Mexican Spanish as well as a bonus task for transforming base 10 numbers into base 20 numbers by exploring the relation between the written numbers in Nahuatl and its numeric representation in Maya. The development of an application that in addition to serving translations, can recollect new variants of Nahuatl and use the community to adjust wrong translations; can really help to adopt Nahuatl from an academic approach and even in day to day usage. This project also helped in expanding the boundaries in terms of available parallel corpus and provided base models than can be improved or used as a foundation for transfer learning and reduce the training time for other models that use Nahuatl in any variant. For further information the code and models can be found on the GitHub repo iTlajtol[2].

Finally the work concluded that the best combination so far for Nahuatl translation turned out to be the use of the architecture **Transformers with a dataset of over 35K pairs, tokenized with SentencePiece and a direction from Spanish to Nahuatl obtaining a 66.45 BLEU score.**

---

[2] iTlajtol repo https://github.com/i-khalil-s/iTlajtol.

5.1 Future Work

Future improvements can be done by refining the training, tweaking the model even more and increasing the size of the corpus. On the other hand the application needs to implement Text-To-Speech and Speech Recognition because many native people do not write or read, also it will make the application sufficiently competitive. Comments given by the reviewers are appreciated for the improvement of this manuscript.

References

1. Aiken, M.: An updated evaluation of Google translate accuracy. Stud. Linguist. Lit. **3**, 253 (2019). https://doi.org/10.22158/sll.v3n3p253
2. Bahdanau, D., Cho, K., Bengio, Y.: Neural machine translation by jointly learning to align and translate. ArXiv 1409, September 2014
3. Bengio, S., Vinyals, O., Jaitly, N., Shazeer, N.: Scheduled sampling for sequence prediction with recurrent neural networks. In: Cortes, C., Lawrence, N., Lee, D., Sugiyama, M., Garnett, R. (eds.) Advances in Neural Information Processing Systems, vol. 28, pp. 1171–1179. Curran Associates, Inc. (2015). https://proceedings. neurips.cc/paper/2015/file/e995f98d56967d946471af29d7bf99f1-Paper.pdf
4. Carolina, E., Cerbón, V., Gutierrez-vasques, X.: Recopilación de un corpus paralelo electrónico para una lengua minoritaria: el caso del español-náhuatl, January 2015
5. Charoenpornsawat, P., Sornlertlamvanich, V., Charoenporn, T.: Improving translation quality of rule-based machine translation. In: COLING-2002: Machine Translation in Asia (2002)
6. Devlin, J., Chang, M., Lee, K., Toutanova, K.: BERT: pre-training of deep bidirectional transformers for language understanding. CoRR abs/1810.04805 (2018). http://arxiv.org/abs/1810.04805
7. Eberhard, D.M., Simons, G.F., Fennig, C.D.: Ethnologue: Languages of the World, 23 edn. SIL International, Dallas (2020). https://www.ethnologue.com/language/nhe
8. Gutierrez-vasques, X., Medina-Urrea, A., Sierra, G.: Morphological segmentation for extracting Spanish-Nahuatl bilingual lexicon. Procesamiento de Lenguaje Natural **63**, 41–48 (2019). https://doi.org/10.26342/2019-63-4
9. Gutierrez-Vasques, X., Sierra, G., Pompa, I.H.: Axolotl: a web accessible parallel corpus for Spanish-Nahuatl. In: Proceedings of the Tenth International Conference on Language Resources and Evaluation (LREC 2016), pp. 4210–4214. European Language Resources Association (ELRA), Portorož, May 2016. https://www.aclweb.org/anthology/L16-1666
10. Gutierrez-Vasques, X., Sierra, G., Pompa, I.H.: Axolotl corpus paralelo náhuatl-español beta (2020). https://axolotl-corpus.mx/search
11. Instituto Nacional de Antropología e Historia (Mexico): CEN juntamente: compendio enciclopédico del Náhuatl. Instituto Nacional de Antropología e Historia (2009). https://books.google.com.mx/books?id=JccvxgEACAAJ
12. Howard, J., Gugger, S.: Fastai: a layered API for deep learning. Information **11**(2), 108 (2020). https://doi.org/10.3390/info11020108
13. Microsoft Inc.: Microsoft translator community partners (2016). https://www.microsoft.com/en-us/translator/business/community/

14. Klein, G., Kim, Y., Deng, Y., Senellart, J., Rush, A.M.: OpenNMT: open-source toolkit for neural machine translation. CoRR abs/1701.02810 (2017). http://arxiv.org/abs/1701.02810
15. Koehn, P.: Statistical significance tests for machine translation evaluation, pp. 388–395, January 2004
16. Koehn, P.: Statistical Machine Translation. Cambridge University Press, Cambridge (2009)
17. Kudo, T.: Subword regularization: improving neural network translation models with multiple subword candidates. CoRR abs/1804.10959 (2018). http://arxiv.org/abs/1804.10959
18. Kudo, T., Richardson, J.: SentencePiece: a simple and language independent subword tokenizer and detokenizer for neural text processing. CoRR abs/1808.06226 (2018). http://arxiv.org/abs/1808.06226
19. SIL International (formerly known as the Summer Institute of Linguistics): ISO 639 code tables (2020). https://iso639-3.sil.org/code_tables/639/data/n?name_3=nahuatl
20. Liu, Q., Wang, J., Zhang, D., Yang, Y., Wang, N.: Text features extraction based on TF-IDF associating semantic. In: 2018 IEEE 4th International Conference on Computer and Communications (ICCC), pp. 2338–2343, December 2018. https://doi.org/10.1109/CompComm.2018.8780663
21. Luong, M., Pham, H., Manning, C.D.: Effective approaches to attention-based neural machine translation. CoRR abs/1508.04025 (2015). http://arxiv.org/abs/1508.04025
22. Mager, M., Gutierrez-Vasques, X., Sierra, G., Meza-Ruíz, I.V.: Challenges of language technologies for the indigenous languages of the Americas. CoRR abs/1806.04291 (2018). http://arxiv.org/abs/1806.04291
23. Mager, M., Meza, I.: Hacia la traducción automática de las lenguas indígenas de méxico, June 2018
24. Papineni, K., Roukos, S., Ward, T., Zhu, W.J.: BLEU: a method for automatic evaluation of machine translation, October 2002. https://doi.org/10.3115/1073083.1073135
25. TheWordPoint: What is the most translated website in the world? (2020). https://thewordpoint.com/blog/worlds-most-translated-website
26. Radford, A., Wu, J., Child, R., Luan, D., Amodei, D., Sutskever, I.: Language models are unsupervised multitask learners (2018). https://d4mucfpksywv.cloudfront.net/better-language-models/language-models.pdf
27. Raffel, C., et al.: Exploring the limits of transfer learning with a unified text-to-text transformer. CoRR abs/1910.10683 (2019). http://arxiv.org/abs/1910.10683
28. Ríos Dolores, J.C., Sierra Martínez, G.E.: Traducción automática náhuatl-español: variables que influyen en la calidad de la traducción. Master's thesis, Universidad Nacional Autónoma de México, September 2019. http://132.248.9.195/ptd2019/septiembre/0795765/Index.html
29. Somers, H.: Example-based machine translation. Mach. Transl. 14(2), 113–157 (1999). https://doi.org/10.1023/A:1008109312730
30. Sutskever, I., Vinyals, O., Le, Q.V.: Sequence to sequence learning with neural networks. CoRR abs/1409.3215 (2014). http://arxiv.org/abs/1409.3215
31. Thouvenot, M.: Gran diccionario náhuatl (2005). http://www.gdn.unam.mx/
32. Vaswani, A., et al.: Attention is all you need. CoRR abs/1706.03762 (2017). http://arxiv.org/abs/1706.03762
33. Villegas, M.R.: Diccionario aulex náhuatl español, April 2019. https://aulex.org/ayuda/nahuatl.php

34. Virpioja, S., Smit, P., Grönroos, S., Kurimo, M.: Morfessor 2.0: Python implementation and extensions for Morfessor Baseline (2013)
35. Williams, R.J., Zipser, D.: A learning algorithm for continually running fully recurrent neural networks. Neural Comput. **1**(2), 270–280 (1989). https://doi.org/10.1162/neco.1989.1.2.270
36. Witnesses, J.: How is our literature written and translated? (2021). https://www.jw.org/en/library/books/jehovahs-will/literature-written-and-translated/
37. Wu, Y., et al.: Google's neural machine translation system: bridging the gap between human and machine translation, September 2016
38. Zhang, S., Frey, B., Bansal, M.: ChrEn: Cherokee-English machine translation for endangered language revitalization (2020)

STClass: A Method for Determining the Sensitivity of Documents

Saturnino Job Morales Escobar[1]([✉]) [iD], José Ruiz Shulcloper[2],
Cristina Juárez Landín[3], José-Sergio Ruiz-Castilla[4] [iD],
and Osvaldo Andrés Pérez García[5]

[1] Centro Universitario UAEM Valle de México, Universidad Autónoma del Estado de México
(UAEM), Atizapán de Zaragoza Estado de México, México city, México
[2] Research Group On Logical Combinatorial Pattern Recognition, Investigations,
University of Informatics Sciences, Havana, Cuba
jshulcloper@uci.cu
[3] Centro Universitario UAEM Valle de Chalco, Universidad Autónoma del Estado de México
(UAEM), Valle de Chalco Solidaridad Estado de México, Valle de Chalco, México
[4] Centro Universitario UAEM Texcoco, Universidad Autónoma del Estado de México (UAEM),
Estado de México, Texcoco, México
jsruizc@uaemex.mx
[5] Equipo de Investigaciones de Minería de Datos, CENATAV - DATYS, La Habana,
Havana, Cuba
osvaldo.perez@cenatav.co.cu

Abstract. The leakage of sensitive information is a pressing problem when information is processed digitally due to the economic, political and social repercussions that it can cause to its owner. Despite the risks and possible threats, the information must always be kept available to users, therefore, alternatives must be available to protect, detect, and prevent the leakage of sensitive information. A particular case of this problem is the leakage of sensitive textual documents. However, the identification of unstructured sensitive information is a problem whose solution is not totally satisfactory despite the development of methods and applications with promising results. Thus, it is necessary to continue developing methods that contribute to the effective solution of the problem based on a critical analysis of existing techniques and their future projections. In this work we start from a taxonomy of the approaches with which this problem has been approached. From the taxonomy, the critical analysis of the techniques and above all considering the practical needs, a method of solution to the problem of determining the sensitivity of textual documents is proposed from the perspective of Logical Combinatorial Patterns Recognition. The problem is approached as a supervised classification problem with two classes: sensitive and non-sensitive textual documents. The proposal in this work is the STClass method to determine the sensitivity of documents, which consists of two phases: the training phase, where the parameters for classification are defined and the classification phase. With the datasets used, 96% of the well classified documents were reached.

Keywords: Data leakage · Sensitivity of documents · Supervised classification · Logical combinatorial pattern recognition

© Springer Nature Switzerland AG 2021
I. Batyrshin et al. (Eds.): MICAI 2021, LNAI 13068, pp. 140–152, 2021.
https://doi.org/10.1007/978-3-030-89820-5_11

1 Introduction

Human activity, especially the ones that involve automated processes, generates and stores a large amount of data, textual documents (hereinafter, documents), images, videos, audios, etc., being undoubtedly one of the most valuable resources for any organization. For this reason, it must be protected, both to be preserved and to prevent its loss, and to prevent its dissemination at unauthorized instances. Documents that can be considered sensitive are of particular interest, but what should be understood by a sensitive document? A sensitive document "It is one that can not be made public" for reasons of personal or organizational privacy [1], or because it contains sensitive information and "the sensitivity of the information can be evaluated based on the impact that may result from its leakage." [2]. In the previous definitions it is assumed that once the sensitivity is determined it will not be modified, however, it is common for it to occur. Therefore, for the authors of this work, *the sensitivity of a document is an assessment of its importance, privacy and confidentiality at a given moment.*

Thus, due to their degree of sensitivity, some documents, such as those corresponding to intellectual property, financial information, patient information and personal data, should be restricted in use. However, in practice, they are used in activities that involve the use of computers and mobile devices, making them vulnerable to their theft or inappropriate use.

Unfortunately, due to the enormous generation and accumulation of these documents and our own human limitations, determining how valuable or sensitive they are, and in terms of this, preventing their escape or the commission of computer crimes, is a problem that it has increased dramatically.

On the other hand, document leakage can also occur intentionally or due to human errors, but it can be increased by the area in which its transmission is carried out (internal or external) or by the means used for its dissemination (electronic mail, instant messages, web page forms, among others) [3]. The risk increases when sensitive documents are shared by clients, business partners, external employees or when made available through social media and online services [4].

Under these conditions, sensitive data leakage can be seen as result of malicious attacks or by the accidental or involuntary distribution of sensitive data to an unauthorized entity [3, 6].

Against this background, the leakage of sensitive documents is considered an emerging problem of threat to personal and organizational security, not only because of its continuous growth and the financial losses it implies, but also because of the impact at the legal level, the possible suspension of operations and the loss of credibility and trust of its customers or users. In this work it is presented STClass, an effective method to address this problem.

The rest of the work is organized as follows. In Sect. 2, an analysis of the work related to the determination of the sensitivity of documents is presented and the proposal of the new method is in the environment of the Systems for the Prevention of Data Leakage. The STClass method, proposed in this work, is presented in detail in Sect. 3. Section 4 describes the datasets used in the training and classification phases, as well as the results obtained. Finally, the conclusions are presented in Sect. 5.

2   Related Work

To solve the problem, systems for Data Leakage Prevention (DLP) have been developed, which can identify, monitor and protect confidential data and detect its misuse. Typically, DLP systems add to traditional security measures by working well for well-defined and structured data [3].

To achieve the success of a system that offers a solution to data leakage considering the challenges it represents: the semantics associated with the data, sensitive data created without classifying, information exposure on social media platforms, electronic commerce, government-provided services, unstructured sensitive data problems described in [7–10] on DLP, it is necessary that, regardless of the application of the techniques for solving document leakage, methods are incorporated to automatically determine its sensitivity from the moment it is generated.

In general, the methods for determining the sensitivity of documents have been developed from two approaches: By context and by content [3, 5].

For context analysis, features related to the environment where the document is located are used, such as: document owner and assigned permissions, network protocols, encryption format, user role, web services used, web addresses, information associated with devices, among others. In some scenarios, it is enough to know the origin of the document to classify it as sensitive or not, making content analysis unnecessary. However, when the context is not categorical with respect to the sensitivity of the document, then it is necessary to perform the analysis of contents. In synthesis, the context analysis is more focused on characterizing the users and their environment than on the data that the document contains.

On the other hand, content-based sensitivity is tied to the meaning that the data may have. It is clear that in itself, each piece of data can contain a large amount of information, however, it can be increased or decreased if it is related to other data.

This work presents an analysis of the proposals developed from the content approach. Among the most used methods are those that are based on: regular expressions, classifiers, document fingerprints, n-grams, weighting or weighting of terms and natural language processing [3]. Here is an overview of these methods and the advantages and disadvantages of each.

Regular Expressions (RE): A set of terms or characters is searched to form detection patterns, they are normally used for partial or exact detection of social security numbers, credit cards, personal and corporate records. With the incorporation of techniques based on state compression [11] and use of specific dictionaries techniques, detection can be accelerated and improved, as shown in [12]. The RE works adequately by verifying predefined rules and quickly identify known data, among the disadvantages are, the difficulty to express the requirements through an RE, they apply only to regular languages, difficulty of developing finite automaton that recognize the generated language by the RE, only identify isolated strings and, where appropriate, the use of specific dictionaries.

The Classifiers: It is known that they depend considerably on an adequate classification of the data, otherwise the prevention systems will not be able to distinguish between sensitive and normal data. The usual practice is that the owner of the data is responsible for determining its sensitivity and the protection policy to apply. Most of the solutions have been based on labels, word lists and use of probabilities with their inheriting limitations, do not maintain semantic relationships between words, most only allow traits of numerical types, randomness and independence between data are assumed, and some require large corpus of text datasets for the training [13–16].

Fingerprint Methods: They are used especially in unstructured data to detect partial or exact matches. It is the most common technique used to detect information leakage. A wide exposition about fingerprinting approach is present in [17]. DLP systems with hashing functions such as MD5, and SHA1 can achieve a high level of accuracy with complete files without alterations, but changes in parts of the document can make this method ineffective [3]. Proposals have been made to overcome data corruption and maintain detection of sensitive data, for example, use of a fuzzy fingerprint algorithm [3] and the use of k-skip-n-grams [17]. Disadvantages: fail to detect small parts of the document, elimination of stop words which can generate loss of context, use of statistics in the selection of terms, excessive use of indexes and failure when sensitive data is altered or modified.

N-gram: Widely used in natural language processing, machine learning and information retrieval by term weighting. The n-grams depend on the frequency analysis of terms and n-grams in the documents. Its application together with Support Vector Machines have been used to classify business documents into two classes: sensitive and non-sensitive [18]; however, depending on the organization, the number of classes can be increased and labeled with different names, for example: public and private; private business, non-public business, and non-business; unclassified, restricted, confidential, secret and top secret [14, 17, 18]. A disadvantage is that once the value of n is set, it can not be changed for every n-gram, another disadvantage, is the elimination of stop words, and finally, they do not maintain semantic relationships between the terms.

Weighting or Term Weighing: The term weighing is a statistical method that indicates the importance of each term in a document, is called the weight of the term. This method is also used in text classification where each document is represented as a vector of dimension n in a vector space [19, 20] and n is the number of terms present in all documents. For term weighing, have been considered from binary weight schemes, the term is present or not [18], to schemes where functions are used to determine the frequencies of the terms based on which their weight is determined [14]. Improvements to the method include the representation of terms by means of n-grams as referred to in [3] or hybrid approaches that combine graphic and vector representations that include term weighing and classifiers [21, 22].

Natural Language Processing: Models to address this problem include the statistical one, in which each document is treated as a bag of words, where only the words and their relative frequencies are of interest to characterize a document. It is also generally assumed that there is a correctly categorized corpus that is used as a training set for supervised machine learning algorithms [14]. Other methods use weighted adaptive graphs, which allow maintaining the semantic sensitivity of the documents [23]. The application of syntactic analysis, the use of probability, identification of domains and corpus in those domains, are other alternatives that have been used to improve the identification of sensitive data from this perspective [24–26]. Among the limitations are: the use of domain corpus, frequently word order and context are ignored, production rules and use of probabilities are required.

It should be noted that in DLP systems, it is where most work has been done on solving the problem of determining the sensitivity of documents, However, due to the aforementioned limitations, it is necessary to continue the development of methods capable of identifying sensitive documents automatically, detecting the semantic content of the data to protect them in a pertinent manner to their sensitivity and prevent their leakage or loss in any of their states: in use, in transit or at rest.

Under these conditions, an important contribution would be aimed at detecting sensitive documents from the moment they are created and before they are released for use. With this objective, STClass was developed, a supervised method capable of determining whether a document is sensitive or not. This method has the following advantages: it does not require a list of words provided by the owner of the data, or specific corpus, it maintains the relationships between the terms to preserve their semantic relationship, it does not presuppose probability distributions over the terms or chains of terms present in documents, the length of sensible strings can be chosen and finally it can be used for document classification. The STClass method is described in the next section of this work.

Considering that the basic architecture of DLP systems is made up of three modules (see Fig. 1). The first detects whether a document is being sent, created or accessed (for printing, copying, editing, sending over the network, etc.) regardless of its content. The second module analyzes the document detected in the filter, reviews it and sends it to the third module for an assessment in accordance with the established policy. This last module responds by allowing access or blocking, if is necessary, the actions on the document to be protected, issuing the corresponding alert.

Is in the analysis module at the content or context level, or both, where the sensitivity of documents must be assessed and based on which will be the response that the system must issue. This answer is qualified by the level of security desired with the DLP application, thus expressing the security policy defined for the system. It is precisely in this module where the theoretical problems related to the determination of the sensitivity of the documents to be protected are located and where the STClass method can be incorporated.

The STClass method is described in the next section.

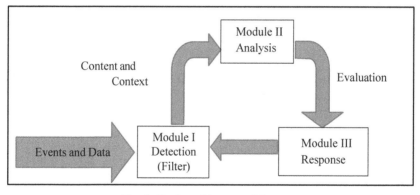

Fig. 1. Basic architecture of the DLP.

3   STClass: Method for Determining the Sensitivity of Documents

Based on the analysis carried out, a new method is presented to determine whether a document is sensitive or not, from the point of view of Logical Combinatorial Pattern Recognition [27, 28]. The method is developed with a content-based approach.

From this perspective, the determination of the sensitivity of documents is approached as a problem of supervised classification considering two stages: training and classification.

In this work, the STClass method is applied with documents classified into two classes: sensitive and non-sensitive documents. Unlike other methods, an initial list of terms is not required.

For the analysis of the document, the point "." is used to delimit the strings of terms that could form sentences or phrases.

In the first instance, as a comparison criterion to decide whether two terms are similar, symbol-by-symbol equality is used, which means that two terms are similar if all the symbols of the term are equal. Without any further modification to the method, other criteria for comparison between terms could be used, e.g., synonyms.

A document will be considered sensitive if it contains a sensitive paragraph and a paragraph is sensitive if it contains a string or substring of terms sensitive, analogously, a string or substring of terms is sensitive if it contains any sensitive term and a term is sensitive, if its frequency in the class of sensitive documents is higher than its frequency in the class of non-sensitive documents by at least a given threshold $\in$, as is show in Eq. (1).

$$S(t) = \begin{cases} 1 \, if \, |F_s(t) - F(t)| \geq \in \\ 0 \, in \, another \, case \end{cases} \tag{1}$$

$Fs(t)$ is the frequency of term t in the class of sensitive documents and $F(t)$ is its frequency in the class of non-sensitive documents.

As can be seen, from Eq. (1), in general, the degree of sensitivity of a term can be expressed as:

$$S_n(t) = \frac{F_s(t) - F(t)}{F_t(t)} \tag{2}$$

$F_s(t)$ y $F(t)$ are defined as in (1) y $F_t(t)$ is the total frequency of the term, given by the Eq. (3)

$$F_t(t) = F_s(t) + F(t) \tag{3}$$

Analogously, the sensitivity of a string or substring of terms, "c", is defined by:

$$S(c) = \begin{cases} 1 \, if \, |F_s(c) - F(c)| \geq \partial \\ 0 \, in \, another \, case \end{cases} \tag{4}$$

Here $F_s(c)$ is the frequency of the string (substring) c in the class of sensitive documents. ∂ is a given threshold and $F(c)$ is its frequency in the class of non-sensitive documents.

It can also define the degree of sensitivity of c as:

$$S_n(c) = \frac{F_s(c) - F(c)}{F_t(c)} \tag{5}$$

$F_s(c)$ y $F(c)$ are defined as (4) y $F_t(t)$ is the total frequency of the term, given by the Eq. (6).

$$F_t(c) = F_s(c) + F(c) \tag{6}$$

The method works as follows, a counter is associated for each term, in such a way that the number of times the term appears in each class is known.

A string of terms is the concatenation of terms delimited by ".".

For the formation of chains, a term is taken and the following terms are linked to it until the delimiter is found. For each substring, the number of times it is present in each class is also stored.

Because of the way the strings are obtained, the relationships between the terms are preserved, which represents an advantage when preserving the information that the terms provide together.

The STClass method consist of 2 phases, and each phase is divided into three steps and in each one the parameters with which the method will work must be provided.

STClass Method

Phase 1. Training

Step 1. Build a training matrix with samples of documents in each class (sensitive and non-sensitive).

Step 2. Construction of chains (substrings) of terms for the training sample.

2.1. Build a list of initial terms of each chain.

2.2. Determine comparison criteria between terms.

2.2.1 Equality

2.2.2 Synonyms

2.3. Build the chains (substrings) of each term in the list.

2.4. For each term and each substring calculate its frequency in each class.

2.5. Determine the sensitivity of each term and each substring of terms using (3) and (4).

Step 3. Definition of parameters for classification.

3.1. Quantity of sensitive terms to use.

3.2. Number of sensitive substrings to use.

3.3. Definition of the similarity function to be used in string comparison.

3.4. Determine sensitivity weights for each substring.

3.4.1. Based on the cardinality of the substrings.

3.4.2. Based on the frequency of terms.

3.5. Classification rule.

Phase 2. Classification

Step 4. Construction of chains (substrings) of terms of the document to classify.

4.1. Build list of initial terms of each chain.

4.2. Build the chains (substrings) of each term in the list.

Step 5. Compare the strings of terms in the document to be classified, with the chains

of terms obtained in step 2 and parameters given in step 3.

Step 6. Classify the document based on the classification rule (step 3.4).

4   Datasets and Experimental Methodology

To test the STClass method a training sample was formed with 80 textual documents and 60 control documents, achieving an efficiency in the 96% classification considering the terms and chains of sensitive terms with an epsilon threshold equal to zero.

Table 1 summarizes the distribution of the documents used in the two phases of the STClass method. For the training phase, a set of 50 sensitive and 30 non-sensitive documents was used. In the classification phase, 60 documents were introduced, of which 40 were sensitive and 20 were non-sensitive. Taking as a function to evaluate the quality the quantity of well classified documents among the total of documents an efficiency of 96% was obtained.

Table 1. Distribution of documents used for training and classification of STClass.

Datasets	Trainning		Classification		Results		Efficiency
	Sensitive	Non-sensitive	Sensitive	Non-sensitive	Well classified	Misclassified	
Documents	50	30	40	20	58	2	96%

In the determination of sensitive documents, seen as a problem of supervised classification, it is essential that the training data set is true and maintained as it is given by the owner of the data. For this reason, the content of the training and classification files should be entered into the program in its original format and content, avoiding the elimination or modification of terms that may be significant in identifying sensitivity and avoiding biases, in some cases, only delimiters were added.

Nevertheless, given the difficulty of obtaining real and current sensitive data, the dataset was formed by taking records published on the internet and were modified to avoid coincidences that compromise some real instance. Below are examples of the contents of the documents used in the training samples and in the classification.

Training sample

Sensitive documents:

D₁: Empresa de Viajes Cia. Ltda
  Guipuzcoa G2-117 y Moreno.
La marqueza / Quito, Ecuador.
EE. UU. Teléfono: 323-675-874 / consulas@andec.com.
En Guipuzcoa.
Licenciado Leonardo Moreno.
Presidente Constitucional de la República de Ecuador.
D₂: Eduardo Estévez Romero.
Investigador Asociado.
Editor asociado de Transactions on Neural Networks Journal.
Correo electrónico: latevez@ing.ucil.cl.
Eduardo Estévez Medina.
Es secretario de cultura.
El presidente de la República es electo por elecciones directas y por un periodo de 6 años.
No hay reelección a la Presidencia de la República.

Non-sensitive documents:
D₃: Alberto Magaña Mercado.
Director del Departamento de Ingeniería Eléctrica.
Profesor titular (2009-).
Editor asociado de IEEE Transactions on Neural Networks Journal (2000-2005).
Copresidente General Congreso Mundial de IEEE sobre Inteligencia Computacional, Río de Janeiro, Brasil, julio de 2004.
D₄: Gerardo Anaya de Isla Galapagos, trabajó como Marino Mercante, ocupando la función de aceitero.
Acuedo con usted para denunciar al señor José Gabriel Olvera Verlanga, de la compañia island travel cia.
Esta compañía y su embarcación trabaja en la provincia de Isla Galapagos pertenece a la compañía ISLANDIA CON RU. No.1U5737001.

Documents to classify:

D₅: Empresa de Viajes Cia. Ltda
  Guipuzcoa G2-117 y Moreno.
D6: Actualmente es profesor de Ingeniería Eléctrica de la Universidad de Chile.
Eduardo Estévez Mediana.
Fue director del Departamento de Ingeniería Eléctrica en los años 2006-2012.

With the previous training documents, the term strings are built and the frequency of the term and the substring in each class is recorded, in such a way that when a document is going to be classified, the strings obtained from the document to be classified are compared with the chains obtained during the training phase.

In this way, all the terms, the order in which they are found and the semantic relationships between them are maintained, it is here that the fulfillment of the similarity functions defined for the comparison of the strings and the comparison criteria of terms is verified.

After applying the method, the strings that were sensitive and that give rise to the classification of the documents as sensitive, are shown below.

This is because the strings were found in the sensitive documents class and are not present in the contents of non-sensitive documents.

As noted in this document, STClass does not require a list of sensitive terms, syntactic rules, specific corpus, or the calculation of probabilities to determine the sensitivity of documents.

Sensitive Chains:
Empresa de Viajes Cia. Ltda.
   Guipuzcoa G2–117 y Moreno.
   Eduardo Estévez Mediana.

5 Conclusion

The problem of determining the sensitivity of documents is a problem that presents great challenges, in principle by itself's nature, the temporality of their sensitivity, the large number of documents that are generated and most significantly, the dependence of sensitivity to natural language semantics.

In this work, based on an analysis of the most used methods to classify sensitive documents and the need to know if a document should be protected or not, limitations and requirements present in these methods were detected, among which are: it must be provided a lists of sensitive words to be able to identify them, the elimination of words can cause the loss of semantic relationships, the comparison between documents is based on numerical vectors, the order of the words is ignored, use of specific corpus, provide grammar rules and the use of probabilities.

Based on this identification, the STClass method was developed to determine the sensitivity of documents from the point of view of the Logical Combinatorial Pattern Recognition. The method is based on content analysis and is approached as a problem of supervised classification considering two phases: training and classification.

In this work, its application to the problem is presented with two classes: sensitive and non-sensitive documents.

Among the advantages offered by STClass are the following: it does not require an initial list of terms, it maintains the order and the semantic relationship between terms, it does not need specific corpus or a priori probabilities, to evaluate the similarity, different comparison criteria can be incorporated between terms and between strings of terms. In addition, its application can be extended to problems with a larger number of classes.

In the tests carried out, an efficiency of 96% was achieved in the classification of new documents.

As a continuation of this work, it is necessary to test the method with public and articles datasets, make comparisons with other methods, and do the extension to include any number of classes and provide degrees of sensitivity.

References

1. Berardi, G., Esuli, A., Macdonald, C., Ounis, L., Sebastiani, F.: Semi-automated text classification for sensitivity identification. In: Proceedings of the 24th ACM International on Conference on Information and Knowledge Management. ACM, pp. 1711–1714, (2015)
2. Alzhrani, K., Ruddy, E., Chow, C., Boulty, T.: Automated U.S diplomatic cables security classification: topic model pruning vs. classification based on clusters. In: Proceedings of the 2017 IEEE International Symposium on Technologies for Homeland Security (HST), pp. 1–6, (2017)
3. Alneyadi, S., Sithirasenan, E., Muthukkumarasamy, V.: A survey on data leakage prevention systems. J. Netw. Comput. Appl. **62**, 137–152 (2016)
4. Salahdine, F., Kaabouch, N.: Social engineering attacks: a survey. Future Internet, **11**(4), 89 (2019)
5. Wynne, N., Reed, B.: Magic quadrant for enterprise data loss prevention. Gartner Group Research Note (2016)
6. Ahmad, N.: Do data almost always eventually leak?: Computer **54**(2), 70–74 (2021)
7. Wadkar, H., Mishra, A., Dixit, A.: Prevention of information leakages in a web browser by monitoring system calls. In: Proceedings of the 2014 IEEE International Advance Computing Conference (IACC), pp. 199–204, (2014)
8. Liu, T., Pu, Y., Shi, J., Li, Q., Chen, X.: Towards misdirected email detection for preventing information leakage. In: Proceedings of the 2014 IEEE Symposium on Computers and Communication (ISCC), pp. 1–6, (2014)
9. Jena, M.D., Singhar, S.S., Mohanta, B.K., Ramasubbareddy, S.: Ensuring data privacy using machine learning for responsible data science. In: Satapathy, S.C., Zhang, Y.-D., Bhateja, V., Majhi, R. (eds.) Intelligent Data Engineering and Analytics. AISC, vol. 1177, pp. 507–514. Springer, Singapore (2021). https://doi.org/10.1007/978-981-15-5679-1_49
10. Ávila, R., Khoury, R., Khoury, R., Petrillo, F.: Use of security logs for data leak detection: a systematic literature review. Secur. Commun. Netw. (2021)
11. Becchi, M., Crowley, P.: An improved algorithm to accelerate regular expression evaluation. In: Proceedings of the 2007 ACM/IEEE Symposium on Architecture for Networking and Communications Systems, pp. 145–154, (2007)
12. Sokolova, M., et al.: Personal health information leak prevention in heterogeneous texts. In: Proceedings of the Workshop on Adaptation of Language Resources and Technology to New Domains, pp. 58–69, (2009)
13. Chen, K., Liu, L.: Privacy preserving data classification with rotation perturbation. In: Fifth IEEE International Conference on Data Mining (ICDM'05), pp. 1–4, (2005)
14. Brown, J.D., Charlebois, D.: Security classification using automated learning (SCALE): optimizing statistical natural language processing techniques to assign security labels to unstructured text. Defense Research and Development Canada, Ottawa (Ontario), (2010).
15. Kowsari, K., Jafari, M., Heidarysafa, M., Mendu, S., Barnes, L., Brown, D.: Text classification algorithms: a survey. Information **10**(4), 150 (2019)
16. Zorarpacı, E., Özel, S.A.: Privacy preserving classification over differentially private data. Wiley Interdisc. Rev. Data Min. Knowl. Discov. **11**(3), e1399 (2021)

17. Shapira, Y., Shapira, B., Shabtai, A.: Content-based data leakage detection using extended fingerprinting. arXiv preprint arXiv:1302.2028 (2013)
18. Hart, M., Manadhata, P., Johnson, R.: Text Classification for data loss prevention. In: Fischer-Hübner, S., Hopper, N. (eds.) PETS 2011. LNCS, vol. 6794, pp. 18–37. Springer, Heidelberg (2011). https://doi.org/10.1007/978-3-642-22263-4_2
19. Salton, G., Wong, A., Yang, C.S.: A vector space model for automatic indexing. Commun. ACM **18**, 613–620 (1975)
20. Carvalho, V.R., Balasubramanyan, R., Cohen, W.W.: Information leaks and suggestions: a case study using mozilla thunderbird. In: CEAS 2009-Sixth Conference on Email and Anti-Spam (2009)
21. Xiang, Y., Zhihong, T., Jing, Q., Feng, J.: A data leakage prevention method based on the reduction of confidential and context terms for smart mobile devices. Wirel. Commun. Mob. Comput. (2018)
22. Katz, G., Elovici, Y., Shapira, B.: CoBAn: a context based model for data leakage prevention. Inf. Sci. **262**, 137–158 (2014)
23. Xiaohong, H., Yunlong, L., Dandan, L.: A novel mechanism for fast detection of transformed data leakage. IEEE Xplore Digit. Libr. **6**, 35926–35936 (2018)
24. Yang, Z., Liang, Z.: Automated identification of sensitive data from implicit user specification. Cybersecurity **1**(1), 1–15 (2018). https://doi.org/10.1186/s42400-018-0011-x
25. Neerbek, J., Assent, I., Dolog, P.: Detecting complex sensitive information via phrase structure in recursive neural networks. In: Phung, D., Tseng, V.S., Webb, G.I., Ho, B., Ganji, M., Rashidi, L. (eds.) PAKDD 2018. LNCS (LNAI), vol. 10939, pp. 373–385. Springer, Cham (2018). https://doi.org/10.1007/978-3-319-93040-4_30
26. Briand, A., Zacharie, S., Jean-Louis, L., Meurs, M.-J.: Identification of sensitive content in data repositories to support personal information protection. In: Mouhoub, M., Sadaoui, S., Ait Mohamed, O., Ali, M. (eds.) IEA/AIE 2018. LNCS (LNAI), vol. 10868, pp. 898–910. Springer, Cham (2018). https://doi.org/10.1007/978-3-319-92058-0_86
27. Martínez-Trinidad, J.F., Guzmán-Arenas, A.: The logical combinatorial approach to pattern recognition, an overview through selected works. Pattern Recogn. **34**, 741–751 (2001)
28. Ruiz-Shulcloper, J.: Pattern recognition with mixed and incomplete data. Pattern Recogn. Image Anal. **18**(4), 563–576 (2008)

Plagiarism Detection in Students' Answers Using FP-Growth Algorithm

Sabina Nurlybayeva[1] , Iskander Akhmetov[1,3](✉) , Alexander Gelbukh[2] ,
and Rustam Mussabayev[3]

[1] Faculty of Information Technology, Kazakh-British Technical University,
Almaty, Kazakhstan
s_nurlybaeva@kbtu.kz
[2] Instituto Politecnico Nacional, CIC, Mexico City, Mexico
gelbukh@gelbukh.com
[3] Institute of Information and Computational Technologies,
Pushkin Street 125, Almaty, Kazakhstan
http://kbtu.edu.kz
http://iict.kz

Abstract. According to statistics, over the past year, the quality of education has fallen due to the pandemic, and the percentage of plagiarism in the work of students has increased. Modern plagiarism detection systems work well with external plagiarism, they allow to weed out works and answers that completely copy someone else's published ideas. Using natural language processing methods, the proposed algorithm allows not only detecting plagiarism, but also correctly classifies students' responses by the amount of plagiarism. This research paper implements a two-step plagiarism detection algorithm. In the experiment, the text was converted into a vector form by the GloVe method, and then segmented by K-means and the result was obtained by the FP-Growth unsupervised learning algorithm.

Keywords: Plagiarism detection · Natural language processing · Machine learning

1 Introduction

Plagiarism is the "wrongful appropriation" and "stealing and publication" of another author's "language, thoughts, ideas, or expressions" and the representation of them as one's own original work. Plagiarism is considered academic dishonesty and a breach of journalistic ethics. The problem of plagiarism is also encountered among the writing and journalistic community, when articles copy the content, and the works have the same plots. Plagiarism has become a problem not only for publicists, but also in educational institutions, this problem is becoming more and more serious. Based on the research of 6,096 undergraduate students at 31 universities, 67.4% was found committed in plagiarism. The

© Springer Nature Switzerland AG 2021
I. Batyrshin et al. (Eds.): MICAI 2021, LNAI 13068, pp. 153–162, 2021.
https://doi.org/10.1007/978-3-030-89820-5_12

results of similar study on several different campuses with more than 6,000 participants from the high school and undergraduate students, showed 76% were found committed in plagiarism [9]. Thus in order to protect academic integrity plagiarism detection has gained a lot of importance these days.

Plagiarism means taking the work or ideas of someone else and passing them off as your own. The most common and well known form being textual plagiarism. For the purpose of this thesis, all references to plagiarism will be to textual plagiarism; copying the text from a source text and presenting it as your own answer. Plagiarism comes in many forms. One can directly copy a text, but detecting pure verbatim plagiarism is a fairly easy task, and plagiarists are quickly caught doing this with current tools. In order to mask an act of plagiarism, the text is often rewritten, words in a sentence rearranged, replaced with synonyms, or the text may be summarized. This makes it harder for automated systems to detect the plagiarised text. Detecting semantic meaning in a text is especially challenging to do with a computer algorithm. They are however very adept at lexical analysis. Most plagiarism detection tools use the structural and lexical similarities of documents.

Machine learning allows users to find optimal settings automatically based on statistics from a data set made up of pre-classified plagiarism and non-plagiarism cases. By defining passages, documents or sentences in a data set as plagiarism, or even the kind of plagiarism methods used on each passage, a system could potentially be tailored to each institution, or even teacher preference.

This study will develop a method for detecting plagiarism and classifying it according to the level of uniqueness of the text using natural language processing techniques. This approach implies a two-stage plagiarism detection algorithm that trains the model without marking, segmentation and searching for frequent elements.

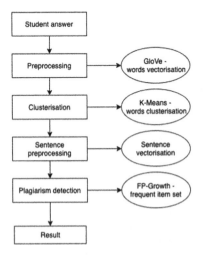

Fig. 1. Algorithm stages

The K-means algorithm is implemented for segmentation of words vectors into similar clusters, from which in the future, using the FP - Growth unsupervised algorithm, frequent sets of elements will be derived. In our context, we receive sentences that are plagiarized. Proposed plagiarism detection algorithm is described in the Fig. 1 above.

2 Related Works

With the development of the internet, people are actively looking for a solution to the plagiarism problem. The most popular tracking systems are Skyline Inc. software, Sherlock software and iThenticate [4].

Skyline. Inc. developed standalone plagiarism-detector anti plagiarism software, which detects plagiarized text. It is an autonomous Microsoft Windows-based computer desktop application made with Visual C # .Net. It follows the exact substrings detection method and it is used in the academic environment. At any rate, it has its shortcomings which is that it runs just on windows operating system, it raises a huge amount of false positives (it flags a sentence as plagiarized even though it is not). It also lacks plagiarism prevention mechanism because there is no module or subsystem in place to deter or discourage plagiarism [3].

Sherlock, is a program used to recognize copyright encroachment for essays, computer source codes files and other kinds of textual documents in digital form. Sherlock works by converting text it receives into digital signatures to measure the similarity between the documents. A digital signature is a number formed by changing several words (3 by default) in the input into a series of bits and joining those bits into a number. Sherlock is developed with C programming language and it requires compilation before being installed either on Unix/Linux or Windows. It doesn't have a GUI as it is a command-line program.

iThenticate compares a given document against the document sources available on the World Wide Web. It also compares the given document against proprietary databases of published works (including ABI/Inform, Periodical Abstracts, Business Dateline), as well as numerous electronic books and produces originality reports. The originality reports provide the amounts of materials copied (in percentages) to determine the extent of plagiarism, was developed using PHP and supported by an MSQL back end database [4].

Over the past decade, Machine Learning solutions have displaced legacy technologies. In the problem of recognizing plagiarism, three main types of solving the problem can be distinguished: distance-meausuring algorithm, character n-gram algorithm and clustering algorithm.

Previously, works such as Plagiarism Detection Using the Levenshtein Distance and Smith-Waterman Algorithm [11] where the Levenshtein distance between two strings is given by the minimum number of operations, and that needed to transform one string into the other, where an operation is an insertion, deletion, or substitution of a single character is seen. A commonly-used bottom-up dynamic programming algorithm for computing the Levenshtein distance involves the use of an $(n + 1) \times (m + 1)$ matrix, where n and m are the lengths of the two strings. This algorithm is based on the Wagner-Fischer algorithm for edit a distance.

The Smith-Waterman algorithm is a classical method of comparing two strings with a view to identifying highly similar sections within them. It is widely-used in finding good near-matches, or so-called local alignments, within biological sequences.

Generally, when researchers compute the similarity of the texts, they first use the Levenshtein distance method to divide the table, after dividing the table and then making some of the portions don't calculate, they applied simplified Smith-Waterman algorithm to the rest of the table, because of the less nodes of the table will be compute than Levenshtein distance.

We also came across Intrinsic Plagiarism Detection Using Character n-gram [1]. This algorithm attempts to quantify the style variation within a document using character n-gram profiles and a style change function based on an appropriate dissimilarity measure originally proposed for author identification.

In this supervised method, the classification model is trained with a small number of features which are the proportions of the n-gram classes. In detail, method is composed of the following steps:

1. Segment each document d into fragments si by using the sliding window technique. Let S denotes the set of these fragments.
2. Build the n-gram class document model without considering numerals. Researchers choose to consider the frequency of a n-gram ngi as the number of its occurrence in d such that it is counted once per fragment. Therefore, the minimum value that could take a frequency is 1 if ngi appears only in one fragment, and its maximum value is —S— (the number of fragments in d) if ngi occurs in each fragment si S.
3. Represent each fragment si by a vector of m features fj, j 0,..., m–1. So that, each fj is the proportion of the n-grams that belong to the class labeled j to the total number of n-grams in si.
4. Combine into one dataset the fragment vectors obtained from all the training corpus documents. Then, label each vector with its authenticity state, i.e. plagiarized, if the fragment plagiarism percentage exceeds 50% and original otherwise.
5. Use the Naïve Bayes algorithm as classifier.

In this project, we used some basic idea from the above methods and implemented a plagiarism detection on a completely different concept. We used unsupervised machine learning algorithm called using Frequent Pattern (FP) Growth Algorithm.

3   Dataset and Features

In this study, the freely available Clough-Stevenson corpus [2] was applied. The corpus consists of answers to five short questions on a variety of topics in Computer Science field. The five short questions are:

- What is inheritance in object oriented programming?
- Explain the PageRank algorithm that is used by the Google search engine.
- Explain the Vector Space Model that is used for Information Retrieval.
- Explain Bayes Theorem from probability theory.
- What is dynamic programming?

Each question has 19 students answers and 1 Wikipedia answer. We are also given which answers are plagiarised.

Table 1. Dataset statistics

Number of questions	5
Number of answers per question	20
Number of Non or lightly plagiarised answers	57
Number of Heavily plagiarised answers	19
Mean number of words per answer	216

There are four different types of answers. They are cut, light, non-plagiarised and heavy. Cut refers to answers that are fully copy-pasted from Wikipedia answer. Heavy refers to answers that are heavily copied from Wikipedia answers, light refers to answers which are slightly copied from Wikipedia answers with extreme changes to the structure of answers. Non refers to non plagiarised work. Statistics about dataset is given in the Table 1 given above.

Thus the input for our system is various documents which contain student answers for various questions. The output is the list of students that have plagiarised work for each question.

4   Methodology

In our experiment we used K-mean algorithm and FP-Growth algorithm. The FP-Growth Algorithm, proposed by Han [10], is an efficient and scalable method for mining the complete set of frequent patterns by pattern fragment growth, using an extended prefix-tree structure for storing compressed and crucial information about frequent patterns named frequent-pattern tree (FP-tree). FP-Growth algorithm is normally used to find frequent item-sets given a number of transactions. In natural language processing, we can model our text data into vectors using word vector vector representation techniques. Many word vector representation techniques have been developed in recent times. We will use GloVe [8] to represent our textual data in form of vectors. Thus we get a vector representing each unique word in our data.

For getting similar words in context and meaning, many methods have been used like Brown Clustering Algorithm [6] or Word2Vec [7]. However in our project, we use K-means [5] Clustering Algorithm because of its features like completeness, exclusivity and fast execution. In our project, clusters of similar words are created. Then a vector for each sentence is built based on those clusters. If the two words belong to the same cluster then, the same cluster number is applied to both the words in the vector. After that a vector for each text document is created based on sentence vectors. If two sentence vectors are similar, then we assign a unique number to those sentences. Thus we get a vector for each document which we can use as item-sets in the FP-Growth Algorithm and the number of documents will be our transactions. Once we get frequent item sets we know which documents are plagiarised from each other.

5   Experiment

Preprocessing. For pre-processing we have to make sure that all the words are lower cased with all the punctuation removed. We use the NLTK sentence tokenizer to get list of sentences so that we know where does each sentence begin and end. There are various latin words in our answers as well so we use "latin1" encoding for reading the text.

Vectorisation. After preprocessing the text we needed a way to cluster similar words. Since, we were using K-means clustering which is a distance based clustering method, we needed each unique word in our corpus to have a numerical value. The choice was between several algorithms: bert glove word2 century. Since the initial task is to determine plagiarism, the word itself is important to us, but not its meaning. The BERT algorithm will generate several vectors for the words of homonyms, since it takes into account the position of the word within the sentence and considers the context of use.

The most famous word2vec word embedding model is the predictive model, that is, it trains itself trying to predict the target word in context (CBOW) or context words from the target (skip gram).

And the GloVe model uses a hit-count matrix to perform attachments that is more suited to this typical task. Each row of the matrix represents a word, while each column represents contexts in which words may appear. Matrix values represent the frequency with which a word occurs in a given context. Downsizing is then applied to this matrix to create the resulting embedding matrix (each row will be a word embedding vector). The main intuition underlying the model is the simple observation that ratios of word-word co-occurrence probabilities have the potential for encoding some form of meaning.

After performing GloVe on our preprocessed data we get vector of each unique word in our corpus. We can use this representation for clustering and further processing.

Implementation. K-means clustering algorithm is that it is not guaranteed to find the most optimal cluster arrangement, if you pick the wrong starting points.

One method for overcoming this is to run the algorithm a number of times with different randomly selected starting points, and then pick the solution that has the lowest total squared Euclidean distance. This approach is used in the scikit-learn package, defaulting to 10 separate repetitions. Since text-based data is usually high-dimensional and sparse, we first use the dimensionality reduction method to reduce the dimension of the high-dimensional text feature vectors. Then use the improved density peaks algorithm to determine the number of clusters and the initial clustering centers, after which the K-means algorithm is used for clustering [12].

In the experiment, two options for implementing the K-means algorithm were proposed: with the use of dimensionality reduction and without, i.e. the algorithm worked with 126 clusters, the number is determined by the number of words in the dataset—1.262 and the size reduction factor is 0.1. For an objective assessment of the method, an iterative selection of K was launched in the range from 10 to 150, and using the Silhouette and Elbow method metrics, it was revealed that the best indicator is at K = 126. Results of two metrics are shown in Fig. 2 below. Since less than 126 clusters according to the WCSS metric shows elements that are too far from the centroids, i.e., little similarity of elements within the cluster, and after 126 clusters, the resulting groups have high similarity and do not have a clear separation boundary by Silhouette metric.

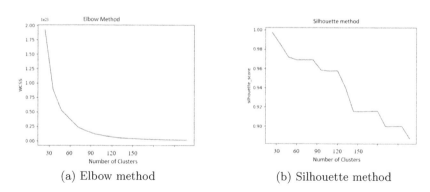

(a) Elbow method   (b) Silhouette method

Fig. 2. K-means algorithm metrics

Scikit-learn implementation of K-Means returns an object that indicates the cluster to which each input vector belongs. Thus after performing K-means clustering, we get similar word clusters. Now, we need to apply FP-growth Algorithm to find frequent item sets. But in order to do that, we first need to represent our data in the form of transactions of various item-sets. In order to do that we created our own vector representation explained below.

Vector Representation. From the obtained clusters and its respective labels from K-means clustering algorithm, we now use these clusters to convert our data in each documents to vectors. For this, we do the following.

- Determine the cluster label for each of the word in sentences and substitute the word with its respective cluster label.
- From the above step, we merge all the words and form sentence vectors.
- From these sentence vector, we form answer vector by assigning a unique number if two sentence vectors are different. If two sentence vectors are same we assign each of them the same number.

Thus we get a vector for each answer. This vector can be viewed as an item-set and each answer can be viewed as a transaction. Thus we get a list of transactions which contain item-sets. We can feed this into FP-Growth Algorithm to get frequent item sets.

FP-Growth Algorithm. The FP-growth algorithm is currently one of the fastest approaches to frequent item set mining. One of the currently fastest and most popular algorithms for frequent item set mining is the FP-growth algorithm. It is based on a prefix tree representation of the given database of transactions (called an FP-tree), which can save considerable amounts of memory for storing the transactions. The basic idea of the FP-growth algorithm can be described as a recursive elimination scheme: in a preprocessing step delete all items from the transactions that are not frequent individually, i.e., do not appear in a user-specified minimum number of transactions. Then select all transactions that contain the least frequent item (least frequent among those that are frequent) and delete this item from them. Recourse to process the obtained reduced (also known as projected) database, remembering that the item sets found in the recursion share the deleted item as a prefix. On return, remove the processed item also from the database of all transactions and start over, i.e., process the second frequent item etc. In these processing steps the prefix tree, which is enhanced by links between the branches, is exploited to quickly find the transactions containing a given item and also to remove this item from the transactions after it has been processed.

Thus after performing FP-Growth Algorithm we get frequent item sets. In our context we get frequent sentences which are plagiarised. We can find which sentences are plagiarised by just looking at the transactions which in our case are student answers. Now it is important to know that we need to consider only three or more frequent item-sets meaning only three or more plagiarised sentences. This is because most of the students can have one one or two similar sentences like "This is called Inheritance". We cannot penalise students for that.

6   Results

As, described in Sect. 2, Each question has 19 students answers and 1 wikipedia answer.

Having launched the proposed solution to the problem of plagiarism detection on the Corpus, we compared the metrics of the classifier with the metrics from the studied articles from Sect. 2.

Of the studies studied using machine learning, the most successful algorithm can be distinguished - it is N-gram classes algorithmBensalem2014, since the metrics of this algorithm are higher than those of Levenshtein Distance and Smith-Waterman Algorithm [11].

Table 2. Comparison of the proposed approach with the most popular algorithms

Model	Precision	Recall	F-score
K-means and FP-Growth algorithm (this work)	**90.4%**	**52.3%**	**66.3%**
Levenshtein Distance and Smith-Waterman Algorithm [11]	39.3%	31.7%	35.1%
N-gram classes [1]	31.3%	49.2%	38.3%

Thus, comparing the indicators of the algorithms from the Table 2, the solution proposed in this work has the best metrics. For example, comparing with the most successful N-gram classes algorithm, our approach has a small gap in the recall metric - only 3% but the precision metric is almost 60% higher.

7   Conclusion

Many methods have been proposed to detect and stop plagiarism. But, still there are many questions which are to be answered. Natural Language Processing has greater possibilities of providing a sound and concrete mechanism which is capable of detecting plagiarism in any document. In this paper we have tried to show finding plagiarism using FP-growth with its advantages and tried to implement clusterisation algorithm with dimension reduction. We have developed a system based on principles of vector representations.

8   Future Work

A s an extension to this work, we can include vector representations using other techniques such as word2vec. Another future work is to change the domain from documents to programming code plagiarism detection. In the task of detection plagiarism in source code, we would need stricter noise removal as well as the support count of FP-growth algorithm will increase.

Acknowledgment. This research is conducted within the framework of the grant num. AP09058174 "Development of language-independent unsupervised methods of semantic analysis of large amounts of text data".

The work was done with partial support from the Mexican Government through the grant A1-S-47854 of the CONACYT, Mexico and grants 20211784, 20211884, and 20211178 of the Secretaría de Investigación y Posgrado of the Instituto Politécnico Nacional, Mexico. The authors thank the CONACYT for the computing resources brought to them through the Plataforma de Aprendizaje Profundo para Tecnologías del Lenguaje of the Laboratorio de Supercómputo of the INAOE, Mexico.

References

1. Bensalem, I., Rosso, P., Chikhi, S.: Intrinsic plagiarism detection using N-gram classes. In: EMNLP 2014 - 2014 Conference on Empirical Methods in Natural Language Processing, Proceedings of the Conference, pp. 1459–1464 (2014). https://doi.org/10.3115/v1/d14-1153
2. Clough, P., Stevenson, M.: Developing a corpus of plagiarised short answers. In: 31, pp. 527–540 (2005)
3. El Tahir Ali, A.M., Dahwa Abdulla, H.M., Snášel, V.: Overview and comparison of plagiarism detection tools. In: CEUR Workshop Proceedings, vol. 706, pp. 161–172 (2011). ISSN: 16130073
4. Foltýnek, T., et al.: Testing of support tools for plagiarism detection. Int. J. Educ. Technol. High. Educ. **17**(1), Article no. 46 (2020). https://doi.org/10.1186/s41239-020-00192-4. arXiv: 2002.04279. ISSN: 23659440
5. Li, Y., Wu, H.: A clustering method based on k-means algorithm. In: Phys. Procedia **25**, 1104–1109 (2012). https://doi.org/10.1016/j.phpro.2012.03.206. ISSN: 18753892
6. Liang, P.: Semi-supervised learning for natural language. In: Massachusetts Institute of Technology. Department of Electrical Engineering and Computer Science, p. 86 (2005). http://hdl.handle.net/1721.1/33296
7. Mikolov, T., et al.: Distributed representations of words and phrases and their compositionality. In: Advances in Neural Information Processing Systems, October 2013. arXiv: 1310.4546. ISSN: 10495258
8. Pennington, J., Richard, S., Manning, C.: GloVe: global vectors for word representation. Br. J. Neurosurg. **31**(6), 682–687 (2017). https://doi.org/10.1080/02688697.2017.1354122. ISSN: 1360046X
9. Scanlon, P.M., Neumann, D.R.: Internet plagiarism among college students. J. College Stud. Dev. **43**(3), 374–385 (2002). ISSN: 08975264
10. Shafiee, A., Karimi, M.: On the relationship between entropy and information. Phys. Essays **20**(3), 487–493 (2007). https://doi.org/10.4006/1.3153419. ISSN: 08361398
11. Su, Z., et al.: Plagiarism detection using the Levenshtein distance and Smith-Waterman algorithm. In: 3rd International Conference on Innovative Computing Information and Control, ICICIC 2008, pp. 1–3 (2008). https://doi.org/10.1109/ICICIC.2008.422
12. Sun, Y., Platoš, J.: High-dimensional text clustering by dimensionality reduction and improved density peak. In: Wireless Communications and Mobile Computing 2020 (2020). https://doi.org/10.1155/2020/8881112. ISSN: 15308677

Determining the Relationship Between the Letters in the Voynich Manuscript Splitting the Text into Parts

Esbolat Sapargali[1], Iskander Akhmetov[1,2](✉), Alexandr Pak[1,2], and Alexander Gelbukh[3]

[1] Faculty of Information Technology, Kazakh-British Technical University, Almaty, Kazakhstan
e_sapargali@kbtu.kz
[2] Institute of Information and Computational Technologies, Pushkin Street 125, Almaty, Kazakhstan
i.akhmetov@ipic.kz
[3] Instituto Politécnico Nacional, CIC, Mexico City, Mexico
gelbukh@gelbukh.com
http://kbtu.kz
http://iict.kz

Abstract. The Voynich Manuscript is an illustrated manuscript code that has not yet been defined the structure of the writing and the relationship to other languages. This study investigated the effectiveness of examining point detail versus examining the full picture all at once in a single study. In the approach of this study, one of these ways, some letter patterns based on frequency and word length were identified, including connections at different combinations of consonant and vowel letters by a statistical approach for a hidden Markov model. A narrowly directed systematic direction can help lead to the unraveling of the manuscript text in progressive steps.

Keywords: Voynich manuscript · Hidden Markov model · Voynich manuscript characters · Natural language processing

1 Introduction

The Voynich manuscript is an illustrated handwritten code written in an unknown language or cipher. It is still one of the main unsolved problems of linguistics and cryptography. The problem of deciphering it is that scientists have not yet been able to determine the structure of the writing and the relationship to other languages.

Previous studies (the first attempts still date back to the 16th century) have tried to decipher the text by all known methods of cryptography and linguistics, including advanced technologies such as neural networks. But large-scale research has failed to make breakthrough advances in deciphering [9].

© Springer Nature Switzerland AG 2021
I. Batyrshin et al. (Eds.): MICAI 2021, LNAI 13068, pp. 163–170, 2021.
https://doi.org/10.1007/978-3-030-89820-5_13

The purpose of this article is to determine the effectiveness of studying point details, compared to studying the whole picture at once in a single study. The approach of this study will use methods that allow statistical analysis of words in the text. Here statistical methods will be used for the hidden Markov model. This will be used to find out to what extent there is a pattern in the various parameters of word frequency, word types, and the removal of spaces between words. The contribution will be that a narrowly directed systematic study will help to arrive at a clue to the manuscript text in small steps.

2 Literature Review

The exact time when the manuscript was made remains unknown, but its history can be traced back to the 16th century. The alphabet of the manuscript bears no visual resemblance to any known writing system, the text has not yet been deciphered, and illustrations (women's clothing and attire as well as a couple of castles) are used to determine the age of the book and its origin. Scholars have concluded that the details are characteristic of 15th- and 16th-century Europe [4].

In 1912 the Society of Jesus was in need of funds and decided to sell some of its property. While sorting through the coffers of books in the Villa Mondragone, Wilfried Voynich stumbled upon a mysterious manuscript, which to this day bears his name [8]. Throughout the century, various methods have been used to decipher the manuscript, and if we focus on them, we can see small steps toward discovery thanks to discoveries made by researchers. Since then, a number of claims have been made about possible decipherment and a number of hypotheses have been advanced, none of which, however, has been unequivocally confirmed and accepted in the scientific community. This literature review will focus on research on word analysis using statistical methods of analysis [3].

Reddy and Knight in their study did not use word-value for character sets divided into words. They did the opposite, dividing them into two types, lexemes and words. They even calculated the exact number of each. The following article says that single-character words occur. They are mostly characters similar to 2 and 9 [6].

In linguistic analysis, there is a lot of discussion about word statistics versus other statistics. There are transliteration issues in addition to word space definition. The most reliable of these is the word length statistic. In a related study, Jorge Stofi concluded that, according to his definition of symbols and spaces, the distribution of word lengths is binomial. This is an unusual phenomenon for natural language, which until now has not been understood or explained [7].

Of more recent research, we can mention Christian Perone, who, using word vectors and visualization of some t-SNE models, has shown how useful word vectors are for analyzing unknown codewords for grouping vector space, for example, for deriving platform names from a lower representation. A University of Adelaide research project led by Dewitt Abbott has developed a research scheme for decoding manuscripts. Including an important questionnaire vector method for statistical analysis [5].

It can be seen from previous studies that one can do the calculations and expect to get different results for the lexeme word length distribution and the word type length distribution, since the more frequent word types tend to be shorter. This is true for ordinary languages as well as for the Voynich text.

The Voynich manuscript was studied using a static Hidden Markov Model (HMM). The HMM is a generative probabilistic model in which the sequence of observed variables is generated by a sequence of internal hidden states. Transitions between latent states are assumed to have the form of a Markov chain. They can be defined by a vector of onset probability and a transition probability matrix a transition probability matrix to determine the probability of the sequence between letters. The outlier probability of the observable can be any distribution with parameters due to the current hidden state [2].

The HMM uses only the variables that are affected by a given state to investigate, so the transition probabilities are the only parameter. Each state has a probability distribution among all possible output values. Therefore, the sequence of generated symbols provides information about sequence of symbol(s) states [1].

3   Methodology

The Voynich manuscript was studied using a static Hidden Markov Model (HMM). In contrast to entropy and mutual information methods, The hidden Markov model can analyze the relations between letters without their prior segmentation, because the sequence of symbols can be extracted from the columns of the scanned symbol image in the same way as from the word image. Segments can then have character sequences (which are jointly optimized by the separation and classification result) extracted from their strings, and the string HMM can be effectively used to check the classification for each segment hypothesized by the column HMM [2].

The diagram below shows the general structure of the HMM. The ovals represent variables with a random value. The random variable x(t) represents the value of the latent variable at time t. The random variable y(t) is the value of the observed variable at time t. The arrows in the diagram symbolize conditional dependencies. It is clear from the diagram that the value of the latent variable x at time t depends only on the value of the latent variable x at time t−1. This is called the Markov property. Although, at the same time, the value of the observed variable y(t) depends only on the value of the latent variable x(t).

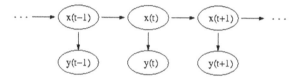

Fig. 1. Temporal evolution of a hidden Markov model

The project used scanned images of the manuscript as well as texts divided into different types of parts to determine the relationship of certain letters as well as substitutions for other characters. Functions were created for tokenization, word counts, and bigram concurrency. Some letter patterns based on word frequency and length have been identified, including relationships at different combinations of consonant and vowel letters.

During tokenization the text is an array. The function written for tokenization selects strings longer than 4 words. The input, of course, is the list of words we want to tokenize. Then a two-part HMM fitting takes place, and we get the tags. The tags themselves are highlighted in green, and all other occurrences are highlighted in blue.

Old manuscripts have folios in which words with the same meaning are arranged together to provide similarity queries. The data are sorted by several properties: by folio, by line, and by word length. Minimal pairs are pairs of words or phrases in a particular language, spoken or written, that differ in only one phonological element.

Word matches in sentences are called bigram frequencies. As you know, for bigrams, the context window is asymmetric by one word to the right of the current word when counting occurrences together. The morpheme boundary runs between the morphemes that make up the word. In some cases, the free stem and suffix are connected by a morpheme boundary, but in most cases the bases are also connected. In the first case, the free base, and in the second case, the connected base.

The "Editing Distance" part of the code calculates the Levenshtein editing distance between two strings. The edit distance refers to the number of characters that must be replaced, inserted, or deleted to convert s1 to s2 [6].

4   Experiment

HMMlearn implements Hidden Markov Models. Each HMM parameter has a symbolic code that can be used to configure its initialization and evaluation. An initial point is required for the EM algorithm to proceed; before training, each parameter is assigned a value, either random or computed from the data. The input data for training is a matrix of combined observation sequences along with sequence lengths.

The Voynich manuscript document is presented as extracted features, not as a line form. When preparing the datasets, The dataset was loaded with Voynich text from vdata. Initially, the text is divided into parts, writing how many words are in each part, which line of the paragraph/folio. A Pandas word dictionary has also been built. The dictionary will be used to preserve the temporal vocabulary and the manuscript word corpus. Only whitespace characters were used for tokenization and then each word was highlighted in lower case.

In addition to the text, there are also scanned images of the manuscript. They are taken from the voinichese website. They were used as a reference in

folio		paragraph	line	text	words
0	f1r	P1	1	fachys ykal ar ataiin shol shory cthres y kor ...	10
1	f1r	P1	2	sory ckhar or y kair chtaiin shar are cthar ct...	11
2	f1r	P1	3	syaiir sheky or ykaiin shod cthoary cthes dara...	9

Fig. 2. The output of Voynich's adapted manuscript line by line

certain situations. Before examining the folio, its integrity was checked. This was done to be sure that we could select one paragraph at a time and combine them.

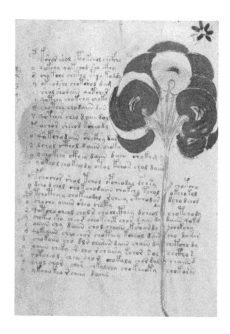

Fig. 3. Fragment of a scanned image of the manuscript

Next we move on to minimal pairs, Such as phoneme, toneme, or chroneme, and have different meanings. They are used to demonstrate that two phonemes are two separate phonemes in a language.

A sliding window was used to look at them, taking 21 sheets, averaging their number of lines, and plotting them on the entire manuscript. Each column is a line on a graph, and the height of the line is the average line length in that window.

Next, we calculate how many times a pair of words occur in sentences, regardless of their position in the sentences. We calculated only half of the matrix, since we only need the editing distance of the equivalent of 1.

5   Result

As a result of the study, the folio integrity check function showed a match after several check attempts. Searching for specific characters and finding a pair gave a successful result. The number of unique words was determined (8078 out of 37886). After that, we displayed a graph of frequently encountered pairs.

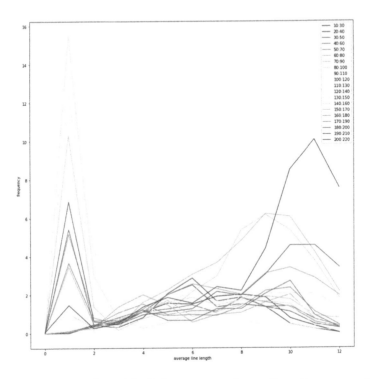

Fig. 4. Sliding window with 21 sheets averaged over the entire manuscript

With the help of the graph and table it was possible to understand the patterns with the help of visualization functions, looking at the pictures. The folio consists of an average of 5 lines of 5 words each (a long row of properties). All the words in the left margin come first.

The data sets are arranged in letter columns. This is interpreted as a 21-window counter capturing more details about the appearance of each word than other methods.

The configuration file generated the best choice of vowels and consonants (some groups of letters were vowels and some were consonants) showed V = ai, e, o, k, C = a, l, dy, n. Loss of vowels between consonants would be 0, with only consonants or only vowels would be 0.1. When in condition 1, the probability of seeing these words will be frequent. But 5.5% when going to state 2 other words.

There are letters that are different. Returns context, letters with state 1 or 2. No difference was detected on the first pass. The first insertion was returned, regardless of editing distance. Some letters (d) replace each other with a higher frequency than others. K t have relations, o replaces a, e and y in many cases.

Some groups of letters turned out to be vowels and some groups turned out to be consonants. The configuration file generated the best selection of vowels and consonants and showed V = ai, e, o, k, C = a, l, dy, n. The loss of vowels between consonants would be 0, with only consonants or vowels would be 0.1.

This could mean when being in condition 1, the probability would be frequent to see these words. But 5.5% when going to state 2 you will see other words.

Got the letters, which is different. Returns context, letters with state 1 or 2. No difference was found in the first pass. The first insertion was returned, regardless of editing distance. Some letters (d) are replaced with each other at a higher frequency than others. K/t have a relationship, o replaces a, e and y in many cases.

6   Conclusion

In this study, using documents, scanned images of manuscripts, as well as text divided into different types of parts, it was possible to determine the relationship of certain letters, as well as their replacement by other characters using the static Markov model and bigram. Scanned images of symbols and words from the manuscript as well as texts divided into different types of parts were examined.

Letter patterns (ratios of certain letters) from the frequency and length of words were determined, including the occurrence of certain letters in English as well as the occurrence of consonants and vowels. Some letters are substituted for each other with greater frequency than others and also have a substituting relationship in some cases.

Some letter patterns based on word frequency and length have been identified, including relationships at different combinations of consonant and vowel letters.

Compared to previous research, it has become clear that different features are required for different applications. The ways in which the Voynich manuscript is handled are varied and depend on applications and languages, which means that they cannot be restricted to any general framework in the subsequent study.

You can then develop a function appropriate to the input format (catalog browsing, eXtensible Markup Language parsing). To get a new list of tokens in each document, the input can be parsed, and the tokens can also be converted into folders to identifiers and displayed inside the repetition with the resulting sparse vector.

Acknowledgment. We gratefully acknowledge the financial support of the Ministry of Education and Sciences, Republic of Kazakhstan (Grant num. AP09260670 "Development of methods and algorithms for augmentation of input data for modifying vector embeddings of words")

The work was done with partial support from the Mexican Government through the grant A1-S-47854 of the CONACYT, Mexico and grants 20211784, 20211884, and 20211178 of the Secretaría de Investigación y Posgrado of the Instituto Politécnico Nacional, Mexico. The authors thank the CONACYT for the computing resources brought to them through the Plataforma de Aprendizaje Profundo para Tecnologías del Lenguaje of the Laboratorio de Supercómputo of the INAOE, Mexico.

References

1. Acedo, L.: A hidden Markov model for the linguistic analysis of the Voynich manuscript. Math. Comput. Appl. **24**, 14 (2019). https://doi.org/10.3390/mca24010014
2. Cave, R., Lee, N.: Hidden Markov models for English. In: Ferguson, J.D. (ed.) Hidden Markov Models for Speech. IDA-CRD, October 1980
3. D'Imperio, M.: An application of cluster analysis and multiple scaling to the question of "hands" and "languages" in the Voynich manuscript. Nat. Secur. Agency Tech. J. **23**, 59–75 (1978)
4. Levitov, L.: Solution of the Voynich Manuscript?: A Liturgical Manual for the Endura Rite of The Cathari Heresi. The Cult of Isis. Aegean Park Press, Laguna Hills (1987)
5. Perone, C.: Voynich Manuscript: word vectors and t-SNE visualization of some patterns (2016). https://blog.christianperone.com/2016/01/voynich-manuscript-word-vectors-and-t-sne-visualization-of-some-patterns/
6. Reddy, S., Knight, K.: What we know about the Voynich manuscript. In: Proceedings of the 5th ACL-HLT Workshop on Language Technology for Cultural Heritage, Social Sciences, and Humanities, pp. 78–86. Association for Computational Linguistics (2011)
7. Stolfi, J.: Voynich Manuscript stuff (2005). https://www.ic.unicamp.br/stolfi/voynich/
8. Voynich, W.: A Preliminary Sketch of the History of the Roger Bacon Cipher Manuscript, pp. 415–430. Transactions of the College of Physicians of Philadelphia, Printed by T. Dobson (1921). http://resource.nlm.nih.gov/2546054R
9. Zandbergen, R.: Voynich MS - history of research of the MS (2019). http://www.voynich.nu/solvers.html

Intelligent Applications and Robotics

The Comparative Approach to Solving Temporal-Constrained Scheduling Problem Under Uncertainty

Alexander Bozhenyuk[1](✉) ⓘ, Alexander Dolgiy[2] ⓘ, Olesiya Kosenko[1] ⓘ,
and Margarita Knyazeva[1] ⓘ

[1] Southern Federal University, Nekrasovsky Street 44, 347922 Taganrog, Russia
[2] Public Corporation "Research and Development Institute of Railway Engineers", 27/1,
Nizhegorodskaya Street, 109029 Moscow, Russia

Abstract. In this paper a network activity planning method based on fuzzy-interval scheduling graphs is introduced. The network activity schedule implementation allows considering temporal-constrained schedules and determining the necessary resources allocation plan for the activities. A case-study example introduces and estimates three methods for constructing and calculating the main indicators necessary for analyzing the scheduling problem. Three mathematical formulations are considered: a crisp temporal statement, a probabilistic model and a newly introduced fuzzy-interval problem formulation for representing the basic temporal parameters of the model. Comparison of the calculation results is presented in this paper, the time lags between activities of the considered network activity model are considered as well. The degree of optimality for the temporal resources allocation for the activities is also considered. The results of comparison for the three methods show that network activity planning in a fuzzy-interval problem formulation provides the best conditions for optimization and transparency of the production process.

Keywords: Network activity planning · Scheduling graph · Decision-making · Uncertainty · Critical temporal path · Fuzzy intervals · Probability

1 Introduction

The current growth rates of industrial production, design and construction activities require the use of such methods of network activity planning and management that can provide the maximum economic effect [1]. Nowadays the network activity planning is a powerful management tool for industry and construction. The advantage lies in the fact that they take into account all the variety of connections between activities, allowing to consider the impact of deviations from the plan on the further course of activities and to construct robust schedules [2, 3]. The necessity to consider all the temporal parameters of the problem is especially important when designing complex technical and organizational systems. At the same time, the costs of implementing solutions in complex multi-parameter systems are continuously increasing, and the consequences of

© Springer Nature Switzerland AG 2021
I. Batyrshin et al. (Eds.): MICAI 2021, LNAI 13068, pp. 173–183, 2021.
https://doi.org/10.1007/978-3-030-89820-5_14

unsuccessful decisions are becoming more serious. Decision-making is usually understood as the choice of the most preferable solution from the set of feasible alternative solutions or, in general, some ordering of this set. In this case, the alternatives differ in the results or the consequences to which they lead. The consequences of choosing different options for decisions are characterized by a certain degree of achievement of the goal of the choice, which reflects preferences. That is, the set of decision options determines the system of preferences in the existing tolerances of values. It should be taken into consideration that decision-making in real production systems is complicated process due to the incompleteness and fuzziness of the initial information. Also, "the best alternative" is not clearly defined in complex production systems. It is clear that in order for an alternative option to become the best, it is necessary to determine by what criterion it is the best and taking into account what parameters. The problem with complex multi-criteria and multi-parameter systems is that there is not always the best solution in the absolute sense. That is, the solution can be considered the best, only in accordance with one of the goals. It is important to highlight the aspects of the influence of the chosen decisions on the possible consequences. The use of the apparatus of fuzzy logic in multi-criteria models makes it possible to compare alternative options taking into account various initial data and limitations of the production system [4, 5].

Formalization of activities is associated with the need to take into account a large number of factors and parameters and the need to link them. Neglect of any factors or parameters when making decisions will inevitably affect the results obtained.

Production systems must operate effectively in a wide variety of activities to be scheduled (roadmaps) and industrial situations. Difficulties in creating an effective system for planning the activities of a complex system are associated with the problems of formalization. This is due to the absence of strict analytical dependencies, with a complex relationship, with the mutual influence of individual tasks, and with the large role of empirical data. Thus, it is necessary to formalize and objectively interpret the parameters of this system in order to avoid intuitive and subjective decisions related to the efficiency of the production system. Correct formalization should reflect the actual values of the system parameters or be as close to them as possible.

In formulation and solving multi-criteria problems, an important role is played by taking into account a large number of conditions and situations for which it is difficult or impossible to give a rigorous mathematical justification. Correct formalization of decision-making problems in real production systems is associated with the need to take into account a large number of factors, the neglect of which inevitably affects the final result.

Usually any initial data, temporal data and the conditions for performing each of the production stages must be estimated, taking into account the constraints and uncertain parameters of the models.

Uncertainty in planning, especially temporal planning can be handled with both probabilistic and fuzzy approaches. The paper [6] discusses different examples of applying temporary, priority Petri network for modeling and optimizing production systems and manufacturing operations, shows the example of fuzzy interference using the Petri network mechanism. Fuzzy Petri nets (FPN) for industrial applications were also discussed in [7] for the implementation of computing reasoning processes and the modeling of systems with uncertainty. Knowledge representation and reasoning with industrial application using interval-valued intuitionistic fuzzy Petri nets and extended TOPSIS was proposed by Y. Weichao and others [8] to handle simultaneously intuitionistic information and fuzzy information of the models.

In this paper we propose a network activity planning method based on fuzzy interval-valued scheduling graph, and the three mathematical formulations are considered: a crisp temporal statement, a probabilistic model and a newly introduced fuzzy-interval problem formulation for representing the basic temporal parameters of the model.

In the second section of the paper a network activity model of the production process in the classical setting is considered. In order to analyze the network activity model, the early and late start and end dates of activity are calculated, and the critical path of this task is determined. Reserves of time are identified. The stress coefficients are determined, which allow interpreting the degree of difficulty in performing the activity of the considered technological process. In the third section, the problem is formalized on the basis of the theory of probability. The tolerances for the deviation of the activity time from the specified values are determined. The probabilities of activity completion within a given time frame are calculated. In the fourth section, the problem of network activity planning is formalized in a fuzzy-interval form. The time intervals are determined in accordance with the α-levels of the fuzzy interval. In conclusion, the results of three methods for solving the problem of network activity planning are considered. The validity, as well as the advantage of using the apparatus of fuzzy logic for solving decision-making problems in complex systems, has been confirmed. Directions for future research are also identified.

2 Solving the Problem of Network Activity Planning in a Non-fuzzy Formulation

Let's consider a production system using a network activity diagram as an example. When constructing network activity schedules, the entire complex of technological process can be divided into separate component parts R (activities or set of activities – partial plans) and the relationship, sequence or precedence relations of those activities are established. At the same time, the so-called fictitious activity F reflects only a logical connection and does not require the expenditure of various resources. Let's denote the fictitious activities on the network activity diagram with a dotted line and the real activities with a solid line. Let's define that any activity connects two events, while the event is considered not as a process of any labor, but its result. An event, unlike activity, has no temporal duration. An event denotes the moment of completion of one or more previous activities. It cannot be expressed in time [9, 10]. In a network activity graph, an event is indicated by the vertex of the graph, inside which a serial number is placed.

Table 1 shows the duration of activities of a certain technological process with an indication of their sequence.

Figure 1 shows the network activity diagram based on the data in Table 1.

The graph indicates the sequence of activities that must be performed to complete a certain technological process.

To analyze the technological process for planning purposes, it is necessary to determine the so-called *critical temporal path*, that is, the sequence of operations or activities performance, which is a set of operations performed and is characterized by the maximum duration of all possible paths. Activities belonging to the critical path are called *critical*. Their untimely implementation leads to the failure to meet the deadlines of the entire project.

Table 1. Duration of activities of technological process.

Activity	Duration of activity	Previous activities
R_1	5	–
R_2	6	–
R_3	3	–
R_4	2	R_1
R_5	2	R_2, R_3
R_6	6	R_2
R_7	7	R_4
R_8	4	R_4, R_5, R_6

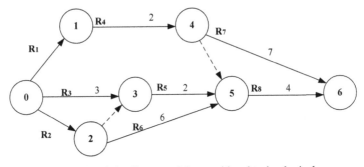

Fig. 1. Network activity diagram of the considered technological process.

Let's calculate the earliest dates of occurrence of events/activities according to the formula [10]:
$$T_p(i) = \max\{T_p(j) + t_{ij}\}.$$

Here the maximum value is taken for all activities j preceding activity i.

$T_p(0) = 0;$
$T_p(1) = T_p(0) + t_{01} = 0 + 5 = 5;$
$T_p(2) = T_p(0) + t_{02} = 0 + 6 = 6;$
$T_p(3) = \max\{T_p(0) + t_{03}, T_p(2) + 0\} = \max\{0 + 3, 6 + 0\} = 6;$
$T_p(4) = T_p(1) + t_{14} = 5 + 2 = 7;$
$T_p(5) = \max\{T_p(2) + t_{25}, T_p(3) + t_{35}, T_p(4) + 0\} = \max\{6 + 6, 6 + 2, 7 + 0\} = 12;$

$T_p(6) = max\{T_p(4) + t_{46}, T_p(5) + t_{56}\} = max\{7 + 7, 12 + 4\} = 16.$

We define the latest dates for the occurrence of activities as follows:

$T_l(i) = m\,in\{T_l(j) - t_{ij}\},$
$T_l(5) = T_l(6) - t_{56} = 16 - 4 = 12;$
$T_l(4) = min\{T_l(6) - t_{46}; T_l(5) - 0\} = min\{16 - 7; 12 - 0\} = 9;$
$T_l(3) = T_l(5) - t_{35} = 12 - 2 = 10;$
$T_l(2) = min\{T_l(3) - 0, T_l(5) - t_{26}\} = m\,in\{10 - 0, 12 - 6\} = 6;$
$T_l(1) = T_l(4) - t_{14} = 9 - 2 = 7;$
$T_l(0) = m\,in\{T_l(1) - t_{01}, T_l(2) - t_{02}, T_l(3) - t_{03}\} = m\,in\{7 - 5, 6 - 6, 10 - 3\} = 0.$

Let's reflect on the network activity diagram the obtained values of the early start and the late start of activity (Fig. 2). The difference between these indicators determines the reserve of time. Events (activities) with zero slack define, in aggregate, the critical production route. In our case, the critical route is: 0–2–5–6, $t_{cr} = 16$.

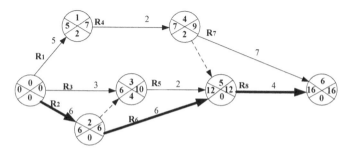

Fig. 2. Network activity graph with time values.

To determine the degree of tension in the performance of individual activity or the entire technological process and to analyze the possibility of redistributing resources, it is necessary to assess some parameters. Let's calculate the early t_E and late t_L start dates. Based on the data obtained, we determine the time reserve of the corresponding activities $r(i,j)$ and the independent time reserve $r_H(i,j)$. In this case, the value $r_H(i,j)$ indicates the duration of the forced waiting for the onset of the final event of this activity. Analysis of this parameter allows you to remove from activity some of the resources to move them to more intense activity. By tension we mean the greatest possibility of failure to meet the deadline. Table 2 shows the results obtained.

The value $r(i,j)$ cannot always accurately characterize how stressful it is to perform a particular activity of the non-critical path. It all depends on how long the calculated reserve applies to, how long this sequence is. It is possible to determine the degree of difficulty of completing each group of activity on a non-critical path on time using the activity intensity factor [10, 11]. The *critical temporal path* or parts of it can be replaced by other non-critical arcs of the presented network activity graph. That is, in order to analyze alternative solutions of this network activity model, it is necessary to calculate the stress coefficients that will help determine the degree of difficulty in completing each of the activity group on time. The values of these coefficients are in the range [0,1]. The

Table 2. Calculation results.

Activity	t_{ij}	t_E	t_L	$r(i,j)$	$r_H(i,j)$
$R_1(0,1)$	5	0	7	2	0
$R_2(0,2)$	6	0	6	0	0
$R_3(0,3)$	3	0	10	7	3
$R_4(1,4)$	2	5	9	2	-2
$R_5(3,5)$	2	6	12	4	0
$R_6(2,5)$	6	6	16	0	0
$R_7(4,6)$	7	7	16	2	0
$R_8(5,6)$	4	12	10	4	0
$F_1(2,3)$	0	6	10	4	0
$F_2(4,5)$	0	7	12	5	-5

closer the stress coefficient is closer to unity, the more difficult it is to complete this activity on time. The corresponding calculations are presented in Table 3:

Table 3. Results of calculating the stress coefficient.

Non-critical arc	t critical arc	t non-critical arc	Arc reserve	Arc stress coefficient
(0,3,5)	12	5	7	0.42
(0,1,4,6)	16	14	2	0.87
(0,1,4,5,6)	16	15	1	0.93
(0,2,3,5)	12	8	4	0.67

It should be noted that the closer the stress coefficient is to unity, the more difficult it is to complete the activity on time, but the greater the opportunity to reduce the activity execution time. The closer to zero, the more reserve a given arc has [10, 12]. At the same time, the inaccuracy of calculating the strength of certain arcs in accordance with the values of the early and late dates of the beginning and end of activity is due to the impossibility of accurately determining the timing.

3 Solving the Problem of Network Planning in a Probabilistic Formulation

The duration of the activity cannot always be specified exactly, but sometimes it can be set by the interval $[t_{minij}; t_{maxij}]$. Here, the minimum t_{minij} characterizes the activity under the most favorable circumstances, and the maximum t_{maxij} – under unfavorable circumstances. Let's calculate the probabilistic characteristics of network activity plans.

It is possible to determine the minimum and maximum possible time to perform a specific operation when sufficient statistical information. Let's correlate the extreme values of time with the given one and determine the expected duration of activity $t_{exp_{ij}}$. We will also calculate the variance of the duration of the activity, to determine how much the tolerances of the activity execution time deviate from the given time [10]. The results are shown in Table 4.

Let's calculate the variance of the critical path R_2-R_6-R_8:

$\sigma^2_{cr} = \sigma^2(R_2) + \sigma^2(R_6) + \sigma^2(R_8) = 3.13$.

The standard deviation of the critical path is determined as $\sigma_{cr} = 1.77$.

Table 4. Estimated duration of activity for a three-parameter model.

Activity	$t_{min_{ij}}$	t_{ij}	$t_{max_{ij}}$	$t_{exp_{ij}}$	$\sigma^2(t_{exp_{ij}})$
R_1	4	5	7	5	0.25
R_2	4	6	8	5	0.44
R_3	2	3	4	3	0.11
R_4	1	2	4	2	0.25
R_5	1	2	3	2	0.11
R_6	4	6	8	5	0.44
R_7	4	7	8	5	0.44
R_8	3	4	12	6	2.25

Based on the obtained characteristics, various parameters of the network activity model can be calculated. In particular, it is possible to calculate the probability that the duration of the critical path does not exceed any given value [10, 12]:

$$p(t_{cr} < t_{pl}) = 0.5 + 0.5\Phi(\text{H}). \tag{1}$$

Here Φ is Laplace function; H is the normalized deviation of a random variable, and is defined as $\text{H} = \frac{|t_{pl} - t_{cr}|}{\sigma_{cr}}$.

Suppose the planned lead time of the production process is $t_{pl} = 19$. According to (1), the probability of completing the project on time is 75%.

Let us consider the inverse problem. Let it be necessary to determine the number of days t_{nec} required to complete the technological process with a probability of 90%. Calculations made according to the following formula:

$$t_{nec} = t_{cr} + \text{H} * \sigma_{cr}. \tag{2}$$

First, we find the value of H, corresponding to a given probability, using the table of values of the Laplace integral function. Then, according to expression (2), we determine the value $t_{nec} = 18$. If we determine the interval of the technological process using the standard deviation, then it will be equal to [14.23, 17.77]. In this case, it is necessary to assume that the standard deviation corresponds to the normal distribution in the example under consideration.

The apparatus of the theory of probability is based on statistical data. When designing a new production system, or a new technological process, such statistics either do not exist or are insufficient. In this case, the application of the theory of fuzzy sets for solving network activity planning problems will help to establish the adequacy of the selected probabilistic model.

4 Solution of the Problem of Network Activity Planning in Fuzzy-Interval Formulation

Since the amount of data is limited and the statistical sample is heterogeneous when planning the dates, there is a need for a tool that takes into account all available data with their possible characteristics. These conditions are reflected in the formalization of the problem in a fuzzy formulation. Let the time interval for performing the activity is set by an expert in a fuzzy-interval form. A fuzzy interval is a set of four parameters [13–15]:

$$(t_{min}, t_{max}, t_{1ij}, t_{2ij}) \tag{3}$$

here t_{min} – left fuzziness index; t_{max} – right coefficient fuzziness; t_{1ij} – lower modal value; t_{2ij} – top modal value (Fig. 3) [16, 17].

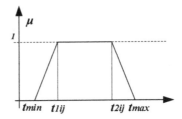

Fig. 3. Fuzzy interval.

Suppose that the duration of operations is determined by a triangular fuzzy interval, that is, $t_{1ij} = t_{2ij} = t_{ij}$. The membership function of a triangular fuzzy interval is written as follows:

$$\mu_{\tilde{t}_{ij}}(t_{ij}) = \begin{cases} \frac{t_{ij}-t_{min_{ij}}}{t_{ij}^m - t_{min_{ij}}}; t_{ij} \in \left[t_{min_{ij}}; t_{ij}^m \right]; \\ \frac{t_{ij}-t_{max_{ij}}}{t_{ij}^m - t_{max_{ij}}}; t_{ij} \in \left[t_{ij}^m; t_{max_{ij}} \right]; \\ 0, \text{ in other cases.} \end{cases} \tag{4}$$

Here t_{ij}^m is a modal value.

Consider the formalization of the network activity planning model in fuzzy mathematics. Table 5 shows the values $t_{min_{ij}}; t_{ij}; t_{max_{ij}}$. The fuzzy value of the duration of activity has been suggested to determine as follows [18, 19]:

$$\tilde{t}_{ij} = \left(t_{min_{ij}}(\alpha); t_{max_{ij}}(\alpha) \right)$$

$$= (t_{min_{ij}} + (t_{ij}{}^m - t_{min_{ij}})\alpha, (t_{max_{ij}} + (t_{ij}{}^m - t_{max_{ij}})\alpha) \tag{5}$$

here α is the level determined by the correspondence of $t_{min_{ij}}$; $t_{max_{ij}}$ and $\mu_{\tilde{t}_{ij}}(\alpha)$.
According to the algebra of fuzzy sets [19], the *critical temporal path* will be equal to:

$$\tilde{t}_{cr_{ij}} = (4 + 2\alpha; 6; 8 - 2\alpha) + (4 + 2\alpha; 6; 8 - 2\alpha) + (3 + \alpha; 4; 12 - 8\alpha).$$

Table 5. Estimated duration of activity for a temporal three-parameter model.

Activity	$t_{min_{ij}}$	t_{ij}	$t_{max_{ij}}$	$t_{min_{ij}}(\alpha)$	$t_{max_{ij}}(\alpha)$
R_1	4	5	7	$4 + \alpha$	$7 - 2\alpha$
R_2	4	6	8	$4 + 2\alpha$	$8 - 2\alpha$
R_3	2	3	4	$2 + \alpha$	$4 - \alpha$
R_4	1	2	4	$1 + \alpha$	$4 - 2\alpha$
R_5	1	2	3	$1 + \alpha$	$3 - \alpha$
R_6	4	6	8	$4 + 2\alpha$	$8 - 2\alpha$
R_7	4	7	8	$4 + 3\alpha$	$8 - \alpha$
R_8	3	4	12	$3 + \alpha$	$12 - 8\alpha$

Suppose it is necessary to determine the time interval during which the technological process will be completed at some value $\mu_{\tilde{t}_{ij}}(\alpha)$. So for $\mu_{\tilde{t}_{ij}}(\alpha) = 90\%$, the time interval will be determined as [15.5, 18.3]. If $\mu_{\tilde{t}_{ij}}(\alpha) = 75\%$, then the process will be executed within the interval [14.75, 19]. These results coincide with the values of the terms of activity calculated in the probabilistic model.

5 Conclusion

Analyzing the results of solving the problem of network temporal activity planning allows considering the following conclusions. When assessing the time values of the activity performance, the results were obtained based on the probabilistic apparatus, on the basis of the classical technique and on the basis of the use of a fuzzy interval apparatus. The solution of the problem by the fuzzy-interval method completely covers the results of solutions in a clear and in a probabilistic formulation.

It should be noted that considering the fact that probabilistic models were not so much practically used in scheduling and the difficulties of operating with the random variables, and the theory of fuzzy sets allows scheduling activities with the help of temporal fuzzy interval values, the latter becomes important here. Thus, the analysis of quantitative characteristics obtained by specifying them in the form of fuzzy intervals is the most effective approach in decision-making problems under conditions of uncertainty, including for network temporal activity planning. At the same time, the calculations in the fuzzy-interval formulation were less cumbersome than when using the theory of probability.

In the future, using the theory of fuzzy sets, it is planned to evaluate the optimization of the activity schedules in terms of material, labor, and financial resources.

Acknowledgments. The reported study was funded by the Russian Foundation for Basic Research according to the research project N20–01-00197.

References

1. Zhang, Y.: WiMAX Network Activity Planning and Optimization. Auerbach Publications, Boca Raton (2009)
2. Mishra, A.: Fundamentals of Network activity Planning and Optimization 2G/3G/4G: Evolution to 5G, 2nd edn. Wiley, New York (2018)
3. Giuliani, M., Castelletti, A.: Is robustness really robust? How different definitions of robustness impact decision-making under climate change. Clim. Change **135**(3–4), 409–424 (2016). https://doi.org/10.1007/s10584-015-1586-9
4. Larsson, C.: 5G Network Activities: Planning. Design and Optimization. Academic Press, London (2018)
5. Seybold, P.M.: Algorithm engineering in geometric network activity planning and data mining. University of Stuttgart (2018)
6. Stryczek, R.: Petri Nets for Computer Aided Group Technology. In: Zawiślak, S., Rysiński, J. (eds.) Graph-Based Modelling in Engineering. MMS, vol. 42, pp. 143–164. Springer, Cham (2017). https://doi.org/10.1007/978-3-319-39020-8_11
7. Zhou, K.-Q., Zain, A.M.: Fuzzy Petri nets and industrial applications: a review. Artif. Intell. Rev. **45**(4), 405–446 (2015). https://doi.org/10.1007/s10462-015-9451-9
8. Yue, W., Liu, X., Li, S., Gui, W., Xie, Y.: Knowledge representation and reasoning with industrial application using interval-valued intuitionistic fuzzy Petri nets and extended TOPSIS. Int. J. Mach. Learn. Cybern. **12**(4), 987–1013 (2020). https://doi.org/10.1007/s13042-020-01216-1
9. Li, Z., Hu, Z., Li, C.: SRv6 Network Activity Programming: Ushering in a New Era of IP Network activitys. CRC Press, New York (2021)
10. Kerzner, H.: Project Management: A Systems Approach to Planning, Scheduling, and Controlling. Wiley, New York (2003)
11. Marchau, V.A.W.J., Walker, W.E., Bloemen, P.J.T.M., Popper, S.W.: Decision Making under Deep Uncertainty: From Theory to Practice. Springer, Heidelberg (2019)
12. Gil-Garcia, J.R., Pardo, T.A., Luna-Reyes, L.F.: Policy Analytics, Modelling, and Informatics: Innovative Tools for Solving Complex Social Problems. Springer, Berlin (2018)
13. Melin, P., Castillo, O., Kacprzyk, J.: Design of Intelligent Systems Based on Fuzzy Logic, Neural Network and Nature-Inspired Optimization. Studies in Computational Intelligence, Springer (2015)
14. Nedosekin, A.O., Shmatko, A.D., Abdoulaeva, Z.I.: Fuzzy preliminary evaluation of industrial risks. In Proceedings of 20th IEEE International Conference on Soft Computing and Measurements (SCM 2017), pp.750 - 751 (2017)
15. Kosenko, O., Bozhenyuk, A., Belyakov, S., Knyazeva, M.: Optimization of Spatial-Time Planning Resource Allocation Under Uncertainty. In: Kahraman, C., Cevik Onar, S., Oztaysi, B., Sari, I.U., Cebi, S., Tolga, A.C. (eds.) INFUS 2020. AISC, vol. 1197, pp. 1475–1482. Springer, Cham (2021). https://doi.org/10.1007/978-3-030-51156-2_171
16. Dubois, D., Prade, H.: Possibility Theory. Plenum Press, New-York (1988)

17. Kosenko, O.V., Sinyavskaya, E.D., Shestova, E.A., Kosenko, E.Y., Antipin, S.O.: Method of rational placement of intermediate centers with setting parameters in the form of the fuzzy intervals. In: Proceedings of 19th IEEE International Conference on Soft Computing and Measurements (SCM 2016), pp. 186–189, (2016).

18. Matveev, M.G., Shevlyakov, A.O., Semenov, M.E., Meleshenko P.A.: Solution of selection problems with fuzzy parameters. In: Proceedings of International Multidisciplinary Scientific GeoConference Surveying Geology and Mining Ecology Management (SGEM), vol. 17, no. 21, pp. 595–602 (2017)

19. Shevlyakov, A.O., Matveev, M.G.: W-algebra for solving problems with fuzzy parameters. J. Phys. Conf. Ser. **973**(1), 012044 (2018)

A Tourist Recommendation System: A Study Case in Mexico

Samuel Arce-Cardenas[1], Daniel Fajardo-Delgado[1],
Miguel Á. Álvarez-Carmona[2(✉)], and Juan Pablo Ramírez-Silva[3]

[1] Tecnológico Nacional de México, Av. Tecnológico 100, 49100 Guzman City, Mexico
{m19291003,daniel.fd}@cdguzman.tecnm.mx
[2] CICESE-UT3, Andador 10 Ciudad del Conocimiento, 63173 Tepic, Mexico
malvarez@cicese.edu.mx
[3] Universidad Autónoma de Nayarit, Ciudad de la Cultura, 63155 Tepic, Mexico
pablor@uan.edu.mx

Abstract. The present work deals with implementing tourist recommendation systems designed to predict the user preferences about a place or tourist activity in Mexico. Three recommendation systems have been proposed: two based on collaborative filtering (user and items) and the other based on demographic issues. To this aim, a corpus has been built by collecting 2,263 ratings from TripAdvisor.com about eighteen tourist places in Mexico. Experimental results show that the demographic-based recommendation system outperforms those based on collaborative filtering, obtaining a mean absolute error of 0.67 and a mean square error of 1.2980. These results also show significant improvement over a majority class baseline based on a sizeable unbalanced corpus.

Keywords: Tourist recommendation system · Collaborative-based filtering · Demographic-based filtering

1 Introduction

Tourism in Mexico has a significant impact on the economy due to its multiplier effects in the generation of added value and employment [13]. Only in 2019, the tourism industry contributed 17.2% of gross domestic product (GDP) in Mexico [7], obtaining sixth place in the international tourism ranking [18]. In terms of economic income, tourism in Mexico represents approximately 22.5 billion dollars per year [21]. Recently, the economic impact generated by the SARS-Cov-2 coronavirus pandemic has repercussions that may extend into the medium term [2,6,23]. Despite this, digital technologies have allowed a reorientation of the social, cultural, and economic models related to the tourism proposals that would alleviate such impact.

Currently, many technologies allow and achieve the scope of tourism at all its levels (transport, restaurants, hotels, events, among others). However, a large number of web pages and online services specialized in tourism usually drown relevant results to informational "noise" that can hinder the best touristic options

© Springer Nature Switzerland AG 2021
I. Batyrshin et al. (Eds.): MICAI 2021, LNAI 13068, pp. 184–195, 2021.
https://doi.org/10.1007/978-3-030-89820-5_15

according to the user preference [8]. One of the technologies that optimize the selection process for suitable tourist places based on the user profile is the recommendation system. A tourist recommendation system seeks to predict a 'score' or preference that users have regarding tourism options, aiming to match tourist attractions with user needs [1].

The main objective of this work is to generate baselines for future researches related to tourist recommendation systems specialized in Spanish-speaking countries, especially in Mexico. With this in mind, three recommendation systems have been proposed. Two of them are based on collaborative filtering, while the other one considers demographic issues. For this aim, a new corpus was built, consisting of 2,263 opinions and ratings about eighteen touristic attractions from the state of Nayarit, Mexico. To the best of our knowledge, this is the first corpus of touristic opinions in Spanish that includes ratings about places in Mexico intended for the training and evaluating of tourist recommendation systems.

The rest of the paper is organized as follows. In Sect. 2, related works on tourist recommendation systems are mentioned. In Sect. 3, the proposed methodology and the database that was built are described. In Sect. 4, the results achieved are described. Finally, in Sect. 5, the conclusions reached in this work and the proposed future work are listed.

2 Related Work

Nowadays, some works in the scientific literature deal with the application of recommendation systems in the tourism domain [10,16,25]. These works are commonly categorized according to three well-known recommendation techniques: content-based filtering, collaborative filtering, and hybrid recommendation systems [25].

In content-based filtering, a user receives recommendations of similar items to the ones the user favored in the past. For the decision-making process, different content factors can be considered from the tourists' preferences [10]. For example, Binucci et al. [4] designed a content analyzer for a content-based travel recommendation system. They use geographical data provided by a set of points of interest (POI) to indicate how much a POI is relevant for a set of possible topics of interest. On the other hand, Vu et al. [22] obtain tourist dining preferences based on restaurant review websites. They use text processing techniques to analyze tourists' preferences concerning dining activities (cuisines, dishes, meals, and restaurant features). Shen et al. [20] use location-based social networks to offer tourists the most relevant and personalized local venue recommendations. However, content-based filtering is not a suitable approach when there is an absence of prior user data to make decisions. Under this perspective, collaborative filtering can offer early data based on user similarities [24].

In collaborative filtering, a user receives recommendations of items establishing relations with people that have similar tastes, or choices preferred in the past. Recent examples of recommendation systems using the collaborative approach are [3,14]. Al-Ghobari et al. [3] proposes a tourist recommendation system that integrates the preferences of users and their geographical information to generate personalized and location-aware recommendations. They used a k-Nearest Neighbor item-based collaborative filtering for this purpose. Their solution aimed to develop a mobile application that uses the service of Google to provides suggestions based on nearby popular attractions. Kuanr et al. [14] present a tourist recommendation system that store the opinions of local users about their preferences on food and purchase. Their system uses the stored information by finding similar users to any querying user and providing him recommendations of the sites with good food and products available on those sites.

Regarding the hybrid recommendation systems, they combine both content-based and collaborative filtering to issue recommendations. For example, Fararni et al. [8] propose a hybrid architecture and a conceptual framework based on big data technologies, artificial intelligence, and operational research. Other research works, like those reviewed in [25], also use hybrid approaches by using linked open data (a concept as the data is shared and built based on semantic web, linked data, and open data) in the tourist domain.

3   Methodology

This study is conducted using two phases: data collection and the design of the recommendation systems, which are described below.

3.1   Data Collection

In order to achieve the proposed goals, a corpus was built by collecting tourism reviews in Spanish and overall ratings of about eighteen domestic tourist places or attractions in the state of Nayarit, Mexico.[1] Data were collected from TripAdvisor.com, a website with user-generated content that captures aspects of travel experiences. A web crawler was used to gather the information via the following two software tools: Selenium WebDriver and Python Selenium [17]. A total of 2,263 online reviews and ratings performed by 2,033 users were collected from May 2012 to January 2021. Each of these ratings consists on a five-point Likert-type scale [15]: 1 (terrible), 2 (poor), 3 (average), 4 (very good) and 5 (excellent). Table 1 shows the distribution of corpus instances according to their rating.

The eighteen tourist places were selected considering eight tourism types based on the purpose for travel: sun and beach, cultural, adventure, religious, natural, gastronomic, ecotourism, and shopping. Table 2 shows the typology of tourism used for these places.

In addition to the reviews and ratings, information about each of the 2,033 users was also obtained via a web crawler. However, manual processing was required to gather the gender of the users and a brief opinion on the rated places. There are no empty fields in the corpus instances, in such a way that if a user did not have any of them, the user and its ratings are omitted. Finally, the username was changed to an ID preserving the privacy of the opinions. Table 3 shows the user information consisting of eight fields.

---

[1] https://sites.google.com/cicese.edu.mx/rest-mex-2021/corpus-request.

Table 1. Distribution of corpus instances according to their rating.

Rating	Number of instances
1	65
2	77
3	239
4	653
5	1229

Table 2. Typology of tourism destinations.

Tourist places	Types of tourism destinations
Bahia de Matanchen	Sun and beach
Playa Los Muertos	Sun and beach
Bucerias Art Walk	Cultural, shopping
Centro Historico de Tepic	Cultural, religious
Galerias Vallarta	Shopping
Isla de Coral	Sun and beach, ecotourism
Islas Marietas	Sun and beach, adventure, ecotourism
Manantial La Tovara	Sun and beach, adventure, ecotourism
Mercado del Pueblo Sayulita	Gastronomic
Mexcaltitan	Natural
Playa Destiladeras	Sun and beach
Playa El Anclote	Sun and beach
Playa Los Ayala	Sun and beach
Splash Water Park	Adventure, shopping
The Jazz Foundation	Cultural
Isla Isabel	Sun and beach, ecotourism
Cerro de la Contaduria	Cultural, adventure
Santuario de Cocodrilos El Cora	Ecotourism

Additionally, a history of opinions of some of the 2,033 users was also collected. This history of opinions consists of comments and observations that each of these users made about the tourist places he/she visited (non-necessarily those listed in Table 2). Table 4 shows the fields of the history of opinions.

Finally, the set of instances in the corpus was split into the following two groups: a training sample consisting of 1,582 randomly selected ratings and a test sample containing 681 randomly selected instances for performance measurement. The split of the corpus instances was made in a stratified K-fold validation based on the distribution of Table 1. Therefore 70% for each rating was ensured for the training sample and 30% for the test sample.

Table 3. User information in the corpus.

Field	Description	Data type
ID	The user ID for each recommendation	Text
Gender	The tourist's gender	[Male, Female]
Place	The tourist place that the tourist is recommended to visit	Text
Location	The place of origin of the tourist (the central, northeast, northwest, west, and southeast regions refer to the regions of Mexico)	Text
Date	Date the recommendation was issued	Date
Type	Type of trip that the tourist would do	[Family, Friends, Alone, Couple, Business]
Rating	The rating represented the level of satisfaction that the tourist will have when going to the recommended place	[1, 2, 3, 4, 5]
Comment	The comment that the tourist granted	Text

Table 4. History of opinions of the users

Field	Description	Data type
Comment	The comment that the user granted (unknown = blank comment)	Text
Rating	The level of satisfaction that the user had regarding an specific place	[1, 2, 3, 4, 5]
Place	The place a user visited (this place can be from anywhere in the world, not necessarily from Mexico)	Text
Location	The place of origin of the user (the central, northeast, northwest, west, and southeast regions refer to the regions of Mexico)	Text
Overall rating	The overall rating that a place has on the TripAdvisor.com site	[1..5]

In the following subsections, the models used for generating recommendations of tourist places are described.

3.2 Collaborative-Based Filtering

Collaborative-based filtering (CF) is a common technique to determine similarity decisions in recommendation systems. CF seeks to predict items for a target user (for whom the recommendation is aimed) using data of other similar users or items. While the user-based approach finds the users who share the same rating patterns with the target user, the item-based approach looks into the set of items the target user has rated and computes how similar they are.

In this work, CF is used applying both user-based and item-based approaches to recommend tourist places. The recommendation models under these approaches are built using the well-known k-Nearest Neighbors (KNN) algorithm or some of its variants. The KNN-type algorithms allow providing recommendations by aggregating the ratings of the closest k neighbors. In particular, the present work uses the algorithm of KNN with means [11], which takes into account the mean rating of each user as well as the mean of k neighbors. Since there is a low number of items compared to the users, different parameters of k were used. The user-based approach was applied with the following values of $k = 10, 20, 25, 30, 35$. These values were chosen following the work of Ghazanfar et al. [9], where they evaluated the optimal value of k from 0 to 100 and computed the mean absolute error for various models of recommendation systems. On the other hand, for the item-based approach, the values of k were $1, 3, 5, 7, 9$. Since there are only 18 items (or tourist destinations), the size of k is limited from 1 to 18 for this approach.

The KNN user-based and item-based approaches were implemented by using the Surprise library[2] which is a Python Scikit for recommendation systems. This library offers a range of recommendation system algorithms, including such variations of KNN and different similarity indexes at ease. Surprise library was also used to compute the following four steps: (1) building the user-item rating matrix, (2) computation of similarity matrix, and (3) compute rating predictions and identify recommendations.

Building the User-Item Rating Matrix. The user-item rating matrix consists of the ratings given by users to items (the tourist places). It relies on the similarities between given user ratings to predict a target user's ratings on particular items. Table 5 shows an example of the user-item rating matrix. In this table, the columns correspond to the tourist places while the rows to the users. The intersection between them is the rating that a user gives to a specific tourist place.

Table 5. Example of the user-item rating matrix.

	Islas Marietas	Manantial La Tovara	Sayulita	...	Mexcaltitan
user_1		5		...	
user_2	3			...	4
user_3		3		...	5
⋮	⋮	⋮	⋮	⋮	⋮
user_n	4		5	...	

Computation of Similarity Matrix. The similarity matrix consists of weights that represents the relation between two elements (users or items). The higher the weight value, the firm of the relation between them. In this work, the

---
[2] https://surprise.readthedocs.io/en/stable.

cosine similarity between all pairs of elements (users or items) was computed to generate the weight values. Let U_{ij} be the set of all users that have rated both items i and j in the recommendation system, and let I_{uv} be the set of items rated by both users u and v. The rating of user u for item i is denoted as r_{ui}.

Equation (1) express the cosine similarity between users u and v, while Eq. (2) describes the similarity between items i and j. Table 6 shows an example of similarity matrix for users.

$$sim(u,v) = \frac{\sum_{i \in I_{uv}} r_{ui} \cdot r_{vi}}{\sqrt{\sum_{i \in I_{uv}} r_{ui}^2} \cdot \sqrt{\sum_{i \in I_{uv}} r_{vi}^2}} \tag{1}$$

$$sim(i,j) = \frac{\sum_{u \in U_{ij}} r_{ui} \cdot r_{uj}}{\sqrt{\sum_{u \in U_{ij}} r_{ui}^2} \cdot \sqrt{\sum_{u \in U_{ij}} r_{uj}^2}} \tag{2}$$

Table 6. Example of similarity matrix for the users-based approach.

	User_1	User_2	User_3	...	User_n
User_1	–	0	0.61	...	0
User_2	0	–	0.45	...	0.4
User_3	0.61	0.45	–	...	0
⋮	⋮	⋮	⋮	⋮	⋮
User_n	0	0.4	0	...	–

Computing Rating Predictions and Identifying Recommendations. The rating prediction is computed considering the mean rating of each user. Let μ_u the mean rating of each user u (or μ_i if the prediction is computed using the item-based approach). The rating prediction $\hat{r}_{ui}$ for user u about item i is expressed in Eq. (3) under the user-based approach and in Eq. (4) under the item-based approach. In these equations, $N_i^k(u)$ denotes the set of k neighbors of u that have rated the item i.

$$\hat{r}_{ui} = \mu_u + \frac{\sum_{v \in N_i^k(u)} sim(u,v) \cdot (r_{vi} - \mu_v)}{\sum_{v \in N_i^k(u)} sim(u,v)} \tag{3}$$

$$\hat{r}_{ui} = \mu_i + \frac{\sum_{j \in N_u^k(i)} sim(i,j) \cdot (r_{uj} - \mu_j)}{\sum_{j \in N_u^k(i)} sim(i,j)} \tag{4}$$

3.3   Demographic-Based Filtering

Demographic-based filtering (DF) categorizes users or items based on their attributes and performs a recommendation based on such demographic categorizations. In the present work, a recommendation model using DF was generated by using the following user information: gender, location, and the type of trip that the tourist did. These fields (described in Table 3) comprised the feature vector for each user instance. Table 7 shows an example of the set of features that characterizes the demographic information on users. Regarding the tourist place instances, each of them consists of a binary feature representation of the typology of tourism destinations (see Table 2). For this binary representation, 0's and 1's indicate whether or not the tourist place fits one or more types of tourism destinations. In order to build the recommendation models, we used the following machine learning algorithms implemented in Python Scikit-Learn: the KNN for $k = 10, 20, 25, 30, 35$, random forest (RF), and neural networks (NN).

Table 7. Demographic information on the users who rated a tourist place.

ID	Gender	Location	Type
User_1	Male	Argentina	Business
User_2	Female	West region of Mexico	Family
User_3	Female	Central region of Mexico	Alone
⋮	⋮	⋮	⋮
User_n	Male	USA	Friends

4   Experimental Results

Experiments were conducted to evaluate the performance of the three proposed recommendation models. The experiments were carried on Google Colab, a free cloud-based service of a Jupyter notebook[3]. The performance of the models was evaluated by using the following error measures:

- Mean absolute error (MAE). It measures the average magnitude of the absolute value differences between the true and the predicted rating [5].
- Mean squared error (MSE). It evaluates the quality of the recommendation models to make predictions computing the average of the squared difference of the predicted ratings.
- Root mean squared error (RMSE). It evaluates the accuracy of the predicted ratings penalizing disproportionately large errors [12].

To use different metrics that allow evaluating other aspects of the recommendation models, the values were transformed from reals to integers through rounding. Thus, the original regression problem was converted to a classification problem considering five classes: 1 (bad), 2 (bad), 3 (fair), 4 (very good), and 5 (excellent). In particular, we use the following two types of statistical measures:

---

[3] https://colab.research.google.com.

- Accuracy. It measures the percentage of cases in which the recommendation model was correct.
- F1-score. It represents the harmonic mean between precision and recall

See [19] to get more details about the metrics for evaluation of the recommendation models.

A majority class baseline was used as the reference value for the experiments. This value is computed by selecting rating 5 as the default response, which corresponds to a 54.1854% of accuracy (see Table 8). Notice that approximately 30% of the corpus instances have a rating equals to 4 while the remaining rating (from 1 to 3) represents almost the 20%.

Table 8. Results for a majority class baseline.

MAE	MSE	RMSE	Accuracy	F1-score
0.72246	1.49779	1.22384	0.54185	0.14057

Table 9 shows the performance of the CF model under the user-based approach. The result with the lowest error measures and the highest accuracy is when $k = 10$. This is not the case for the F1-score and Accuracy measure, where the highest value results when $k = 25$. Notice that there is no significant difference concerning the remaining results. Regarding the majority class baseline, this approach obtains lower MSE and RMSE values; however, it does not outperform the rest of the metrics.

Table 9. Performance of the CF model under the user-based approach.

k value	MAE	MSE	RMSE	Accuracy	F1-score
10	**0.79083**	**1.07988**	**1.03917**	0.32599	0.13035
20	0.79374	1.0937	1.0458	0.32452	0.12993
25	0.79348	1.09309	1.04551	**0.32745**	**0.13188**
30	0.79354	1.09302	1.04548	0.32599	0.13091
35	0.79359	1.09314	1.04553	0.32599	0.13091

Table 10 shows the performance of the CF model under the item-based approach. The result with the lowest error measures and the highest accuracy is when $k = 9$. For the F1-score measure, the highest value was obtained when $k = 1$. Similar to the CF model under the user-based approach, there is no significant difference concerning the remaining results. In addition, this approach also obtains lower MSE and RMSE values than those of the majority class baseline, but it does not outperform the rest of the metrics.

Table 10. Performance of the CF model under the item-based approach.

k value	MAE	MSE	RMSE	Accuracy	F1-score
1	0.79588	1.11894	1.0578	0.32599	**0.13167**
3	0.78267	1.07929	1.03889	0.32892	0.12528
5	0.79882	1.11894	1.0578	0.32158	0.12819
7	0.79735	1.11747	1.05711	0.32305	0.12969
9	**0.78120**	**1.07489**	**1.036768**	**0.328928**	0.12517

Finally, Table 11 shows the performance of the DF models trained by the machine learning algorithms: random forest (RF), neural networks (NN) and KNN with $k = 10, 20, 25, 30, 35$ (see Sect. 3.3). All DF models outperform the majority class baseline in all the used evaluation metrics (although lower MSE and RMSE values are obtained with the CF models). The overall best result is obtained for the DF model trained by RF.

Table 11. Performance results for the demographic system

Model	MAE	MSE	RMSE	Accuracy	F1-score
KNN 10	0.69456	1.33186	1.15406	0.51982	0.19155
KNN 20	0.70778	1.39207	1.17986	0.52569	0.18355
KNN 25	0.70044	1.37885	1.17424	0.53010	0.18286
KNN 30	0.69603	1.36857	1.16986	0.53303	0.18070
KNN 35	0.68428	1.3392	1.15724	0.53597	0.18438
RF	**0.66666**	**1.29809**	**1.13933**	**0.54478**	**0.20378**
NN	0.68428	1.3392	1.15724	0.54185	0.17582

5 Conclusions and Future Work

In this work, three recommendation models were proposed: two based on collaborative filtering (user and items) and the other based on demographic issues. These methods serve as baselines for future work on recommendation systems for sites in Mexico. A corpus was built, collecting tourism reviews in Spanish and overall tourist places in Nayarit, Mexico. This is the first corpus, as far as the authors are aware of, which includes ratings about places in Mexico intended for tourist recommendation systems. Experimental results show that the demographic-based filtering approach outperforms a majority class baseline (used as a reference). This is not the case for the collaborative-based filtering (users and items) approaches, although they obtained the lower overall MSE and RMSE values.

As future work, it would be interesting to explore other recommendation approaches such as context-based models or others using deep learning and natural language processing.

Acknowledgements. This work was partially supported by the Tecnológico Nacional de México (Grants No. 8288.20-P and 9518.20-P).

References

1. Adomavicius, G., Tuzhilin, A.: Context-aware recommender systems. In: Ricci, F., Rokach, L., Shapira, B., Kantor, P.B. (eds.) Recommender Systems Handbook, pp. 217–253. Springer, Boston, MA (2011). https://doi.org/10.1007/978-0-387-85820-3_7
2. Aguirre Quezada, J.P.: Caída del turismo por la covid-19. desafío para méxico y experiencias internacionales. In: Instituto Belisario Dominguez, **186**, 1–13. Senado de la republica (2020)
3. Al-Ghobari, M., Muneer, A., Fati, S.M.: Location-aware personalized traveler recommender system (lapta) using collaborative filtering KNN. Comput. Mater. Continu. **68** (2021)
4. Binucci, C., De Luca, F., Di Giacomo, E., Liotta, G., Montecchiani, F.: Designing the content analyzer of a travel recommender system. Expert Syst. Appl. **87**, 199–208 (2017)
5. Chai, T., Draxler, R.R.: Root mean square error (RMSE) or mean absolute error (MAE)? - arguments against avoiding RMSE in the literature. Geosci. Mod. Dev. **7**(3), 1247–1250 (2014). https://doi.org/10.5194/gmd-7-1247-2014
6. EFE, A.: Estimas caida del 10% en el pib turistico de mexico (2020). https://www.efe.com/efe/america/mexico/estiman-caida-del-10-en-el-pib-tu-ristico-de-mexico/50000545-4233506
7. El economista (2019). https://www.eleconomista.com.mx/empresas/Sector-de-viajes-y-turismo-crecio-mas-que-el-PIB-20190301-0003.html
8. Fararni, K.A., Nafis, F., Aghoutane, B., Yahyaouy, A., Riffi, J., Sabri, A.: Hybrid recommender system for tourism based on big data and AI: a conceptual framework. Big Data Min. Anal. **4**(1), 47–55 (2021). https://doi.org/10.26599/BDMA.2020.9020015
9. Ghazanfar, M.A., Prugel-Bennett, A.: A scalable, accurate hybrid recommender system. In: 2010 Third International Conference on Knowledge Discovery and Data Mining, pp. 94–98. IEEE (2010)
10. Hamid, R.A., et al.: How smart is e-tourism? a systematic review of smart tourism recommendation system applying data management. Comput. Sci. Rev. **39**, 100337 (2021). https://doi.org/10.1016/j.cosrev.2020.100337
11. Hedlund, J., Nilsson Tengstrand, E.: A comparison between different recommender system approaches for a book and an author recommender system (2020)
12. Herlocker, J.L., Konstan, J.A., Terveen, L.G., Riedl, J.T.: Evaluating collaborative filtering recommender systems. ACM Trans. Inf. Syst. **22**(1), 5–53 (2004). https://doi.org/10.1145/963770.963772
13. INEGI: Estadísticas a propósito del día mundial del turismo (2019). https://www.inegi.org.mx/contenidos/saladeprensa/aproposito/2019/turismo2019_Nal.pdf
14. Kuanr, M., Mohanty, S.N.: Location-based personalised recommendation systems for the tourists in India. Int. J. Bus. Intell. Data Min. **17**(3), 377–392 (2020)

15. Likert, R.: A technique for the measurement of attitudes. Arch. Psychol. **140**, 55 (1932)
16. Ranjith, S., Paul, P.V.: A survey on recent recommendation systems for the tourism industry. In: Accelerating Knowledge Sharing, Creativity, and Innovation Through Business Tourism, pp. 205–237. IGI Global (2020)
17. Salunke, S.S.: Selenium Webdriver in Python: Learn with Examples, vol. 70. CreateSpace Independent Publishing Platform, USA (2014)
18. SECTUR: Ranking mundial de turismo internacional (2018). https://www.datatur.sectur.gob.mx/SitePages/RankingOMT.aspx
19. Shani, G., Gunawardana, A.: Evaluating Recommendation Systems, pp. 257–297. Springer, US, Boston, MA (2011). https://doi.org/10.1007/978-0-387-85820-3_8
20. Shen, J., Deng, C., Gao, X.: Attraction recommendation: towards personalized tourism via collective intelligence. Neurocomputing **173**, 789–798 (2016)
21. UNWTO: Unwto world tourism barometer and statistical annex, UNWTO World Tourism Barometer **18**(1), 1–48 (2020)
22. Vu, H.Q., Li, G., Law, R., Zhang, Y.: Exploring tourist dining preferences based on restaurant reviews. J. Travel Res. **58**(1), 149–167 (2019)
23. Welle, D.: El impacto al turismo arrastrará a la economía mexicana. (2020). https://www.dw.com/es/el-impacto-al-turismo-arrastra-a-la-econom%C3%ADa-mexicana/a-53137428
24. Xiong, H., Zhou, Y., Hu, C., Wei, X., Li, L.: A novel recommendation algorithm frame for tourist spots based on multi-clustering bipartite graphs. In: 2017 IEEE 2nd International Conference on Cloud Computing and Big Data Analysis (ICCBDA), pp. 276–282. IEEE (2017)
25. Yochum, P., Chang, L., Gu, T., Zhu, M.: Linked open data in location-based recommendation system on tourism domain: a survey. IEEE Access **8**, 16409–16439 (2020). https://doi.org/10.1109/ACCESS.2020.2967120

Detecting Traces of Self-harm in Social Media: A Simple and Interpretable Approach

Juan Aguilera[1], Delia Irazú Hernández Farías[2]([✉]) [ID],
Manuel Montes-y-Gómez[1] [ID], and Luis C. González[3] [ID]

[1] Instituto Nacional de Astrofísica, Óptica y Electrónica, Puebla, Mexico
{jaguilera,mmontesg}@inaoep.mx
[2] División de Ciencias e Ingenierías, Campus León, Universidad de Guanajuato,
Leon, Mexico
di.hernandez@ugto.mx
[3] Universidad Autónoma de Chihuahua, Chihuahua, Mexico
lcgonzalez@uach.mx

Abstract. Social networks have become the main means of communication and interaction between people. In them, users share information and opinions, but also their experiences, worries, and personal concerns. Because of this, there is a growing interest in analyzing this kind of content to identify people who commit self-harm, which is often one of the first signs of suicide risk. Recently, methods based on Deep Learning have shown good results in this task, however, they are opaque and do not facilitate the interpretation of decisions, something fundamental in health-related tasks. In this paper, we face the detection of self-harm in social media by applying a simple and interpretable one-class-classification approach, which, supported on the concept of the attraction force [1], produces its decisions considering both the relevance and distance between users. The results obtained in a benchmark dataset are encouraging, as they indicate a competitive performance with respect to state-of-the-art methods. Furthermore, taking advantage of the approach's properties, we outline what could be a support tool for healthcare professionals for analyzing and monitoring self-harm behaviors in social networks.

1 Introduction

Nowadays, social networks are the preferred communication channel around the world. They offer a forum for people to share their daily activities, thoughts, and ideas. Furthermore, they are also a face-saving platform for sharing worries, personal concerns, even related to very personal health issues. This has drawn attention for research purposes, since on these platforms people tend to express themselves more freely than in other circumstances, providing a priceless chance for understanding and modeling the relation of language and users' profiles. Accordingly, some recent efforts have been done to study the content generated by users suffering from different mental health problems like depression, schizophrenia, anorexia, and self-harm.

© Springer Nature Switzerland AG 2021
I. Batyrshin et al. (Eds.): MICAI 2021, LNAI 13068, pp. 196–207, 2021.
https://doi.org/10.1007/978-3-030-89820-5_16

Mental health is a major challenge for social well-being. Self-harm, in particular, is a mental health problem that involves deliberately harming the body[1], and whose extreme cases can lead to suicide [13]. Recent studies [9,21] have shown that social media platforms are widely used by people who commit self-harm to seek information, as well as advice and support. However, due to the enormous amount of information that is generated in these media, it is very difficult for experts to manage it to identify users at risk and then support them. To address this issue, computational tools are being developed to help professionals performing such a complex task. This paper presents our effort in this direction.

Identifying self-harm is a very challenging problem from the computational linguistics perspective. It has been addressed considering user-generated content in different platforms like Flickr [20], Reddit [10,11,21], Twitter [3], and Instagram [19]. Self-harm content has been mainly studied by modeling the posts' content by means of bag-of-words and word embeddings, together with well-known traditional classifiers (like logistic regression and support vector machines) as well as with complex deep learning models (like convolutional, recurrent and attention-based NNs) [10,11,21]. Other works have developed frameworks that consider different features like online activity and visual content [20]. In addition, some others have attempt to further explore discussion forums on self-harm [3], or to exploit information regarding to the emotional changes shown on this type of content [4]. Language used in self-harm content is strongly related to the one used in suicide.

Attempting to promote research on mental health related topics, some shared tasks have been organized. One of the best known is the *Computational Linguistics and Clinical Psychology Workshop* (CLPsych[2]), which, in its 2016 edition [17] included a task aimed to classify posts from the ReachOut.com site[3] according to four levels of risk of harming. The majority of the participating teams used word-based approaches with traditional classifiers as well as some lexical resources related to affective information. On the other hand, in the framework of the *Early Risk Prediction on the Internet Lab* (eRisk[4]), a task dedicated to self-harm detection on Reddit posts was organized in 2019 [22] and 2020 [14]. Most participating teams also employed basic representations like the BOW, and traditional classifiers like Random Forest and SVM (the most widely used); nonetheless, the best results were obtained by deep learning models, in particular by BERT-based classifiers [15]. From these previous works, it is important to highlight that, despite deep learning methods offering outstanding results, they have a major drawback: they are not easy to interpret [7].

In this paper, we propose to face the task of self-harm detection in social media by means of a *one-class classification* (OCC) approach [12]. The observation that motivates our choice is that the posts from users who do not harm

---

[1] https://www.mayoclinic.org/es-es/diseases-conditions/self-injury/symptoms-causes/syc-20350950.
[2] https://clpsych.org/.
[3] It is an online community of Australian youth.
[4] https://early.irlab.org/.

themselves, who indeed are the vast majority, are very diverse in topics and style, making the negative class very complex to model, and, in consequence, not really useful to discriminate the users who actually harm themselves. In contrast, we assume the posts from the latter group are more homogeneous, since this kind of users tend to talk about their emotional state as well as to share about the actions of self-injury they have carried out.

Out of the existing OCC approaches, we decided to use the *Global Strength Classifier* [2] (henceforth denoted as gSC), a novel and transparent instance-based classifier supported on the concept of the gravitational attraction force. It evaluates the relation among instances by their strengths, considering their distances as well as their masses (relevance) with respect to the target task. Accordingly, in the task at hand, gSC classifies an unlabeled user as a "case of self-harm", if he/she shows a significant attraction to all training positive users, although the most relevant users, those who post more information related to self-harm, will have a greater influence on the classification decision.

gSC was originally evaluated in the depression and anorexia detection tasks, showing very competitive results compared to more complex models [2]. In this paper, we move a step forward by extending its evaluation and proposing new functionalities for it. The main contributions of this work are:

i) We present for the first time gSC in the task of self-harm detection. This model, besides offering competitive results also provides some degree of intuition of the classification decisions it takes, then contributing to the understanding and diagnosis of this important mental disorder.

ii) We carry out an in-depth analysis of gSC properties and their correlation with the classification errors, providing insights on its robustness for detecting and monitoring mental disorders in social media.

iii) We outline a user-friendly interface to support health professionals for the detection and follow-up of users who harm themselves. This interface takes advantage of the different characteristics of gSC to allow the interpretation of results, a key aspect in any health-related task.

The rest of the paper is organized as follows: The gSC method is introduced in Sect. 2. Section 3 presents the experimental settings. Section 4 shows the obtained results as well as an analysis carried out on them. The proposed support tool for helping health professionals is described in Sect. 5. Finally, in Sect. 6 we pointed out some conclusions and directions for future work.

2   gSC: A One-Class Approach for Detecting Mental Disorders

gSC is a supervised classification method based on the attraction force concept build for depression and anorexia detection [2]. It works under the intuition that only by observing the *positive* users (i.e., target class) it is possible to characterize the associated mental disorder. Thus, gSC uses only information from one single class for its decision-making. The gSC criterion for classifying an unlabeled user

x_u as positive is that the strength with which he/she is attracted to the training set X (*target strength*, S_{trg}) has to be similar to the strength with which all elements in the training set are attracted to each other (*reference strength*, S_{ref}). The above is illustrated in Fig. 1.

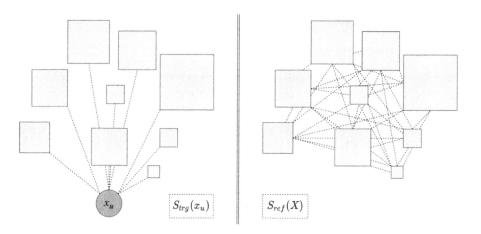

Fig. 1. Graphical representation of gSC.

Formally, gSC works as follows: Given a training set belonging to the positive class $X = \{x_1, x_2, x_3, \ldots, x_N\}$ and an unlabeled user x_u, S_{trg} and S_{ref} are calculated with Eq. 1 and 2, respectively. Observe that both equations use Eq. 3.

$$S_{trg}(x_u) = \frac{1}{N} \sum_{x_i \in X} strength(x_u, x_i) \tag{1}$$

$$S_{ref}(X) = \frac{1}{(N)(N-1)} \sum_{\substack{\forall x_i, x_j \in X \\ i \neq j}} strength(x_i, x_j) \tag{2}$$

$$strength(x_u, x_i) = G\frac{m(x_u)m(x_i)}{dist^2(x_u, x_i)} \simeq \frac{m(x_u)m(x_i)}{dist^2(x_u, x_i)} \tag{3}$$

where N is the cardinality of the training set (denoted as X); $strength(\bullet, \bullet)$ is the attraction force between two given users, and $m(\bullet)$ represents the mass of each user, which is nothing more than a measure of his/her relevance or relation to the target domain. G is the gravitational constant and $dist(\bullet, \bullet)$ is the distance between the two users in the given feature space. It is important to specify three things, first, that each user is represented by a single *document* that comprises all of his/her writings; second, that different metrics, other than the cosine distance, can be used to measure the distance between users; and third, that constant G is omitted from Eq. 3 since it is only a scaling factor.

Once both strengths are calculated, the decision of whether or not x_u belongs to the positive class is made up according to Eq. 4, where the resulting quotient between both strengths is compared against a predefined threshold β.

$$c(x_u) = \begin{cases} 1 \ (positive), & if \ \frac{S_{trg}(x_u)}{S_{ref}(X)} \geq \beta \\ 0 \ (negative), & otherwise \end{cases} \tag{4}$$

2.1 Mass Assignment to Users

The criterion for determining the relevance or mass that a given document (i.e., user) has is one of the main concepts in gSC. In this case, each document has a mass value that is proportional to the amount of terms related to a given vocabulary containing on it. Hence, the more terms it comprises, the greater mass it has. Formally, the mass of each sample is calculated according to Eq. 5.

$$mass(x) = \frac{1 + \sum_{\forall w_i \in \mathcal{L}} f(w_i, x)}{1 + |x|} \tag{5}$$

Where $\mathcal{L}$ is a lexicon related to the task at hand (in this case, the vocabulary includes terms related to self-harm), $f(w_i, x)$ is the number of occurrences of the term w_i in the document x, and $|x|$ is its length.

3 Experimental Settings

3.1 Dataset

To evaluate the performance of gSC for self-harm detection in social media, we take advantage of the dataset developed for the eRisk-2020 [14] shared task. It is composed by a collection of posts from Reddit users. Two categories were included: *self-harm*, which includes users who explicitly said that they had self-injured, and a *control* group which comprises users that have not mentioned to commit self-injury. In the rest of the paper, the latter is sometimes also referred as the *negative* class. Table 1 shows some characteristics of the dataset. It is important to highlight that, given the fact that gSC works under an OCC approach, only the *self-harm* group was used during training. While, both *self-harm* and *control* instances were exploited for evaluation purposes.

Table 1. Dataset main characteristics.

	Training		Test	
	Self-harm	Control	Self-harm	Control
No. of users	41	299	104	319
No. of posts	1322	45006	11691	92138
Avg. posts per user	32.24	150.52	112.41	288.83

3.2   Text Representations

As mentioned before, gSC needs to compute the distance among all users. For evaluation purposes we considered different feature spaces, defined by the following text representations:

- **Word Embeddings.** All posts belonging to a given user were concatenated, thus, each user is represented by a single document containing all his/her posts. As pre-processing, all posts were converted to lower-case, and hashtags, user mentions, urls, punctuation marks, and stopwords were removed. Regardless of the type of embeddings used, users were represented by the average vector of *all* their words. We used the following three types of embeddings:
  - *Word2Vec* [16]. Vectors of 300 dimensions trained on the Google News dataset.
  - *GloVe* [18]. Vectors of 200 dimensions trained on Twitter data.
  - *FastText* [6]. Vectors of 300 dimensions trained on Wikipedia, and on the UMBC and statmt.org news datasets.
- **BERT Embeddings.** We followed a standard design for sentence classification tasks using BERT [8], which considers the hidden state h of the final layer over the special token [CLS] as the full representation of the input sequences. In particular, we used the *bert-base-uncased* pre-trained model[5]. In this case, each post of a given user was treated individually; afterwards, the obtained vectors were averaged and the resulting vector used as the final user representation.

3.3   Self-harm Vocabulary for Mass Calculation

As in other related tasks, lexical resources for addressing self-harm detection are scarce, therefore, a common practice is to build in-house resources for experimental purposes. In the case of gSC, having a lexicon to calculate the mass of the instances is essential. A lexicon composed by 61 terms, which are shown in Table 2, was created. The starting point of this resource was the vocabulary of self-harm terms found in [20], which were collected from a wide set of Flickr posts related to the topic at hand. We manually enriched this list by adding terms that could be relevant for capturing self-harm content.

Table 2. Lexicon used for mass assignment.

addiction, alone, anemia, angry, anorexia, anxious, arm, arms, bath, bathroom, blade, blades, bleeding, blood, body, bruised, bulimia, cut, cuts, cutting, dark, depressed, depression, die, failure, finger, fingers, hand, hands, harm, harming, hate, help, illness, kill, killme, knife, leg, legs, mental-illness, night, pain, palm, plan, plans, razor, sad, sadness, scar, scars, self, selfharm, selfhate, skin, sh, sleeve, sleeves, stress, suffer, suffering, suicide

---

[5] https://huggingface.co/transformers/pretrained_models.html.

3.4　Parameters' Tuning

For using gSC, some parameters must be tuned. In a similar fashion than in [2], we decided to evaluate different values of the parameter $\beta = \{0.5, 1, 2\}$. It serves to adjust gSC for being lenient or strict in decision-making. To calculate the distance between two instances, the cosine distance was used. For what concerns to the baselines, for kNN-based methods we considered $k = \{1, 3, 5, 7\}$ and for OCC-kNN we evaluated $\beta = \{0.5, 1, 2\}$. For SVM and OCC-SVM, the parameters used were $kernel = \{linear, poly, rbf, sigmoid\}$, as well as $C = \{0.5, 1.0, 1.5, \ldots, 10.0\}$ and $nu = \{0.05, 0.1, 0.15, \ldots, 0.95\}$, respectively.

4　Results

As in the eRisk-2020 shared task, and for comparison purposes, we use the F_1-score over the positive class as main evaluation measure; precision and recall are also included for completeness. We compare the performance of gSC against well-known machine learning methods: kNN and SVM, as well as their OCC versions, denoted as OCC-kNN and OCC-SVM, respectively. Besides, we also include the best ranking model in the eRisk-2020 shared task [15], denoted as *B-eRisk-M*. This model used a variety of BERT-based classifiers that were trained with additional data[6] than the provided for official training. Table 3 shows the results of the baseline methods as well as the ones obtained with gSC for self-harm detection. The results of all methods correspond to their best parameter settings. For gSC, Word2Vec embeddings and $\beta = 1$ generated the best result.

Table 3. Performance of *gSC* and baseline methods in the self-harm detection task.

Method	F_1-score	Precision	Recall
gSC	0.679	0.697	0.663
OCC-kNN	0.434	0.291	0.856
OCC-SVM	0.548	0.500	0.606
kNN	0.395	0.246	1.000
SVM	0.642	0.927	0.490
B-eRisk-M	0.754	0.828	0.692

According to the results in Table 3, gSC outperforms all baseline models in terms of $\mathbf{F_1}$-score. Although gSC does not outperform *B-eRisk-M*, it should be noted that the latter is a complex binary classification BERT-based model and it does not use the same information than our method during training. Instead, gSC only exploits data from the target class for making decisions. Considering the official eRisk-2020 results, gSC would have ranked in the 4th position, being

---

[6] Martínez-Castaño et al. exploited data collected from Pushshift Reddit Dataset [5].

surpassed only by three variations of the *B-eRisk-M* model. We applied the z-test of significance between gSC and *B-eRisk-M* with p-value = 0.01, concluding that there is no significant difference between them, which means that gSC is a statistically similar method.

Furthermore, we also calculated the $P@10$ value considered as *confidence level* for the quotient of the division of S_{trg} by S_{ref}, described in Eq. 4. A $P@10 = 1$ was obtained by ordering the classified instances from highest to lowest, according to their confidence level. The higher the confidence level, the higher the amount of evidence that a user has traces of self-harming.

4.1   Error Analysis

Attempting to further analyze the results obtained by gSC, we decided to rank all the users in the test set in terms of their classification confidence level, as described at the end of the previous section. After this ranking, we noticed that most users having a confidence level higher than 2 were correctly classified. In particular, 37 users felt into this situation, from them, only one was a false positive. Reading the posts from this user, we realized that although not marked as positive, he/she mentioned many terms associated with self-harm (corresponding to Table 2) in his/her writings. This particular case highlights one of the main drawbacks of gSC, which is that the classification decisions strongly depends on the vocabulary used for measuring the masses. On the other hand, the majority of misclassifications occurred for confidence levels between 1 and 2. In this case, only 33 out of 62 users were correctly classified.

An additional analysis was carried out aimed to infer the reasons for the false positives and false negatives obtained by gSC in the experiments. In this case, we considered two aspects: the *masses* of the test users and their *distances* to the training users. Figure 2 shows two boxplots regarding four classification metrics, namely, True Positives (TP), False Positives (FP), True Negatives (TN), and False Negatives (FN), for the masses (in the left) and distances (in the right).

With respect to the *masses*, it can be observed that instances with high mass values tend to be correctly classified as positive. On the other hand, instances with low mass values were identified as negative, but in many cases incorrectly. That is, the mass values from TN and FN are very similar, which indicates that it is very complex to detect users who harm themselves when they do not show the signals of self-harm in an explicit way or, in other words, when their writings do not use the words from the reference lexicon.

Regarding the *distances* to the training set users, Fig. 2 shows an opposite story. Correctly classified instances in the positive class mostly show small distance values with respect to the training data. However, false positives seem to have even lower distance values. The distances observed in the TP and FP sets are very similar, indicating that it is very difficult to distinguish the users who harm themselves, when they do not share similar posts to other positive users, in other words, it seems to be very complicated for gSC to distinguish a positive user when he/she shares different experiences and sentiments than the rest of the positive users, even when he/she does so explicitly and frequently. On the

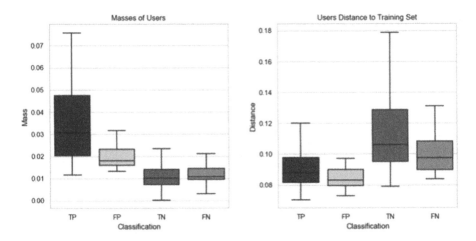

Fig. 2. Masses and distances of the instances in the testset with respect to classification metrics.

other hand, the TN shows the highest distance values, which could indicate that there are indeed term differences in the posts written by healthy users and those generated by self-harming users.

5   Decision-Making Support Tool

Nowadays, novel NLP models are increasingly sophisticated and complex, which has led to improve state-of-the-art results on a wide variety of problems. However, one of the most important drawbacks of these models is its interpretability. A task like the one discussed in this paper, where the interpretation of the results is crucial, needs to be addressed by methods allowing a simpler interpretation. In this sense, taking advantage of the properties of gSC that allow us to extract relevant information for interpretation purposes, we developed a prototype of a *Decision-Making Support Tool* that could serve to health professionals to establish a diagnosis on the basis of the social media content. Figure 3 illustrates a proposal of the interface developed as a potential support tool.

Within this interface, a user (expected to be a health professional) could find the following:

– On Point 1, through a color palette the self-harm level associated to a given subject is shown. Levels are represented from the lowest degree of evidence in green to the highest one in red. Pressing on any color shows an ordered list of subjects according to their self-harm level, (it is obtained as the confidence level).
– On Point 2, the user can select any subject, then information like its confidence level, mass, average distance to the training set, N most frequent words,

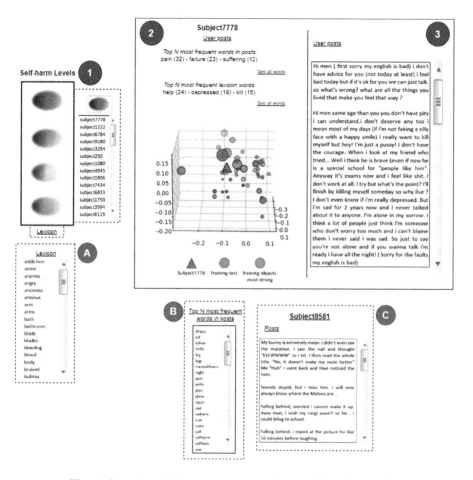

Fig. 3. Interface of the support system for health professionals.

and N most frequent lexicon-words will be displayed. Besides, a 3D model of the subject features space is also shown. Here, the instances in training set and the subject itself are shown; those instances which exert the greater strength on the subject can be explored.

- On Point 3, all post of the selected subject are displayed.
- Pop-up windows are also considered in this interface. Window A shows the lexicon used to calculate the masses. Window B shows the whole list of most frequent words or the list of the most frequent lexicon-words of the selected subject. When any user in the 3D model is selected, all her post are displayed through Window C.

6   Conclusions

In this paper, we tackle self-harm detection in social media. Such a complex task was approached by using gSC, a one-class classification method based on the concept of textual attraction forces proposed in [2]. According to the experimental setting performed, gSC outperformed baseline methods from both perspectives binary and one-class classification; besides, the obtained results are very competitive and encouraging against the state-of-the-art. Given the features of gSC, its outcomes are easier to interpret than other state-of-the-art models. An error analysis was carried out, the findings seem to confirm the ability of the aspects considered in gSC for classifying self-harm content. The first version of an outline support tool for healthcare professionals was also introduced. Such application leverages the properties of gSC for presenting not only the label assigned to a given user but also which aspects were considered by the model during classification. As future work we are interested on evaluating the approach on data from other social media as well as to consider an early risk detection perspective.

Acknowledgments. This research was funded by the CONACYT project CB-2015-01-257383.

References

1. Aguilera, J., González, L.C., Montes-y-Gómez, M., López, R., Escalante, H.J.: From neighbors to strengths - the k-strongest strengths (kSS) classification algorithm. Pattern Recogn. Lett. **136**, 301–308 (2020)
2. Aguilera, J., Hernández Farías, D.I., Ortega-Mendoza, R.M., Montes-y Gómez, M.: Depression and anorexia detection in social media as a one-class classification problem. Appl. Intell. 1–16 (2021)
3. Alhassan, M.A., Inuwa-Dutse, I., Bello, B.S., Pennington, D.R.: Self-harm: detection and support on twitter. CoRR abs/2104.00174 (2021)
4. Aragón, M., López-Monroy, A.P., y Gómez, M.M.: INAOE-CIMAT at eRisk 2020: detecting signs of self-harm using sub-emotions and words. In: CLEF (2020)
5. Baumgartner, J., Zannettou, S., Keegan, B., Squire, M., Blackburn, J.: The pushshift reddit dataset. In: Proceedings of the International AAAI Conference on Web and Social Media, vol. 14, no. 1, pp. 830–839 (2020)
6. Bojanowski, P., Grave, E., Joulin, A., Mikolov, T.: Enriching word vectors with subword information. Trans. Assoc. Comput. Ling. **5**, 135–146 (2017)
7. Danilevsky, M., Qian, K., Aharonov, R., Katsis, Y., Kawas, B., Sen, P.: A survey of the state of explainable AI for natural language processing. In: Proceedings of the 1st Conference of the Asia-Pacific Chapter of the Association for Computational Linguistics and the 10th International Joint Conference on Natural Language Processing, pp. 447–459. ACL, Suzhou, China, December 2020
8. Devlin, J., Chang, M.W., Lee, K., Toutanova, K.: BERT: pre-training of deep bidirectional transformers for language understanding. In: Proceedings of the 2019 Conference of the North American Chapter of the Association for Computational Linguistics: Human Language Technologies, Volume 1 (Long and Short Papers), pp. 4171–4186. ACL, Minneapolis, Minnesota, June 2019

9. Gkotsis, G., et al.: The language of mental health problems in social media. In: Proceedings of the Third Workshop on Computational Linguistics and Clinical Psychology, pp. 63–73. ACL, San Diego, CA, USA, June 2016

10. Gkotsis, G., et al.: Characterisation of mental health conditions in social media using informed deep learning. Sci. Rep. **7**(1), 45141 (2017)

11. Ive, J., Gkotsis, G., Dutta, R., Stewart, R., Velupillai, S.: Hierarchical neural model with attention mechanisms for the classification of social media text related to mental health. In: Proceedings of the Fifth Workshop on Computational Linguistics and Clinical Psychology: From Keyboard to Clinic, pp. 69–77. ACL, June 2018

12. Khan, S.S., Madden, M.G.: One-class classification: taxonomy of study and review of techniques. Knowl. Eng. Rev. **29**(3), 345–374 (2014)

13. Laye-Gindhu, A., Schonert-Reichl, K.: Nonsuicidal self-harm among community adolescents: understanding the "whats" and "whys" of self-harm. J. Youth Adolesc. **34**, 447–457 (2005)

14. Losada, D.E., Crestani, F., Parapar, J.: Overview of eRisk at CLEF 2020: early risk prediction on the internet (extended overview). In: Cappellato, L., Eickhoff, C., Ferro, N., Névéol, A. (eds.) Conference and Labs of the Evaluation Forum. CEUR Workshop Proceedings (2020)

15. Martínez-Castaño, R., Htait, A., Azzopardi, L., Moshfeghi, Y.: Early risk detection of self-harm and depression severity using BERT-based transformers. In: Working Notes of CLEF 2020 - Conference and Labs of the Evaluation Forum, Thessaloniki, Greece, 22–25 September 2020. CEUR Workshop Proceedings, vol. 2696. CEUR-WS.org (2020)

16. Mikolov, T., Chen, K., Corrado, G., Dean, J.: Efficient estimation of word representations in vector space. In: Bengio, Y., LeCun, Y. (eds.) 1st Workshop Track Proceedings International Conference on Learning Representations, ICLR 2013, Scottsdale, Arizona, USA, 2–4 May 2013 (2013)

17. Milne, D.N., Pink, G., Hachey, B., Calvo, R.A.: CLPsych 2016 shared task: triaging content in online peer-support forums. In: Proceedings of the Third Workshop on Computational Linguistics and Clinical Psychology, pp. 118–127. ACL, June 2016

18. Pennington, J., Socher, R., Manning, C.D.: GloVe: global Vectors for Word representation. In: Empirical Methods in Natural Language Processing (EMNLP), pp. 1532–1543 (2014)

19. Scherr, S., Arendt, F., Frissen, T., Oramas, M.J.: Detecting intentional self-harm on instagram: development, testing, and validation of an automatic image-recognition algorithm to discover cutting-related posts. Soc. Sci. Comput. Rev. **38**(6), 673–685 (2020)

20. Wang, Y., Tang, J., Li, J., Li, B., Wan, Y., Mellina, C., O'Hare, N., Chang, Y.: Understanding and discovering deliberate self-harm content in social media. In: Proceedings of the 26th International Conference on World Wide Web, pp. 93–102. WWW 2017, International World Wide Web Conferences Steering Committee, Republic and Canton of Geneva, CHE (2017)

21. Yates, A., Cohan, A., Goharian, N.: Depression and self-harm risk assessment in online forums. In: Proceedings of the 2017 Conference on Empirical Methods in Natural Language Processing, pp. 2968–2978. ACL, September 2017

22. Zirikly, A., Resnik, P., Uzuner, Ö., Hollingshead, K.: CLPsych 2019 shared task: predicting the degree of suicide risk in reddit posts. In: Proceedings of the Sixth Workshop on Computational Linguistics and Clinical Psychology, pp. 24–33. ACL, Minneapolis, Minnesota, June 2019

Finite-Field Parallel Adder Circuit Over Prime Numbers Based on Spiking Neural P Systems

Emmanuel Tonatihu Juárez-Velázquez[1,2], Derlis Hernández-Lara[1,2(✉)], and Carlos Alfonso Trejo-Villanueva[1,2]

[1] Instituto Politécnico Nacional, Escuela Superior de Ingeniería Mecánica y Eléctrica, Ciudad de México, México
{emmanuel.juarez,dderlis-lara,carlostrejo}@tese.edu.mx
[2] Tecnológico Nacional de México, Tecnológico de Estudios Superiores de Ecatepec, Ecatepec Estado de, México

Abstract. Nowadays, the arithmetic operations precision is one of the most critical aspects in the development of efficient finite-field arithmetic circuits, because they are involved in several applications, for example, in advanced cryptographic algorithms such as AES (*Advanced Encryption Standard*), elliptic curves and RSA (*Rivest Shamir Adleman*). Most of these algorithms have been implemented on general purpose machines. However, the performance of recent computational systems could not satisfy the computational needs to perform finite-field arithmetic computations of large bit-length numbers, because the word length of these processors is too small compared with the bit-length of these numbers and thus suffer from the resulting increase in execution time. One potential solution can be found in the development of advanced highly parallel computing systems. Recently, an emerging branch of natural computation has created arithmetic circuits based on parallel computing (*Spiking Neural P Systems*). Most of them perform basic arithmetic operations sequentially despite of having intrinsic parallelism. In this paper, we introduce for the first time, the design of a finite-field parallel adder circuit, which is highly inspired by neural processing of the soma, synaptic weights and rules on the synapses, to process numbers with large bit-length efficiently.

Keywords: Parallel adder · Finite-field · Spiking neural P system (SN P)

1 Introduction

Finite-field arithmetic operations over Galois Field (GF(p)) [1, 2], such addition and multiplication are involved in advanced encryption standard (AES) [3], Rivest-Shamir-Adleman algorithm (RSA) [4] and elliptic curves algorithm [5]. They have been considered as main public-key crypto-systems and have been widely used in many practical applications, such as secure data transmission, wireless sensor networks, key exchange and digital signature. One of the main features of these algorithms is linked to their easy implementation and have a better industry support. However, RSA algorithm is going to require a considerable increase in the length of public keys to keep the integrity and security of the information in the near future, as stated by members of the national institute

© Springer Nature Switzerland AG 2021
I. Batyrshin et al. (Eds.): MICAI 2021, LNAI 13068, pp. 208–215, 2021.
https://doi.org/10.1007/978-3-030-89820-5_17

of standards and technology (NIST). Hence, there is a large challenge in the development of new computing schemes to support finite-field multiplication and addition over *GF(p)* efficiently and they can be used in practical implementations on limited-resource devices.

Neural-like computing models are versatile computing mechanisms in the field of artificial intelligence. Spiking Neural P Systems (SN P systems for short) are one of the recently developed spiking neural network models inspired by the way neurons communicate. The communications among neurons are essentially achieved by spikes, i.e., short electrical pulses. In terms of motivation, SN P systems fall into the third generation of neural network models [6].

During the last decade, computational scientists have dedicated enormous efforts to create new computational schemes based on spiking neural P systems (shortly called SN P systems) [7] that is considered as a class of parallel computing. Here, the basic processing units of the spiking neural P systems are called neurons and are connected through their synapses. These neural SN P systems are mainly based on the way biological neurons communicate via electrical impulses (spikes) and the soma processing. The soma processes these spikes by means of two types of spiking rules, forgetting and firing. The firing rule is defined as follows: $E/a^c \rightarrow a^p$: d, where a form regular expression under E. The natural numbers are represented by the symbols $c, p, d, d \geq 0, c \geq 1, p \geq 1$. If a spiking neuron has k input spikes, where $a^k \in L(E)$ and $k \geq c$ then it consumes c spikes and produces p spikes as an output, after a delay d. Finally, the forgetting rule is defined in the form $a^s \rightarrow \lambda$ implying that $s \geq 1$ spikes are deleted, if s spikes are contained in the neuron. Recently, several variants of SN P systems have been proposed to increase the computational capabilities of conventional SN P systems inspired by diverse neurobiological phenomena, such as rules on the synapses [7]; dendritic delays [8]; among others.

In particular, some authors have proposed sequential arithmetic circuits (adders, subtractors, multipliers and divisors) based on conventional SN P systems. However, they have had difficulties in adequately designing parallel circuits to exploit at maximum their intrinsic parallel processing. Besides, none of them has been proposed finite-field arithmetic circuits. This paper presents the design of an advanced finite-field parallel adder considering new variants of SN P systems (synaptic weights and rules on the synapses) [9]. The use of these neurobiological phenomena has allowed us to reduce the complexity of connectivity and spiking rules and take advantage of their intrinsic parallel processing.

2   An Introduction to the Finite-Field Addition Over *GF(p)*

The finite-field $\mathbb{F}$ is called prime field when its order is p [1]. Hence, the finite-field $\mathbb{F}$ p contains a set Zp of integers $\{0, 1, \ldots, p-1\}$ along with the modular arithmetic operations $(mod)\,p$. The addition over $GF(p)$ of two prime numbers (and) can be defined as follows:

$$u + v \, mod \, p \tag{1}$$

where u and $v \in Zp$ and the integer p is called the modulus. As can be observed from (1), the addition is one of the simplest finite-field operations that is heavily used in many cryptographic algorithms such as AES, RSA and Diffie-Hellman.

3   Proposal of a Finite-Field Neural Adder Circuit

The proposed finite-field neural adder $\Pi_{add\_GF(p)}$ performs the addition of two natural numbers (u and v) with many digits ($u_0, \ldots, u_{n-2}, u_{n-1}$ and $v_0, \ldots, v_{n-2}, v_{n-1}$) over $GF(p)$, $u + v \bmod p$. The proposed circuit is mainly composed of a set of adder neurons ($\sigma_{A0}, \sigma_{A1}, \cdots, \sigma_{An-2}, \sigma_{An-1}$) with rules on synapses, a set of neurons ($\sigma_0, \sigma_1, \cdots, \sigma_{n-2}, \sigma_{n-1}$) with synaptic weights and a module neuron (σ_{mod}), as shown in Fig. 1.

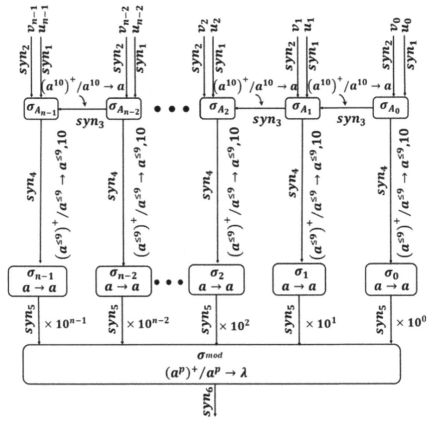

Fig. 1. The structure of the proposed finite-field parallel SN P adder $\Pi_{add\_GF(p)}$ with synaptic weights and rules on the synapses.

The formal definition of the finite-field neural adder $\Pi_{add\_GF(p)}$ and its operation are described as follows:

$$\Pi_{add\_GF(p)} = (O, \sigma_{An-1}, \sigma_{An-2}, \cdots, \sigma_{A1}, \sigma_{A0}, \sigma_{n-1}, \sigma_{n-2}, \cdots, \sigma_1, \sigma_0, syn, in, out)$$

where:

1. $O = \{a\}$;
2. $\sigma_{An-1}, \sigma_{An-2}, \cdots, \sigma_{A1}, \sigma_{A0} = \{(0, R_A,) \, with \, R_A = \{0\}$;
3. $\sigma_{n-1}, \sigma_{n-2}, \ldots \sigma_1, \sigma_0 = \{(0, R,) \, with \, R = \{a \to a\}$;
4. $\sigma_{mod} = \{(0, R_{mod},) \, with \, R_{mod} = \{(a^p)^+ / a^p \to \lambda\}$;
5. $in = \{syn_1, syn_2\}$;
6. $out = \{syn_6\}$;

Here, we define the synapse with weight and spiking rules:

$$syn = (\sigma i; \sigma j; w; R) \tag{2}$$

$$syn = \{syn_1(u, \sigma_A), syn_2(v, \sigma_A), syn_3(\sigma_x, \sigma_{x+1}, R_3);$$

$$with \, R_3 = \left\{\left(a^{10}\right)^+ / a^{10} \to a\right\}, syn_4(\sigma_A, \sigma, R_4);$$

$$with \, R_4 = \{(a \leq 9) + /a \leq 9 \to a \leq 9, 10\};$$

$$syn_5(\sigma, \sigma_{mod}, w_5) \, with \, w = \left\{1x10^{(0, 1, \cdots n-2, n-1)}\right\}\}.$$

where $w \geq 1$ is the synaptic weight and R is the spiking rule. If is not assigned, then it is equal to 1. In contrast, if the rule on the synapse R is not specified, then it is considered as a simple connection.

First, the natural numbers (u and v) must satisfy two format specifications to be processed by the proposed finite-field parallel SN P adder $\Pi_{add\_GF(p)}$. The first format specification is linked to the segmentation process of these numbers as single units (i.e., segmenting them into units, tens, hundreds, thousands, etc.). The second format is related to the codification process (i.e., every single digit is encoded as a train of spikes). For example, the digit 5 is encoded as a train of 5 spikes. Once the above conditions are met, the proposed finite-field parallel SN P adder $\Pi_{add\_GF(p)}$ performs the finite-field operation over $GF(p)$ as follows:

As can be observed in Fig. 1, each neuron σ_A has three input synapses (syn_1, syn_2, syn_3). From simulation step ($t = 1$) to simulation step ($t = 5$), neurons ($\sigma_{A0}, \sigma_{A1}, \cdots, \sigma_{An-2}, \sigma_{An-1}$) store their respective input spikes ($u_0, \ldots, u_{n-2}, u_{n-1}$ and $v_0, \ldots, v_{n-2}, v_{n-1}$) that are received through their respective synapses (syn_1, syn_2). At $t = 5$, if neurons ($\sigma_{A0}, \sigma_{A1}, \cdots \sigma_{An-2}, \sigma_{An-1}$) contain ten spikes, the spiking rule on synapse $syn_3\left(\left(a^{10}\right)^+ / a^{10} \to a\right)$ of each of neuron ($\sigma_{A0}, \sigma_{A1}, \cdots \sigma_{An-2}, \sigma_{An-1}$) generates a spike (carry) and consumes the spikes that are contained in each neuron σA.

Therefore, any neuron (σ_{Ax}) "ripples" the carry spike to the next neuron (σ_{Ax+1}) through their respective synapses (syn_3). From simulation step $(t = 6)$ to simulation step $(t = 9)$, neurons $(\sigma_{A0}, \sigma_{A1}, ..., \sigma_{An-2}, \sigma_{An-1})$ store the remaining spikes of the digits $(u_0, \ldots, u_{n-2}, u_{n-1}$ and $v_0, \ldots, v_{n-2}, v_{n-1})$. At $t = 10$, the spiking rule on synapsis (syn_4) of each neuron σ_A is set and reads the spikes that are contained in neuron σ_A. At this moment, neurons $(\sigma_{A0}, \sigma_{A1}, ..., \sigma_{An-2}, \sigma_{An-1})$ start to fire trains of spikes that represent the result of the addition of multiple digits $(u_0, \ldots, u_{n-2}, u_{n-1}$ and $v_0, \ldots, v_{n-2}, v_{n-1})$. These trains of spikes are sent to its respective neurons $(\sigma_0, \sigma_1, ... \sigma_{n-2}, \sigma_{n-1})$. According to the firing rule of neurons $(\sigma_0, \sigma_1, ... \sigma_{n-2}, \sigma_{n-1})$, these neurons fire a spike by receiving an input spike. Here, we use neurons $(\sigma_0, \sigma_1, \cdots \sigma_{n-2}, \sigma_{n-1})$ to allocate the synaptic weights per each synapse syn_5. Hence, the result is provided in units, tens, hundreds, etc.

From simulation step $(t = 10)$ to simulation step $(t = 20)$, neuron σ_{mod} receives the input spikes, which are generated by neurons $(\sigma_0, \sigma_1, ... \sigma_{n-2}, \sigma_{n-1})$, to perform the modulo operation. This operation is achieved by adding these trains of spikes with their synaptic weights and subtracting them with the value of the modulus p simultaneously, only if the sum of weights is equal to the value of the modulus p. At $t = 20$, the spikes, which are contained in neuron σ_{mod}, represent the result of the finite-field addition over $GF(p)$ of two natural numbers. Here, a single neuron σ_A calculates up to $9 + 9$ by processing two trains of spikes sequentially. However, all neurons σ_A are updated in parallel while neuron σ_{mod} performs the modulo operation concurrently.

Therefore, the finite-field addition over $GF(p)$ adds two natural numbers with multiple digits using mainly addition and subtraction operations. This aspect takes on special relevance since the division operation, which is one of the most demanding operations, is highly required for performing the modulo operation. Therefore, the use of adders and subtractors potentially allow creation of low-area and high-speed systems since these operations are far less complex than division operation.

4   Experiment and Results

Figure 2 shows an example $(19 + 5 mod 23)$ using the proposed finite-field adder over $GF(p)$. Here, two natural numbers $(u$ and $v)$ are segmented in units, tens and converted into spikes. From $t = 1$ to $t = 5$, neurons $(\sigma_{A0}, \sigma_{A1})$ store the input spikes $(v_0, v_1$ and $v_0, v_1)$. At $t = 5$, the spiking rule on synapse syn_3 of neuron σ_{A1} is set, because the neuron σ_{A0} contains ten spikes. Therefore, neuron σ_{A0} fires the carry spike to be stored in neuron σ_{A1} and its spikes are consumed, as shown in Table 1. From $t = 6$ to $t = 9$, neuron σ_{A0} stores the remaining spikes of u_0. At $t = 10$, the spiking rule on synapse syn_4 of each neuron σ_A is set. Hence, neurons σ_A fires their spikes that were stored from $t = 6$ to $t = 9$.

These spikes are sent to their respective neurons (σ_0, σ_1) to generate the input spikes of neuron σ_{mod}. At $t = 10$, neuron σ_{mod} contains 11 spikes by receiving two spikes with synaptic weights (x_1, x_{10}). At $t = 11$, neuron σ_{mod} again receive two spikes with synaptic weights (x_1, x_{10}). Therefore, neuron σ_{mod} has 22 spikes. At $t = 12$, the spiking rule of neuron σ_{mod} is set by receiving a single input spike with synaptic weight (x_1), i.e., neuron σ_{mod} contains 23 spikes and thus reaches the value of the modulus $p = 23$. At this moment, the spiking rule of neuron σ_{mod} indicates that 23 spikes must be consumed, i.e., neuron σ_{mod} does not contain spikes. At $t = 13$, neuron σ_{mod} receives the last input spike that is generated by neuron (σ_0) with synaptic weight (x_1). This spike represents the result of the finite-field addition over $F(p)$ $(19 + 5 \, mod \, 23) = 1$.

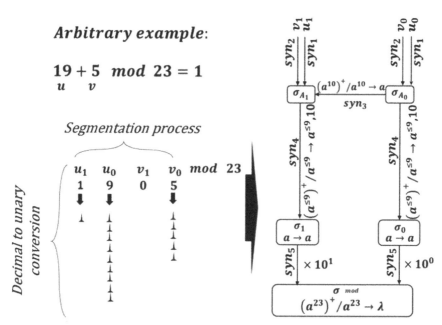

Fig. 2. Experiment using the proposed finite-field parallel SN P adder $\Pi_{add\_GF(p)}$ to perform the addition of two natural numbers over GF(p) $(19 + 5 \, mod \, 23)$.

Table 1. Simulation of the experiment $(19 + 5 \, mod \, 23)$ step-by-step.

Neurons ➡	σ_{A_0}			σ_{A_1}				σ_0	σ_1	$\sigma_{mod}(23)$
Time ↓	syn_1	syn_2	Σ	syn_1	syn_2	syn_3	Σ	x1	x10	
t=1	1	1	2	1	0	0	1	0	0	0
t=2	1	1	4	0	0	0	1	0	0	0
t=3	1	1	6	0	0	0	1	0	0	0
t=4	1	1	8	0	0	0	1	0	0	0
t=5	1	1	10	0	0	1	2	0	0	0
t=6	1	0	1	0	0	0	2	0	0	0
t=7	1	0	2	0	0	0	2	0	0	0
t=8	1	0	3	0	0	0	2	0	0	0
t=9	1	0	4	0	0	0	2	0	0	0
t=10	0	0	3	0	0	0	1	1	1	(1+10)=11
t=11	0	0	2	0	0	0	0	1	1	(11+1+10)=22
t=12	0	0	1	0	0	0	0	1	0	(22+1)-23=0
t=13	0	0	0	0	0	0	0	1	0	0+1=1

5 Conclusions and Future Work

The modular addition operation described in this paper, in addition to the modular multiplication operation, are used to implement some of the most reliable public key encryption algorithms at present time [10], and due to the mathematical complexity, these finite-field operations offer, are fundamental for contemporary cryptography.

This paper presents a new finite-field parallel SN P adder $\Pi_{add\_GF(p)}$ with a reduced number of neurons/synapses and simple and homogenous spiking rules. We stress that the inclusion of new variants, such as synaptic weights, rules on the synapses into the conventional SN P systems allows the development of efficient parallel circuits. Part of the future work is to develop a finite-field SN P multiplier based on the proposed finite-field parallel SN P adder $\Pi_{add\_GF(p)}$ in order to be used in cryptographic algorithms. In addition, the proposed finite-field parallel SN P adder $\Pi_{add\_GF(p)}$ will be implemented in advanced FPGAs to validate its performance as has been done in previous proposal [8]. This circuit potentially will allow the creation of cutting-edge applications for cryptography in an efficient and quick manner.

Has been stablished the need of increase the length of public keys in several thousands of bits for some cryptographic algorithms in the near future. Thus, an enormous processing power is required without increase the area consumption. In this paper we propose a new alternative to efficiently parallel process a lot of bits oriented to perform finite-field arithmetic additions.

Acknowledgments. The authors would like to thank Instituto Politécnico Nacional, Tecnológico Nacional de México and Tecnológico de Estudios Superiores de Ecatepec (TESE) for the support given.

References

1. Lidl, R., Niederreiter, H.: Finite fields, Cambridge. Cambridge University Press, UK (1997)
2. Dickson, L.E.: Linear Groups, with an Exposition of the Galois Field Theory, Mineola. BiblioLife, New York (2009)
3. Daemen, J., Rijmen, V.: The design of Rijndael: AES-the advanced encryption standard, Berlín. Springer-Verlag, Berlin Heidelberg, Germany (2020)
4. Rivest, R.L., Shamir, A., Adleman, L.: A method for obtaining digital signatures and public-key cryptosystems. Commun. ACM **21**(2), 120–126 (1978)
5. D. Hankerson and A. Menezes, "Elliptic Curve Cryptography. In: van Tilborg H.C.A., Jajodia S. (eds) Encyclopedia of Cryptography and Security," Springer, Boston, MA, 2011.
6. X. Wang, T. Song, F. Gong and P. Zheng, "On the Computational Power of Spiking Neural P Systems with Self-Organization," *Scientific Reports,* vol. 6, no. 27624, 2016.
7. Ionescu, M., Păun, G., Yokomori, T.: Spiking neural P systems. Fund. Inform. **71**(2–3), 279–308 (2006)
8. Song, T., Zou, Q., Liu, X., Zeng, X.: Asynchronous spiking neural P systems with rules on synapses. Neurocomputing **151**(3), 1439–1445 (2015)
9. Zeng, X., Song, T., Zhang, X., Pan, L.: Performing four basic arithmetic operations with spiking neural P systems. IEEE Trans. Nanobiosci. **11**(4), 366–374 (2006)

10. Stallings, W.: Cryptography and network security: principles and practices, 5th edn. Pearson Education, India (2006)
11. Diaz, C., Sánchez, G., Duchen, G., Nakano, M., Perez, H.: An efficient hardware implementation of a novel unary spiking neural network multiplier with variable dendritic delays. Neurocomputing **189**, 130–134 (2016)

A Rapid HMI Prototyping Based on Personality Traits and AI for Social Connected Thermostats

Juana Isabel Méndez[1](✉) ⓘ, Pedro Ponce[1] ⓘ, Marcel Pecina[1] ⓘ,
Gustavo Schroeder[1] ⓘ, Sergio Castellanos[2] ⓘ, Therese Peffer[3] ⓘ, Alan Meier[4] ⓘ,
and Arturo Molina[1] ⓘ

[1] School of Engineering and Sciences, Tecnologico de Monterrey, México City, México
{A01165549,A01337182,A01650799}@itesm.mx, {pedro.ponce,
armolina}@tec.mx
[2] Department of Civil, Architectural and Environmental Engineering,
The University of Texas at Austin, Austin, TX, USA
sergioc@utexas.edu
[3] Institute for Energy and Environment, University of California, Berkeley, CA 94720, USA
tpeffer@berkeley.edu
[4] Energy and Efficiency Institute, University of California, Davis, CA 95616, USA
akmeier@ucdavis.edu

Abstract. Residential energy efficiency decreases electricity consumption and saves energy worldwide. Moreover, 86% of the residential buildings use thermostats that control the Heating, Ventilation, and Air-Conditioning (HVAC) system. The energy consumption can decrease from 11% to 18% due to user behavior modifications accompanied by strategies such as feedback and gamification. Social products use gamification features to interact with the end-user and other devices. However, tailored gamified Human-Machine Interfaces (HMI) must consider five personality traits. As a result, implementing Artificial Neural Networks (ANN) within the HMIs can classify the type of user and deploy a tailored strategy to save energy and promote behavioral changes. Thus, this paper shows a three-step framework to develop a rapid prototype using Arduino and MATLAB/Simulink to predict which type of gamified interface is needed depending on the personality traits.

Keywords: Connected thermostat · Gamification · Tailored HMI · ANN · Arduino · Personality traits

1 Introduction

In Mexico, the residential sector consumes 22.7% of Mexican electrical energy consumption [1]. Studies reveal that 2/5 to 3/5 of the residential consumption relies on the Heating, Ventilation, and Air-Conditioning (HVAC) systems [2–4]; whereas, more than 4/5 of the homes have thermostats that control the HVAC systems [5, 6]. A connected thermostat reduces energy consumption from 10% to 35% [7]. Thus, end-users interact

© Springer Nature Switzerland AG 2021
I. Batyrshin et al. (Eds.): MICAI 2021, LNAI 13068, pp. 216–227, 2021.
https://doi.org/10.1007/978-3-030-89820-5_18

directly with the thermostat to change the setpoint or even let it as the default schedule of the thermostat. Research indicates that feedback, financial information, social influence, goal setting, tips, and gamification strategies can reduce energy up to 21.7% [8]. Gamification strategies or game elements within products and services promote goal-oriented activities. For instance, end-users can reduce energy through gamification without feeling compromised and become energy aware [9–14]. Gamification uses environments as online platforms, mobile applications, or Human-Machine Interfaces (HMIs) to teach, engage, and motivate individuals to shape attitudes like energy and environmental concern [6, 10, 11].

Personalizing interfaces expand the horizon in how customers use gamified applications as strategies fit with their interests [10]. Besides, social features with gamification strategies must be included in the design process to stimulate consumer behavior [6, 15]. For example, in [10], they proposed to tailor gamified interfaces into a connected thermostat interface to reduce energy consumption; they outlined that knowing the type of consumer allows tailored interfaces to promote energy concern. Thus, knowing the types of users allows them to understand their needs to propose tailored interfaces [10, 16–21].

Rapid prototyping provides a preliminary version of the final product to evaluate its design and technology [22]. Smart Hybrid Prototyping encourages interdisciplinary fields to create digital prototypes that evolve from a virtual to a physical product [23]. This type of prototyping combines mechanical engineering, software, electrics, electronics, and design. Arduino boards are used for rapid prototyping because they are low-cost, energy-efficient, use cross-platform software, and are easy to interface with [24]. V-Model for Systems Development iterates from the user requirements to the implemented solution by defining the project and integrating it [25].

On the other hand, Artificial Intelligence (AI) tries to reproduce the solution process of the brain. Artificial Neural Networks (ANN) generalize extracted information from experimental data, tables, or databases determined by human experts. The two most used topologies are the feed-forward or forward propagation network and the recurrent network. In the first type, the information flows from inputs to outputs and is exclusively forward. It spreads through multiple layers of units with no feedback connection and uses supervised learning methods. The second type has feedback connections, which can be derived in the evolution towards a stable state with no changes in the activation state of neurons [26]. This paper uses the feed-forward topology to propose a rapid prototype that predicts the required gamified interface based on the personality traits in an Arduino board.

2 Material and Methods

An online survey with 89 questions was launched from December 2020 to March 2021 [27]. This survey collected 130 responses with the following sections:

1. Survey title and objective: Explain to the respondent the aim of this survey.
2. Informed consent: This section provided information about the final usage and anonymity of the survey.

3. Characteristics of the respondent: gender, age, educational level, employment, income, annual income, home type, and resident location.
4. Gamified interface: The respondent selected one of three gamified connected thermostat interfaces proposed by Ponce et al. [10] to reduce energy consumption.
5. Big Five personality traits: 44 questions were originally developed by the Berkeley Personality Lab [28] and translated into Spanish and deployed in Mexico by Zamorano et al. [29]. These questions classified five types of personality traits.
6. Type of gamification user: 24 questions to classify six types of gamified users. The questions were validated in the Spanish-speaking community [17].
7. Type of energy user: 10 questions to classify five types of energy-end user segmentation [20].

Table 1 displays the software and hardware required for the rapid prototype.

Table 1. Rapid prototype requirements

Software	Hardware
Neural network pattern recognition toolbox from MATLAB	Arduino UNO board, USB Cable, Breadboard, jumpers, and 220 Ω resistors
MATLAB/Simulink	Five digital inputs: buttons
Neural network block library	Five analog inputs: potentiometers
	Six digital/analog inputs: LEDs

2.1 New Dataset Creation as a Result of the Survey

The 130 observations with the personality traits and the gamified connected thermostat interface generated a new dataset. This normalized dataset had nine variables: ID, Openness, Conscientiousness, Extraversion, Agreeableness, Neuroticism, Interface A, Interface B, and Interface C.

3 Methodology

Exploratory analysis and a predictive model were developed from the survey explained in Sect. 2. Table 2 describes the characteristics of each personality trait used in this paper for rapid prototyping.

This paper considered the Big-Five personality traits for the deployment of rapid prototyping as these traits are greatly supported and accepted [21, 28]. In addition, the survey questions were validated for the Mexican sample [29].

3.1 Two-Layer Feed-Forward ANN Classification

Interconnected perceptrons form a multilayer feed-forward ANN in which data and calculation flow in a single direction, from the input to the output data. The number of layers in an ANN is the number of layers of perceptrons [26]. Figure 1 shows the main structure of the ANN. This ANN was a two-layer feed-forward network, with a hidden sigmoid layer and SoftMax output neurons, and whose input data flow forward to the output data. The network was trained with scaled conjugate gradient backpropagation. The input values were each personality trait, and the output values were the gamified interface selected from the survey (Interface A, B, or C).

Table 2. Personality traits and their characteristics are commonly known as the Big Five [21]

Personality trait	Characteristics
Openness (O)	They appreciate divergent thinking and prefer learning new things on online platforms
Conscientiousness (C)	They are rule followers with clear goals in life and with a positive attitude regarding energy conservation
Extraversion (E)	They are optimistic, assertive, and energized by social interactions. Stronger extraversion personalities are inclined to save energy
Agreeableness (A)	They are tolerant, sympathetic, altruistic, modest, and cooperative with inclinations to save energy
Neuroticism (N)	They are impulsive, stressed, and bad. Besides, higher levels of neuroticism indicate a higher attitude to save energy

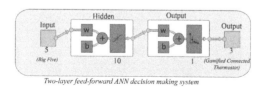

Two-layer feed-forward ANN decision making system

Fig. 1. Two-layer feed-forward network, with hidden sigmoid layer and SoftMax output neurons. This ANN was trained with scaled conjugate gradient backpropagation

3.2 Rapid Prototyping Using Arduino UNO and MATLAB/Simulink

Once the ANN was trained, an NNET block was exported into Simulink and programmed using the Arduino library to deploy the network into an Arduino UNO board. The prototype used five digital inputs as push buttons for each personality and digital outputs as LEDs for the first case. For the second case, the analog inputs were the potentiometers, and the analog outputs were the LED dimming. These prototypes predicted which type of gamified interface was needed depending on the personality traits. The difference was that the second case considered wider personality traits to predict the level of interest of the gamified interface. Thus, multiple personalities can be chosen in both cases.

4 Proposed Framework

Figure 2 depicts the proposed three-step framework. During the first step or the knowledge base step, a survey was conducted to relate the personality traits with three proposed gamified interfaces. The second step, or the decision system step, consisted of creating a database for training and validating the multilayer feed-forward ANN; the input values were the personality traits. The output values were the gamified interface. Finally, during the third step or evaluation step, the ANN was uploaded onto the Arduino board. One of the three interfaces will appear on the connected thermostat gamified interface depending on the output value. The feedback and adjustments give insights regarding user engagement and interest in saving energy; real-time reductions can be visualized by connecting this interface with the electric bill.

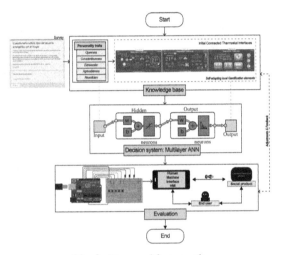

Fig. 2. Proposed framework.

4.1 Knowledge Base

The survey explained in Sect. 2 was considered to classify the user type: personality traits, gamified user, and energy consumer. The survey had 130 responses, once removed the outliers, the responses were 124: 11 responses for Interface A; 56 responses for Interfaces B; and 57 responses for Interface C. Figure 3 shows the histogram of each interface and personality trait with the minimum, maximum, mean and standard deviation for each personality trait. Hence, medium openness and agreeableness traits preferred interface B and C. Medium levels of conscientiousness, extraversion, and neuroticism had an equal preference for the three interfaces.

Being one the maximum degree of the personality and zero the minimum. In interface A, seven respondents had an openness trait with a degree from 0.55 to 0.98, 8 respondents had a conscientiousness trait with a degree from 0.51 to 0.78, 6 respondents had an extraversion trait from 0.33 to 0.6. Agreeableness had six votes with a degree of 0.56 to 0.84 and 5 votes with a degree of 0.28 to 0.56, meaning that this type of user had a higher or lower degree of this trait for this interface. The same happened with the neuroticism trait; six votes went to the mid-high level of neuroticism, whereas five votes went to the low-mid level. The interface B had 20 votes for a medium to a high level of openness; it had 19 votes for a medium level of conscientiousness, 21 votes for a low level of extraversion, 17 votes for high levels of agreeableness, and a medium to low level of neuroticism. Interface C, like the previous interface, had 23 votes for medium to a high level of openness, had a medium level of conscientiousness with 26 votes, had 19 votes for medium to low level of extraversion, had equally 16 votes for a range of medium to a high level of agreeableness, and had a low level of neuroticism.

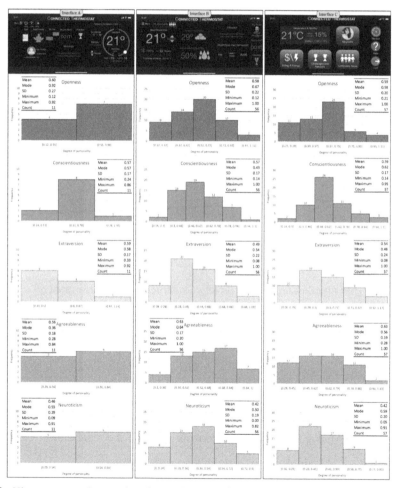

Fig. 3. Histogram graphs per interface. The three interfaces display the minimum, mean, maximum, and standard deviation per personality trait.

4.2   Decision System

This subsection presents the two cases; both cases used the Simulink Support Package for Arduino Hardware to program both cases and uploaded it into an Arduino UNO board. Figure 4 depicts the Neural Network tools used for each case.

Case 1: Digital Inputs and Outputs
The Neural Pattern Recognition tool solves a pattern-recognition problem with a two-layer feed-forward network. It has a sigmoid hidden and SoftMax output neurons to classify vectors arbitrarily, and it was trained with scaled conjugate gradient backpropagation. This tool requires digital inputs and outputs; therefore, a dataset with the 124 observations presented in Subsect. 4.1 was created considering values greater or equal to 0.5 as one and below 0.5 as zero; regarding the type of interface, interface A equal to 0, interface B to 1, and interface C to 2. Nevertheless, this tool required digital outputs; thus, the dataset was split into two new datasets. The first dataset considered the answers selected for interface A and interface B. In contrast, the second dataset considered interface A and interface C answers, meaning that interface C equaled one instead of two. The dataset was divided this way because Interface A had few observations, and the tool would easily solve the pattern recognition with higher accuracy. Thus, both ANN had five inputs (personality traits) and one output (Interface A or B, or Interface C or D).

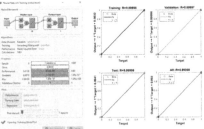

(a) Digital case: Neuronal Network structure and performance

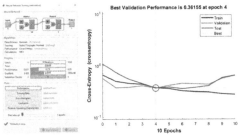

(b) Analog case: Neuronal Network structure and regression

Fig. 4. Neural network structure from each case.

Case 2: Analog Inputs and Outputs

The Neural Network Tool (nntool) is a graphical user interface that opens the Network/Data Manager window to create the ANN [30]. During this case, the network type was the Feed-forward backpropagation, with a network training function that updates weight and bias values using the Levenberg-Marquardt optimization method. Gradient descent with momentum weight and bias learning function and a mean squared error performance function. This ANN uses a two-layer feed-forward network with ten neurons in its hidden layer and uses a hyperbolic tangent sigmoid transfer function. Hence, the values from the original dataset were multiplied by 1023 due to the voltage used for Analog inputs in Arduino. For the output values, an additional column was added to later manage in Simulink the ANN. As a result, the output values considered two ranges 0 or 255 depending on the selected interface.

4.3 Evaluation

Table 3 exemplifies three of the 124 responses explained in Sect. 4.1 for case 1 and case 2. The complete table can be found at [31]. This table compared the answers from the survey with the ANN. Thus, the answers were transformed into digital and analog values (explained in the previous section). The table shows the respondents' selected interface and the ANN interface to validate the prediction of this network. The ANN correctly predicted the 124 responses. Some respondents had the same combination of personalities but selected different interfaces; for instance, they selected interface B or C; therefore, the ANN displayed both interfaces. For example, ID 116 selected interface B, but the ANN also proposed interface C due to ID 23 selected interface C [31]. In addition, a fifth row was proposed to see what happened if the digital and analog inputs had zero values. Thus, as an initial state, where no users' profiling exists, the predicted interface for the digital case suggests proposing the three interfaces. In contrast, the analog case only proposes interface C.

Figure 5 (a) displays the MATLAB/Simulink dashboard for the digital case, and Fig. 5 (b) for the analog case helps as a guideline to visualize the interfaces to propose. The input values are the personality traits, and the output value is the type of interface. For example, interface A was on both Neural Network blocks; thus, the values below 0.5 belong to Interface A, and greater or equal than 0.5 belongs to Interface B or C. The Custom Neural Network 2 considered Interface A for the analog case because R's regression model equals 0.99.

5   Results: Arduino Prototype

The artificial neural network configuration trained in Matlab and implemented in Simulink was deployed into an Arduino board (See Fig. 6). Figure 6 (a) shows the digital prototype that considered five digital input values as push buttons and three digital output values as LEDs. Thus, when a digital input was activated, it emulated that the end-user was high in certain or multiple personality traits. Multiple buttons can be pushed simultaneously, meaning that this person had one or more personality traits. Hence, the analog case implies that the individual had or not had that personality trait.

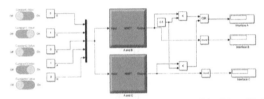

(a) Digital case dashboard programmed in Simulink

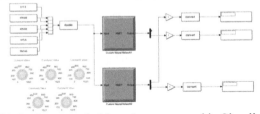

(b) Analog case dashboard programmed in Simulink

Fig. 5. Programmed Simulink dashboard. (a) Digital case and (b) Analog case.

Table 3. Exemplification of inputs and outputs as a result of the survey. The complete table is reported in [31]. The inputs and outputs belong to the data transformed for cases 1 and 2 and are explained in Sect. 4.2.

ID	Type	Inputs (personality traits)					Selected HMI (survey)	Predicted output (Interface)		
		O	C	E	A	N		A	B	C
127	*Digital*	0	0	1	0	1	A	1	0	0
	Analog	0.38	0.24	0.58	0.28	0.27		0.99	2E–4	9E–4
116	*Digital*	1	0	0	1	1	B	0	1	1
	Analog	0.5	0.43	0.42	0.6	0.55		0	1	1
73	*Digital*	0	1	0	1	0	C	1	1	1
	Analog	0.42	0.62	0.46	0.68	0.32		0	1	1
Proposed	*Digital*	0	0	0	0	0	None	1	1	1
	Analog	0	0	0	0	0		1E–8	2E–5	1

Figure 6 (b) depicts the analog experiment that considered five analog input values as potentiometers and three analog output values as LEDs; a led with different input voltage value changes; hence, the light intensity generated by the LED changes this implies the level of personality traits. Multiple potentiometers can be rotated simultaneously, meaning that this person had a degree of each personality trait.

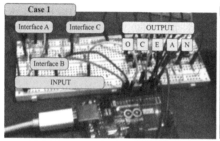
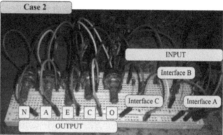

(a) Arduino prototype for the digital case.

(b) Arduino prototype for the analog case.

Fig. 6. Arduino prototype for each case.

6 Discussion

Rapid prototyping implements low-cost solutions to solve specific goals. There are models as the V model that helps to propose projects by understanding the end-user requirement and giving a human-centered approach. This paper proposes an Arduino rapid prototype that considers personality traits to propose a possible interface that these users could prefer and help save energy through this gamification strategy. On the other hand, implementing tailored gamified interfaces on connected thermostats reduces energy at home while it is fun and rewarding. Moreover, using ANN to predict the interface to be used on an HMI help in understanding which type of gamification strategies and the interface can teach the end-user to save energy.

This survey brought insights regarding end-users preferences toward selecting interfaces based on the visual display. Unfortunately, interface A had few responses; thus, two possible options come from that insight. The first option is to change the interface and propose another based on the majority of the personality traits and consider the Octalysis framework proposed by Chou [11] and complimented for energy applications by Ponce et al. [10]. The second option is to ask the respondents which type of gamification element they would prefer to watch on the HMI.

7 Conclusion

Saving energy in smart homes by connected devices is not good enough since HMI requires a tailored design that profiles the end-user to help them become energy aware and learn the benefits of saving energy or money, depending on the users' interests. This paper proposes a topology for designing interfaces tailored using ANN into a connected thermostat interface. The results show that the characteristics of each personality are covered and, thus, end-users select tailored interfaces.

Moreover, a rapid prototype for validating the implementation on a low-cost digital controller is proposed to support profiling end-user types to deploy tailored interfaces.

As a result, this structure can design tailored gamified HMI that engages and motivates individuals to save energy and interact with household appliances or devices as the connected thermostats.

Acknowledgments. Research Project supported by Tecnologico de Monterrey and CITRIS under the collaboration ITESM-CITRIS Smart thermostat, deep learning, and gamification project (https://citris-uc.org/2019-itesm-seed-funding/).

References

1. Secretaría de Energía: SENER | Sistema de Información Energética | Electricidad. https://sie.energia.gob.mx/bdiController.do?action=cuadro&subAction=applyOptions. Accessed 15 June 2021
2. Bienvenido-Huertas, D., Sánchez-García, D., Rubio-Bellido, C., Pulido-Arcas, J.A.: Influence of the improvement in thermal expectation levels with adaptive setpoint temperatures on energy consumption. Appl. Sci. **10**, 5282 (2020). https://doi.org/10.3390/app10155282
3. Tomat, V., Ramallo-González, A.P., Skarmeta Gómez, A.F.: A comprehensive survey about thermal comfort under the IoT paradigm: is crowdsensing the new horizon? Sensors **20**, 4647 (2020). https://doi.org/10.3390/s20164647
4. Chaudhuri, T., Soh, Y.C., Li, H., Xie, L.: A feed-forward neural network based indoor-climate control framework for thermal comfort and energy saving in buildings. Appl. Energy **248**, 44–53 (2019). https://doi.org/10.1016/j.apenergy.2019.04.065
5. Peffer, T., Pritoni, M., Meier, A., Aragon, C., Perry, D.: How people use thermostats in homes: a review. Build. Environ. **46**, 2529–2541 (2011). https://doi.org/10.1016/j.buildenv.2011.06.002
6. Méndez, J.I., Ponce, P., Meier, A., Peffer, T., Mata, O., Molina, A.: S4 product design framework: a gamification strategy based on type 1 and 2 fuzzy logic. In: McDaniel, T., Berretti, S., Curcio, I.D.D., Basu, A. (eds.) ICSM 2019. LNCS, vol. 12015, pp. 509–524. Springer, Cham (2020). https://doi.org/10.1007/978-3-030-54407-2_43
7. Cetin, K.S., O'Neill, Z.: Smart meters and smart devices in buildings: a review of recent progress and influence on electricity use and peak demand. Curr. Sustain./Renew. Energ. Rep. **4**(1), 1–7 (2017). https://doi.org/10.1007/s40518-017-0063-7
8. Chatzigeorgiou, I.M.: Andreou, GT: a systematic review on feedback research for residential energy behavior change through mobile and web interfaces. Renew. Sustain. Energ. Rev. **135**, 110187 (2021). https://doi.org/10.1016/j.rser.2020.110187
9. Avila, M., Méndez, J.I., Ponce, P., Peffer, T., Meier, A., Molina, A.: Energy management system based on a gamified application for households. Energies **14**, 3 445 (2021). https://doi.org/10.3390/en14123445
10. Ponce, P., Meier, A., Mendez, J., Peffer, T., Molina, A., Mata, O.: Tailored gamification and serious game framework based on fuzzy logic for saving energy in smart thermostats. J. Clean. Product. **262** 121167 (2020) .https://doi.org/10.1016/j.jclepro.2020.121167.
11. Chou, Y.: Actionable Gamification Beyond Points, Badges, and Leaderboards. CreateSpace Independent Publishing Platform (2015)
12. AlSkaif, T., Lampropoulos, I., van den Broek, M., van Sark, W.: Gamification-based framework for engagement of residential customers in energy applications. Energ. Res. Soc. Sci. **44**, 187–195 (2018). https://doi.org/10.1016/j.erss.2018.04.043
13. Wee, S.-C., Choong, W.-W.: Gamification: Predicting the effectiveness of variety game design elements to intrinsically motivate users' energy conservation behaviour. J. Environ. Manag. **233**, 97–106 (2019). https://doi.org/10.1016/j.jenvman.2018.11.127
14. Schiele, K.: Utilizing gamification to promote sustainable practices. In: Marques, J. (ed.) Handbook of Engaged Sustainability, pp. 427–444. Springer, Cham (2018). https://doi.org/10.1007/978-3-319-71312-0_16

15. Ponce, P., Meier, A., Miranda, J., Molina, A., Peffer, T.: The next generation of social products based on sensing, smart and sustainable (S3) features: a smart thermostat as case study. In: 9th IFAC Conference on Manufacturing Modelling, Management and Control, p. 6 (2019)

16. Shen, M., Lu, Y., Tan, K.Y.: Big five personality traits, demographics and energy conservation behaviour: a preliminary study of their associations in singapore. Energ. Procedia. **158**, 3458–3463 (2019). https://doi.org/10.1016/j.egypro.2019.01.927

17. Tondello, G.F., Mora, A., Marczewski, A., Nacke, L.E.: Empirical validation of the gamification user types hexad scale in English and Spanish. Int. J. Hum. Comput. Stud. **127**, 95–111 (2019). https://doi.org/10.1016/j.ijhcs.2018.10.002

18. Ponce, P., Peffer, T., Molina, A.: Framework for communicating with consumers using an expectation interface in smart thermostats. Energ. Build. **145**, 44–56 (2017). https://doi.org/10.1016/j.enbuild.2017.03.065

19. Milfont, T.L., Sibley, C.G.: The big five personality traits and environmental engagement: Associations at the individual and societal level. J. Environ. Psychol. **32**, 187–195 (2012). https://doi.org/10.1016/j.jenvp.2011.12.006

20. Frankel, D., Heck, S., Tai, H.: Using a consumer-segmentation approach to make energy-efficiency gains in the residential market **9** (2013)

21. John, O.P., Srivastava, S.: The big five trait taxonomy: history, measurement, and theoretical perspectives. In: Handbook of personality: Theory and research, 2nd ed, pp. 102–138. Guilford Press, New York, NY, US (1999)

22. What is Rapid Prototyping, protyping techniques, benefits and limitations, https://engineeringproductdesign.com/knowledge-base/rapid-prototyping-techniques/. Ac-cessed 16 June 2021

23. Gengnagel, C., Nagy, E., Stark, R. (eds.): Rethink! Prototyping. Springer, Cham (2016). https://doi.org/10.1007/978-3-319-24439-6

24. Kondaveeti, H.K., Kumaravelu, N.K., Vanambathina, S.D., Mathe, S.E., Vappangi, S.: A systematic literature review on prototyping with arduino: applications, challenges, advantages, and limitations. Comput. Sci. Rev. **40**, 100364 (2021). https://doi.org/10.1016/j.cosrev.2021.100364

25. Ponce, P., Mendez, E., Molina, A.: Teaching fuzzy controllers through a V-model based methodology. **17**

26. Ponce, P.: Inteligencia Artificial con Aplicaciones a la Ingeniería. Marcombo (2011)

27. Cuestionario sobre tipo de usuario energético en el hogar. https://docs.google.com/forms/d/e/1FAIpQLSf138hb55q2isxsRO_ag0lyINvEOH4ju32U5W8Gcian-8rdSA/viewform?usp=send_form&usp=embed_facebook. Accessed 16 June 2021

28. Berkeley Personality Lab: The Big Five Inventory, https://www.ocf.berkeley.edu/~johnlab/bfi.htm. Accessed 09 Nov 2020

29. Zamorano, E.R., Carrillo, C.Á., Silva, A.P., Sandoval, A.M., Pastrana, I.M.R.: Psychometric. **37**, 8 (2014)

30. MathWorks: Open Network/Data Manager - MATLAB nntool, https://www.mathworks.com/help/deeplearning/ref/nntool.html. Accessed 21 June 2021

31. Méndez, J.I., et al.: Table_3_CompleteAnswers.xlsx. https://docs.google.com/spreadsheets/d/17UH7lPAVJHZ_f4B3k45OX9tQUnydUqY1/edit?usp=sharing&ouid=117422985426650013513&rtpof=true&sd=true. Accessed 26 Aug 2021

Machine Learning Framework for Antalgic Gait Recognition Based on Human Activity

Juan-Carlos Gonzalez-Islas[1,2], Omar-Arturo Dominguez-Ramirez[1(✉)],
Omar Lopez-Ortega[1], Rene-Daniel Paredes-Bautista[3],
and David Diazgiron-Aguilar[2]

[1] Autonomous University of the Hidalgo State, Hidalgo, Mexico
{juan_gonzalez7024,omar,lopezo}@uaeh.edu.mx
[2] Technological University of Tulancingo, Hidalgo, Mexico
1718110586@utectulancingo.edu.mx
[3] Integral Rehabilitation Centre of Hidalgo, Hidalgo, Mexico
direccioncrih.dif@hidalgo.gob.mx

Abstract. Antalgic gait is one of the most common abnormalities in human beings during the walking. This work presents a framework for the automatic recognition for antalgic and non-antalgic gaits, using the gyroscope of a smartphone for data acquisition. The test carried out was 10-meter walk, with a population of 30 subjects, 40% antalgics, and 60% non-antalgics; 80% was used in the training stage, and the rest for the test. A hypothesis testing and p-value method were developed to determine the statistical difference between both datasets and validate the usefulness of data in the features selection and classification approach. The classification algorithms used were: i) K-Nearest Neighbors (k-NN), ii) Naive Bayes (NB), iii) Support Vector Machines (SVM), iv) Discriminant Analysis (DA), v) Decision Trees (DT), and vi) Classification Ensembles (CE). The performance of the algorithms was evaluated using the metrics: Accuracy (ACC), Sensitivity (R), Specificity (SP), Precision (P), and F-measure (F). k-NN and SVM were the models with better performance with Accuracy of 99.44% and 98.88%, respectively. The obtained results allow to determine the feasibility of implementing this framework in real scenarios for its use in the improvement of diseases diagnosis and decision-making to antalgic gait diseases.

Keywords: Automatic gait recognition · Gait analysis · Antalgic gait · Activity recognition · Hypothesis testing

1 Introduction

Gait analysis is the systematic study of human motion during the walk, to obtain detailed diagnoses and planning optimal treatments. This analysis is usually based on the experience of the specialist, however, it has been improved by

© Springer Nature Switzerland AG 2021
I. Batyrshin et al. (Eds.): MICAI 2021, LNAI 13068, pp. 228–239, 2021.
https://doi.org/10.1007/978-3-030-89820-5_19

advances in instrumentation to measure the biomechanics of the human body when performing this function [24]. A large amount of data and multivariate, multidimensional, heterogeneous, and uncertain nature of the gait analysis problem, can be solved from an approach based on machine learning known as automatic gait recognition. This refers to a computational approach to pattern recognition, in which the walking patterns or properties of different subjects are evaluated and compared to determine styles of walk or pathologies, based on the human locomotion assessment [4, 6].

In some areas such as robotics, biomechanics, gender classification, surveillance, sports, rehabilitation, diagnosis of diseases affecting the neuromuscular and musculoskeletal systems such as Parkinson's disease, muscular dystrophy, arthritis, cerebral palsy, idiopathic scoliosis, stroke, myelodysplasia, multiple sclerosis, among others, gait assessment has been used [14, 25, 27]. Antalgic gait is one of the most common abnormalities, the majority of alterations in bones, muscles, joints, and soft tissues derived in this type of gait are not so evident, one of its characteristics is the presence of lameness in the gait pattern, which causes the support and swing phases to be shortened. The conditions that generally lead to this type of gait are: i) knee osteoarthritis [2, 15], ii) rheumatoid arthritis [18] or iii) arthritis due to trauma or infection [13].

Nowadays, there are multiple platforms for gait analysis, mainly based on markers, markerless [10], wearable sensors [22] and floor sensors [3], which have advantages and disadvantages depending on the purpose. The acceleration and angular velocity of the joints of the musculoskeletal system of a person during the gait cycle, are very useful variables to differentiate and identify a person concerning others. Commonly, sensors are placed on the parts of the body to be tested [19]. The technological development of wearable sensors and portable electronics has allowed their integration into smartphones, which in addition to being used for the recognition of activities [1], can be used to acquire signals such as acceleration and speed while walking [26].

1.1 Related Work

Automatic gait recognition to classify normal and 5 types of abnormal gaits such as antalgic have been reported in [12], which was based on a closed recurrent unit (GRU) and artificial vision, with an Accuracy of 90.13%, and in [16] it is reported up to 88.68% recognition rate using Bayesian networks and an RBG-D sensor to recognize this kind of walk. In [6], with the same purpose and also using computer vision techniques, it was shown that the use of other classification algorithms such as artificial neural networks (ANN), convolutional neural networks (CNN), and k-nearest neighbors (k-NN), can produce high recognition rates, but that can still be improved.

Although systems based on computer vision are useful options, there are factors associated with both, the sensor and the environment, that limit its performance. Therefore, the use of inertial units is useful, as demonstrated at the time with an Accuracy of 94.4% in [23], using kNN as a classification algorithm. In [9] it was shown that the use of accelerometers for the same purpose allows a recognition rate of 83.3% through statistical techniques. Increasing the number of inertial units (2 accelerometers) increases the processing complexity but improves the rates of the gait recognition [8]. In the same way, [19] have generated one of the largest databases (OUISIR) using 4 accelerometers and gyroscope units to identify 3 types of walking surface: i) horizontal, ii) positive slope and iii) negative slope, significantly improving the performance of previous systems. However, the tests carried out do not have a practical application in the diagnosis of diseases related to antalgic gait.

The use of sensors embedded in a smartphone partially solves the problem of instrumentation and signal conditioning, in [1] this approach has been used to recognize human activities such as walking with an Accuracy of 95.6% implementing SVM or quantify Parkinson's disease severity [28]. In [5] gait recognition is reported with a recognition rate of 87.6% and 86.7% using LibSVM and tree logistic model, respectively. In [11] author uses the accelerometer embedded in a smartphone and Support Vector Machines (SVM) which to this end reports an accuracy of 91%.

1.2   Problem Statement and Solution Proposal

Although there are many works on automatic gait recognition, few are developed to identify antalgic gait based on the musculoskeletal biomechanics using a inertial sensor embedded in a smartphone as data acquisition platform. In addition, it is necessary to improve the classification performance in the framework based on optimization of the features extraction and selection, as well as classification stages. Therefore, in this paper, the problem of recognizing people with an antalgic (A) gait pattern and a non-antalgic (NA) (non-diagnosed gait diseases) gait is addressed. The development of an automatic gait recognition framework to classify between both types of gait is presented, using the embedded gyroscope of a smartphone as a data acquisition device.

1.3   Paper Organization

To describe this work, the article is organized as follows: Sect. 1, the introduction and contributions to the literature on the automatic recognition of antalgic gait are presented. The automatic antalgic gait recognition framework and each of its modules are described in Sect. 2. The experimental results and a discussion about them are provided in Sect. 3. Finally, the conclusions and future work are presented.

2   Antalgic Gait Recognition Framework

The antalgic gait recognition framework proposed in this work as shown in Fig. 1, consists of two phases: the training phase using 80% of data and testing one with 20% of data. The phases included are: i) gait data acquisition, ii) data access and pre-processing, iii) feature extraction, iv) feature selection, v) model training, and vi) classification [15,17].

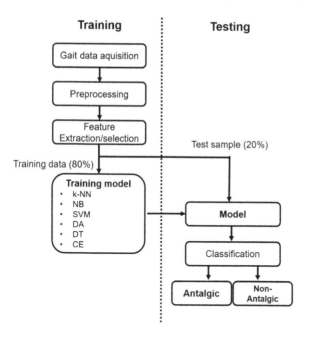

Fig. 1. Antalgic gait recognition framework.

2.1   Data Acquisition

Data acquisition is the first stage, this module is required for collecting human gait data [26]. The temporal-spatial dataset set was acquired during the 10-meter walk test on a flat surface as shown in Fig. 2a, which is generally used to evaluate walking speed over a short distance [21]. As there is no difference between the gait pattern of men and women, so much in the magnitude of the parameters evaluated, in this work as the first stage, the experimental test was carried out with only 30 men between 18 and 49 years old [27], obtaining 18 (NA) and 12 (A) gait sequences. The gyroscope (BOSCH $bmi160$, $accuracy = 0.0001\,rad/s$, $maximum\,interval = 34.9\,rad/s$) embedded in a smartphone was used to collect the 3-axes angular velocity (ω) with a sample rate 406 Hz, and to eliminate high frequencies, a digital low-pass filter with a cutoff frequency of 0.5 Hz was applied. The device was arranged over the right knee joint as shown in Fig. 2b. The correspondence between the anatomical axes of the human body [27] and the axes of the gyroscope is: anterior with axis x, upper with axis y, while the right corresponds with axis z (Fig. 2c), respectively.

Data access and exploration is the next step after data acquisition. In this step, some examples are inspected through [20] visualizations. The raw data contains variable windows between 12 and 19 s of the gyroscope signals of both types of gait. An example of the original signals of the 3 axes Gx, Gy, and Gz of the gyroscope in the window of 2 and 8 s is shown in Fig. 3.

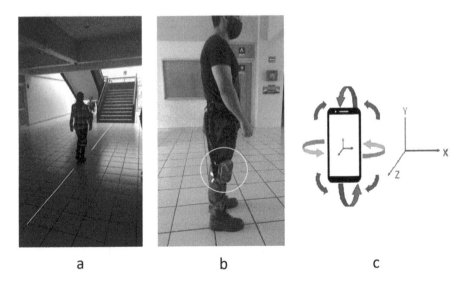

Fig. 2. Antalgic gait recognition framework.

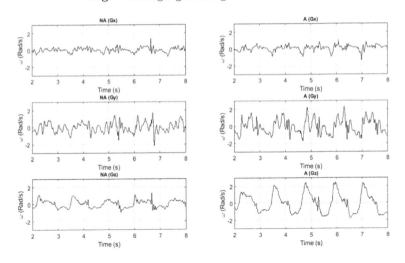

Fig. 3. Gyroscope signals (Gx, Gy, and Gz) without preprocessing for a sequence of: i) Non-Antalgic gait (left column) and ii) Antalgic gait (right column).

As it is shown in Fig. 3, the values of both non-antalgic and antalgic signals are different; it is possible to differentiate by simple visual inspection, however it does not represent the required numerical formality. To this end, a statistical proof for analytical argumentation is presented in subsect. 2.3.

2.2   Preprocessing

Unit preprocessing tasks such as data cleaning, data integration, data reduction, and data transformation, are used to solve problems of missing, noise, inconsistency, multiple sources, and redundancy in data [15]. In this work, to contain the 3 gyroscope signals Gx, Gy and Gz in the same dataset have been integrated. In addition, by extracting the data from the window between (4–8) s with a sample rate 100 Hz, a dimensionality reduction was made, which results in vectors of 407 data per signal with the same representativeness as the raw data.

2.3   Feature Extraction and Selection

To identify individuals in a general and non-redundant way, the gait recognition system must extract useful features from the raw data [26]. In the proposed approach, because the gait is a cyclic process, the basic characteristics to detect it from the signals acquired from the gyroscope Gx, Gy and Gz are: the arithmetic mean $\overline{X}$, the standard deviation (SD), the root mean square value (RMS) and the value of the principal components analysis (PCA) [26]. As a result of this stage, a dataset is obtained with 30 instances with 12 attributes and the corresponding class (antalgic and non-antalgic). The boxplot in Fig. 4 shows in summary the dataset obtained from this stage and allows to compare the data distribution for the arithmetic mean and standard deviation and Fig. 5 shows the distribution for the RMS and PCA for the antalgic a non-antalgic datasets.

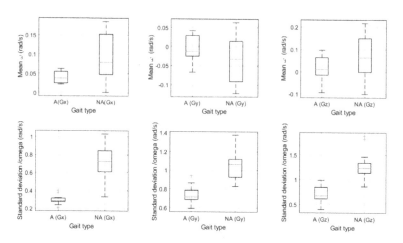

Fig. 4. Statistical representation of the distributions of the arithmetic mean and standard deviation of the preprocessed dataset of the signals of the 3 axes of the gyroscopes.

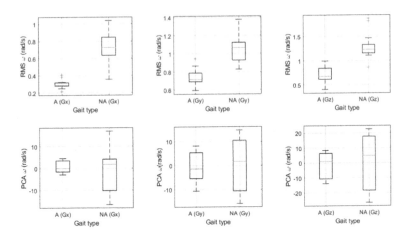

Fig. 5. Statistical representation of the distributions of the RMS and PCA values of the preprocessed dataset of the signals of the 3 axes of the gyroscopes.

Although the preview of the raw data and the boxplots of the dataset of the extracted features give graphic evidence of the differences between the antalgic and non-antalgic subjects, a more rigorous statistical proof is necessary. The hypothesis testing and the p-value method allows to determine if any observation could have occurred by chance, to test the similarity between 2 datasets and in data science it is used to improve the models in the feature selection stage. In this work, this approach is used to differentiate statistically both datasets. In addition, the results obtained from the test allow to support the selection of features. Firstly, once the extracted features dataset is available, the null hypothesis H_0: An antalgic subject is a casual measurement of non-antalgic group and alternative hypothesis H_1: Subjects with antalgic gait have a different distribution than non-antalgic subjects, are established. The value of statistical significance established for all cases is $\alpha = 0.05$. Subsequently, the Z-score (Z) for each feature dataset is calculated using Eq. 1.

$$Z = \frac{\overline{X} - \mu}{\frac{\sigma}{\sqrt{n}}} \tag{1}$$

Where, $\overline{X}$ is arithmetic mean of the non-antalgic dataset, σ is the (NA) standard deviation, μ is the mean of the antalgic dataset, $n = 12$. As following, using the Z-score table the p-value (p) is calculated and this value is compared whith the α value to reject or not reject H_0. If $p < \alpha$ then H_0 is rejected, else $p \geq \alpha$ H_0 is not rejected. Table 1 summarize the statistical values used for the hypothesis testing and p-value method. As it can be seen in Table 1, the hypothesis test and the p-value method allows to determine, that both datasets (NA) and (A) are statistically different concerning the mean, standard deviation and RMS value, that means, antalgic subjects belong to own distribution and the dataset can be classified into two classes. Therefore, the proof for PCA values states that

Table 1. Statistical values of the extracted features dataset, for the hypothesis testing and p-value method. Where R represents reject of H_0 and NR is no-reject H_0.

	$\overline{X}_{Gx}$	$\overline{X}_{Gy}$	$\overline{X}_{Gz}$	SD_{Gx}	SD_{Gy}	SD_{Gz}	RMS_{Gx}	RMS_{Gy}	RMS_{Gz}	PCA_{Gx}	PCA_{Gy}	PCA_{Gx}
$\overline{X}$	−0.092	−0.036	0.067	0.715	1.062	1.283	0.724	1.062	1.287	−0.411	0.185	0.774
σ	0.062	0.056	0.099	0.190	0.172	0.244	0.182	0.171	0.242	9.028	10.887	17.828
μ	0.030	−0.007	0.019	0.298	0.737	0.709	0.300	0.736	0.710	0.617	−0.278	−1.162
X	2.95	−1.75	−1.67	7.59	6.54	8.14	8.08	6.57	8.26	−0.40	0.15	0.38
p	0.001	0.040	0.040	0.000	0.000	0.000	0.000	0.000	0.000	0.350	0.440	0.350
H_0	R	R	R	R	R	R	R	R	R	NR	NR	NR

this feature cannot be applied to classify both datasets. Generally, due to the high dimensionality and redundancy of the extracted features, it is necessary to select the features that efficiently describe the input features and are optimal for classification, avoiding overfitting [20]. For this purpose, in adittion to the above, over the tuples:$\{\overline{X}_{Gx}, SD_{Gx}, RMS_{Gx}, PCA_{Gx}\}$; $\{\overline{X}_{Gy}, SD_{Gy}, RMS_{Gy}, PCA_{Gy}\}$ and $\{\overline{X}_{Gz}, SD_{Gz}, RMS_{Gz}, PCA_{Gz}\}$ the brute force method was used on the prototype-based partition clustering algorithm k-means [7], clustering 100% of the examples. From which it was determined that the mean, the standard deviation and the RMS value are the characteristics that best represent the data set of each instance with its respective class.

2.4   Training Model

The last step in the antalgic gait recognition framework is to classify the test gait sequences of each instance with the selected optimized features. For which the classification model is previously trained through supervised learning. At random, 80% of the dataset was used in the training phase, while the other 20% in the testing phase. The most used algorithms for gait recognition are i) K-nearest neighbors (kNN), ii) Naive-Bayes (NB), and iii) Support Vector Machines (SVM) [26], which in addition to Discriminant Analysis (DA), Decision Trees (DT), and Classification Ensembles (CE) are used in this work as a comparative study with the purpose to select the best method for this task.

2.5   Classification

For classification problems like this one, to determine which model is the best option to evaluate the performance of each classification algorithm for n repetitions, the most common metrics are accuracy (Acc) and F-measure (F). The first one is used when the true positives (TP) and true negatives (TN) are more important, while (F) is useful when the false negatives (FN) and false positives (FP) are crucial [25]. In this work, TP are correctly classified instances of antalgic gait, TN are correctly classified instances of non-antalgic gait, FP are instances misclassified as antalgic, and FN are instances misclassified as non-antalgic. Other metrics such as: Sensitivity (R), Specificity (SP), Precision (P) [12], are used to evaluate the performance. As following, the equations to calculate the metrics are described.

– Accuracy (Acc)

$$\overline{Acc} = \frac{1}{n} \sum_{i=1}^{n} \frac{TP_i + TN_i}{TP_i + TN_i + FP_i + FN_i} * 100 \tag{2}$$

– F-measure (F)

$$\overline{F} = \frac{1}{n} \sum_{i=1}^{n} \frac{2P_i R_i}{P_i + R_i} * 100 \tag{3}$$

– Sensitivity or Recall (R)

$$\overline{R} = \frac{1}{n} \sum_{i=1}^{n} \frac{TP_i}{TP_i + FN_i} * 100 \tag{4}$$

– Specificity (SP)

$$\overline{SP} = \frac{1}{n} \sum_{i=1}^{n} \frac{TN_i}{TN_i + FP_i} * 100 \tag{5}$$

– Precision (P)

$$\overline{P} = \frac{1}{n} \sum_{i=1}^{n} \frac{TP_i}{TP_i + FP_i} * 100 \tag{6}$$

3   Results and Discussion

A dataset of 30 measurements obtained from a 3-axes gyroscope was used to assess the performance of the proposed framework to classify between non-antalgic (60%) and antalgic (30%) gaits. To evaluate the performance of the framework of the proposed system with each algorithm, 30 repetitions with 80% of the data for training and 20% for randomly selected tests were carried out. Table 2 summarizes the average value of the proposed metrics.

Table 2 shows the accuracy and F-measure of each classifier. As it can be seen, the algorithms with the highest accuracy are k-NN (99.44%) and SVM

Table 2. Performance of the classification algorithms (%).

Model \ Metric	Acc (%)	R (%)	SP (%)	P (%)	F (%)
k-NN	99.44	100.00	99.33	98.33	98.88
NB	96.11	91.66	100.00	100.00	94.82
SVM	98.88	97.77	100.00	100.00	98.66
DA	98.33	99.16	98.33	98.33	98.41
DT	89.44	86.66	93.72	89.16	84.12
CE	89.44	88.22	91.22	87.22	87.34

(98.88%), and the worst models are DT and CE with (89.44%). Similarly, k-NN and SVM are the models with the best performance when evaluating the F-measure with 98.88% and 98.66%, respectively. In this work, due to the importance of the medical purpose, TP and TN are important for diagnosing patients with a disease derived from antalgic gait or who are healthy, for that reason, it is so useful accuracy than F-measure. Sensitivity (R) is the fraction of relevant instances recovered, it is the probability of correctly identifying antalgic gait in people characterized by this type of gait. Table 2 also summarizes the sensitivity, specificity, and precision of each model during the test stage.

Finally, Precision is the rate of relevant instances among retrieved instances, which implies the probability of correctly classifying antalgic individuals overall subjects with this condition, being very useful in this work. NB and SVM are the best models with this capacity, with a rate of 100% and with the lowest rank CE (87.22%). In general, on average, under the experimental conditions proposed, according to Table 2, the model with the best performance for the problem of classification of the antalgic and non-antalgic gaits treated is k-NN, with SVM being the ranked as second classifier and the worst option is CE.

4   Conclusions

In this paper, a framework for automatic antalgic gait recognition by using a smartphone was presented. The good performance of the system in the data acquisition stage allows determining the feasibility to implement low-cost instrumentation platforms based on inertial units in this type of studies, particularly to measure the amount of human activity through the use of embedded sensors on a smartphone during the gait cycle. Data cleaning, data reduction, and data integration techniques used in the pre-processing module of this work, based on filtering, sampling, and dimension reduction techniques, are necessary and sufficient according to the properties of the gyroscope signals. In the same way, the basic features extracted such as RMS value, arithmetic mean, standard deviation, and principal component analysis (PCA), maintained the integrity and essence of the raw data. The hypothesis testing and the p-value method over the features extracted except PCA, determined that both datasets (antalgic and non-antalgic) are statistically different and can be classified in two distinct classes. Using the force method as an input of the clustering algorithm (KMeans) to select the optimal features that cluster the datasets in its respectively class, founding the same result that in the previous approach. In this stage, for a larger dataset of features, another algorithm is necessary, such as independent component analysis (ICA), for example.

The classification models used in the framework such as k-NN, NB, SVM, DA, DT, CE are initially, according to its performance an option for the antalgic gait classification problem, being k-NN and SVM the best ranked in terms of classification Accuracy. The most common metrics used in automatic learning systems are: Accuracy, F-measure, Sensitivity, Specificity, and Precision, allowed to objectively evaluate the performance of classifiers, as well as to discern the scope of its application in the identification of people with an antalgic gait. Dividing the dataset into 80% for the training stage and 20% for testing, and performing 30 repetitions supports the performance of the framework in terms of statistical significance, however, it is necessary to have a number of greater instances of antalgic and non-antalgic gaits, of another age group and another gender. The proposed antalgic gait classification framework can be used in medical scenarios or home-based approaches to obtain objective diagnosis and support decision-making in treatments in conditions related to antalgic gait. In addition, the analysis in this type of gait and some others can be improved and expanded by carrying out other type of tasks in an experimental procedure such as going up and down stairs or by integrating multiple sources of biomechanical, clinical, demographic, and environmental data.

References

1. Anguita, D., Ghio, A., Oneto, L., Parra, X., Reyes-Ortiz, J.L.: Human activity recognition on smartphones using a multiclass hardware-friendly support vector machine. In: Bravo, J., Hervás, R., Rodríguez, M. (eds.) IWAAL 2012. LNCS, vol. 7657, pp. 216–223. Springer, Heidelberg (2012). https://doi.org/10.1007/978-3-642-35395-6_30

2. Brahim, A., et al.: A decision support tool for early detection of knee osteoarthritis using x-ray imaging and machine learning: data from the osteoarthritis initiative. Comput. Med. Imaging Graph. **73**, 11–18 (2019)

3. Brenton-Rule, A., Mattock, J., Carroll, M., et al.: Reliability of the tekscan matscan® system for the measurement of postural stability in older people with rheumatoid arthritis. J. Foot Ankle Res. **5**(1), 21 (2012)

4. Connor, P., Ross, A.: Biometric recognition by gait: a survey of modalities and features. Comput. Vis. Image Underst. **167**, 1–27 (2018)

5. Derawi, M., Bours, P.: Gait and activity recognition using commercial phones. Comput. Secur. **39**, 137–144 (2013)

6. Fathima, S.S.S., Banu, W.R.: Abnormal walk identification for systems using gait patterns. Biomed. Res. India **27**, S112–S117 (2016)

7. Frigui, H.: Clustering: algorithms and applications. In: 2008 First Workshops on Image Processing Theory, Tools and Applications, pp. 1–11. IEEE (2008)

8. Gafurov, D., Helkala, K., Søndrol, T.: Gait recognition using acceleration from mems. In: First International Conference on Availability, Reliability and Security (ARES 2006), p. 6. IEEE (2006)

9. Gafurov, D., Snekkenes, E., Bours, P.: Gait authentication and identification using wearable accelerometer sensor. In: 2007 IEEE Workshop on Automatic Identification Advanced Technologies, pp. 220–225. IEEE (2007)

10. Gu, X., Deligianni, F., Lo, B., Chen, W., Yang, G.Z.: Markerless gait analysis based on a single RGB camera. In: 2018 IEEE 15th International Conference on Wearable and Implantable Body Sensor Networks (BSN), pp. 42–45. IEEE (2018)

11. Hoang, T., Nguyen, T., Luong, C., Do, S., Choi, D.: Adaptive cross-device gait recognition using a mobile accelerometer. J. Inf. Process. Syst. **9**(2), 333–348 (2013)

12. Jun, K., Lee, Y., Lee, S., Lee, D.W., Kim, M.S.: Pathological gait classification using kinect v2 and gated recurrent neural networks. IEEE Access **8**, 139881–139891 (2020)

13. Khera, P., Kumar, N.: Role of machine learning in gait analysis: a review. J. Med. Eng. Technol. **44**(8), 441–467 (2020)
14. Kitade, I., et al.: Kinematic, kinetic, and musculoskeletal modeling analysis of gait in patients with cervical myelopathy using a severity classification. Spine J. **20**(7), 1096–1105 (2020)
15. Kokkotis, C., Moustakidis, S., Papageorgiou, E., Giakas, G., Tsaopoulos, D.: Machine learning in knee osteoarthritis: a review. Osteoarthritis Cartilage Open, 100069 (2020)
16. Kozlow, P., Abid, N., Yanushkevich, S.: Gait type analysis using dynamic Bayesian networks. Sensors **18**(10), 3329 (2018)
17. MathWorks, I.: Heart sound classifier. https://la.mathworks.com/matlabcentral// fileexchange/65286-heart-sound-classifier (2021). Accessed 06 Apr 2021
18. Nair, S.S., French, R.M., Laroche, D., Thomas, E.: The application of machine learning algorithms to the analysis of electromyographic patterns from arthritic patients. IEEE Trans. Neural Syst. Rehab. Eng. **18**(2), 174–184 (2009)
19. Ngo, T.T., Makihara, Y., Nagahara, H., Mukaigawa, Y., Yagi, Y.: The largest inertial sensor-based gait database and performance evaluation of gait-based personal authentication. Pattern Recogn. **47**(1), 228–237 (2014)
20. Paluszek, M., Thomas, S.: MATLAB Machine Learning. Apress, New York (2016)
21. Physiopedia: 10 metre walk test. https://physio-pedia.com.html (2021). Accessed 19 June 2021
22. Recher, F., Banos, O., Nikamp, C.D., Schaake, L., Baten, C.T., Buurkc, J.H.: Optimizing activity recognition in stroke survivors for wearable exoskeletons. In: 2018 7th IEEE International Conference on Biomedical Robotics and Biomechatronics (Biorob), pp. 173–178. IEEE (2018)
23. Rong, L., Jianzhong, Z., Ming, L., Xiangfeng, H.: A wearable acceleration sensor system for gait recognition. In: 2007 2nd IEEE Conference on Industrial Electronics and Applications, pp. 2654–2659. IEEE (2007)
24. Sharif Bidabadi, S., Tan, T., Murray, I., Lee, G.: Tracking foot drop recovery following lumbar-spine surgery, applying multiclass gait classification using machine learning techniques. Sensors **19**(11), 2542 (2019)
25. Singh, J.P., Jain, S., Arora, S., Singh, U.P.: Vision-based gait recognition: a survey. IEEE Access **6**, 70497–70527 (2018)
26. Wan, C., Wang, L., Phoha, V.V.: A survey on gait recognition. ACM Comput. Surv. (CSUR) **51**(5), 1–35 (2018)
27. Whittle, M.W.: Gait Analysis: An Introduction. Butterworth-Heinemann, UK (2014)
28. Zhan, A., et al.: Using smartphones and machine learning to quantify Parkinson disease severity: the mobile Parkinson disease score. JAMA Neurol. **75**(7), 876–880 (2018)

A New Approach for the Automatic Connection of Sensors to an IoT Platform

Hugo Estrada$^{(\boxtimes)}$ ⓘ, Juan José Flores, Alicia Martínez ⓘ, Jassón Flores ⓘ,
and Yasmin Hernández ⓘ

Tecnologico Nacional de México/CENIDET, Cuernavaca, Morelos, México
{hugo.ee,m20ce084,alicia.mr,jasson.fp,
yasmin.hp}@cenidet.tecnm.mx

Abstract. Today there are several platforms that allow the development of smart applications with the Internet of Things approach. These platforms process the context information produced by smart applications through different devices and sensors connected to the Internet. FIWARE is an open-source platform that impulses the standards creation for the development of smart applications and services of different domains, in the cloud. However, one of the main issues in the development of smart applications with these platforms has been the complexity associated to the connection between hardware and software. This paper presents a new approach for carrying on the automatic creation of software components that manage the communication between sensors and the FIWARE Platform. The proposed approach is based on the IoT agent mechanisms proposed by FIWARE Platform as an intermediary between devices and a IoT Platform. The paper also presents some examples of the software system that implements the proposed approach to automatically produce the code of the modules to manage the connection between sensor and FIWARE IoT Platform.

Keywords: Internet of Things · FIWARE platform · Software components · Agents

1 Introduction

Today, the Internet of Things and Artificial Intelligence are among the most important transformative technologies. The main idea of Internet of Things is creating an environment where objects recognize themselves and, they use the information of context to perform smart behaviors. In this sense, the objects can take decisions considering the information that, they can communicate about their context [1]. However, the Internet of Things faces significant challenges that could make it difficult to realize its potential benefits.

The complexity of solutions in the Internet of Things has required platforms that help to manage and combining physical devices and software systems. Some of these solutions implement technologies of the Internet of the Future based on platforms such as: Google Cloud Platform [2], Amazon Web Services IoT [3] or FIWARE [4].

© Springer Nature Switzerland AG 2021
I. Batyrshin et al. (Eds.): MICAI 2021, LNAI 13068, pp. 240–251, 2021.
https://doi.org/10.1007/978-3-030-89820-5_20

The FIWARE Platform offers software components (generic enablers) to perform big data analysis and provision of real-time metrics, manipulation of context information, real-time event analysis, collection of sensor information and action on actuators. in this platform the connections between physical devices and the cloud using Agents. Agents allow manage groups of devices and integrate the data they collect into a combined flow and send it back to smart Internet of Things applications. Currently, the configuration of the connection of the devices to the FIWARE cloud is done manually. This increases the complexity for unskilled developers of smart applications in the Internet of Things.

The difficulty of connecting a device or sensor with the FIWARE platform could increase with the use of agents. However, when a direct connection between sensors and FIWARE is created, this could cause severe security problems. This direct connection scheme can be broken allowing unauthorized access to the sensors data.

The objective of this paper is to present a new approach that allows the automatic creation of software components that manage communication between physical devices and an IoT platform using the concept of agents. This approach allows to reduce the complexity in the development of Internet of Things applications. Our approach permits to isolate to the developers from the manual configuration of software components to execute following actions: (a) obtain data readings from sensors, (b) translate the sensor data to FIWARE NGSI format; (c) configure a specific IoT agent, and finally (d) stablish the connection of Agent with the FIWARE Cloud.

This paper is organized as follows. Section 2 shows background and the related work. Section 3 presents the overview of the proposed approach. Section 4 presents our approach to connectivity between sensors and FIWARE. Section 5 shows the software system, which implement our proposed approach, and finally, Sect. 6 details the conclusions and future work.

2   Background and Related Work

2.1   Internet of Things

Some events in the world were relevant for the birth of the Internet of Things (IoT): the constant growth in the number of "things" connected to internet, the cheapening of electronic devices (sensors and actuators), the need for new solutions that permit the collection and analysis of data coming from sensors, and the need for solutions to enable the Things to modify their environment. As a result, the current IoT technology supports devices and Applications of IoT, which includes the services and standards necessary to connect, manage and protect different devices and applications of IoT.

The devices on IoT approach can be sensors, actuators, mobile devices, etc. All the data collected by these devices are stored in the cloud, so that they can have easy access to them, as well as providing greater security in the event of a mishap [5].

2.2   FIWARE Platform

FIWARE is a IoT platforms for the development and deployment of Internet of the Future applications. FIWARE aims to provide a fully open architecture that allows developers, service providers, enterprises and other organizations to develop products that meet their needs. FIWARE comprises a set of technologies called generic enablers which provide open interfaces for APIs and support interoperability with other generic enablers. These enablers arise as a proposal to respond to the need for approaches to the chosen in cities [6].

IoT Agents in FIWARE

Connecting "objects" or "things" implies the need to overcome a set of problems that arise in the different layers of the communication model. Due to the lack of globally accepted standards, a heterogeneous environment is required for positive devices using different protocols. For this reason, IoT agents were created together with the FIWARE platform, in order to allow a group of devices to send their data to the Orion Context Broker using their own native protocols. these agents act as intermediaries between the devices and IoT platforms. Thus, a developers must first determine the protocol with which the device communicates and thus select the appropriate IoT agent [7].

Mechanisms to Connect IoT Sensors with FIWARE

One of the current challenges in IoT is the current connection between IoT devices and the FIWARE platform, this connection that is currently made manually involves the configuration of physical devices to be able to link them with the appropriate IoT Agent.

This IoT agent requires to be configured for each communication protocol, which implies a thorough knowledge of the operation of the protocol and the agent in question. When an Agent uses a communication protocol that does not already have a standard will be necessary to create a specific IoT agent. This will involve coding the commands and attributes necessary for the IoT agent to function correctly.

Therefore, if exist an appropriate IoT agent then will be possible carry out the connection with the Orion Context Broker. This connection involves knowledge of the physical device, knowledge of IoT agents and knowledge the Orion Context Broker. The difficulty of making this connection is that the one that has caused that at present the connection is made in a direct way between the devices and the Orion Context Broker, which breaks with the ideal scheme and allows unauthorized access to the data read from the sensors [8].

2.3 Related Work

The main research works related to the proposed approach are described below. The research paper [9] presents an architecture that allows to capture sensors data from Programmable Logic Controllers (PCL) of old generations, also permits the transformation of the data to an IoT communication standard, and provides contextual information of data sources on demand to enable plug and play IoT connectivity. This paper also proposes a method that stores, processes and visualizes the data obtained from the connected sensors. The proposed architecture was evaluated with three temperature sensors and three CO_2 sensors connected to a Programmable Logic Controller PLC [9]. This paper proposes a mechanism to reduce the current complexity of connecting sensors with PCL. In the case of our proposal, we also follow the same approach to reduce the complexity in IoT development but in our case for the connectivity of sensors with a software platform.

In research work [10], an autonomous agent trust model is proposed to reduce security problems, increasing reliability and credibility in IoT environments. The authors proposed an architecture called TAEC (Trustworthy Agent Execution Chip) using a high-security and cost-effective software and hardware platform for the secure operation of the Agent [10]. The proposed model can operate in a centralized or distributed IoT topology. In that model, each sensor node can register its name, network address, security requirement, and digital certificate. The latter is issued by the TAEC manufacturer. TAEC manufacturer is verified by the TAEC public key copy, which is responsible for using a specific encryption coprocessor to generate the pair key to ensure that the private key cannot be spied on by anyone. The silicon chip with an architecture and functions of the system was selected to be the hardware of TAEC, in addition the integrated Linux operating system was selected to be the operating system that runs the platform, and in the end the J2ME was used to be the development tool. The aim of this approach is to manage the security aspects in the definition of IoT systems. In the case of our proposed approach, the security is implemented by using IoT agents that encapsulates the communication among sensors and a IoT Platform.

The research work [11] proposes an agent-based IoT architecture and its middleware to perform autonomous and resilient service delivery in IoT systems. The paper also proposes the Agent-based Internet of Things application architecture of IoT devices, as well as an autonomic Agent-based Internet of Things organization, and re-organization schema that enables those applications can be autonomously composed and operated using IoT agent devices. The authors of paper evaluated the effectiveness of the proposed architecture in autonomous logistics experiment. To do this, an autonomous logistics application was implemented by using small robots with sensors. The experimentation confirmed that, in terms of design and implementation, the proposed AIoT architecture mitigates the administrative burden on the organization and reorganization that implies IoT applications. The results of the comparison between the proposed AIoT architecture and the conventional architecture-based logistics application reveals the architectural flexibility and resilience of the agent-based IoT application [11]. This paper demonstrates that the creation of mechanisms that permits mitigate the complexity in the implementation of IoT systems at architectural level. In the case of our proposed approach, it also follows the objective of reducing the complexity in the development of IoT system, but, in the case of our proposal, the simplification is in the connection between sensors an IoT platform.

The research work [12] presents an analysis of the fundamental gaps that exist in the connection between physical devices and integrated IoT software. The authors have found that a critical difficulty in the security of IoT systems is the implementation of the mechanism to isolate the physical devices from the services they offered. The authors propose an architecture of IoT agent platform where virtual clones of the physical devices will be housed, which permits to separate the devices from the functions they perform allowing the execution of functions in isolation. The proposed architecture restricted application services by nature, for example, personalized services based on private information. As a result, the IoT agent platform provides a more secure way to manage sensor values in the cloud without any modification of IoT agent/device programs. This research work explores the use of IoT agents as a mechanism to ensure de security in managing sensors values in the cloud. In our research work, the IoT agent is used to manage the secure connection of sensors with a specific IoT Platform, this solution also has positive effect to ensure the security in the connection with several sensors.

3   Overview of Our Approach Proposed

The FIWARE IoT Agents are an appropriated mechanism to manage, in a secure and well-defined manner, the connection between sensors and a IoT Platform. However, currently, all the software components required for enabling the connection between sensors to the IoT Agents and later to the FIWARE Platform is done manually, encoding the data entry of each sensor, creating the specific of an IoT Agent for the protocol handled by the sensors and finally, encoding the connection configuration between the IoT Agents and the FIWARE Platform.

The current architecture to connect devices through IoT agents with the FIWARE approach is shown in Fig. 1. In this architecture, FIWARE defined several IoT Agents to consider most of the current communication protocols implemented in sensors, such as IoTAgent-JSON, IoTAgent-LWM2M, IoTAgent-Utralight, IoTAgent loRanWAN, IoTAgent OPC-UA, IoTAgent sigfox. The IoT developer need to select a specific IoT Agent depending on the sensor protocol. The IoT Agents transform the sensor information into the NGSI protocol of FIWARE.

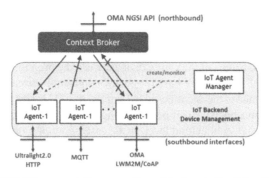

Fig. 1. The FIWARE approach for connection of devices to the Orion Context Broker.

Our proposed approach enables the connection between sensors and the FIWARE platform to be carried out semi-automatically. The connection of the devices is made through IoT Agents, which allows multiple communication protocols to be translated into the universal FIWARE language: the NGSI protocol. It is important to point out that sending data directly from the sensor to an IoT platform compromises the security of the data, since a malicious service could easily access the data sent by the sensor. This is the reason why the use of IoT Agents allows us to manage the security in the access to the information adding a layer of security to communications.

The main idea of the solution presented in this paper is to reduce the complexity of current process by proposing the automatic code generation for connecting sensors and FIWARE. To do this, the IoT developers use the proposed system to define the characteristics of the device's sensors that will generate the information and also in obtaining the data from the FIWARE Orion Context Broker where data will be sent. Our approach takes this information to automatically generates the code of a IoT system that performs the following actions: (a) obtain data readings from sensors, (b) translate the sensor data to FIWARE NGSI format; (c) configure a specific IoT Agent according to the sensors protocol, and d) configure the communication between the IoT Agent and FIWARE Orion Context Broker to send the sensor data to the cloud (See Fig. 2). The proposed approach permits the IoT developers focus in the sensors and the specific FIWARE Cloud in place of focus on the development of code for communicate sensor and FIWARE.

4 Our Approach for the Automatic Connection of Sensors to an IoT Platform

This section presents details of the proposed approach for the automatic creation of software components to enable the communications between agents and the IoT FIWARE Platform.

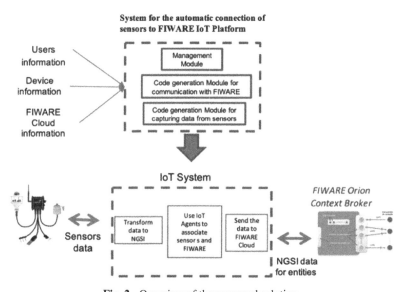

Fig. 2. Overview of the proposed solution.

It is important to point out that that expected user of the proposed system is an IoT developer that wanted to create a IoT system that captures data from sensors and sends this data to a specific IoT Platform.

The proposed architecture is composed by three main modules: Management Module, Code generation Module for communication with FIWARE, and the Code generation Module for capturing data from sensors. The input of the proposed system is the information of users, devices, and the data of the specific FIWARE Cloud where data will be sent. The output of the system is the code of a IoT system that, one compiled, permits the communication of defined sensors and the FIWARE Cloud (see Fig. 3). The Following, each of the components is described in detail.

4.1 Management Module

This module has the objective of managing sensors characteristics, users' information, authentication aspects and the details of the FIWARE Cloud. This module is composed by three sub-modules: User Management, Device Management and Authentication Management.

The User Management sub-module offer the functionality to register users in the system. The expected users for this module are IoT developers that wanted to create an IoT system using sensors connected to FIWARE.

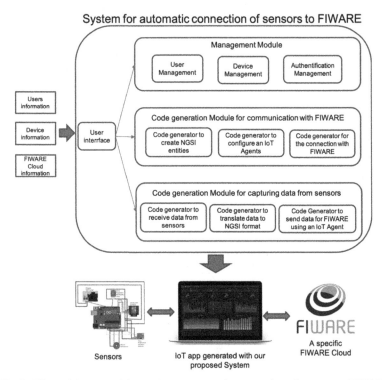

Fig. 3. The architecture of the system to automatic connection of sensors to FIWARE

The system only can be used by register users that provided their user's name, email and password. The validation of the user is made by using the sub-module of Authentication Management. Only the authorized users can register sensors in the system. It is important to point out that register the sensors that will provide data to final IoT system to be automatically developed.

The registered users need to define the name of the sensors and the type of readings of each sensor using the Device Management Sub-module. These sensors characteristics are relevant because they are used to create the code of the IoT System that obtains the data from sensors and sent the information to the FIWARE Cloud.

4.2 Code Generation Module for Communication with FIWARE

This module has the objective of generating the necessary code to define the FIWARE entities corresponding with devices that will provide data to the IoT System, the creation of NGSI Entities and the generation of code for the connection with FIWARE. This module is composed by three sub-modules: Code generator to create NGSI entities, Code generator to configure an IoT Agents and Code generator for the connection with FIWARE.

The FIWARE approach is based on the concept of Entities that relate and Entity with attributes and metadata. Therefore, the values that are captured from the sensors need to be represented using the concept of Entities. The users need to use the Code generator to create NGSI entities sub-module to define the map between the several sensors defined in the system and the several predefined entities by FIWARE.

The users need to select a specific IoT Agent using the sub-module Code generator to configure and IoT Agent according to the protocol defined in the sensor. This information is very relevant because it enables the system to construct a specific code that implements a FIWARE IoT Agent for IoT to be created. The configuration of each agent is different for each protocol type.

The submodule Code generator for the connection with FIWARE produce the code for the connection of the selected IoT Agent with the specific FIWARE Cloud that user defined in the Management Module. This code will enable the IoT System automatically produced to stablish a stable link with the FIWARE Cloud to send the data of the sensors represented in FIWARE Entities.

4.3 Code Generation Module for Capturing Data from Sensors

This module has the objective of producing the necessary code to enable the IoT System to obtain data from the sensors previously registered. Also, this module has the objective of generate the code to enable the transformation of the sensors data to the NGSI format (NGSI REST API) to be sent to the Orion Context Broker through a specific IoT Agent. This module is composed by 3 sub-modules: Code generator to receive data from sensors, Code generator to translate data to NGSI format and Code Generator to send data for FIWARE using an IoT Agent.

The sub-module Code generator to receive data from sensors generates the code to access to the several sensors defined in the Management Module. In this case, no user intervention is needed because the system recovers the sensors information and its corresponding typo de reading of previous Modules. This code, to be later compiled will enable the IoT System to take data from each sensor.

The sub-module Code generator to translate data to NGSI format generates the code to map the sensors data with the Entities defined in previous Module. In this case, no user intervention is needed. This code, to be later compiled will enable the IoT System to map the specific sensors readings into values of the Entity attributes.

The sub-module Code Generator to send data for FIWARE using an IoT Agents generates the code that enables the connection of the running instance of the IoT Agent with the URL address of the FIWARE Cloud.

Once the three system modules have been executed, all the code have been generated and it need to be compiled to generate a IoT System that implements the functionalities to: obtain data from sensors, to transform this data in FIWARE Entities, to stablish the communication with a IoT Agent that will be the intermediate between sensors and FIWARE, and finally, to send the data to the FIWARE cloud through a IoT Agent.

5 Software System for the Automatic Connection of Sensor to FIWARE IoT Platform

In this section we present some examples of the functionality of our proposed approach. In Fig. 4. (a) shows a view of the information requested for user registration. Meanwhile Fig. 4. (b) shows the user profile of the system, where users can modify their personal data if they need it. It is important to point out that an authentication mechanism was implemented to avoid nonauthorized user.

(a)   (b)

Fig. 4. View of user registration and user profile of the proposed software system

The software system developed allows the user to register the devices that he wishes to configure to connect to the FIWARE platform. The form that the user must fill in to register the device is shown in Fig. 5 (a). The information requested is: Device name. For example: Temperature_Sensor; Readings, that is to say the type of reading of the device, for example: "temperature"; the units in which the reading will be measured. In the case of temperature, it can be: Fahrenheit or Celsius; The maximum value of the reading, as well as the minimum value of the reading. For the example of the temperature sensor, the maximum value can be: 150 and the minimum value can be -40, in degrees Celsius.

A user can register different devices, so it is possible to view the registered devices. Figure 5, (b) shows the view of this option in the software system. The system allows you to edit or delete registered devices.

(a)   (b)

Fig. 5. Views of (a) Device registration form, and (b) devices list

Fig. 6. Orion Context Broker entity definition.

The definition of FIWARE entities is shown in Fig. 6. In this option, the system generates the JSON code that define an entity. This entity generation enables the system to send the data of a specific device to the Orion Context Broker of the FIWARE platform. The device information is obtained from the database that contains the information of each registered device. Thus, the software system only requests the address of the Orion context broker, in order to automatically generate the device connection code.

6   Conclusions and Future Work

The Internet of Things of one of the technologies that more impact has in the everyday life. Today, we found that any object can be provided with sensors that communicates its state and the state of the context where the object is located. This information is currently used to analyze the object and context patterns and also, to take decision that modify the current state of the object to match with changes in the context.

The IoT has face the developer with several challenges related to the several physical and software components of the solutions. One of the key challenges is the creation of software components to obtain the data from sensors, to transform the data in entities, and to send these entities to a IoT Platform. These software components need to be manually created for each new IoT system. In some cases, the technical difficulties to create these communication modules causes that IoT developers create a direct communication among sensors and the IoT Platform.

In this paper we proposed a novel system that generates the necessary code for a IoT System that stablish the communication among sensors and the IoT FIWARE Platform using IoT Agents. To do this, the IoT developers use the proposed system to define the characteristics of the device's sensors that will generate the data and also to define the information of the FIWARE Orion Context Broker where data will be sent. Our approach takes this information to automatically generates the code of a IoT system that performs the following actions: a) transform the sensors data into the NGSI protocol, b) configure a specific IoT Agent according to the sensors protocol, and c) configure the communication between the IoT Agent and FIWARE Orion Context Broker to send the sensor data to the cloud. In this manner, we reduce the complexity in using IoT application using the FIWARE Platform.

Our future work is focused on consider the creation of mechanisms to consider sensors with new communication protocols that currently don't have a corresponding IoT Agent.

Acknowledgments. This research was supported by Projects: TecNM 10265.21-P, and PRODEP 31535 CENIDET-CA-18.

References

1. Aldein Mohammed, Z., Ali Ahmed, E.: Internet of Things applications, challenges and related future technologies. World Sci. News J. **67**(2), 126–148 (2017)
2. Google Cloud (s.f): Cloud Computing, servicios de alojamiento y APIs de Google Cloud | Google Cloud

3. Amazon Web Services (s.f): Plataforma AWS IoT – Amazon Web Services (2017). https://aws.amazon.com/es/iot-platform/
4. IBM Cloud (s.f): About Watson IoT Platform. https://console.bluemix.net/docs/services/IoT/iotplatform_overview.html#about_iotplatform
5. Fiware-orion (s.f): «Welcome to Orion Context Broker». https://fiwareorion.readthedocs.io/en/master/
6. Ray, P.P.: A survey of IoT cloud platforms. Future Comput. Inform. J. **1**(1–2), 35–46 (2016). https://www.sciencedirect.com/science/article/pii/S2314728816300149
7. FIWARE-ABOUT US, "ABOUT US» FIWARE (2016). https://www.fiware.org/about-us/
8. Bliznakoff del Valle, D.J.: IoT: Tecnologías, usos, tendencias y desarrollo futuro (2014). http://openaccess.uoc.edu/webapps/o2/bitstream/10609/40044/6/dbliznakoffTFM0115memoria.pdf
9. FIWARE: "Desarrolla tu primer aplicación en FIWARE". https://fiware-training.readthedocs.io/es_MX/latest/casodeestudio/descripcion/
10. John, T., Vorbröcker, M.: Enabling IoT connectivity for ModbusTCP sensors. In: 2020 25th IEEE International Conference on Emerging Technologies and Factory Automation (ETFA), vol. 1, pp. 1339–1342. IEEE (2020). https://ieeexplore.ieee.org/document/9211999
11. Xu, X., Bessis, N., Cao, J.: An autonomic agent trust model for IoT systems. Procedia Comput. Sci. **21**, 107–113 (2013). https://www.sciencedirect.com/science/article/pii/S187705091300809090
12. Kato, T., Takahashi, H., Kinoshita, T.: Multiagent based autonomic and resilient service provisioning architecture for the Internet of Things. IJCSNS, **17**(6), 36 (2017). https://www.researchgate.net/publication/318338583_Multiagent-based_Autonomic_and_Resilient_Service_Provisioning_Architecture_for_the_Internet_of_Things
13. Shimojo, S., Nakagawa, I.: Secure IoT agent platform with m-cloud distributed statistical computation mechanism. In 2018 IEEE 42nd Annual Computer Software and Applications Conference (COMPSAC), vol. 2, pp. 528–533. IEEE (2018). https://ieeexplore.ieee.org/document/8377917

A Hybrid Model for the Prediction of Air Pollutants Concentration, Based on Statistical and Machine Learning Techniques

Carlos Minutti-Martinez[1]([✉]) [iD], Magali Arellano-Vázquez[2] [iD],
and Marlene Zamora-Machado[3] [iD]

[1] Artificial Intelligence Consortium, CONACyT-CIMAT, Guanajuato, Mexico
carlos.minutti@iimas.unam.mx
[2] INFOTEC Center for Research and Innovation in Information and Communication
Technologies, Aguascalientes, Mexico
magali.arellano@infotec.mx
[3] Autonomous University of Baja California, Mexicali, Mexico
zamora.marlene@uabc.edu.mx

Abstract. In large cities, the health of the inhabitants and the concentrations of particles smaller than 10 and 2.5 µm (PM_{10}, $PM_{2.5}$) as well as ozone (O_3) are related, making their prediction useful for the government and citizens. Mexico City has an air quality forecast system, which presents a forecast by pollutant at hourly and geographic zone level, but is only valid for the next 24 h.

To generate predictions for a longer time period, sophisticated methods need to be used, but highly automated techniques, such as deep learning, require a large amount of data, which are not available for this problem. Therefore, a set of predictor variables is created to feed and test different Machine Learning (ML) methods, and determine which features of these methods are essential for the prediction of different pollutant concentrations, to develop a hybrid *ad-hoc* model that includes ML features, but allowing a level of explainability, unlike what would occur with methods such as neural networks.

In this work we present a hybrid prediction model using different statistical methods and ML techniques, which allow estimating the concentration of the three main pollutants in the air of Mexico City two weeks ahead. The results of the different models are presented and compared, with the hybrid model being the one that best predicts the extreme cases.

Keywords: Pollutant forecasting · Machine learning · Particulate matter · Urban ambient air pollution

1 Introduction

In large cities, particles smaller than 10 and 2.5 µm (PM_{10}, $PM_{2.5}$) as well as ozone (O_3), correspond to the most dangerous air pollutants. Particularly in

© Springer Nature Switzerland AG 2021
I. Batyrshin et al. (Eds.): MICAI 2021, LNAI 13068, pp. 252–264, 2021.
https://doi.org/10.1007/978-3-030-89820-5_21

Mexico City (CDMX) these are also the pollutants that have most commonly given rise to the activation of environmental contingencies.

Coarse particles (PM_{10}) can penetrate into the deepest part of the lungs, such as the bronchioles or alveoli, and ultrafine particles ($PM_{2.5}$) tend to penetrate the gas exchange regions of the lung, and ultrafine particles can pass through the lungs to affect other organs [10]. Ozone is formed mainly from photochemical reactions between organic compounds and nitrogen oxides. Ozone has been shown to affect the respiratory, cardiovascular and central nervous systems. A link has also been found between premature death and reproductive health problems associated with ozone exposure [5].

According to the current version of the air quality index, concentrations greater than 96 (parts per billion) ppb of O_3, 76 µg/cubic meter (µg/m^3) of PM_{10} or 45.1 µg/m^3 of $PM_{2.5}$, fall into air quality that is considered poor.

In recent years, Artificial Intelligence (AI) methods have been used to address environmental problems, including air quality prediction. Carbajal et al. [2] use data from Mexico City and fuzzy logic to classify the concentrations of different pollutants into an air quality category and an autoregressive model to predict and classify the next day's air quality. Zhao and Hasan [19] use tree-based classification algorithms to predict whether a critical $PM_{2.5}$ value will be exceeded on the next day in Hong Kong, using historical pollutant data. Di et al. [8] combine estimates from neural network, random forest, and gradient boosting models to predict daily $PM_{2.5}$ values in the United States using different data sources, including meteorological data. Jihoon et al. [18] use Random Forest (RF), Gradient boosting (GBM), Regression as well as meteorological and pollutant data to predict next-day $PM_{2.5}$ and PM_{10} values in Seoul, with GBM being the best model, followed by RF. Ditsuhi et al. [11] review multiple papers about air pollutants forecasting concluding that the most predicted pollutant is $PM_{2.5}$, usually for next-day predictions, with neural networks being the most used method. Ali Shah et al. [17] use Empirical Mode Decomposition (EMD) to decompose time series of $PM_{2.5}$ and PM_{10} and test different ML algorithms, with data from different locations, with different algorithms generating better results at each location, but the best being those whose input data were pre-processed with EMD.

In these studies a benefit of using ML methods as well as meteorological data sources can be observed, but generally these models are not generated for predictions longer than one day, nor to be more sensitive to detect extreme cases, which are the main interest of making these predictions.

Mexico City is located within the Valley of Mexico basin, a flat area surrounded by mountains with an average height between 600 and 800 m above the valley floor. The mountains known as the Sierra de Guadalupe, surround the city to the north, the Sierra de las Cruces to the west, the Sierra del Ajusco to the south and the Sierra Nevada to the east, the latter including the volcanoes Iztlacihuatl (5200 m above sea level) and Popocatepetl (5400 m above sea level).

The number and distribution of mountains make Mexico City and its metropolitan area a highly complex terrain, influencing the meteorology and how pollutants behave in the atmosphere. Local winds influence air quality and the distribution of pollutants.

Studies have been conducted on local winds in Mexico City, in which the presence of three winds throughout the day has been identified (Fig. 1), which are affected when there are weather fronts in the Pacific Ocean and the Gulf of Mexico [6, 7, 9, 12], other authors have identified up to 9 wind patterns throughout the year [3].

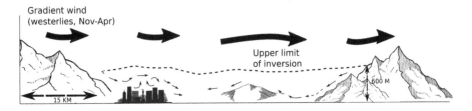

Fig. 1. Schematic illustration of drainage airflow over the CDMX basin [12].

Prediction of the concentrations of different air pollutants in the air, is very useful for citizens and governments to take actions that allow them to reduce the impact that these can reach and if possible, reduce the phenomenon itself in terms of magnitude and occurrence. A wind state is defined as a region in velocity phase space that contains available wind speeds that have a standard probability distribution function that characterizes them as a group [16]. In previous research [1] has been possible to characterize in an automated way the different wind states, replicating the classifications made by experts without having trained the classification method to reproduce that classification, resulting in a validation of both classifications.

Historical analysis of these data also followed that there is a correlation between the absence of some of these wind states and the subsequent occurrence of pollutants in sufficient concentration to result in a contingency. It is the use of this information and its variables that we intend to analyze in order to develop AI/ML methods for predicting the different states of poor air quality within Mexico City.

2   Methodology

The process by which the different ML models were arrived at, as well as the decisions taken for their development, are presented below. The coding and analysis were performed using the R language/environment [14].

2.1   Data

For the pollutants to be studied (O_3, PM_{10} and $PM_{2.5}$) we resorted to the Mexico City's Automatic Air Quality Monitoring Network (RAMA[15]), which has data since 1995 for O_3, 2011 for PM_{10} and 2003 for $PM_{2.5}$, whose data can be obtained at hourly level, for different monitoring stations.

The meteorological data come from stations located in the Mexico City area of the Automatic Weather Stations operated by the National Water Commission (CONAGUA [4]). These stations are shown in Fig. 2, and include the following variables: *wind speed and direction, air temperature, atmospheric pressure, relative humidity, barometric pressure, precipitation and solar radiation.* The data presents measurements every 10 min and data are available for the period from January 1, 2010 to March 31, 2019.

Although there are several monitoring stations, some of them disappeared over time and new ones appeared, and also many have missing data, so in order to characterize the levels of pollutants in the area of the CDMX, the 5 stations with the highest density of data were determined and the maximum value (as well as the mean, median and minimum) observed for each day.

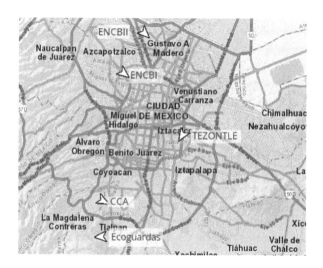

Fig. 2. Geographic location of the meteorological stations used for the predictor variables.

As for the meteorological data, the daily maximum, minimum, mean and median values for the different observed variables are used to generate the predictor variables, for each of the 5 stations in Fig. 2. However, it was observed that using information from 2 or more stations did not increase the accuracy of the methods. The station with the highest density of data and that produced the highest accuracy is the Tezontle station (Tezon), which is located in the central part of the CDMX, therefore, all the reported results are using the Tezon station data.

When looking for other predictor variables, it was observed that pollutant concentrations have a well-defined trends over different time scales. When the data was analyzed for different years, at the level of the day of the year and the week, it was also observed that for all pollutants there is a trend defined by the time of the year. Thus, the following variables are added to the predictor variables: the year, week, month, four-month period, day of the year and day of the week to be predicted.

Taking into consideration the temporal relationship between the years, days of the week and the trend within each year, the variables corresponding to the minimum, maximum, average and daily median of each pollutant and meteorological variable for the previous 52 weeks are also added as predictors, always using the same day of the week as the one to be estimated.

This process results in a database with 2,979 records and 2,563 variables, of which 2,550 are predictor variables. If there are missing data, the median (for numerical variables) and mode (for categorical variables) are used as imputation methods. This database is available in [13].

The relationships of the different variables are intended to be studied with statistical methods to determine the best way to incorporate the meteorological and temporal variables into the ML models. This is because there is no enough data to let the method itself to determine in a completely automated way all this information (new non-linear variables, interactions, etc.), so a careful statistical analysis is also required.

After testing the models, it was observed that it is possible to predict up to 2 weeks into the future, without excessive loss in accuracy, so the results reported are for this time range.

2.2 AI/ML Methods

As an exploratory method of the variables of importance and the base prediction capacity, the Spearman correlation with the pollutant to be predicted is measured, the 1,000 most correlated variables were chosen to form the basis of each of the models, these variables being chosen independently for each pollutant. Even though there are several methods for variable selection, Spearman was used to account for a nonlinear relationship and, due to the large number of variables and redundancy of information (collinearity), there was no appreciable difference using other variable selection methods. Although some ML methods can work with a high number of variables without overfitting the model, poorly related variables only introduce noise to the method, reduce robustness and complicate the training process.

As an initial model, a regression model analysis is performed. Despite the initial selection of variables, cross-validation suggests that the regression model is over-fitted, so the *stepwise* method is used. Although the regression model allows us to determine the most important variables, due to the over-fitting of the model by using all the variables, it is not possible to determine the base prediction level, so regularized regression (ridge regression, LASSO and Elastic Net) is used to explore this base prediction capability.

Subsequently, a Neural Network was tested, however, due to the scarcity of records, the depth of the network could only go up to 3 layers, even though the parameter *threshold* was controlled to avoid over-fitting.

The use of a regression tree model was also tested, which can give hints of variables of importance, but with reduced predictive power, so a *Random forest* model was also tested, using 5,000 training models.

After analyzing the results of the different models, it was observed that many of the variables have valuable information for the prediction of pollutants, but their use is limited due to the number of records, so an hybrid *ad-hoc* model was developed for the problem. This model combines the characteristics of *Random forest* that fits multiple models and those of a Neural Network that can include new non-linear variables and their interactions.

The new model is named `CM-MLPred` and consists of the generation of new nonlinear variables (polynomials of degree 2 and 3 of the original variables) and interaction of multiple variables, in this case, interaction of 2–6 variables. Subsequently, multiple regression models are fitted by means of a random selection of the base variables and the new variables, this selection of variables can follow a probability distribution of how many variables to use (the highest number of variables is prioritized). Subsequently, a random selection of records to predict is also performed, this in order to (1) not over-fit the final model, (2) give different selection probability to each record to simulate adjustment weights, if it is desired to prioritize the error reduction for a certain type of value and (3) to be able to use the data not used during the training/adjustment of the model, to obtain an estimate of the prediction error (cross-validation).

Another additional feature of the model is that since there are multiple models with different variables and number of variables, it is not necessary to impute missing data, since only those models for which the value of the variables is available can be used for the final estimate. In addition, having a multiplicity of models prevents an outlier or erroneous value of a predictor variable from considerably affecting the estimation.

Finally, the model can give a prediction interval, which can use the different estimates of each sub-model to obtain a probability distribution of the estimate. For the calculation of the probability distribution of the estimate, the weight of each sub-model is used, which is given by a *score* that is calculated by the product of the coefficient of determination of each model (adjusted R^2), the AIC[1] (*Akaike information criterion*) and a coefficient of determination for prediction. Thus, a sub-model with a high *score* generally implies an adequate performance in the 3 different measures. The final estimate is given by the estimate value that maximizes the likelihood of the probability distribution of the estimate.

3   Results

The results for the 3 different pollutants are presented below, starting with PM_{10}, for which a greater level of detail of the process and results obtained are given, and for $PM_{2.5}$ and O_3 the results obtained by performing the same process described in PM_{10} are presented. When observing the distribution of the

---

[1] Since models with lower AIC are better, 1-(AIC-min(AIC))/(max(AIC)-min(AIC)) is used so that higher values correspond to better models.

different contaminants along the data set, it was observed (Fig. 3) that the distribution is very asymmetric, with very large values being infrequent. However, the very high values are of special interest for prediction, that is why the first decision taken was to predict the logarithm of the pollutant concentration, which has a more symmetric distribution (and more similar to a Gaussian), which will make all methods more efficient in the prediction of high concentrations.

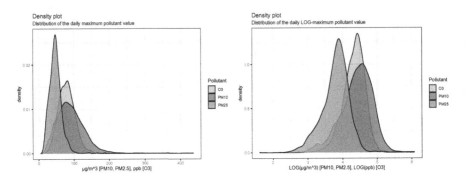

Fig. 3. Distribution of daily maximum values, observed for each pollutant (left) and for its logarithm (right).

To calculate the prediction error for each of the models, a random set of data was selected for cross-validation, which corresponds to 13% of the total records (384 records). This validation data set was selected by means of a random sample where the probability of selection of each record is inversely proportional to its frequency, in order to determine how good each model is at predicting extreme cases, which are the ones of main interest. This validation set was never used in the training of any of the models, and its error is measured by the formula $err = \left(\frac{C_i^{obs} - C_i^{est}}{C_i^{obs}} \right)^2$, where C_i^{obs} is the i-th observation of the pollutant $C = PM_{10}, PM_{2.5}, O_3$ and C_i^{est} is the model prediction corresponding to the i-th observation. That is, it is a quadratic error relative to the measured value. err results into a vector for which its different quartiles and mean are estimated.

All models (Regression [REG], Regularized regression [RIDGE], Neural Networks [NN], Random Forest [RF], Regression Trees [TREE]) were calibrated to maximize their prediction power avoiding overfitting. For regression we used *stepwise*, for regularized regression, ridge regression (LASSO and Elastic Net were tested, and an optimal value of the regularization parameter was used, being the Ridge regression always the one with better results). In the case of Neural Networks, the number of hidden layers and the threshold parameter were optimized, and different initial values for the weights were tested. This process was done for each pollutant, having the following results.

3.1 PM10

The hybrid model (`CM-MLPred`) aims to combine the advantages of new nonlinear variables and interactions that a Neural Network provides, as well as the multiplicity of predictors that a model such as Random Forest has. For the training of this model, 5,000 sub-models were used, and they add 900 new variables, consisting of 300 non-linear transformations (polynomials of degree 2–3 and logarithms) as well as 600 variable interactions ranging from 2–6 variables, where each sub-model contains 2–350 variables. A sample of the base variables can be seen in Fig. 4, where the importance of the variables for the RF model is presented.

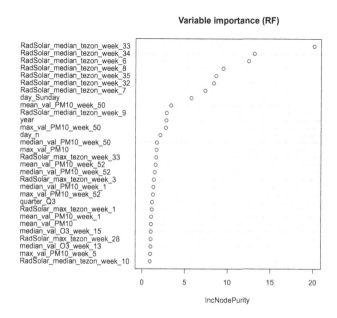

Fig. 4. Variable importance for PM_{10} in the RF model

Here we show different comparisons of the different models with respect to the validation data set, which was never used to train the models or to calibrate their parameters.

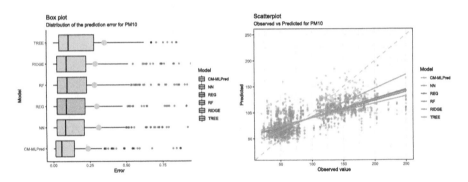

Fig. 5. Comparison of the different models for the prediction error of PM_{10}, in the validation set

Figure 5 shows the distribution of the prediction squared error as well as the box plot. From both graphs it can be seen that the hybrid method, `CM-MLPred` presents a higher number of cases with low errors, in relation to the other models, and has a lower variability in its errors.

Table 1 shows the different quartiles for the error obtained with each model, as well as their mean.

Table 1. Errors for the validation data set using the different models tested, for PM_{10}

Model	Min.	1st Qu.	Median	Mean	3rd Qu.	Max.
CM-MLPred	0.0000	0.0138	0.0545	0.2349	0.1419	8.4287
REG	0.0000	0.0244	0.0890	0.2969	0.2176	10.5835
RIDGE	0.0000	0.0242	0.0897	0.2879	0.2242	7.5782
NN	0.0000	0.0230	0.0828	0.3087	0.2110	9.8603
TREE	0.0000	0.0387	0.1036	0.3495	0.2795	15.3808
RF	0.0000	0.0273	0.0948	0.2821	0.2291	7.4604

Taking these results into account, the best performing model was `CM-MLPred` with the difference in the third quartile being more relevant, indicating a lower probability of making large errors. Neural Networks (NN) is the one that could be considered the second best model.

Figure 5 shows the observed vs estimated values of PM_{10} for each model, so the model that is closer to a straight line with slope 1 (dotted line) is the best one. In this graph it can be seen that `CM-MLPred` is the closest to that line and that the other models tend to have problems when predicting extreme values, especially for very high PM_{10} values, which are precisely the values we are interested in predicting.

3.2   PM2.5

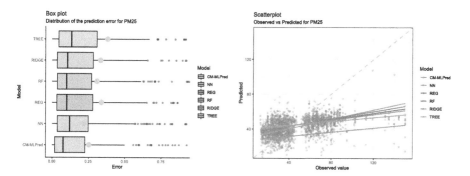

Fig. 6. Comparison of the different models for the prediction error of $PM_{2.5}$, in the validation set

Figure 6 shows the distribution of the prediction errors in a box plot, it can be seen that the hybrid model, CM-MLPred, has a higher number of cases with low errors, in relation to the other models, and has a lower variability in its errors. Figure 6 also shows the observed vs predicted values of $PM_{2.5}$ for each model.

Table 2 shows the different quartiles for the error obtained with each model, as well as their mean.

Table 2. Errors for the validation data set using the different models tested for $PM_{2.5}$

Model	Min.	1st Qu.	Median	Mean	3rd Qu.	Max.
CM-MLPred	0.0000	0.0181	0.0761	0.2527	0.2250	6.8016
REG	0.0000	0.0328	0.1003	0.3392	0.2799	10.4971
RIDGE	0.0000	0.0345	0.1054	0.3334	0.2823	8.2566
NN	0.0000	0.0355	0.1205	0.2152	0.2478	6.7171
TREE	0.0000	0.0453	0.1325	0.3819	0.3086	8.4904
RF	0.0000	0.0364	0.0989	0.3088	0.2712	5.9467

The best performing model was CM-MLPred with the difference in the third quartile being more relevant, indicating a lower probability of making large errors. Neural Networks (NN) is the one that could be considered the second best model.

Although CM-MLPred performed better than the other models, it is also observed that for $PM_{2.5}$ it is more difficult to make adequate predictions, and the difference between the methods is smaller (compared to PM_{10}), which may be expected given the low correlations of the predictor variables.

3.3 O3

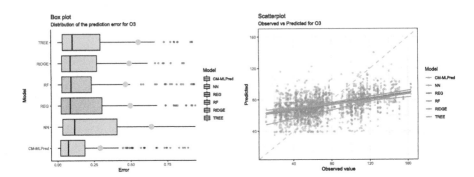

Fig. 7. Comparison of the different models for the prediction error of O_3, in the validation data set

Table 3 shows the different quartiles for the error obtained with each model, as well as their mean.

Table 3. Errors for the validation dataset using the different models tested for O_3

Model	Min.	1st Qu.	Median	Mean	3rd Qu.	Max.
CM-MLPred	0.0000	0.0185	0.0740	0.2897	0.1865	13.3532
REG	0.0000	0.0230	0.0873	0.4950	0.3019	14.2492
RIDGE	0.0000	0.0281	0.0882	0.4896	0.2684	19.4817
NN	0.0000	0.0341	0.1160	0.6401	0.4048	17.9026
TREE	0.0000	0.0332	0.1031	0.5523	0.2925	27.3900
RF	0.0000	0.0278	0.0924	0.4630	0.2312	22.3349

Figure 7 shows the distribution of the prediction errors for O_3 as well as a plot of observed vs predicted values for each model.

The best performing model was `CM-MLPred` with the difference in the third quartile being very relevant, indicating a lower probability of making large errors. Unlike PM_{10} and $PM_{2.5}$, Neural Networks (NN) performed worse in this case, with the second best model being Random Forest.

Although `CM-MLPred` performed better than the other models, it is also observed that for O_3 it is more difficult to make adequate predictions, and the differences between the other methods are smaller (compared to PM_{10}), which may be expected given the low correlations of the predictor variables.

4   Summary and Conclusions

A data set of meteorological variables and previous air pollutant concentrations was constructed in order to study different AI/ML models to predict future air pollutant concentrations. By analyzing the results and performance of these models in a cross-validation data set, an hybrid *ad-hoc* model was developed including the most relevant features of the studied models. The following conclusions are drawn from the results obtained:

- PM_{10} is the pollutant that was more correlated to the meteorological variables and the one in which better predictions are achieved.
- $PM_{2.5}$ is the pollutant that presented the greatest prediction problems.
- O_3 is mainly dominated by solar radiation and the time of the year.
- For all pollutants, the hybrid model (CM-MLPred) was the one that obtained the best predictions and the one that performed better in predicting extreme values.
- The developed model can be adapted to other pollutants and cities.
- Because these pollutants show a pattern related to the day of the week, the effect of human activity is evident, therefore the inclusion of related variables, such as human mobility, could significantly improve the results.

In future work we will include human mobility data as well as orography data, to improve the results.

Data Availability Statement

The data that support the findings of this study are openly available in figshare at https://dx.doi.org/10.6084/m9.figshare.16589822, under the Creative Commons Attribution CC BY.

References

1. Arellano-Vázquez, M., Minutti-Martinez, C., Zamora-Machado, M.: Automated characterization and prediction of wind conditions using gaussian mixtures. In: Martínez-Villasenor, L., Herrera-Alcántara, O., Ponce, H., Castro-Espinoza, F.A. (eds.) Advances in Soft Computing, vol. 12468, pp. 158–168. Springer, Cham (2020). https://doi.org/10.1007/978-3-030-60884-2_12
2. Carbajal-Hernández, J.J., Sánchez-Fernández, L.P., Carrasco-Ochoa, J.A., Martínez-Trinidad, J.F.: Assessment and prediction of air quality using fuzzy logic and autoregressive models. Atmos. Environ. **60**, 37–50 (2012). https://doi.org/10.1016/j.atmosenv.2012.06.004
3. Carreón-Sierra, S., Salcido, A., Castro, T., Celada-Murillo, A.T.: Cluster analysis of the wind events and seasonal wind circulation patterns in the Mexico city region. Atmosphere **6**(8), 1006–1031 (2015)
4. CONAGUA: Automated weather stations, August 2021. https://smn.conagua.gob.mx/tools/GUI/EMAS.php

5. Council, N.R.: Estimating Mortality Risk Reduction and Economic Benefits from Controlling Ozone Air Pollution. The National Academies Press, Washington, DC (2008). https://doi.org/10.17226/12198

6. De Foy, B., et al.: Mexico city basin wind circulation during the MCMA-2003 field campaign. Atmos. Chem. Phys. Discuss. **5**(3), 2503–2558 (2005). https://hal.archives-ouvertes.fr/hal-00303903

7. De Foy, B., Clappier, A., Molina, L.T., Molina, M.J.: Distinct wind convergence patterns in the Mexico city basin due to the interaction of the gap winds with the synoptic flow. Atmos. Chem. Phys. **6**(5), 1249–1265 (2006). https://doi.org/10.5194/acp-6-1249-2006

8. Di, Q., et al.: An ensemble-based model of PM2.5 concentration across the contiguous united states with high spatiotemporal resolution. Environ. Int. **130**, 104909 (2019). https://doi.org/10.1016/j.envint.2019.104909

9. de Foy, B., et al.: Basin-scale wind transport during the MILAGRO field campaign and comparison to climatology using cluster analysis. Atmos. Chem. Phys. **8**(5), 1209–1224 (2008). https://doi.org/10.5194/acp-8-1209-2008

10. Heinzerling, A., Hsu, J., Yip, F.: Respiratory health effects of ultrafine particles in children: a literature review. Water Air Soil Pollut. **227**(1), 32 (2015). https://doi.org/10.1007/s11270-015-2726-6

11. Iskandaryan, D., Ramos, F., Trilles, S.: Air quality prediction in smart cities using machine learning technologies based on sensor data: a review. Appl. Sci. **10**(7) (2020). https://doi.org/10.3390/app10072401

12. Jauregui, E.: Local wind and air pollution interaction in the Mexico basin. Atmósfera **1**(3) (2011). https://www.revistascca.unam.mx/atm/index.php/atm/article/view/25944

13. Minutti, C.: Pollutant and meteorological data for the prediction of air pollutants in Mexico city, September 2021. https://doi.org/10.6084/m9.figshare.16589822.v1

14. R Core Team: R: A Language and Environment for Statistical Computing. R Foundation for Statistical Computing, Vienna, Austria (2021). https://www.R-project.org/

15. RAMA: Automatic air quality monitoring network (2021). http://www.aire.cdmx.gob.mx/default.php?opc=%27aKBh%27

16. Sánchez-Pérez, P.A., Robles, M., Jaramillo, O.A.: Real time Markov chains: wind states in anemometric data. J. Renew. Sustain. Energy **8**(2), 023304 (2016). https://doi.org/10.1063/1.4943120

17. Shah, S.A.A., Almaraashi, W.A.M., Nadeem, M.S.A., Habib, N., Shim, S.O.: A hybrid model for forecasting of particulate matter concentrations based on multiscale characterization and machine learning techniques. Math. Biosci. Eng. **18**(3), 1992 (2021). https://doi.org/10.3934/mbe.2021104

18. Yoo, J., Shin, D., Shin, D.: Prediction system for fine particulate matter concentration index by meteorological and air pollution material factors based on machine learning. In: Proceedings of the Tenth International Symposium on Information and Communication Technology, SoICT 2019, pp. 479–485. Association for Computing Machinery, New York (2019). https://doi.org/10.1145/3368926.3369684

19. Zhao, Y., Hasan, Y.A.: Fine particulate matter concentration level prediction by using tree-based ensemble classification algorithms. Int. J. Adv. Comput. Sci. Appl. **4**(5) (2013). https://doi.org/10.14569/IJACSA.2013.040503

Mexican Automotive Industry Sales Behavior During the COVID-19 Pandemic

Jorge Ramírez$^{(\boxtimes)}$, Joaquín Alarcón, Gustavo Calzada, and Hiram Ponce

Facultad de Ingeniería, Universidad Panamericana, Augusto Rodin 498,
Ciudad de México 03920, Mexico
{0231937,0189971,0241903,hponce}@up.edu.mx

Abstract. This work shows the results of forecasting the behavior of sales in the Mexican automotive industry in a simulated scenario without COVID-19 and comparing it with the actual sales numbers. As this pandemic has caused traditional forecasting techniques to show poor performance and low prediction quality, this work aims to estimate the number of sales lost during the pandemic, using a machine learning model based on several explanatory variables and predicting those variables without the influence of the COVID-19 pandemic. Three different regression models were tested (Linear regression, Random Forest and Neural Network) creating scenarios and incorporating different variables into the models. Random Forest with 3 variables shows the highest predictive power. This model applied on forecast variables without pandemic's impact predicts 1,342,028 units sold between February 2020 and January 2021, representing a 29.76% drop in sales and a total impact of 416,324 sales lost due to the pandemic.

Keywords: Total industry volume · Economic cycles · Indicators · Predictors · Automotive industry

1 Introduction

The COVID-19 pandemic has had a severe impact on the global automotive industry. It has caused a dramatic decrease in retail sales in the Mexican market, and has intensified the downward trend that Mexican brands have experienced since 2017. According to The Economist, car sales in Mexico have decreased 28% in 2020, to less than 950,000 units sold, the largest decline since 1995 [3]. In Mexico, the automotive industry also contributes to around 17% of manufacturing Gross Domestic Product (GDP) and 3% of the national GDP [13]. Their behavior makes it one of the most important complementary economic indicators in Mexico. Therefore any movement, drop or upturn of this industry is in the spotlight of Mexican economy.

© Springer Nature Switzerland AG 2021
I. Batyrshin et al. (Eds.): MICAI 2021, LNAI 13068, pp. 265–276, 2021.
https://doi.org/10.1007/978-3-030-89820-5_22

This has created many problems in demand planning and forecasting, and traditional techniques have shown poor performance and low prediction quality. Intense pressure has been placed on the industry since they are currently dealing with low mergers, overstock and an aggressive competition. Estimating the impact of the pandemic on the sales is important to plan measures and adjustments to demand and production for the players in the market.

Machine Learning models are an alternative approach to forecasting that could have advantages over current methods. It is expected that these models can better capture unexpected variations in the time series, and that those variations can be explained in terms of macroeconomic variables. The use of publicly available information about macroeconomic indicators can produce a predictive model that is easily reproducible, without requiring private data from car companies.

The purpose of this study is to provide a new forecasting option by predicting TIV (Total Industry Volume) through Machine Learning techniques, using macroeconomic indicators as predictors. The results of this work attempt to explain the effect of the pandemic on the volume of sales. First, a number of candidate explanatory variables are selected and their correlations to the car sales are calculated. The variables with the highest correlation, both positive or negative, are selected. Then, three models are applied to those variables: Linear Regression, Random Forest Regression, and Neural Network Regression. Data from 2010 through 2017 is used as a train set, and data from 2018 to 2019 is used as the test set. The model with the best performance across three metrics is chosen: Coefficient of Determination, Mean Squared Error and Mean Absolute Error.

Once the right variables and model have been found, a hypothetical scenario is created by forecasting the explanatory variables into 2020, disregarding their actual behavior in that period. Applying the regression model to those alternate variables will produce a hypothetical value for the sales as if the COVID-19 pandemic had not occurred. Finally, the difference between the simulated scenario and the actual numbers will provide a quantitative measure of the lost sales.

With the proposed model, car companies are expected to have a better perspective on the evolution of the COVID-19 pandemic impact in the short term. As TIV is an important macroeconomic indicator and quite sensitive to economic cycles, this project will also bring visibility to anyone interested in Mexico's economic outlook.

The rest of the paper is organized as follows. Section 2 explores similar work and related studies. Section 3 details the process for selecting explanatory variables, describes regression algorithms and the metrics used to assess them. In Sect. 4, the algorithms are applied to the selected variables and their performance is compared to find the best predictive model, then an alternate scenario is created without effects from COVID-19 to calculate the difference with the true values. Section 5 presents the conclusions of this work.

2   Related Work

The behavior and health of car sales is of great importance to the automotive industry and to the general macroeconomic indicators. Several articles are published every year dealing with the forecasts and variables affecting this indicator. In general, these sources do not disclose the methodology used to estimate expected sales. This paper aims to produce a model that can reproduce those estimations using publicly available information.

The use of global indicators specific to the Mexican economy is a key feature of this paper. A related paper, "Predicting the Selling Price of Cars Using Business Intelligence with the Feed-forward Backpropagation Algorithms" [6], proposes an approach for car price prediction based on the vehicle's technical specifications, and is focused on one manufacturer for the U.S market. This work covers a wider range of brands and manufacturers, and doesn't require detailed knowledge of the technical features of each vehicle.

In 2020, Deloitte made an analysis of the automotive industry perspective, forecasting over a million sales for 2021; it is now expected that sales won't reach 2019 levels until 2024 [2]. According to a forecast by Jato Dynamics, in March 2020 vehicle sales would have amounted to 1.3 million units, similar to 2019 [12].

An article by Lozano [8] states that the last two months of every year usually concentrate 20% of annual car sales transactions. The article reinforces the expectation that sales will climb back to 2019 numbers by 2024.

The work by Heath [4] for INEGI provides information about the available data and methods for using it. It highlights the relevance of the automotive industry to the indicators of national economic activity. It also notes that car sales are closely linked to the credit penetration of each country, in which Mexico lags far behind other countries.

This study deals extensively with time series and economics. An article by Mauricio [9] describes the ARIMA technique, while the article by Ezequiel [14] helps in understanding the homoscedasticity property and its importance in modeling.

3   Description of the Proposal

The purpose of this project is to provide a numerical estimate of the amount of sales lost to COVID-19 by the automotive industry in the Mexican Market. With this information, governments and decision makers can know the real impact of the pandemic in economic terms and devise recovery strategies

3.1   Exploration of Variables and Data Sources

Most of the data sources in this study are provided by INEGI [7]. The first step is exploring the automotive sales time series and the candidate explanatory variables. Figure 1 shows that sales reach a peak around 2016, then start a downwards trend in the following two years and have a dramatic drop in 2020 because of the pandemic. This time series has a notorious seasonal component, with the highest point around November-December of each year, and the lowest on May.

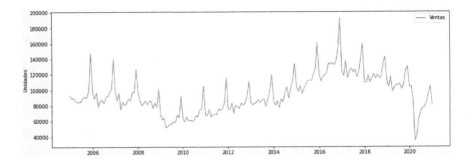

Fig. 1. Sales of cars from 2005 to 2021 in Mexico.

Working with the raw sales numbers as a time series proved too difficult, since the machine learning models would overfit the signal following the seasonality and trend in the training period. To solve this, the data was converted to monthly percentage variations. This change centers the signal and turns large variations in relative values between −100 to 100, as shown in Fig. 2. This is the target variable.

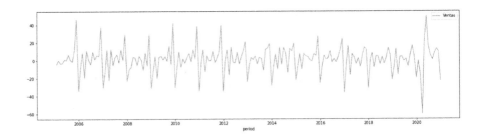

Fig. 2. Monthly percentage variation of car sales.

The next step is selecting the macroeconomic variables with the best predictive power. Each of the candidate variables was transformed to monthly percentage variations and its Pearson Correlation Coefficient (PCC) with the target variable was calculated. The PCC is a measure of the linear correlation between two variables, and is calculated as the covariance of the variables divided by the product of their standard deviations. The result always has a value between −1 and 1. Table 1 shows the result of this analysis. The variables marked with * were selected because they have the highest absolute PCC coefficient.

Table 1. Candidate explanatory variables and their correlation to the target variable.

	Candidate variable	PCC with target variable
	Indicador Global de Actividad Económica (IGAE) desestacionalizado	0.63
*	IGAE original	0.63
*	Month	0.58
	IGAE desestacionalizado, efecto calendario	0.45
	Indicador de Confianza del Consumidor (ICC)	0.33
	Exports	0.31
	Gas price	0.19
	Working days in month	0.15
	Índice de Precios al Consumidor (IPC) General	0.12
	Inflation	0.12
	Exchange rate	0.043
	Tasa de Interés Interbancaria de Equilibrio (TIIE) a 28 días	−0.0076
	IPC Autos	−0.37
	Inflación autos	−0.37
*	Relative price	−0.45
*	Total daily salary	−0.49

*: highest absolute PCC coefficient.

The Global Indicator of Economic Activity (Indicador Global de Actividad Economica, IGAE), is provided by INEGI with and without seasonal adjustment, and with effects of vacation periods. Since those variables have similar PCC, the one without any adjustments was selected. The month has a high PCC score, and to use it the modeling, the month numbers were turned into categorical values using one-hot encoding. Relative price and Total daily salary have the highest inverse correlation with the target variable. The rest of the candidates have PCC scores considered too low to impact the precision of the regression model.

The full dataset used as input to the models is available at: https://github.com/0231937/micaipaper91.

3.2 Model Analysis and Selection

The next step is to perform regression methods on the time series to forecast it, based on the selected predictive variables. The algorithms selected for this study: Multiple Linear Regression, Random Forest Regression, and Neural Network

Regression (Multilayer Perceptron, MLP), were chosen because of their low time complexity and ease of understanding and interpretation. These features allow for simple implementation, quick feedback, and easy error detection.

Multiple Linear Regression [15] fits a curve described by a linear equation to the observed data. The equation has a coefficient for each explanatory variable plus a constant called the intercept. Because it is a very simple algorithm to implement and understand, it provides a baseline for comparing other algorithms.

Random Forest Regression [5] is an algorithm that builds multiple decision trees at training time. Then, for a regression task, the mean prediction of all the trees is returned. Using random decision forests helps reduce the natural overfitting of a single decision tree on its training set. Another advantage of this algorithm is that it can provide accurate results with a relatively low number of samples, and it can measure the weight of each feature on the final result.

The Multilayer Perceptron algorithm (MLP) [10] is a kind of feed-forward neural network composed of several layers of perceptrons with threshold activation. For this paper, the algorithm uses 100 hidden layers, with a ReLU activation function and a maximum of 500 iterations. This algorithm works better with a large number of samples, and there is a possibility that it will not produce more accurate forecasts than the other two methods.

The data was split in two sets, for training and testing. Instead of taking random samples of certain percentages of the data, the split was made by a cutoff date because of the auto-regressive nature of the series. The training set, using data from 2010 to 2017, contains 96 samples, and the test set, from 2018 to 2019, has 24.

3.3 Experimentation

To decide which of the three algorithms produces a better forecast, the results must be compared using metrics that describe their accuracy. In the following definitions, for n observations:

y_i is the true value, the actual sales data,
y_i' is the predicted value, the result of the model, and
$\bar{y}$ is the mean of all y_i.

The coefficient of determination, written as R^2 [1], is a measure of correlation. It is the proportion of the variance in the dependent variable that is predictable from the independent variables. A correlation closer to 1 means a strong positive relationship, while -1 means a stronger negative relationship. A value closer to 0 means that relationship between the variables is weak. This metric can be expressed as follows:

$$R^2 = 1 - \frac{\sum_{i=1}^{n}(y_i - \bar{y})^2}{\sum_{i=1}^{n}(y_i' - y_i)^2}$$

The Mean Squared Error or MSE [1] is the average of the the squared difference between the values predicted by a regression and the actual values of the time series. A value of MSE closer to 0 means that there is a small difference between the forecast produced by a model and the real data. This metric is sensitive to outliers, with large differences causing a higher value. MSE is computed with the following expression:

$$MSE = \frac{1}{n} \sum_{i=1}^{n} (y'_i - y_i)^2$$

The Mean Absolute Error or MAE [1] is the sum of the absolute differences between a prediction from a regression model and the actual data. Values of MAE closer to zero indicate a better model, and it is measured in the same units as the data. MAE is calculated as:

$$MAE = \frac{1}{n} \sum_{i=1}^{n} |y'_i - y_i|$$

4   Results and Discussion

All three regression methods were applied to the data and their predictions were compared using the three metrics: R^2, MAE and MSE. After the results were measured, an effort was made to try and improve the forecast by using time windows. The time windows separate yearly data into four periods of 3 months each, then those windows are concatenated with the original data set, and the performance is measured again.

Regressions over raw time series data result in poor predictions because of overfitting. One way to solve this issue is using monthly percentage variations calculated from the time series. Another impact of working with a time series is that the datasets for training and testing are chosen by cutoff date instead of random sampling. The results of these processes are summarized in Table 2.

Table 2. Regression model metrics.

Algorithm	R^2_{Train}	R^2_{Test}	MSE_{Test}	MAE_{Test}
Linear regression	0.860	0.569	49.082	5.280
Random forest (no windows)	0.971	0.828	19.560	3.587
Random forest (with windows)	0.963	0.743	29.216	4.030
Neural network	0.880	0.688	35.505	4.180

Linear regression and Neural Network models overfit the data. This can be concluded because the predictions are good on the training dataset, but poor on the testing dataset. The time window technique was discarded as it did not improve the performance of any of the models. Random Forest produces the best results across all metrics, so it is the chosen model to make a forecast.

Since the goal of the study is to produce a new scenario that is not impacted by COVID-19, new data for the independent variables is needed. The objective is to produce hypothetical time series for the explanatory variables: IGAE, relative car price, and daily salary, that will follow the trend they had before March 2020. The new simulated data will be fed to the trained Random Forest model to produce a new time series that will represent the behavior of the automotive industry as though the pandemic had not taken place.

Because the independent variables are time series, the ARIMA technique was used to produce the hypothetical, non-COVID projections. The ARIMA models are trained with data up to February 2020. The models are then used to forecast the data through February 2021, and this process simulates time series that are not impacted by the pandemic, as seen in Figs. 3, 4, and 5.

The trained Random Forest model is applied to the new simulated variables and a new time series for TIV can be produced, which represents what would have happened to car sales without COVID-19. This prediction is compared with the real data, what actually happened.

Figure 6 shows that the monthly percentage variations predicted by the model have a large difference with the actual values, starting in March-April 2020, when the pandemic restrictions were imposed in Mexico.

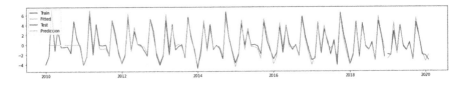

Fig. 3. IGAE forecast with ARIMA.

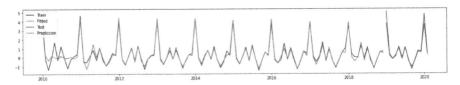

Fig. 4. Daily salary forecast with ARIMA.

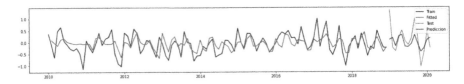

Fig. 5. Relative car price forecast with ARIMA.

Table 3 shows the results of applying the model to an alternate scenario with no effects from the COVID-19 pandemic. The prediction is expressed as monthly percentage variations, which are used to calculate the expected number of units sold. The difference between the predicted and actual sales is the amount of lost sales per month.

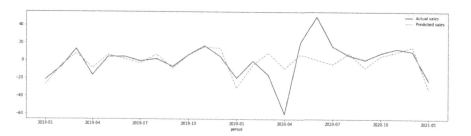

Fig. 6. Percentage change of actual sales vs. sales forecast without COVID-19

Table 3. Prediction results and comparison.

Period	Actual sales (with COVID, units)	Predicted sales (no COVID, units)	Predicted variation	Lost sales (units)	Total sales lost (units)
Feb 2020	104,338	104,338	0%	0	0
Mar 2020	87,541	113,421	8.70%	25,880	25,880
Apr 2020	34,927	103,252	−8.97%	68,325	94,205
May 2020	42,034	110,175	6.70%	68,141	162,346
Jun 2020	62,861	111,347	1.06%	48,486	210,832
Jul 2020	72,921	106,902	−3.99%	33,981	244,813
Aug 2020	77,120	115,446	7.99%	38,326	283,139
Sep 2020	77,808	106,608	−8.12%	28,260	311,399
Oct 2020	84,331	111,458	5.08%	27,127	338,526
Nov 2020	95,485	122,452	9.86%	26,967	365,493
Dec 2020	105,135	141,446	15.51%	36,311	401,804
Jan 2021	81,203	95,723	−32.33%	14,520	**416,324**
Total	**925,704**	**1,342,028**			

The results show a total impact of 416,324 sales lost to the pandemic until January 2021. Compared to the 1,317,931 units sold in 2019, the model predicted an increase of 1.83% or 24,097 additional units had the pandemic not taken place. Instead, the year-to-year loss is 29.76%.

The value of sales obtained from this calculation can be compared to the actual sales, as seen in Fig. 7. Percentage variations are converted to number of units sold. A clear drop is observed starting on March 2020, and a recovery starting on May 2020 is not strong enough to return to the original levels before the pandemic.

This study shows that it is possible to predict the behavior of the automotive market by using only three explanatory variables: IGAE, daily salary and relative car price. The decision to buy a car in Mexico seems to be influenced by the strength of the economy, the relative prices of the cars, and the amount of money a person makes.

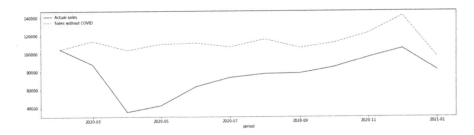

Fig. 7. Comparison chart with and without COVID.

Unexpectedly, the price of gas and associated IEPS tax were found to reduce model accuracy when included in the regression as independent variables. The low correlation with the car sales could be explained because the price of oil is difficult to predict, so potential buyers do not take it into account to make a decision to purchase a car.

The regression with the best performance for this dataset is Random Forest. The data for training spans the period from 2010 to 2017, which results in only 96 monthly data samples, too few for a neural network to be effective. Other advantages of Random Forest are that it does not overfit data as much as a linear regression, it is not too computationally expensive and it provides a feature importance score, which helps to identify variables that do not help the model accuracy.

The results of this study match those found in a study from July 2020 [11], in units and percentage of sales lost.

5   Conclusions

This document presented a machine learning-based approach to predict car sales comparing three types of regression using three explanatory variables. The prediction using random forest regression had the best performance across all metrics. An alternate scenario without the effects of COVID-19 was created by forecasting the explanatory variables and generating a prediction with the new values. By comparing the alternate scenario with the actual data, it was possible to calculate the amount of sales lost during the pandemic.

The importance of this work is that it can be used to predict the behavior of car sales in future scenarios using only global indicators for the market in Mexico, without having access to private data from automotive makers.

Future work on this topic may include separating the car market by segment or by manufacturer, which will possibly require additional variables to get an accurate prediction. The existing model could be improved by using other regression methods over time series, e.g. Recurrent Neural Networks.

References

1. Botchkarev, A.: Performance metrics (error measures) in machine learning regression, forecasting and prognostics: properties and typology. Interdisc. J. Inf. Knowl. Manag. **14**, 45–79 (2018). https://doi.org/10.28945/4184
2. Deloitte: Perspectiva Industrial - Industria Automotriz (2020). https://www2.deloitte.com/content/dam/Deloitte/mx/Documents/finance/2020/Perspectiva-Industria-Automotriz-DEconosignal.pdf
3. González, L.: Sales of Cars in Mexico Decreased 28 Percent in 2020. The Economist, Westminster (2021)
4. Heath, J.: Lo Que Indican Los Indicadores (2020). http://internet.contenidos.inegi.org.mx/contenidos/Productos/prod_serv/contenidos/espanol/bvinegi/productos/estudios/indican_indi/indica_v25iv12.pdf
5. Ho, T.: Random decision forests. In: Proceedings of 3rd International Conference on Document Analysis and Recognition, vol. 1, pp. 278–282 (1995). https://doi.org/10.1109/ICDAR.1995.598994
6. Idris, N.O., Achban, A., Utiarahman, S.A., Karim, J., Pontoiyo, F.: Predicting the selling price of cars using business intelligence with the feed-forward back-propagation algorithms. In: 2020 Fifth International Conference on Informatics and Computing (ICIC), pp. 1–6 (2020). https://doi.org/10.1109/ICIC50835.2020.9288594
7. INEGI: Programa Anual de Investigación del INEGI (2021). https://sc.inegi.org.mx/repositorioNormateca/Od_28Ene21.pdf (2021)
8. Lozano, L.F.: Industria Automotriz Espera Mejores Ventas En último Bimestre de (2020). https://www.forbes.com.mx/negocios-industria-automotriz-mejores-ventas-ultimo-bimestre-2020/
9. Mauricio, J.: Temporal series analysis. In: UCM (2013)
10. Murtagh, F.: Fionn, m.: Multilayer perceptrons for classification and regression. Neurocomputing **2**, 183–197 (1990). https://doi.org/10.1016/0925-2312(91)90023-5
11. Paz, K.: La evolución en la venta de vehículos en tiempos de COVID 19 (2020). https://www.jato.com/mexico/la-evolucion-en-la-venta-de-vehiculos-en-tiempos-de-covid-19/
12. Rodríguez, I.: Car sales in Mexico grow for the first time in three years (2020). https://expansion.mx/empresas/2020/03/04/la-venta-de-autos-en-mexico-crece-febrero-2020-amda
13. Thornton, G.: Boletín de Economía (2020). https://www.grantthornton.mx/globalassets/1.-member-firms/mexico/pdf/boletin-de-economia-febrero-2020-v.1.pdf

14. Uriel, E.: Introducción a la Econometría (2019). https://www.uv.es/uriel/manual/Introducci%C3%B3n%20a%20la%20econometr%C3%ADa%202012-09-2019%20B.pdf
15. Wei, W.: Time series regression. In: International Encyclopedia of Statistical Science, pp. 1607–1609 (2011). https://doi.org/10.1007/978-3-642-04898-2_596

Modeling Self-efficacy and Self-regulated Learning in Gamified Learning Environments Through Educational Data Mining

Yasmín Hernández$^{(\boxtimes)}$![ORCID], Alicia Martínez ![ORCID], Javier Ortiz ![ORCID], and Hugo Estrada ![ORCID]

Tecnológico Nacional de México, CENIDET, Interior Internado Palmira, 62490 Cuernavaca, México

{yasmin.hp,alicia.mr,javier.oh,hugo.ee}@cenidet.tecnm.mx

Abstract. The increasing usage of computers in education have produced cumulus of data. Educational Data Mining emerged to take advantage of growing educational data. There has been an extensive application of educational data mining to improve Learning Environments, such as Intelligent Tutoring Systems. The gamification is integrated to educational systems to engage students and produce a better learning. We are developing a gamified tutoring system, and we want to know the relevant characteristics of students to be considered in a gamified learning context. In a first stage, we want to promote motivation, self-efficacy, and self-regulated learning. Therefore, we are analyzing several educational datasets, and we are developing online courses to obtain data and in turn to obtain insights about the relationship between diverse characteristics of students and learning.

Keywords: Data mining · Educational data mining · Gamification · Intelligent tutoring systems · Intelligent learning environments

1 Introduction

The presence of electronic devices in daily life generates cumulus of data every second. The analysis of this data allows us to obtain information about processes, people, relationships, behaviors, and about ourselves, which in turn allows us to make decisions and take actions in an easier way. Data mining emerged with the aim to take advantage of growing data. Data mining seeks to discover patterns in large volumes of data, to extract information and to transform it into an understandable structure for later use [20]. The advancement of technology has made possible to store and process a huge amount of data, that is why data mining has more and more successful applications in different fields, for example, commerce, banking, and health. However, education is one of the fields where data mining has arisen the most interest and research.

Education is one of the fields that has benefited the most from computers and electronic devices, and therefore there are an incredible volume of data on the interaction of students with learning environments. This is result of the increasing use of learning environments, such as intelligent tutor systems (ITS), e-learning systems, educational

I. Batyrshin et al. (Eds.): MICAI 2021, LNAI 13068, pp. 277–288, 2021.
https://doi.org/10.1007/978-3-030-89820-5_23

games, learning management systems (LMS) and massive open online courses (MOOC), in addition to administrative computer-based systems. With these data we could know the students, understand different aspects of the interaction of the students with the systems and comprehend the learning process itself.

Educational Data Mining (EDM) is an emerging discipline, interested in the development of methods to explore the exceptional data that comes from educational environments, and concerned in the use of these methods to understand students and the environments in which they learn [16].

The designing of Intelligent Tutoring Systems has taken advantage of EDM. These educational programs simulate the behavior of human tutors. Namely, ITS teach students in the same way that a human tutor does [21]. To have a more precise and adaptive behavior, several elements have been integrated to ITS behaviors such as the recognition of emotions and personality, as well as the modeling of different cognitive states such as motivation, self-efficacy, and self-regulated learning. These elements allow a more personal and motivating interaction with ITS.

In recent years, game techniques have been included due to their proven ability to motivate students. Gamification in education is a learning technique that transfers the elements of games to the educational field to achieve better results. Its main function is to motivate and engage students through challenges and missions, with the expectation of obtaining rewards.

Gamification is defined as the use of game elements in non-playful contexts, such as: points, badges, levels, trophies, challenges, and missions, among others [17]. The application of gamification in education is a research field of recent birth and promises important results, since it has shown the ability to motivate and engage students, which leads to learning. Through playful teaching, students could internalize knowledge and develop important skills such as critical thinking, problem solving, collaboration and communication.

As known, some subjects are perceived as difficult; thus, students are apathetic, do not do homework, and do not study in their account, and consequently they have a low achievement in their studies. We want to promote motivation and self-efficacy in students, and to provide them with tools for self-regulated learning. These constructs have been identified as important players in learning [11].

With this aim, we are developing a gamified ITS for mathematics for elementary school. As first steps, towards building the student model, we are analyzing several educational datasets to know which are the relevant characteristics for learning and to include them in our ITS. We are applying machine learning algorithms like Classification and Regression Tree, Naïve Bayes, k-Nearest Neighbors and Random Forest for classification, and k-means for clustering to public datasets. In addition, we are developing online courses to obtain data about self-efficacy via self-reports.

In this paper we present our proposal to build a gamified ITS to promote self-efficacy and self-regulated learning. The paper is organized as following: Sect. 2 presents a brief review of literature on educational data mining; Sect. 3 describes how ITS have been extended with gamification and presents some relevant research; Sect. 4 depicts our proposal to build the gamified ITS to promote self-efficacy and self-regulated learning. Finally, Sect. 5 outlines our conclusions and future work.

2 Data Mining in Education

Educational data can be used to improve our understanding of learning, of students, and to create a better, smarter, more interactive, engaging, and effective education. This requires advances in artificial intelligence and machine learning, human intelligence understanding and learning theories [8]. Educational data mining is an emerging discipline that still has many pending solutions; but it has a potential to support the development of other fields related to education.

EDM and, its technical basis, the machine learning techniques play an important role in augmenting and improving learning environments. Machine learning is concerned with the ability of a system to acquire and integrate new knowledge through observations of users and with improving and extend itself by learning rather than by being programmed with knowledge [20]. These techniques organize existing knowledge and acquire new knowledge by intelligently recording and reasoning about data. For example, observations of the previous behavior of students will be used to provide training examples that will form a model designed to predict future behavior.

As in data mining, in EDM several computing paradigms and algorithms converge, such as decision trees, artificial neural networks, machine learning, Bayesian learning, logic programming, statistical algorithms, among others. However, traditional mining algorithms need to consider the characteristics of the educational context to support instructional design and pedagogical decisions [16].

Educational data have meanings with multiple levels of hierarchy, which need to be determined by means of the properties of the data itself. Time, sequence, and context play an important role in the study of educational data [7]. EDM supports the development of research on many problems in education, since it not only allows to see the unique learning trajectories of individuals, but it also allows to build increasingly complex and sophisticated learning models [4].

The knowledge uncovered by EDM algorithms can be used not only to help teachers manage their classes, understand learning processes of their students, and reflect it in their own teaching methods, but also to support reflections of the student about the situation and give feedback to them [13]. Although one might think that there are only these two stakeholders in EDM, there are other groups of users, who see EDM from different points of view, according to their own objectives [16]. For example, education researchers, universities, course developers, training companies, school supervisors, school administrators, could also benefit from the knowledge generated by EDM [8]. Figure 1 shows the interrelationships of educational environments, stakeholders and the EDM process.

The growing of EDM is due, in part, to the advancement of computing in processing and storage; nowadays it is possible to store and process huge data which some years ago it was impossible. In recent years, educational technologies have been instrumented to collect large amounts of data that are available for free. An example is DataShop which consists of an open data repository and a set of analysis and visualization tools. DataShop is owned by the Pittsburgh Science of Learning Center, and currently stores more than 350 datasets including more than 200,000 student hours of data from thousands of students at an average of 10 s per share, producing more than 90 million student shares [8].

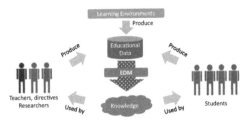

Fig. 1. Educational data mining knowledge discovery cycle [16].

The different components of ITS have been improved by applying knowledge produced by EDM. Many data-driven student models have been built. For example, a data-driven student model was built with educational data coming from a training system. In this research, several machine learning algorithms were evaluated such as Bayesian search, essential graph search, greedy thick thinning, tree augmented naive Bayes, augmented naive Bayes, and naive Bayes. The resulting model was evaluated by comparing it with a model based on expert knowledge [23].

EDM has been used to identify behavioral patterns related to self-regulated learning. The aim is to measure self-regulated behavior and identify significant behavioral indicators in computer-assisted language learning courses. Data is coming from behaviors stored on a log data from 2454 freshman university students from Art and Science departments for a year. The attributes analyzed are the degree of self-regulation, including anti-procrastination, irregularity of study interval, and pacing. Clustering analysis was conducted to identify typical patterns of learning pace, and hierarchical regression analysis was performed to examine significant behavioral indicators in the online course. The results of learning pace clustering analysis revealed that the final course point average in different clusters increased with the number of completed quizzes, and students who had procrastination behavior were more likely to achieve lower final course points. Furthermore, the number of completed quizzes and study interval irregularity were strong predictors of course performance in the regression model. It clearly indicated the importance of self-regulation skill, in particular completion of assigned tasks and regular learning [12].

Another research is interested in providing teachers with tools to make decisions for the classes and courses. Authors compare different data mining methods and techniques for classifying students based on their Moodle usage data and the final marks obtained in their respective courses. They developed a specific mining tool for making the configuration and execution of data mining techniques easier for instructors. Real data from seven Moodle courses with college students were used. Authors apply discretization and rebalance preprocessing techniques on the original numerical data to verify if better classifier models are obtained. Researchers state that a classifier model appropriate for educational use must be both accurate and comprehensible for instructors in order to be of use for decision making [15].

Massive Open Online Course (MOOC) is a new modality for learning which offer a high flexibility and open access via the Web to unlimited participants. However, they do not offer personalization neither adaptation, in this sense a Framework for User Model and Adaptation has been developed to augment MOOC, shown in Fig. 2.

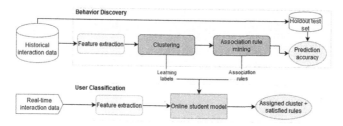

Fig. 2. Framework for user model and adaptation [9].

This framework consists of two main phases to guide the delivery of adaptive support. In the Behavior Discovery phase, interaction data of previous students is first pre-processed into feature vectors. Next, clustering is applied to these vectors to identify students with similar interaction behaviors. The resulting clusters are analyzed by comparing the learning performance of the students in each cluster relatively to the other clusters. Next, association rule mining is used to identify the distinctive behavior in each cluster. The values of features are discretized into bins to avoid producing many fine-grained rules that are difficult to interpret, a well-known problem with association rules learnt on continuous features. Hyper-parameters such as the number of clusters, the minimum support of the association rules, and the number of bins to be used for discretization, are learnt as part of the training process. In the User Classification phase, the labeled clusters and the corresponding association rules extracted in Behavior Discovery are used to train a classifier student model. As new students interact with the target MOOC, they would be classified in real-time into one of the identified clusters, based on a membership score that summarizes how well the student's behaviors match the association rules for each cluster. In addition to classifying students, this phase returns the subset of association rules satisfied by the students that caused the classification. These rules can be used to trigger adaptation meant to encourage productive behaviors and discourage detrimental ones [9].

3 ITS and Gamification

Intelligent Tutoring Systems are educational programs which teach students by simulating the behavior patterns of a human tutor, namely, they decide what and how to teach based on the characteristics and particular needs of every student. The intelligence of the ITS is represented through its components: student model, tutor module, expert module, and interface module. These components interact with each other to fulfill different functions to present adaptive teaching [21]. The architecture of an ITS is shown in Fig. 3.

Games as learning tools represent a promising approach due to their abilities to teach and reinforce knowledge, as well as to develop important skills such as problem solving, critical thinking, communication, and collaboration. In addition, they have a strong ability to motivate and engage people in the interaction.

The aim of educational games is not only fun, but it also seeks learning, training, skill development, rehabilitation, among other purposes. Serious games have been applied in

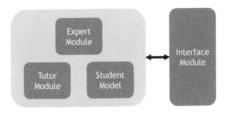

Fig. 3. Intelligent tutoring system architecture [21].

different sectors and industries with great success. For example, in health and education we can find research to support children with learning disabilities [2].

Gamification in education proposes the use of elements of game in the design of learning environments to improve student engagement and motivation. Gamification is the use of game design elements in non-playful contexts [17]. This new field differs from educational games or serious games in that educational games involve the design of entire games for non-entertainment purposes, while gamification applications only include elements of the games in the learning environments [3].

Gamification has seen rapid adoption in different sectors due to its potential to influence user behavior. For example, platforms such as Stackoverflow.com, codeacademy.com and khanacademy.org, among others, use game elements to attract and motivate users [3].

As a result of this growing interest, design principles for the application of gamification in education have been identified. Some of the design principles are fundamental and they are always present in education systems, but they may need to be adapted to fit the gamification paradigm. For example, feedback should be immediate or with shorter cycles. Learning tasks must be clear, concrete, and actionable with increasing complexity [3].

These design principles are implemented trough different gamification elements which are classified into mechanics and dynamics. Mechanical techniques consist of the way to reward the user based on the objectives achieved, namely badges, points, medals, gifts, levels, among other. While dynamic techniques refer to the user's own motivation to play and continue to achieve their objectives which are implemented by means of rewards, status, achievements, and competitions [5].

Gamification have been implemented in ITS as a fundamental way to improve interaction with students and to motivate them. *EasyLogic* is a learning environment that integrates affective recognition with gamification techniques. This environment teaches algorithmic logic and programming to engineering students. In *EasyLogic*, students earn points every time they perform an exercise correctly, and every certain number of points they receive a trophy. It also keeps a table of classifications showing the students with the highest scores. The performance of *EasyLogic* was evaluated by comparing it to the performance of the same system without emotion recognition and without gamification elements. Results and statistical tests showed that student learning is better when the affective state of the student is considered and gamification techniques are used [23]. The *EasyLogic* interface is shown in Fig. 4.

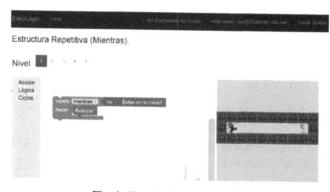

Fig. 4. EasyLogic interface [23].

SQL-Tutor is a mature ITS that teaches SQL and has been proven effective in multiple studies. The authors developed a version of SQL-Tutor with gamification to understand the effects of gamification on learning. In this playful version they included goals, evaluation, and challenges, these are three categories of elements of the game of the Theory of Gamified Learning [10]. These elements were implemented through 13 types of badges divided into three categories: basic, classic, and elite. A notification of winning a badge in gamified *SQL-Tutor* is shown in Fig. 5. The authors found that badges can positively increase student performance on the ITS. They also found evidence that goal setting, challenges, and self-assessment behaviors implemented as badges indirectly and significantly affect learning outcomes through time spent on task as mediator [18].

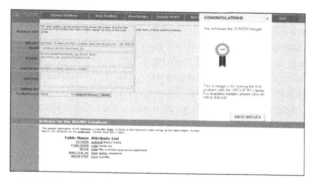

Fig. 5. Example of winning a badge in Gamified *SQL-Tutor*.

This study provides initial evidence that badges can positively increase student achievement in ITS, and that this relation can be mediated by the amount of time participants spend on the task. The results show the impact of gamification on learning through behavioral change, supporting the theory of gamified learning with the time-on-task as a valid behavior target for gamification. From the statistical analysis, it was determined that time-on-task correlates and predicts learning outcomes. We did not find a difference between gamified and non-gamified groups in terms of time spent in *SQL-Tutor*, problems completed, and learning outcomes. A possible explanation for this finding is that the students are already highly motivated and used SQL-Tutor to prepare for the lab test. However, we found evidence that goal setting, challenges and self-testing behaviors implemented as badges indirectly and significantly affect learning outcomes through the time-on-task as the mediator.

4 Data-Driven Construction of a Gamified ITS

Educational data mining (EDM) and machine learning techniques play an important role in augmenting educational models and systems. Machine learning is concerned with the ability of a system to acquire and integrate new knowledge through observations of students and with improving and extend itself by learning rather than by being programmed in an explicit way [20]. These techniques organize existing knowledge and acquire new knowledge by intelligently recording and reasoning about data. For example, observations of the previous behavior of students will be used to provide training examples that will form a model designed to predict future behavior [22].

It has been recognized that self-regulated students develop skills and habits to be effective learners, exhibiting effective learning strategies, effort, and persistence. Self-regulated learning refers to one's ability to understand and control one's learning environment. Self-regulation abilities include goal setting, self-monitoring, self-instruction, and self-reinforcement [14].

Self-efficacy is a personal judgment of how well or poorly a person can cope with a given situation based on the skills they have and the circumstances they face. Self-efficacy affects every area of human endeavor. By determining the beliefs, a person holds regarding their power to affect situations, self-efficacy strongly influences both the power a person actually has to face challenges competently and the choices a person is most likely to make [1].

Also has been recognized that self-efficacy is a key trait of self-regulated learners [14]. Self-efficacy for self-regulated learning refers to the beliefs that individuals hold in their capabilities to think and behave in ways that are systematically oriented toward or associated with their learning goals. Students with a robust sense of efficacy in their self-regulatory capabilities believe they can manage their time effectively, organize their work, minimize distractions, set goals for themselves, monitor their comprehension, ask for help when necessary, and maintain an effective work environment [19].

We are developing an ITS to promote self-efficacy in students. We are integrating gamification techniques to engage students. Despite there are extensive research in gamification in education, there are several elements which needs to be understood such the relationship between game engagement with motivation, self-efficacy, and self-regulated learning.

Firstly, we need to identify the relevant attribute in students which can be indicators of self-efficacy and self-regulated learning to include them in the student model of the ITS. In our previous research, we have identified emotions, personality, and goals as important players in motivation and learning. But now, we want to explore other relationships. In this sense, we are building a model to identify self-efficacy, and we will include them as important component of the student model. Figure 6 shows the initial model to represent self-efficacy in the student model.

Fig. 6. Initial model to identify self-efficacy.

As important component of the ITS, we are building a data-driven student model; therefore, we are evaluating and applying several EDM techniques to find patterns and relationships in educational data. We are following two strategies. The first one consists of analyzing public datasets and the second one is interested in gathering our own data. We are analyzing several public datasets at repositories as DataShop, which is a big repository of learning interaction data. Such data can be used to help advance our understanding of student learning and learning process itself, therefore to create better, more intelligent, interactive, engaging, and effective education [8].

On the other hand, we want to have a deeper understanding of self-efficacy, learning and gaming; therefore, we are designing some experiments to gather our own data, therefore. We are designing two online courses with some elements of gamification where we will ask students to fill self-reports on emotions, motivation, and self-efficacy. We are building a course on math for sixth grade of elementary school and a course on Mathematical Logic for under-graduated and graduated students. Figure 7 shows an exercise in the first course (in Spanish). The self-reports will be designed with base on the guide to build self-efficacy scales proposes by Bandura [1]. Figure 8 presents a very preliminary self-report for self-efficacy in academic performance. However, we are studying how to ask kids about self-efficacy and how to evaluate this construct in kids.

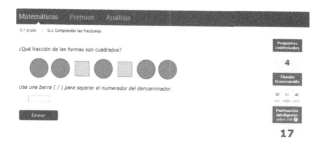

Fig. 7. Example of an exercise of the math course for sixth grade.

Tutors and teachers know students by means of observation and interacting with them, and in this way, they adapt their instruction to needs of students. The interaction between teachers and students provide data about knowledge, goals, skills, motivation, and interests of the students. In an ITS this knowledge is stored in the student model, which is a representation of the different student states. The student model ensure that the system has principled knowledge about each student, and hence it can respond effectively, engage students, and promote learning [22].

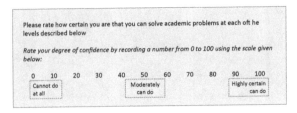

Fig. 8. Preliminary self-report for self-efficacy in academic performance.

Typically, an ITS decides what and how to teach based on a representation of the knowledge of the student; however, there is some evidence that motivated, self-effective and self-regulated students learn in a better way. Therefore, the student representation structure needs to be augmented to include knowledge about self-efficacy, self-regulated learning, and motivation. Thus, students can be provided with a tutorial action which fulfills knowledge requirements, and at the same time promotes motivation and self-efficacy and in turn, promotes self-regulated learning in students. Figure 9 shows our initial proposal for student modelling.

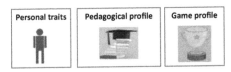

Fig. 9. Student model for the gamified ITS.

As we mentioned, we have identified some traits and states of students and, also, some strategies to deliver the appropriate tutorial action and feedback, and they are integrated in the different components of the ITS. An important element is the gamification which is included with the aim to motivate and engage students and is integrated as a module in the architecture. Figure 10 (left) shows the initial architecture for the gamified ITS and which traits are included in each module. Since the process of understanding the different traits and states of students involves uncertainty, we rely on Bayesian networks for this task. Bayesian networks have strong mechanisms for managing uncertainty which allows to reach a conclusion with limited evidence. The components of the ITS will be implemented by means of Bayesian networks to probabilistically relate the states of student state with the appropriate tutorial actions. Figure 10 (right) snows a high-level Bayesian network representing the student model.

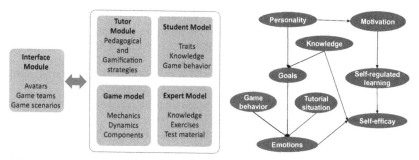

Fig. 10. Initial architecture for the for the gamified ITS (Left), and Bayesian network for the student model (Right).

5   Conclusions and Future Work

Educational data can be used to improve our understanding of learning and students, and which in turn allows to have better educational technologies and a better education. These objectives require further advances in artificial intelligence and in human learning theories. Educational data mining is an emerging discipline that can be useful towards these aims due its potential to support the development of fields related to education.

In this paper, we propose a gamified ITS to promote self-efficacy, self-regulated learning, and motivation to improve learning. The ITS is building by means of applying several educational data mining techniques. We are analyzing public educational datasets, but also, we are gathering data by means of a controlled experiment with an online course and under graduated and graduated students participating.

Despite, this research is in an initial stage, it promises encouraging results as we appreciate potential in the educational data mining techniques and based on our previous research in intelligent learning environments.

Acknowledgments. This research was supported by Projects TecNM 10463.21-P, TecNM 10265.21-P, and PRODEP 31535 CENIDET-CA-18.

References

1. Bandura, A.: Guide for constructing self-efficacy scales. Self-efficacy Beliefs Adolesc. 307–337 (2006). https://doi.org/10.1017/CBO9781107415324.004
2. Cornejo, R., et al.: Serious games for basic learning mechanisms: reinforcing Mexican children's gross motor skills and attention. Pers. Ubiquit. Comput. **25**(2), 375–390 (2021). https://doi.org/10.1007/s00779-021-01529-0
3. Dicheva, D., et al.: Gamification in education: a systematic mapping study. Educ. Technol. Soc. **18**(3), 75–88 (2015)
4. Fischer, C., et al.: Mining big data in education: affordances and challenges. Rev. Res. Educ. **44**(1), 130–160 (2020). https://doi.org/10.3102/0091732X20903304
5. Gaitan, V.: Gamificación: el aprendizaje divertido. https://www.educativa.com/blog-articulos /gamificacion-el-aprendizaje-divertido/#:~:text=LaGamificaciónesuna   técnica,concretas %2Centreotrosmuchosobjetivos. Accessed 03 Apr 2021

6. Hernández, Y., Cervantes-Salgado, M., Pérez-Ramírez, M., Mejía-Lavalle, M.: Data-driven construction of a student model using bayesian networks in an electrical domain. In: Pichardo-Lagunas, O., Miranda-Jiménez, S. (eds.) MICAI 2016. LNCS (LNAI), vol. 10062, pp. 481–490. Springer, Cham (2017). https://doi.org/10.1007/978-3-319-62428-0_39

7. International Educational Data Mining Society: Educational Data Mining. http://www.educationaldatamining.org/

8. Koedinger, K.R., et al.: New potentials for data-driven intelligent tutoring system development and optimization. AI Mag. **3**, 27–41 (2013)

9. Lallé, S., Conati, C.: A data-driven student model to provide adaptive support during video watching across MOOCs. In: Bittencourt, I.I., Cukurova, M., Muldner, K., Luckin, R., Millán, E. (eds.) AIED 2020. LNCS (LNAI), vol. 12163, pp. 282–295. Springer, Cham (2020). https://doi.org/10.1007/978-3-030-52237-7_23

10. Landers, R., et al.: How to use game elements to enhance learning: applications of the theory of gamified learning. In: Serious Games and Edutainment Applications, vol. II, pp. 1–702 (2017). https://doi.org/10.1007/978-3-319-51645-5

11. Lavasani, M.G., et al.: The effect of self-regulation learning strategies training on the academic motivation and self-efficacy. Procedia - Soc. Behav. Sci. **29**, 627–632 (2011). https://doi.org/10.1016/j.sbspro.2011.11.285

12. Li, H., Flanagan, B., Konomi, S., Ogata, H.: Measuring behaviors and identifying indicators of self-regulation in computer-assisted language learning courses. Res. Pract. Technol. Enhanc. Learn. **13**(1), 1–12 (2018). https://doi.org/10.1186/s41039-018-0087-7

13. Merceron, A., et al.: Learning analytics: from big data to meaningful data. J. Learn. Anal. **2**(3), 4–8 (2016). https://doi.org/10.18608/jla.2015.23.2

14. Panadero, E.: A review of self-regulated learning: six models and four directions for research. Front. Psychol. **8**(APR), 1–28 (2017). https://doi.org/10.3389/fpsyg.2017.00422

15. Romero, C., et al.: Data mining algorithms to classify students. In: Proceedings of the 1st International Conference on Educational Data Mining, pp. 8–17 (2008)

16. Romero, C., Ventura, S.: Educational data mining and learning analytics: an updated survey. Wiley Interdiscip. Rev. Data Min. Knowl. Discov. **10**(3), 1–21 (2020). https://doi.org/10.1002/widm.1355

17. Van Roy, R., et al.: Uses and gratifcations of initiating use of gamifed learning platforms. In: Proceedings of the Conference on Human Factors in Computing Systems (2018). https://doi.org/10.1145/3170427.3188458

18. Tahir, F., et al.: Investigating the effects of gamifying SQL-Tutor. In: ICCE 2020 - 28th Proceedings of the International Conference on Computers in Education, vol. 1, pp. 416–425 (2020)

19. Usher, E.L.: Self-efficacy for self-regulated learning (2012). https://doi.org/10.1007/978-1-4419-1428-6_835

20. Witten, I.H., et al.: Data Mining: Practical Machine Learning Tools and Techniques. Morgan Kaufmann, Cambridge (2017)

21. Woolf, B.P.: Building intelligent interactive tutors student-centered strategies for revolutionizing e-learning (2010)

22. Woolf, B.P.: Student modeling. Stud. Comput. Intell. **308**, 267–279 (2010). https://doi.org/10.1007/978-3-642-14363-2_13

23. Zatarain Cabada, R.: Reconocimiento afectivo y gamificación aplicados al aprendizaje de Lógica algorítmica y programación. Rev. Electrónica Investig. Educ. 20(3), 115 (2018). https://doi.org/10.24320/redie.2018.20.3.1636

Parallelization of the Array Method Using OpenMP

Apolinar Velarde Martínez[(✉)]

Instituto Tecnológico el Llano Aguascalientes, Carretera Aguascalientes-San Luis Potosí, Km. 18 El Llano, Aguascalientes, Mexico
apolinar.vm@llano.tecnm.mx

Abstract. Shared memory programming and distributed memory programming, are the most prominent ways of parallelize applications requiring high processing times and large amounts of storage in High Performance Computing (HPC) systems; parallel applications can be represented by Parallel Task Graphs (PTG) using Directed Acyclic Graphs (DAGs). The scheduling of PTGs in HPCS is considered a NP-Complete combinatorial problem that requires large amounts of storage and long processing times. Heuristic methods and sequential programming languages have been proposed to address this problem. In the open access paper: Scheduling in Heterogeneous Distributed Computing Systems Based on Internal Structure of Parallel Tasks Graphs with Meta-Heuristics, the Array Method is presented, this method optimizes the use of Processing Elements (PE) in a HPCS and improves response times in scheduling and mapping resource with the use of the Univariate Marginal Distribution Algorithm (UMDA); Array Method uses the internal characteristics of PTGs to make task scheduling; this method was programmed in the C language in sequential form, analyzed and tested with the use of algorithms for the generation of synthetic workloads and DAGs of real applications. Considering the great benefits of parallel software, this research work presents the Array Method using parallel programming with OpenMP. The results of the experiments show an acceleration in the response times of parallel programming compared to sequential programming when evaluating three metrics: waiting time, makespan and quality of assignments.

Keywords: Parallel Task Graphs (PTG) · High Performance Computing (HPC) Systems · Scheduling tasks · Univariate Marginal Distribution Algorithm (UMDA) · Array method

This research work is funded by Tecnológico Nacional de México TecNM. Special Thanks to Instituto Tecnológico El Llano Aguascalientes.

I. Batyrshin et al. (Eds.): MICAI 2021, LNAI 13068, pp. 289–308, 2021.
https://doi.org/10.1007/978-3-030-89820-5_24

1   Introduction

Shared memory programming and distributed memory programming are the most prominent ways of parallelizing applications that require high processing times and large amounts of storage in High Performance Computing (HPC) Systems; these types of programming have been used to convert sequential applications to parallel applications [2–4] in different areas of science, to obtain results in shorter execution times. The development of parallel programming is performed on different hardware platforms with support for programming with centralized memory and distributed memory such as Clusters of SMP (Symmetric Multi-Processors) [5], multicomputers and clusters [6]. Clusters are groupings of Processing Elements (PE) dispersed in different geographical areas, which can be accessed by communication links to execute programs requiring high processing times [7]. The processing power of clusters is based on the number of processors of each cluster contains and is available for use; the distinguishing feature is the heterogeneity of their PE since not all clusters contain processors with the same communication speeds, processing speeds and number of cores. The parallel structure of the clusters makes them suitable for processing Parallel Task Graphs (PTGs) with parallel programs requesting different numbers of processors to process the PTG subtasks, and communication links to transfer information between tasks.

PTGs represented by Directed Acyclic Graphs (DAGs), have been used to represent parallel programs, where vertices represent tasks while the edges represent communication relationships between subtasks. PTGs are scheduled in the target system using a scheduler, which is executed in two phases, scheduling of resources and mapping. In the scheduling phase the best assignments of resources to tasks are searched for to reduce the waiting time (the time the task waits in queue) and makespan namely, the time since tasks arrival in the queue until the completion of the execution of the task on the system. The most common way to evaluate the performance in a scheduler is with the results obtained with these two performance metrics: Waiting time and Makespan [1,8]. Other metrics supporting the performance of the scheduler are the quality of the allocations, which obtains the percentage of HPCS processors used in the execution of the allocations, and the time consumed by the scheduler in searching the resources. To measure the overall performance of a scheduler with these metrics, different synthetic workloads or real application workloads are used. The mapping phase maps the tasks to the resources that were assigned to them in the scheduling phase.

The Array Method (described in Sect. 4) is a scheduler for an HPC System, which uses the metaheuristic algorithm UMDA (Univariate Marginal Distribution Algorithm) [9] for scheduling and resource mapping in a HPC System [1]; a sequential version of the algorithm executes the method in a cluster of servers and synthetic workloads are used to evaluate the performance metrics. From the results obtained with the experiments of the sequential algorithm we propose that the times obtained, with the performance metrics evaluated, can be improved by scaling the scheduling phase of the algorithm to a parallel version, using C language and OpenMP libraries to carry out shared memory programming. The justification for the use of these libraries is given in Sect. 3 with the explanation of advantages of some applications that have been scaled with the OpenMP libraries and in Sect. 4 with the data structures used in the programming of scheduling phase.

This research work describes the design of the parallel program for the scheduling phase of the array method, using shared memory programming. For the explanation of the parallel program design, a flowchart and a set of pseudocode blocks have been used. The parallel program and the sequential program proposed in [1], for comparison purposes, are executed on an HPC System consisting of a set of clusters and a server farm. Synthetic loads are used for the execution of experiments and the metrics waiting time, makespan, quality of allocations and resource search time are evaluated; in Sect. 5 results obtained with the experiments are explained. The following subsection summarizes the contributions of this work.

1.1 Contributions of the Paper

- Describes and presents a parallel version of the algorithm for resource scheduling in an HPC System based on the sequential algorithm proposed in [1].
- Evaluates and compares the performance metrics and quality of the allocations of the parallel and sequential versions of the resource scheduling algorithms.
- Execution of experiments with a parallel approach to the UMDA algorithm.
- Compare the results obtained from a sequential programming method with a parallel programming method, highlighting the benefits of using each type of programming.
- Performs extensive experimentation in different scenarios to show the results obtained with different synthetic loads and different number of PE in the clusters.
- Addresses shared memory programming and its application to resource scheduling in HPC systems.

The paper is structured as follows: Sect. 2 presents a set of definitions to understand the scheduling phase of the scheduler and the parallel algorithms developed. Section 3 describes the technologies used in this work, as well as the work related to this paper. Section 4 describes the arrays method data structures along with the proposed parallel algorithms to fill these structures. Experiments have been developed with the proposed parallel algorithm comparing it with the sequential algorithm, the results are presented in Sect. 5. The conclusions are presented in Sect. 6 and future work in Sect. 7.

2   Basic Definitions

The definitions in this section are used in this research work and in the algorithms proposed in the following sections. The definitions in [1] have been extended for further explanation of the proposed parallel algorithms.

Definition 1. The target system consists of C_l clusters, $C_1, C_2, ..., C_l$ where l is the number of clusters contained in the HPC System. Each cluster contains m heterogeneous processors with n processing cores. Therefore, $C_{l,m,n}$ is cluster k, processor m, processing core n.

Definition 2. PTG can be modeled by an Directed Acyclic Graph (DAG) $T = (N, E)$ where:

$N = \{n_i : i = 1, 2, ..., N\}$ is a set of N vertices or subtasks that constitute the task, and
$E = E_{i,j} : i, j = 1, 2, ..., N$ is a set of E edges.
A PTG can be characterized by

$$(n_i, \{1 \leq j \geq n_i | T_i\}, G_i, V_i, W_i) \tag{1}$$

where:
n_i : is the number of subtasks in T_i.
$\{1 \leq j \leq n_i | T_i\}$: is the set of subtasks.
G_i : is the set of directed relationships between the subtasks.
V_i : is the number of levels of T_i.
W_i : is the width of each level T_i represented by an array.
The PTG consists of a set of N nodes and a set E of edges (directed relationships). The nodes represent execution requirements of the task T. The requirement of each task is represented by w_{n_i}. The directed relationships show the flow of execution of the subtask $\tau_{i,j}$ to subtask $\tau_{i,k}$ of task T_i. Each of the terms used in this definition are explained below.

Definition 3. The processing time of a task $t_{i,k} \in T_i$ is the cost of executing the task in a $C_{l,m,n}$ and is represented by:

$$EC_{\tau_{i,j}} \tag{2}$$

Definition 4. The processing time of a task T_i, is the sum of the execution time of all its subtasks and is denoted by:

$$\sum_{\forall \tau_{i,k} \in T_i}^{N} EC_{\tau_{i,k}} \tag{3}$$

Definition 5. The cost of the execution flow or cost of communication between the subtasks $\tau_{i,j}$ and $\tau_{i,k}$ represented by $CC_{\tau_{i,j} \to \tau_{i,j}}$ is expressed in bytes.

Definition 6. PTG density is the number of links between PTG subtasks. It is represented by:

$$|G_i| \tag{4}$$

The communication percentage of a task is obtained by counting the total number of edges and the number of subtasks of PTG.

Definition 7. A directed relationship from subtask $\tau_{i,j}$ to $\tau_{i,k}$ means $\tau_{i,k}$ can start its execution only if $\tau_{i,j}$ completes its own. In this case we call $\tau_{i,j}$ a parent sub-task of $\tau_{i,k}$ and $\tau_{i,k}$ the child of $\tau_{i,j}$. Each sub-task in a given DAG task can have several parents and children. An initial subtask is a subtask without parents, while a final subtask is a subtask without children. A PTG has a start subtask and a finish subtask.

Definition 8. The width of a level V_l is traditionally defined as

$$\omega(V) = \sum v \in V_l \tag{5}$$

And the width of a layered network (divided into layers or levels) is defined by the equation:

$$\omega = max_{1 \leq l \leq h} w(V_l) \tag{6}$$

Definition 9. Layering. Given T, where each node $n_i \in N$ has positive width W_i, a division by layers or levels of T_i also called stratification of T_i is a partition of the set of nodes V into disjoint subsets $V_1, V_2, ..., V_h$ such as if $(u,v) \in E$ and $u \in V_i$ and $v \in V_j$ then $i > j$. A DAG with a stratification or division by levels is called a stratified digraph.

Definition 10. A synthetic workload is constituted by a set of DAG Tasks and is denoted by:

$$S = T_1, T_2, ..., T_n \tag{7}$$

Each T_n consists of a random number of subtasks and a random number of edges. n is defined in the workload generation algorithm.

Definition 11. Calculation of the DAG routes, is the calculation of all paths from the initial subtask to the final subtask. For the critical path, the algorithm chooses the path that satisfies the following two conditions:

$$max \sum v \in w_{n_i} \tag{8}$$

$$max \sum CC_{\tau_{i,j} \to \tau_{i,j}} \tag{9}$$

Where the sum of the execution requirements and the cost of the execution flow on the route is greater than all other routes.

Definition 12. The critical path length (CP Length) of a DAG task is denoted by:

$$M = \lceil \frac{\sum w_{n_i}}{CPLength} \rceil \tag{10}$$

Where M is the minimum number of processors and w_{n_i} is the processing time of task T_i.

Definition 13. Threshold μ_1 is a value that is satisfied when any subtask $T_{i,j}$ is connected with 75% or more of the subtasks of T_i.

Definition 14. Threshold μ_2 is the percentage of edges of a subtask in relation to N, and is expressed by:

$$\mu_2 = \left(\frac{100}{|E| - 1} \right) * |A_{\tau_{i,j}}| \tag{11}$$

Where:

$|E|$ is the absolute value of the finite set E of edges

$|A_{\tau_{i,j}}|$ is the absolute value of the edges set of any subtask $\tau_{i,j}$

Definition 15. A densely connected vertex. A vertex n_i is densely connected, if the following condition is true:

$$\mu_2 \geq \mu_1 \tag{12}$$

Definition 16. Densely connected PTG. A PTG is densely connected if the following condition is true:

$$P_{HL} = \left(\left(\frac{100}{|E|} \right) * Number\ of\ densely\ connected\ vertices\ of\ \tau_i \right) \leq \mu_2 \tag{13}$$

Definition 17. Start time of the task, is the start time of each DAG task and is calculated according this formula:

$$S_t(T_n) = EX_t \left(\sum_{T_1}^{n-1} EC_{T_n} \right) + DCT_t \left(\sum_{T_1}^{n-1} CC_{\tau_{i,1} \to \tau_{i,n}} \right) + ST_{T_n \to \pi_m} \tag{14}$$

Where: $S_t(T_n)$, is start time of the task, $EX_t \left(\sum_{T_1}^{n-1} EC_{T_n} \right)$ is execution time of its predecessor nodes, $DCT_t \left(\sum_{T_1}^{n-1} CC_{\tau_{i,1} \to \tau_{i,n}} \right)$, corresponds to data communication time of its predecessor nodes, and $ST_{T_n \to \pi_m}$ is sending time of task to the processor.

Definition 18. The task completion time (TCT), is the time recorded in the matrix once the task has finished its execution in the processor; parameter calculated by the formula:

$$TCT = S_t(T_n) + TaskExecutionTime \tag{15}$$

Definition 19. Quality of the assignments. Represents the percentage of occupied processors in each allocation made by the algorithms, and is calculated with the total sum of processors occupied in the allocation, among the total number of processors in the target system, times 100: the quality of the allocations is obtained with the formula:

$$Q_a = \left(\frac{\sum_{i=0}^{m} \forall \pi_m\ that\ contains\ a\ \eta_i}{|\pi|} \right) * 100 \tag{16}$$

Definition 20. Waiting time. Time consumed by the task from the arrival of the queue to the start of its execution on a processor.

Definition 21. Makespan, is the time difference between the start and finish of a sequence of jobs or tasks.

The aforementioned definitions represent an HDCS in which the Array Method schedules synthetic loads, upholding the execution requirements of each task, the directed hierarchical relationships and the start time of each DAG Task.

3 Related Works

Clusters are a prominent way to process large amounts of information and develop parallel programs. The languages used for cluster programming have been OpenMP [10] for shared memory programming, MPI for distributed memory programming and parallelization of applications with a hybrid model: OpenMP and MPI; for the case of this research, only shared memory programming with Open MP is used to parallelization of Arrays Method scheduling phase; future works currently under development include the use of programming with the hybrid model for the resource allocation phase.

OpenMP is an open specification for shared-memory parallelism that extends the base languages, such as Fortran, C and C++ [11,12]; by itself is not a language, it provides an API for portably expressing parallelism and concurrency and across of the three languages, thus the OpenMP provides a simple and flexible model for developing parallel applications for plataforms ranging from embedded systems and accelerator devices to multicore system [11] and is the de facto standard for shared-memory parallel programming, providing a simple but powerful method for specifying shared work between threads [13].

OpenMP programmers can start from simple usage of OpenMP directives and incrementally increase the level of complexity to expose more and more control over the code transformations applied and parallel execution to achieve higher performance [11]. Therefore, OpenMP has literally become a posible programming for distributed memory parallel machines, notably clusters, for implementing of distributed virtual shared memory software which allow near-shared-memory programming [6].

Although applications based on OpenMP libraries have been developed, a method for scheduling PTGs using pure OpenMP as the base programming language does not appear in the literature. Some works from different areas of science scaled from a sequential algorithmic solution to a parallel solution in a cluster computational environment using OpenMP libraries, are described in the following paragraphs; these works have been considered as examples for the development of this research.

In the research works listed below, the performance and acceleration improvements that come with scaling an application are described. These papers are referenced not only because they used OpenMP but because of the compelling results that each paper brings in different areas of science.

In [2], an application of simplex method parallelization based on OpenMP parallel programming technology is developed to improve, the acceleration and efficiency of the method as well as a comparison with the conventional simplex method; the objective is to take advantage of modern trends in multi-core processor architecture, with the parallelization of the algorithm of the simplex method, to achieve maximum acceleration and efficiency in the processing of large volumes of input data; the results obtained in this work show the acceleration factor increases with the increase in the number of cores, which means the acceleration and efficiency of the parallel algorithm depends directly on the computer architecture, and the threads number of the processor.

In [3], the parallelization of the multiple precision Taylor series method with OpenMP is proposed and the use of the C programming language and the GMP library (The GNU Multiple Precision Arithmetic Library), changing the sequential program into a parallel program step by step one code block at a time, looking for acceleration results; the aim is present a simple and effective OpenMP parallelization of the multiple precision Taylor series method, which uses a moderate computational resource, namely one CPU-node; the results obtained are very good parallel performance scalability and parallel efficiency inside one computation node of a CPU-cluster.

In [4] a high performance implementation of MARSA-LFIB4, a high quality recursive multiple pseudo-random recursive number generator based on OpenMP is presented, to improve performance and acceleration on multicore architectures and to make the application more energy efficient; this implementation uses an algorithmic approach combining language-based vectorization techniques together with a new parallel divide-and-conquer algorithm, can exploit the special sparse structure of the obtained matrix. This parallel implementation outperforms a simple (non-optimized) and SIMD (vectorized but not parallel) implementation in terms of performance, speedup and energy efficiency.

3.1 Parallel Application Design

Research works [12, 14–16] have proposed a set of steps or criteria for the design of a parallel application such as: the specification of the hardware or architecture where the application runs, the parallelization model to be used, the programming methodologies, the workload partitioning scheme, the implementation strategy, the synchronization, the software libraries and the communication model. Each of the steps specifies the work to be performed by the programmer during the design of a parallel system. Based on the aforementioned, in this research work the following stages are considered:

- Hardware specification. The parallel program design for the scheduling phase of the array method is performed for a multi-core processor with shared cache memory on a single microprocessor. These systems are more prominent in the commercial market and therefore the processing can be implemented not only in HPC architectures, but also in low-cost personal computers and workstations using standard software components [14].

– The workload partitioning scheme. To partition the workloads, the regions of the code that consume the most processing time and can be parallelized were identified, along with a trace of the program flow to debug and resolve performance issues. The GNU gprof tool [17], was used in this phase of the algorithm design.
– Software library. The OpenMP standard has been chosen. OpenMP allow the multi-threaded execution of a program due to compiler directives exploit loop level paralelism [10,14]. Parallel loops are an important part of OpenMP programs. Loop-level parallelism is a very important part of many OpenMP applications that frequently contain computationally-intensive and large data parallel loops. Such OpenMP applications are typically executed on HPC platforms which are increasingly complex, large, heterogeneous, and exhibit massive and diverse parallelism [18].

4   Array Method Parallelization Using OpenMP

The array method [1], is a dynamic scheduler for scheduling and mapping tasks in an HPC system; this scheduler works with a set of arrays that store the results generated in each function.

Why is C language and OpenMP libraries used as the base language to parallelize the array method? Because for each of the arrays, iterative processes or loops are executed. The loops are parallelized through a master that creates additional threads covering all iterations of the loop (one thread per core), producing for each processing cores the division of work. In order to parallelize the functions of Arrays Method, OpenMP data parallelism and shared memory-based directives or pragmas were used. The scope of the variables shared by all the functions (shared variables) and the variables used by each function (private variables) were defined. Handling of concurrencies in the program is done by declaring critical sections that ensure mutual exclusion in the execution of code blocks and prevent simultaneous execution of code segments by different threads. Finally, using explicit parallelism, the parallel work per core was distributed based on the number of cores contained in the processor.

The code blocks in Table 1 through Table 8 show the main pseudo code functions of the parallel algorithm and how each matrix is used and filled within The Matrix Method, using OpenMP programming. Flowchart in Fig. 1 depicts the interaction between the blocks of pseudocode; the program starts with the verification of the resources in the target system (Resource_Verification) and updates the resource matrix, then each PTG is extracted from the queue and the characteristics are extracted from each PTG (PTG_Characteristics) with the Depth First Search algorithm and the matrix features is updated; with the characteristics' matrix, the search process for the best assignment is carried out with the UMDA. By obtaining the best characteristics, the start times of the tasks are calculated; finally the process of freeing up resources is executed every time the tasks are finished without execution.

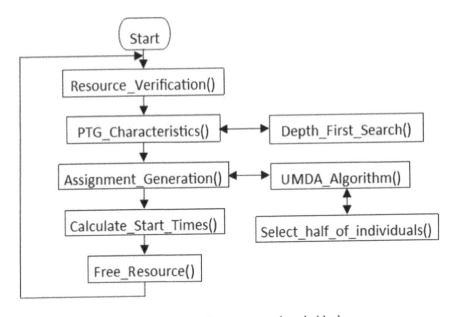

Fig. 1. Interaction between pseudocode blocks.

4.1   Arrays of the Array Method

The arrays used by The Array Method are: The resource matrix, the matrix of the characteristics of the PTGs, the allocation matrix and the matrix of task start times. On next paragraphs, every array is explained.

1. The resource matrix is an array whose values are obtained by an iterative process of checking the resources in the HPC system. Each time a processing element or a cluster is added to the HPC system, this array is updated; it stores two characteristics of each PE: its number of cores and the distances between the PE and the PE of the HPC system.

The algorithm in Table 1 shows an iterative process of searching for new resources in the HPC system for updating the resource matrix; this algorithm is executed in set time lapses and a procedure performs the sensing in the HPC system.

If new resources are located, a loop is executed to extract the resource characteristics and compute the distances from the processing element to each of the EPs; finally the resource is added to the resource matrix for utilization.

Resource status. A resource in the resource matrix can have a busy state or an idle state. A resource's busy state indicates a task is using the resource, and a resource's idle status indicates resource has not been occupied by a task or has already been released by the completion of task's execution. Algorithm in Table 2 release a resource when a task has already finished execution.

Once the Free Resource ($C_{k,n,m}$) function is executed, resources are released for the execution of other subtasks or tasks.

Table 1. Algorithm 1. Search algorithm performs the search for new resources in the HPC system.

```
Resource_Verification {
  Resource Detection in HPCS (Num_New_Res);
  #pragma omp parallel num_threads(THreads) shared(Num_New_Res)
  if (Num_New_Resources > 0) then
    for (j = 0; j < Num_New_Res; j++) do
      Extract_Characteristics_Res();
      Compute_Distances();
      Add_Resources_Matrix();
    end_for
  end_if
} // Resource_Verification
```

Table 2. Algorithm 2. Free_Resource function, Algorithm for release of resources from a $C_{k,n,m}$ when a task has finished its execution.

```
#pragma omp parallel num_threads(THreads) shared(j, Res_in_Cluster)
Free_Resource (C_{k,n,m}) {
# pragma omp for
  for (j = 1; j < Res_in_Cluster; j++) do
    if (C_{k,n,m}_in_Array_Resources) then
      (C_{k,n,m}) is free;
    end_if
  end_for
} // Free_Resource
```

2. The Characteristics Matrix. The PTG characteristics matrix stores the features extracted from each PTG using the Depth First Search Algorithm (DFS Algorithm): PTG identification number, number of PTG routes according to Definition 11, number of PTG levels according to Definition 9, number of vertices per level according to Definition 8 and PTG density according to Definition 6. The algorithm in Table 3 generates the characteristics of the PTGs and calls the first depth search algorithm proposed in Table 4. For space reasons, a reduced version of the Deep Search Algorithm (DSA) is shown; the development of this algorithm is based on [19].

With the DFS Algorithm the characteristics of each PTG are obtained, which are: number of PTG paths, critical path, number of PTG levels, number of vertices per level and the density of the DAG. The whole set of features obtained is stored in the feature matrix.

3. The assignment matrix, is a dynamic matrix that takes values from each assignment produced by the algorithm. The PTGs in the feature matrix are iteratively assigned to the free processors in the HPC System by applying two free processor search criteria. These criteria are applied based on the density of the DAG. If the DAG density is greater than the established threshold criterion

Table 3. Algorithm 3. Algorithm for the generation of PTG characteristics.

PTG_Characteristics {
   while (PTG_in_ S) do
      Select_Next_PTG_from S ();
      Depth_First_Search();
      Store_in_Characteristics_Matrix();
   end_while
} // PTG_Characteristics

Table 4. Algorithm 4. Depth First Search Algorithm [19].

Depth_First_Search (T) {
  stack is empty;
  stack.push$\tau_{i,k}$
  while (stack is not empty)
   $\tau_{i,k}$ =stack.pop()
   if $\tau_{i,k}$ is not visted
    label $\tau_{i,k}$ as visted
#pragma omp parallel num_threads(THreads) shared(i, Adjacent_Edges)
    for all $E_{i,j}$ from i to j in adjacent Edges $\tau_{i,k}$ do
 # pragma omp critical
      stack.push(j)
  Return: PTG Characteristics

2 (according to Definitions 13 and 14) is applied otherwise criterion 1 is used. An explanation of each criterion is given in the paragraphs below.

Criterion 1. Determines if the allocation of HPC System resources is based on the paths generated from the DAG. The path with the highest allocation priority is the critical path M (according to Definition 12). A pruning process for the PTG is performed once each route is assigned. The number of cores of each selected EP is considered for the path assignment; the divide and conquer method is applied recursively in case the PTG path is greater than the number of cores of the selected EP.

Criterion 2. Determines if the PTG is densely connected, according to Definition 16, the resource allocation process is carried out using the DAG levels (according to Definition 9) and the number of subtasks per PTG level (according to Definition 8). Depending on the number of subtasks per level, these are the processing cores to be searched for in the EPs, so that the processing data flow in the same direction. In cases where the algorithm does not find a EP with the number of cores equal to or less than the number of tasks per level, it iteratively applies the divide and conquer method.

The algorithm in Table 5 is the process for generating solutions and calculating the parameters of each population to store the data in the allocation matrix.

Table 5. Algorithm 5. Process for generating solutions and calculating the parameters of each population.

```
Input: characteristics matrix
 stack is empty;
Input: characteristics matrix
Output: assignment matrix for T
Assignment_Generation {
 Search_for_resources_available_in_HPC_System ;
 while ((resources_available) and (T in Charactersitics_Array)) do
   if not true (P_HL) }
     criterion_1_is_applied
   } else {
     criterion_2_is_applied
   }
 end_while
} //Assignment_Generation
```

An iterative process generates the assignments in this matrix. Each time the process iterates, a solution is generated which is the assignment of the task to the PEs of the HPC System, according to the two assignment criteria.

The solution generation process is iterated until a certain number of assignments is reached (maximum number of populations indicated in the algorithm) or when the population does not improve with respect to the best of the individuals obtained in the previous generations.

Generation of Populations. With the matrix of assignments the solution matrices are constructed. The solution matrices store three parameters: Hamming distance, state of the processors, and the distance to the target cluster. These solution matrices are the populations used by the UMDA algorithm for its execution

UMDA Algorithm. The following steps are performed by the UMDA algorithm (appearing in Table 7) for the generation of the best allocation.

Step 1. The solutions generated and stored in the assignment matrix represent the initial population P_0; the following generated solutions represent the next populations used by the algorithm to iterate.

Step 2. Some individuals are selected from P_0 by the standard truncation method to select half of the initial population, denoted by $p_0^{S_0}$; the selection is carried out by the function that minimizes the values of the following three parameters: Hamming distance, state of the processors and the distance to the target cluster; the algorithm in Table 6 shows the function to minimize these parameters. In case of a tie between the values when evaluating the individuals, the selection is carried out probabilistically.

The Best Assignment Determined by the UMDA Algorithm

Once the UMDA algorithm completes execution, the best assignment for T is provided. This phase of the algorithm determines whether the task can start

Table 6. Algorithm 6. Algorithm for the minimization of the UMDA algorithm parameters.

Select_half_of_individuals() {
  Min(Hamming_Distance, State_Processors, Distance_to_the_Target_Cluster);
} //Select_half_of_individuals

Table 7. Algorithm 7. UMDA algorithm [9]

UMDA_Algorithm {
  D_0 ← Generate_M_Allocations (the initial population) randomly
  Repeat for $l = 1, 2, ...$ until the stop criterion is verified
  D_{l-1}^{Se} ← Select $N \leq$ individuals from D_{l-1} according to the selection method
  $p_l(x) = p(x|D_{l-1}^{Se})$ ← Estimate the probability distribution of finding
        an individual in the selected individuals
  D_l ← Sample M individuals (the new population) of $p_l(x)$
} //UMDA_Algorithm

its execution or is queued waiting for the processors that are occupied by other tasks.

4. The matrix of the start times of the tasks

Once the algorithm determines the best assignment for the PTG, the start times for each of the PTG subtasks are calculated; these values are stored in the matrix of task start times. Algorithm in Table 8 calculates the execution start times for each PTG. This process is executed in one cycle when more than one task has been scheduled and must be assigned to the matrix of task start times.

Table 8. Algorithm 8, calculates the execution start times for each PTG.

while (T in Task_Scheduling_Queue) {
  Record the PTG arrival time in the matrix of task start times.
  Computes task start time (according to Definition 17)
  Calculates task completion time (according to Definition 19)
} //end_while

5 Results

To perform the experiments, an HDCS is simulated, based on 50 clusters, with the generation of a random number of resources per cluster. The number of clusters and the number of resources per cluster is fixed, in order to obtain the results of the 3 parameters evaluated: waiting time, makespan and quality of assignment.

For a better understanding of the experiments carried out in this research work, this section defines the hardware, software, the way in which the workloads are constituted and the way in which the comparisons of the proposed algorithms are made. Due to space, explanation of every experiment was reduced considering the most important comments.

Hardware. Programming of the scheduler is done on a Dell server EMC Power Edge Rack Server Intel Xeon generation 2 with 8 cores. Dell Technologies 701 E. Parmer Lane, Bldg PS2, Austin, TX 78753, USA.

Software. The programming language used in the scheduler programming is the standard C language, with the OpenMP libraries; both technologies are used for the generation of the PTGs that are in the host memory. The resident operating system is Linux.

Workload. The sizes of the workloads are constituted in incremental amounts from 25 to 1000, with increments of 25 PTGs. These loads are stored in physical files that are read at each experiment performed and are not modified during the execution of the experiments.

Algorithm Comparison. In this work, a comparison is made between the sequential array method algorithm proposed in [1] and the parallel array method algorithm proposed and developed in this research work. The experiments were classified as follows: the makespan and waiting time were evaluated with synthetic loads generated with the Markov Chain algorithm. Partial execution times are not considered in these experiments. The time presented in the graphs is considered from the time the algorithm starts to process the first PTG until it processes the last PTG of the workload.

5.1   Experiments to Evaluate the Makespan Metric

Experiments are carried out with the makespan (according to Definition 21), using the sequential algorithm and the parallel algorithm; Fig. 2 shows the comparisons of the times that each of the algorithms consumes with different workloads.

Observation points. The Markov chain algorithm for the generation of synthetic loads produces PTGs with a greater distribution of subtasks in the initial phase, which generates an early search for resources to perform the PTG subtask assignments. At the beginning of the execution of the algorithms, with an average of less than 350 PTGs, the algorithms generate very similar times in the evaluation of the makespan. When the number of PTGs increases, there are differences between both algorithms; the number of PTGs in the synthetic loads, allow to observe a differentiation in the execution speeds of the algorithms.

5.2   Experiments to Evaluate the Waiting Time Metric

The evaluation parameter waiting time (according to Definition 20), allows to observe the time that the tasks must wait to be attended. It is an exponential parameter that increases as the workloads increase the number of PTGs.

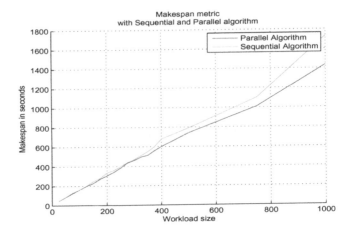

Fig. 2. Results of the comparisons between parallel and sequential algorithm of the consumed times with makespan metric.

The main objective of this experiment is to determine whether the parallel algorithm outperforms the makespan of the sequential algorithm. The makespan results obtained using parallel algorithm and sequential algorithm are shown in Fig. 3.

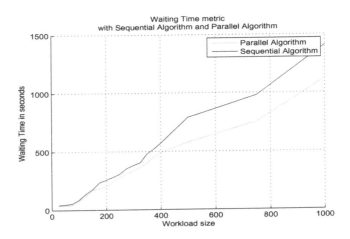

Fig. 3. Results of the comparisons between parallel and sequential algorithm of the consumed times with waiting time metric.

Observation points. Differences in the results obtained occur when the workloads are substantially increased. The parallel algorithm outperforms the sequential algorithm when the loads are greater than 150 PTGs on average.

5.3 Experiments to Evaluate the Quality of Assignments When Experimenting with the Makespan Metric

Quality of Assignments. The evaluation of this metric (according to Definition 19), specifies the resources used during the assignments that the algorithms perform. The experiment is performed when the workload is equal to 500 PTGs, and the availability of resources is 100%, and is made to decrease in each experiment, i.e., only 90% is made available in the second experiment, 80% in the third experiment, and so on until having approximately 10% of the available resources of the system.

The comparison of the results of this metric with both algorithms was performed as follows: 10 experiments were performed with the same workload 300 PTGs and the percentage of resource utilization after the allocations was measured; both algorithms present very similar percentages, results obtained using parallel algorithm and sequential algorithm are shown in Fig. 4; the parallel algorithm exceeds the sequential algorithm by only one percentage point. Based on this experimentation, it was decided to perform the following experimentation: to measure the time consumed by each of the algorithms during the search for resources in the clusters for the assignment of tasks. This experimentation is explained in the following paragraphs.

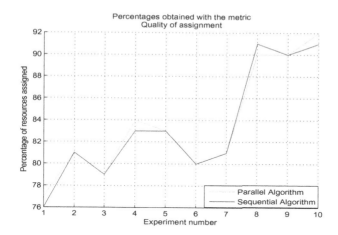

Fig. 4. Results of evaluating the sequential and parallel algorithm with the quality assignment metric; different workloads are applied.

Observation points. A good allocation quality is found when the number of resources is low, but when the number of resources increases, the results of the allocation percentages of both algorithms may vary, the sequential algorithm is able to outperform the parallel algorithm. The dispersion of subtasks in the clusters, during the scheduling fase is produced by the sequential search, performed by both algorithms. Experiments with this metric led to the following experimentation: Time to search for resources in the clusters for the assignment of tasks, which is explained in the following paragraphs.

5.4   Time to Search for Resources in the Clusters for the Assignment of Tasks

For this experimentation, the same workloads used for the measurement of the makespan and waiting time metrics were used. In this experimentation, the parallel algorithm shows shorter search times when the number of resources in the clusters is less or equal to 500 (experiments 1 to 5), which means that this algorithm is faster during execution. But when the number of resources in the cluster increases considerably (more than 500 PEs in experiments 6 to 10) both algorithms present very similar times, which shows that the search for resources in the clusters when the number of PEs is very dense requires a more sophisticated algorithm than the sequential algorithm of resource search. Results obtained using parallel algorithm and sequential algorithm are shown in Fig. 5.

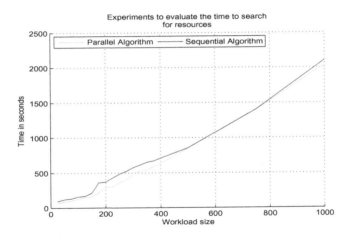

Fig. 5. Results of time to search for resources in the clusters for the assignment of tasks.

This experiment shows the need to modify the resource search method in the clusters. It is clear that a high number of resources in the HDC System makes it difficult to locate resources faster.

6   Conclusions

The Array Method is a PTGs scheduler for an HPC System. This scheduler has two phases: scheduling and allocation. The array method is made up of a set of arrays; repetitive cycles are used for filled these arrays during the scheduling phase, which allows parallelize array method; OpenMP libraries are used with multi-threaded methodologies that consist of an analysis, design, debugging and tuning of the proposed algorithms. The experiments were carried out with the sequential version of the algorithm against a parallel version using the makespan and waiting time metrics. The results obtained show a decrease in the convergence times in the metrics evaluated with the parallel algorithm. Two more evaluations were carried out: the quality of the assignments and the time spent searching for resources in the cluster; the results when evaluating these two metrics have shown similar times in both algorithms (sometimes the sequential algorithm exceeds the parallel algorithm), which makes it necessary to develop a resource search strategy in the clusters.

7 Future Works

To continue with this research, the parallelization of the mapping phase of the resources to the PTGs is proposed; to develop this future research, OpenMP and MPI hybrid programming will be used. Similarly, comparisons with a meta-heuristic approach are proposed for the planning phase and the resource mapping phase.

References

1. Velarde Martinez, A.: Scheduling in heterogeneous distributed computing systems based on internal structure of parallel tasks graphs with meta-heuristics. Appl. Sci. **10**(18), 6611 (2020)
2. Mochurad, L., Boyko, N., Petryshyn, N., Potokij, M., Yatskiv, M.: Parallelization of the simplex method based on the OpenMP technology. In: Lytvyn, V., et al. (ed.) Proceedings of the 4th International Conference on Computational Linguistics and Intelligent Systems (COLINS 2020), vol. I, 23–24 April 2020, Lviv, Ukraine (2020). http://ceur-ws.org/Vol-2604/paper62.pdf
3. Dimova, S., et al: OpenMP parallelization of multiple precision Taylor series method. Cornell University, 25 August 2019. arXiv:1908.09301v1, https://arxiv.org/pdf/1908.09301.pdf
4. Stpiczyński, P.: Algorithmic and language-based optimization of Marsa-LFIB4 pseudorandom number generator using OpenMP, OpenACC and CUDA. J. Parallel Distrib. Comput. **137**, 238–245 (2020)
5. Jost, G., Jin, H., an Mey, D., Hatay, F.F.: Comparing the OpenMP, MPI, and Hybrid Programming Paradigm on an SMP Cluster. https://ntrs.nasa.gov/api/citations/20030107321/downloads/20030107321.pdf
6. Rabenseifner, R., Hager, G., Jost, G.: Hybrid MPI/OpenMP parallel programming on clusters of multi-core SMP nodes. In: 2009 17th Euromicro International Conference on Parallel, Distributed and Network-based Processing, Weimar, Germany, pp. 427–436 (2009). https://doi.org/10.1109/PDP.2009.43
7. Jiao, Y.Y., Zhao, Q., Wang, L., Huang, G.H., Tan, F.: A hybrid MPI/OpenMP parallel computing model for spherical discontinuous deformation analysis. Comput. Geotech. **106**, 217–227 (2019). https://doi.org/10.1016/j.compgeo.2018.11.004 ELSEVIER

8. Xafa, F., Abraham, A.: Computational models and heuristic methods for grid scheduling problems. Future Gener. Comput. Syst. **26**(4), 608–621 (2010). https://doi.org/10.1016/j.future.2009.11.005

9. Larrañaga, P., Lozano, A.: Estimation of Distribution Algorithms A New Tool for Evolutionary Computation. Springer, Cham (2002). https://doi.org/10.1007/978-1-4615-1539-5, Hardcover ISBN: 978-0-7923-7466-4

10. https://www.openmp.org/

11. de Supinski, B.R., et al.: The ongoing evolution of OpenMP. Proc. IEEE **106**(11), 2004–2019 (2018). https://doi.org/10.1109/JPROC.2018.2853600

12. Kasim, H., March, V., Zhang, R., See, S.: Survey on parallel programming model. In: Cao, J., Li, M., Wu, M.Y., Chen, J. (eds.) Network and Parallel Computing, NPC 2008, Lecture Notes in Computer Science, vol. 5245, pp. 266–275. Springer, Heidelberg (2008). https://doi.org/10.1007/978-3-540-88140-7_24

13. Chorley, M.J., Walker, D.W.: Performance analysis of a hybrid MPI/OpenMP application on multi-core clusters. J. Comput. Sci. **1**(3), 168–174 (2010). https://doi.org/10.1016/j.jocs.2010.05.001

14. Baños, R., Ortega, J., Gil, C., de Toro, F., Montoya, M.G.: Analysis of OpenMP and MPI implementations of meta-heuristics for vehicle routing problems. Appl. Soft Comput. **43**, 262–275 (2016). https://doi.org/10.1016/j.asoc.2016.02.035

15. Chapman, B., Jost, G., Van Der Pas, R.: Using OpenMP, Portable Shared Memory Parallel Programming. The MIT Press, Cambridge (2008)

16. Ma, H., Wang, L., Krishnamoorthy, K.: Detecting thread-safety violations in hybrid OpenMP/MPI programs. In: 2015 IEEE International Conference on Cluster Computing, Chicago, IL, USA, pp. 460–463 (2015). https://doi.org/10.1109/CLUSTER.2015.70

17. https://ftp.gnu.org/

18. Kale, V., Iwainsky, Ch., Klemm, M., Müller Korndürfer, J.H., Ciorb, F.M.: Toward a standard interface for user-defined scheduling in OpenMP, August 2019. https://www.researchgate.net/publication/333971657_Toward_a_Standard_Interface_for_User-Defined_Scheduling_in_OpenMP, https://doi.org/10.1007/978-3-030-28596-8_13

19. Freeman, J.: Parallel Algorithms for Depth-First Search. University of Pennsylvania Department of Computer and Information Science Technical Report No. MS-CIS-91-71, October 1991

Best Paper Award, Third Place

Sign Language Translation Using Multi Context Transformer

M. Badri Narayanan[1]([envelope]), K. Mahesh Bharadwaj[1], G. R. Nithin[1],
Dhiganth Rao Padamnoor[1], and Vineeth Vijayaraghavan[2]

[1] Sri Sivasubramaniya Nadar College of Engineering, Chennai, India
mbadri@ieee.org, maheshbharadwaj18089@cse.ssn.edu.in,
{nithin18100,dhiganth18037}@ece.ssn.edu.in
[2] Solarillion Foundation, Chennai, India
vineethv@ieee.org

Abstract. Sign Language Translation (SLT) is an important sequence-to-sequence problem that has been challenging to solve, because of the various factors which influence the meaning of a sign. In this paper, we implement a *Multi Context Transformer* architecture that attempts to solve this problem by operating on batched video segment representations called *context vectors*, intending to capture various temporal dependencies present between the frames to accurately translate the input signs. This architecture, being end-to-end also eliminates the need for sign language intermediaries known as *glosses*. Our model produces results that are on par with the state-of-the-art (98.19% score retention in the ROUGE-L score and 86.65% in the BLEU-4 score) while simultaneously achieving a 30.88% reduction in model parameters, which makes the model suitable for real-world applications. Our implementation is available on GitHub.([1]https://github.com/MBadriNarayanan/MultiContextTransformer)

Keywords: Sign language · Sign language translation · Transformer · Multi-context · Context vectors

1 Introduction

Communication is an integral part of our daily lives. In a society where auditory communication is the most predominant form of communication, people who make use of sign language are deprived of effective methods to communicate with others. Sign Language Translation is defined as either converting written languages into a video of sign language; or extracting an equivalent spoken language sentence from a video, which is the objective of this paper.

Implementing SLT systems is a challenging task as sign language does not follow the conventional grammatical and linguistic structure of spoken language; signs in a sequence do not maintain a one-one relationship with the output translation. Recent research, however, has provided a breakthrough with the usage

© Springer Nature Switzerland AG 2021
I. Batyrshin et al. (Eds.): MICAI 2021, LNAI 13068, pp. 311–324, 2021.
https://doi.org/10.1007/978-3-030-89820-5_25

of Transformer architecture [1,2], which processes the whole video sequence and produces a fairly accurate translation. With regards to continuous sign language translation, a simple unification of isolated signs is not sufficient to correctly recognize, translate or generate a complete sentence due to the above-mentioned challenges. We devise an easy-to-use and assistive technology that facilitates hearing-impaired people to communicate better with the world around them using accessible devices with moderate computational power. We posit a hybrid architecture that groups the video sequence into blocks of 8, 12 & 16 frames to provide more context in the global and local perspectives. In our architecture, we reduce the parameters to a large extent while simultaneously not compromising on the results.

2   Related Work

Sign Language Translation stemmed from Sign Language Recognition (SLR), which is the process of generating intermediate representations (*glosses*) of the sign being performed given the video of the sign. *Sign Glosses* are shortened representations of spoken sign language sentences. SLR can be divided into 2 sub-categories:

2.1   Isolated Sign Language Recognition

Isolated Sign Language Recognition (ISLR) is the task of classifying signs one at a time. ISLR is similar to video action recognition wherein the action being performed is classified by the model. This task is easier than Continuous Sign Language Recognition due to its isolated nature. Initial approaches for ISLR involved manually selecting features [3,4]. With an increase in the computational capabilities of machines, isolated sign recognition lost its significance due to the negligible real-world impact it has in improving the ability of the speech & hearing-impaired community to communicate with others.

2.2   Continuous Sign Language Recognition

Continuous Sign Language Recognition (CLSR) is the process of identifying the signs as they are being performed by the signer. CSLR is not restricted to recognizing each of the frames but also learning the mapping between the entire video input and the corresponding glosses [5]. This was first introduced by deep learning based works [6,7]. [8] proposed a CNN-LSTM model which made use of bidirectional LSTMs. Recurrent Neural Networks also have been used for this task [9,10]. A drawback of CSLR is the fact that this generates a stream of glosses that requires prior knowledge to comprehend.

2.3   Continuous Sign Language Translation

In Continuous Sign Language Translation (CSLT), the spoken language sentence is generated given the input video. Current SLT approaches involve two independent steps. First, a tokenization system (SLR) generates glosses from sign language videos. Second, a translation system translates the recognized glosses into spoken language. The first step has been addressed in the previous sections, but there have been no implementations improving on the translation system from glosses to text. [11] proposed a CNN-HMM encoder-decoder architecture and also released the current benchmark dataset for German Sign Language Translation, named RWTH-PHOENIX-2014T. [2] created a novel architecture, Spatio-Temporal Multi Cue-Transformers, a Sign-to-Gloss-to-Text (S2G2T) model; and further demonstrated that the claim that translation using ground truth glosses acts as an upper bound for SLT performance was incorrect.

S2G2T models are not feasible in real-world applications, as glosses require sign language expertise to annotate which is a time-consuming and expensive process. Furthermore, multiple annotators are required to produce usable glosses without human error. Finally, there are no existing pre-trained representations for glosses which models can readily use. As a result, it is inherently better to mitigate the requirement of glosses by introducing end-to-end CSLT models; to which end, [1] has made some advances.

Improving on the existing methodologies, the characteristics of the proposed architecture are:

- No requirement for glosses in the training or translation phase.
- Uses lesser parameters than the aforementioned approaches making it more suitable for devices with limited resources.
- Achieves comparable scores with respect to the state-of-the-art models. [11,12]

3   Continuous Sign Language Translation

Continuous Sign Language Translation is a sequence-to-sequence problem of learning the mapping between the input signing video and its output translation. Specifically, given a video consisting of a sequence of n frames $X = \{x_1, x_2, \ldots, x_n\}$ where x_i denotes the frame at the ith position, the model learns the conditional probability $P(Y/X)$ where $Y = \{y_1, y_2, \ldots, y_n\}$ is the output translation, and y_i is the corresponding word at the ith position. Usually, sign language translation models comprise of two networks: (i) A 2D convolution network like VGG [13] to extract spatial features in a d-dimensional feature space from the video by processing individual frames; (ii) A sequence model like Long Short-Term Memory [14] to map the extracted d-dimensional feature vectors to the output translation sequence. However, there is an inherent problem associated with processing the frames individually. The model captures the spatial information present in the individual frames of the video but neglects the temporal relationships existing between the frames. For instance, a sign appearing in a later part of the video might influence the context in which an earlier sign must be interpreted; thus affecting the output translation. This approach also requires the sequence model to learn these complex temporal factors from merely the feature vectors of the individual frames. To solve this problem, the video must be processed in segments; frames in the video must be grouped to form overlapping segments. The video segments could be defined by the parameters stride (s) and window size (w) and the information present could be projected onto an a dimensional vector space by learning a 3D convolutional network. We modify the problem statement by changing the input structure from individual frames to batched video segments $\bar{X} = \{\bar{x}_1, \bar{x}_2, \bar{x}_3, \ldots \bar{x}_k\}$ where $\bar{x}_i$ is a video segment. We learn the conditional probability $\mathrm{P}(\mathrm{Y}/\bar{X}_{w,s},\ w,s \in \mathbb{Z}^+)$ where several batched video segment representations can be formed by varying w & s.

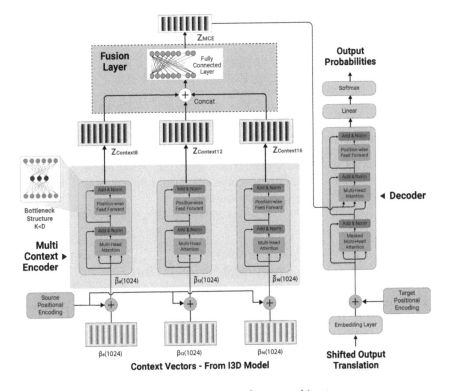

Fig. 1. Multi context transformer architecture

4   Multi Context Transformer

Multi Context Transformer is an encoder-decoder architecture based on Transformers [15] consisting of parallel Transformer Encoder blocks, each operating on different context vectors created using the preprocessing framework described in Sect. 4.1. Figure 1 provides an overview of our proposed architecture. Our architecture comprises of a Multi Context Encoder, Fusion Layer, and a Decoder which we define in Sects. 4.4, 4.5 and 4.6.

4.1 Context Vectors

We follow the preprocessing framework as defined by [12] to obtain *context vectors*. The collection of video segments characterized by window size w and stride s, denoted by $\alpha(x, w, s)$, is defined as

$$\alpha(x, w, s) = \{x_{ks,w} \mid 0 \leq k < \lfloor \frac{N}{w} \rfloor\}$$
$$x_{ks,w} = \{x_{ks}, x_{ks+1}, x_{ks+2}, \dots, x_{ks+w-1}\} \tag{1}$$

where $x_{ks,w}$ is a subsequence of the input video X starting from the frame $k \times s$ and having a length of w frames with a stride of s. We make use of an I3D network [16] to convert $\alpha(x, w, s)$ into a sequence of a dimensional vectors.

$$\beta(a) = \{V_{ks,w} \in \mathbb{R}^a\}$$
$$V_{ks,w} = I3D(x_{ks,w} \ \forall \ x_{ks,w} \in \alpha(x, w, s)) \tag{2}$$

where each vector $\beta^i_w(a) = V_{is,w}$ is the encoded representation of a windowed segment $x_{is,w}$. We refer to the sets of $\beta_w(a)$ as simply β_w, or simply as the set of context vectors as they contain either local, intermediate , or global context information depending on the window size w. When w is small, the video segments are short; they capture sign details well but fail to contain more information about the other signs; however, if the video segments are made longer by increasing w, more information is captured but sign details may be compromised. Hence, we consider video segments with three values of w: 8, 12 and 16 and a stride of 2. We hypothesize that this setup can successfully capture both "local" details and general information in a "global" context; a window size of 8 ensures that finer details of the sign performed are captured, a window size of 12 captures intermediary gestures and a window size of 16 captures the global context. We also fix a to 1024.

4.2 Positional Encoding

The context vectors alone do not contain explicit information embedded in them about the position in which the vectors occur in the original sequence. Our model is a customized extension of Transformer networks, and to preserve the temporal data of the signs, we employ the same Sinusoidal Positional Encoding mechanism introduced by [15]. We add the generated positional vectors $pe(a)$ to $\beta_w(a)$ to obtain the position informed context vectors $\bar{\beta}_w(a)$.

$$\bar{\beta}_w(a) = F(\beta_w(a)) = \beta_w(a) + pe(a) \ \forall \ w \in \{8, 12, 16\} \tag{3}$$

4.3   Transformer Block

Transformer Encoder Layer. The Transformer encoder layer consists of two fundamental units namely, Multi Head Self-Attention and a Feed Forward Network. Self-Attention is an attention mechanism introduced by [17] which relates different positions of a single sequence in order, to compute a representation of the same sequence. To compute Self-Attention, the model learns three weight matrices W_q, W_k and W_v which are then passed onto a softmax layer based on the equation given below

$$Self - Attention = Softmax(\frac{Q \cdot K^T}{\sqrt{a}}) \cdot V \tag{4}$$

W_q, W_k and W_v stands for Query (Q), Key (K) and Value (V) weight matrices. Multi Head Self-Attention is a variant of Self-Attention wherein the model learns multiple Q, K & V weight matrices $W_{q,k,v} = \{W_{q,k,v_1}, W_{q,k,v_2}, \ldots, W_{q,k,v_n}\}$ where n is the number of heads and computes attention scores on each of the heads independently.

$$MultiHead(Q, K, V) = Concat(head_1, \ldots, head_h)W^O$$
$$\text{where } head_i = Attention(QW_i^Q, KW_i^K, VW_i^V) \tag{5}$$

The computations involved in Self-Attention are essentially matrix multiplications, so compared to other attention mechanisms [11], scaled dot product attention is faster and has constant space complexity. Self-Attention scales linearly with input and target sequence size, so when we cluster the frames with stride 2, the sequence size is reduced to half the original value, hence reducing the number of computations and providing faster inference time.

The non-linear point-wise Feed Forward part learns a transformation that projects the D-dimensional Self-Attention representation into an L-dimensional latent space, and back to D-dimensions. This helps to learn enriched features from the Self-Attention representation.

$$FFN(Z) = (Z \cdot W_1^T + B_1) \cdot W_2^T + B_2 \tag{6}$$

where W_1 and W_2 are shared weight matrices across the sequence. We observe that a large number of the parameters are concentrated in the Feed Forward layers. So, to reduce the parameters and model size, we invert the bottleneck to have an intermediate latent space of dimensionality $L < D$ instead of following the traditional $L = 4D$ recommended by the original paper.

Transformer Decoder Layer. The Transformer Decoder Layer has a similar structure to the Transformer Encoder layer. However, in addition to the masked multi head attention layer operating over word embeddings of the sequence, there is an additional multi head attention layer present which operates with Queries (Q) generated from the previous multi head attention layer's output and the Key (K) and Value (V) pairs being generated from the output representation of the Encoder. We use a similar pointwise feed-forward network with an inverted bottleneck to learn the transformation.

4.4 Multi Context Encoder

We define the Multi Context Encoder as $MCE = \{T_8, T_{12}, T_{16}\}$, as the set of Transformer Encoder layers defined in Sect. 4.3 stacked in parallel. Each encoder layer takes in position informed context vectors $\bar{\beta}_n(a)$ as input and uses the multi head attention layer followed by the pointwise non-linear feed forward layer to form a context inclusive representation of the input sequence.

$$Z_{Context_N} = FFN(MultiHead(Q^N, K^N, V^N)) \tag{7}$$

Each Transformer encoder learns the contextual information depending on the temporal granularity of the preprocessed vectors. Building on our hypothesis, the T_8 encoder in MCE learns to differentiate between sign gestures and model sign transitions, therefore reinforcing local context with respect to adjacent sign gestures, while the T_{12} and T_{16} encoders are responsible for learning the relationship between spaced out, global contextual information while compromising on finer-grained information between the signs themselves.

4.5 Fusion Layer

The multiple Self-Attention based representations obtained from the MCE layer are concatenated and fused with a Fully Connected layer to provide a single representation summarizing the whole video input. This representation is analogous to the final vector representation of a sentence at the end of an encoder in an Encoder-Decoder architecture used for standard seq-to-seq tasks. We define the Fully Connected layer as

$$G = FC_d(V) = W^T \cdot V + B \text{ where } V \in \mathbb{R}^a \text{ and } G \in \mathbb{R}^d \tag{8}$$

W and B are the associated weight matrices and bias and a and d are the input and output dimensions of the vectors. We proceed to define the Fusion process as

$$Z_{MCE} = FC_S(Z_{Final})$$
$$Z_{Final} = Concat(Z_{Context_8}, Z_{Context_{12}}, Z_{Context_{16}}) \tag{9}$$

S is the decoder side multi head attention dimension and $Z_{MCE} \in \mathbb{R}^S$ is the final condensed representation of the input video sequence. The concatenation of the inbound encoder outputs is a simple way to provide a complete yet elaborate representation of the video. The fully connected layer essentially computes a weighted linear combination on the concatenated vectors, which allows the model to highlight and select pieces of data that contribute the most towards producing high quality and semantically correct translations at the decoder side. Through this layer, we not only intend to fuse the representations but also to effectively reduce the dimension which helps in constructing a condensed representation while also ensuring dimensional compatibility at the decoder side's multi head attention process.

4.6   Decoder

We use the Transformer Decoder layer defined in Sect. 4.3 coupled with a softmax function to produce the output translation probabilities. The queries (Q) are generated from the word embeddings of the shifted ground truth sequence while the condensed representation Z_{MCE} gives rise to the key-value (K, V) pairs. The output translation probabilities contain the probability of each word appearing at the ith position across the entire sequence.

5   Dataset

5.1   Introduction

The benchmark dataset, RWTH-PHOENIX 14T, released by [11] contains German Sign Language or Deutsche Gebärdensprache (DGS) in the context of weather forecasts and as a reason of this, the content is influenced by the grammatical structure of the spoken weather forecast and features speech effects such as hesitations & false starts. The signing was recorded by a color camera placed in front of the sign language interpreters who wear dark-colored clothes in front of a grey background. The corresponding German translation sentence and the *gloss* representation for each video are provided in the dataset.

5.2   Features and Statistics

There are a total of 9 signers present in the dataset, out of which 1 signer is unique to the test set. The videos are sampled at a frame rate of 25 frames per second. The duration of the videos is between 1–18 s with an average duration of 4.64 s. On average each sign performed takes about half a second [18]. Other details about the dataset are listed in Table 1.

Table 1. Features of RWTH-PHOENIX14T dataset

Features	Train	Dev	Test
Instances	7,096	519	642
Frames	827,354	55,775	64,627
Vocab	2,887	951	1,001
Total words	99,081	6,820	7,816
Out of vocabulary (OOV)	N/A	57	60
Singletons	1,077	N/A	N/A
Frame rate	25 FPS		
Resolution	210 × 260 pixels		

6   Experimental Details

6.1   Hyperparameter Details

The models were implemented using PyTorch [19]. The RWTH dataset split was used as given by [11]. We perform our experiments on an NVIDIA 2080 Super GPU. We employ the standard sinusoidal positional encoding, perform word-level tokenization, manually add <SOS> and <EOS> tokens to the start and end of each sentence and replaced the unknown words in the dev and test sets with <OOV> token. We initialize model parameters using the Xavier initialization method [20] to ensure all weights are initialized in a suitable range.

6.2   Evaluation Metrics

We adopt BLEU [21] and ROUGE-L F1 [22] scores, two commonly used machine translation metrics, for evaluating model performance. BLEU-n measures the precision of translation up to n-grams. BLEU is a measure of how well a predicted translation compares to the actual translations. The ROUGE-L metric is a measure of the performance of the model based on the longest common sub-sequences between predictions and ground-truth translations. BLEU and ROUGE-L scores complement each other; BLEU is a measure of the precision while ROUGE is a measure of the recall of the model. A higher BLEU and ROUGE-L score is indicative of a good model; a BLEU-4 score of 60–70 implies that the model is producing translations bettering human translators. We further experiment to empirically determine the ideal embedding dimension, the number of Multi Context Encoders and Decoders and the details of the experiments are given in Sects. 6.3 and 6.4. For all the experimental comparisons, we keep certain hyperparameters constant: The learning rate is set at 5×10^{-4} and all models are trained for 400 epochs using a Stochastic Gradient Descent optimizer and with Cross-Entropy Loss as the loss function.

6.3   Word Embeddings

Experimental Setup. We experiment using FastText German embeddings [23] and custom embedding vectors in our models to determine which suits this task better. For this experiment, we set other hyperparameters constant based on experimental analysis: The number of Multi Context Encoders and Decoders to be 1 and 6 respectively; the attention heads were set to be 4 on both the encoder and decoder sections. The bottleneck layers in the feed forward network in the encoder half were set to be 300 units. We modify the bottleneck in the feed forward network in the decoder side based on the model embedding dimension to ensure compatibility.

Results and Inferences. From the results obtained on the dev set given in Table 2, it is observed that the models trained using a custom embedding layer outperformed the models utilizing FastText embedding vectors. The custom embeddings learn to better represent weather-specific vocabulary in comparison with pre-trained FastText embedding vectors. Hence, custom embeddings are used throughout further analysis of our model's performance. In the next section, we perform encoder and decoder layer analysis to find the ideal pairing for this task.

Table 2. Impact of embedding type on model performance

Decoder			Dev set scores				
Hidden units	Embedding						
	Type	Dim	ROUGE-L	BLEU-1	BLEU-2	BLEU-3	BLEU-4
512	FastText	300	34.55	34.66	21.5	15.27	11.78
512	**Custom**	**300**	**34.79**	**35**	**21.97**	**15.7**	**12.17**
300	FastText	100	32.98	33.79	20.6	14.21	10.74
300	**Custom**	**100**	**33.16**	**33.48**	**20.62**	**14.37**	**10.93**

6.4 Multi Context Encoder and Decoder Analysis

Experimental Setup. The number of Multi Context Encoders and Decoders was experimented with the values of 1, 2 & 4 for the encoder and 4, 6 & 8 for the decoder. Similar to the Embedding Comparison experiment in Sect. 6.3 we set other hyperparameters constant based on experimental analysis: For both the Multi Context Encoder and Decoder the bottleneck layer in the feed forward network was set as 300 and the attention heads were also set to be 4.

Results and Inferences. From the results obtained on the dev set given in Table 3, it can be inferred that the ideal number of Multi Context Encoders is 1, while the ideal number of Multi Context Decoders is 6. With an increase in the number of Multi Context Encoders, there is a commensurate increase in the parameters of the model. When more than one Multi Context Encoder is used, the performance drops which goes against the usual hypothesis that increasing computation power produces better performance. We theorize that as the I3D network already provides a comprehensive encoding of the segment of frames, using more than one encoder layer results in significant information loss; thereby reducing model performance and caused a significant drop in the BLEU and ROUGE-L which can be seen in Table 3. Based on this hypothesis, we use only 1 Multi Context Encoder. On the other hand, the performance increases with an increase in the number of Decoders, which is in line with the usual hypothesis. The configuration mentioned above (1 Multi Context Encoder and 6 Decoders) is significant to achieving comparable performance with state-of-the art models while simultaneously reducing the parameters. Based on the results of the above experiments performed in Sects. 6.3 and 6.4, going further we use

1 Multi Context Encoder, 6 Multi Context Decoders, and Custom Embeddings for optimal performance.

Table 3. Multi context encoder and decoder comparison

Encoder layer(s)	Decoder layers	Parameters (in millions)	Dev set scores				
			ROUGE-L	BLEU-1	BLEU-2	BLEU-3	BLEU-4
1	4	15.91	33.71	33.99	20.49	14.04	10.68
1	**6**	**16.19**	**33.16**	**33.48**	**20.62**	**14.37**	**10.93**
1	8	16.47	33.23	32.95	19.69	13.46	10.22
2	4	30.36	31.99	32.6	19.36	13.31	10.08
2	6	30.64	32.12	32.85	19.5	13.17	9.82
2	8	30.93	30.6	29.94	17.65	11.92	8.91
4	4	59.27	29.42	29.27	16.82	11.4	8.59
4	6	59.55	29.5	29.35	17.12	11.7	8.79
4	8	59.84	28.67	26.77	15.4	10.43	7.8

7 Results and Comparisons

We perform experiments by varying important hyperparameters as shown in Table 4 and the corresponding results obtained are shown in Table 5. The metrics BLEU and ROUGE-L scores defined in Sect. 6.2 are used to evaluate the performance of models. Our best performing model (**v4**) produces a ROUGE-L score of **34.33** and a BLEU-4 score of **11.62** with just **17.75** million parameters. In comparison with other end-to-end approaches like [12] which requires **25.68** million parameters to achieve ROUGE-L and BLEU-4 scores of **34.96** and **13.41** respectively, the Multi Context Transformer retains **98.19%** of the ROUGE-L score and **86.65%** of the BLEU-4 score and reduces the parameters by **30.88%** in comparison with the same model. Our approach also outperforms [11], improving on their ROUGE-L and BLEU-4 score of **31.80** and **9.58** by a factor of **7.9%** and **21.2%** respectively.

Table 4. MultiContext transformer model description

Model	Encoder		Decoder			Parameters (in millions)
	Num heads	Hidden units	Num heads	Dimension	Hidden units	
v1	4	300	4	100	300	16.19
v2	4	300	4	100	512	16.44
v3	8	300	4	100	512	16.44
v4	4	512	4	100	512	17.75

Table 5. Comparison of our models with the state-of-the-art

Model	Test set scores					Dev set scores				
	ROUGE-L	BLEU-1	BLEU-2	BLEU-3	BLEU-4	ROUGE-L	BLEU-1	BLEU-2	BLEU-3	BLEU-4
v1	33.3	33.85	20.7	14.2	10.69	33.16	33.48	20.62	14.37	10.93
v2	33.43	33.94	21.05	14.51	10.96	34.34	34.63	21.45	15.03	11.42
v3	33.39	34.02	20.99	14.66	11.18	33.64	33.86	20.77	14.55	11.02
v4	**34.33**	**34.86**	**21.89**	**15.33**	**11.62**	32.84	**33.51**	**20.33**	**13.83**	**10.41**
[12] (Joint)	34.96	36.1	23.12	16.88	13.41	Not mentioned in the paper				
[11] (S2T)	31.80	32.24	19.03	12.83	9.58	31.80	31.87	19.11	13.16	9.94

Table 6. Sample predictions made by the proposed model

Ground truth	Prediction
und nun die wettervorhersage für morgen freitag den fünfzehnten oktober	und nun die wettervorhersage für morgen freitag den dreizehnten oktober
am samstag regnet es im südosten und an der ostsee dort ist es teilweise windig sonst regnet es nur vereinzelt teilweise zeigt sich die sonne	am samstag regnet es im süden und osten und osten teilweise stark bewölkt an der ostsee ist es windig und gewitter möglich und gewitter möglich
und nun die wettervorhersage für morgen samstag den achtzehnten juli	und nun die wettervorhersage für morgen montag den dreizehnten juli
liebe zuschauer guten abend	liebe zuschauer guten abend
und nun die wettervorhersage für morgen montag den vierundzwanzigsten januar \<OOV\>	und nun die wettervorhersage für morgen montag den neunundzwanzigsten januar

8   Conclusion

In this paper, we introduce Multi Context Transformer for end-to-end SLT. The input video sequence is broken down into smaller subsequences of frames and then converted into *context vectors* of uniform dimensionality. The Multi Context Encoder operates on these vectors to capture contexts across different temporal intervals of the input sign video. This process mitigates the problems associated with discerning sign transitions. Our approach uses **17.75** million trainable parameters and obtains a BLEU-4 score of **11.62** and a ROUGE-L score of **34.33**. Our model can be deployed in accessible devices, thereby ensuring that these devices can efficiently carry out Sign Language Translation. Future scope can involve a further reduction in model size by improving the attention mechanism and further working on varying the embedding size.

References

1. Camgoz, N.C., Koller, O., Hadfield, S., Bowden, R.: Sign language transformers: joint end-to-end sign language recognition and translation. IEEE Conference on Computer Vision and Pattern Recognition (CVPR) (2020)
2. Yin, K., Read, J.: Better sign language translation with STMC-transformer. In: Proceedings of the 28th International Conference on Computational Linguistics, Barcelona (2020)
3. Quan, Y.: Chinese sign language recognition based on video sequence appearance modeling. In: 2010 5th IEEE Conference on Industrial Electronics and Applications, pp. 1537–1542 (2010)
4. Grobel, K., Assan, M.: Isolated sign language recognition using hidden markov models. In: 1997 IEEE International Conference on Systems, Man, and Cybernetics, Computational Cybernetics and Simulation, vol. 1, pp. 162–167 (1997)
5. Rastgoo, R., Kiani, K., Escalera, S.: Sign language recognition: a deep survey. Expert Syst. Appl. **164**, 113794 (2021)
6. Koller, O., Ney, H., Bowden, R.: Deep hand: how to train a CNN on 1 million hand images when your data is continuous and weakly labelled. In: Proceedings of the IEEE Conference on Computer Vision and Pattern Recognition (CVPR) (2016)
7. Koller, O., Zargaran, S., Ney, H., Bowden, R.: Deep sign: hybrid CNN-HMM for continuous sign language recognition. In: Proceedings of the British Machine Vision Conference (2016)
8. Camgoz, N.C., Hadfield, S., Koller, O., Bowden, R.: Subunets: end-to-end hand shape and continuous sign language recognition. In: 2017 IEEE International Conference on Computer Vision (ICCV), pp. 3075–3084 (2017)
9. Cui, R., Liu, H., Zhang, C.: Recurrent convolutional neural networks for continuous sign language recognition by staged optimization. In: Proceedings of the IEEE Conference on Computer Vision and Pattern Recognition (CVPR) (2017)
10. Koller, O., Zargaran, S., Ney, H.: Re-sign: re-aligned end-to-end sequence modelling with deep recurrent CNN-HMMs. In: 2017 IEEE Conference on Computer Vision and Pattern Recognition (CVPR), pp. 3416–3424 (2017)
11. Camgöz, N.C., Hadfield, S., Koller, O., Ney, H., Bowden, R.: Neural sign language translation. IEEE Conference on Computer Vision and Pattern Recognition (CVPR), Salt Lake City (2018)
12. Li, D., et al.: Tspnet: hierarchical feature learning via temporal semantic pyramid for sign language translation. In: Advances in Neural Information Processing Systems, vol. 33 (2020)
13. Simonyan, K., Zisserman, A.: Very deep convolutional networks for large-scale image recognition. arXiv:1409.1556 (2014)
14. Hochreiter, S., Schmidhuber, J.: Long short-term memory. Neural comput. **9**, 1735–80 (1997)
15. Vaswani, A., et al.: Attention is all you need. In: Proceedings of the 31st International Conference on Neural Information Processing Systems, NIPS 2017, pp. 6000–6010. Curran Associates Inc., Red Hook (2017)
16. Carreira, J., Zisserman, A.: Quo vadis, action recognition? a new model and the kinetics dataset (2018)
17. Luong, M.T., Pham, H., Manning, C.D.: Effective approaches to attention-based neural machine translation (2015)
18. Buehler, P., Zisserman, A., Everingham, M.: Learning sign language by watching tv (using weakly aligned subtitles). In: 2009 IEEE Conference on Computer Vision and Pattern Recognition, pp. 2961–2968 (2009)

19. Paszke, A., Gross, S., et al.: An imperative style, high-performance deep learning library. In: Wallach, H., Larochelle, H., Beygelzimer, A., d'Alché-Buc, F., Fox, E., Garnett, R. (eds.) Advances in Neural Information Processing Systems, vol. 32, pp. 8024–8035. Curran Associates, Inc. (2019)
20. Glorot, X., Bengio, Y.: Understanding the difficulty of training deep feedforward neural networks. J. Mach. Learn. Res. Proc. Track **9**, 249–256 (01 2010)
21. Papineni, K., Roukos, S., Ward, T., Zhu, W.J.: Bleu: a method for automatic evaluation of machine translation (2002)
22. Lin, C.Y.: ROUGE: a package for automatic evaluation of summaries. In: Text Summarization Branches Out, pp. 74–81. Association for Computational Linguistics, Barcelona (2004)
23. Bojanowski, P., Grave, E., Joulin, A., Mikolov, T.: Enriching word vectors with subword information. arXiv preprint arXiv:1607.04606 (2016)

Optimized Fuzzy Control with Genetic Algorithms and Differential Evolution for Tracking the Trajectories of an Ankle Prosthesis

Rocío Ambrocio-Delgado[1(✉)], Arturo Téllez-Velázquez[2],
Esther Lugo-González[3(✉)], and Francisco Espinosa-Garcia[1]

[1] División de Estudios de Posgrado, Universidad Tecnológica de la Mixteca,
Carretera a Acatlima km. 2.5, 69007 Huajuapan de León, Oaxaca, México
rocio.ambrocio.delgado@gmail.com, fjeg_1234@hotmail.com
[2] Cátedras Conacyt, Universidad Tecnológica de la Mixteca, Carretera a Acatlima
km. 2.5, 69007 Huajuapan de León, Oaxaca, México
atellezv@mixteco.utm.mx
[3] Instituto de Electrónica y Mecatrónica, Universidad Tecnológica de la Mixteca,
Carretera a Acatlima km. 2.5, 69007 Huajuapan de León, Oaxaca, México
elugog@mixteco.utm.mx

Abstract. This work presents a comparison between three Mandani controllers (trial and error, optimized with Genetic Algorithms (GA), and Differential Evolution (DE)) and a traditional PID controller in the trajectory tracking application in the sagittal/frontal planes of an ankle, considering a disturbance that simulates the existence of an irregularity in the walking surface. The controller rulebase design uses only the error signals and the error derivative. For the implementation of the mentioned controllers, a co-simulation is presented using the MatLAb fuzzy Toolbox, Simulink PID block of Matlab, and Adams View. From the results obtained, a comparison is made to determine the computation time and the position error to choose the best one for the tracking the trajectories of an ankle prosthesis.

Keywords: Fuzzy control · Genetic algorithms · Differential evolution · Trajectory

1 Introduction

From fuzzy sets, fuzzy systems are made by incorporating common language sentences to interpret the variables state of a certain process, assigning them a degree of membership, which are interpreted by logical operators. The fuzzy systems' performance depends on the choice of linguistic control rules and membership functions. In general, the rules adjustment is carried out by trial and error, which takes a lot of time and uncertainty. To simplify this task, optimization methods such as Genetic and Differential Evolution Algorithms are used.

© Springer Nature Switzerland AG 2021
I. Batyrshin et al. (Eds.): MICAI 2021, LNAI 13068, pp. 325–336, 2021.
https://doi.org/10.1007/978-3-030-89820-5_26

Mitra et al. [6] introduced a fuzzy control technique, using a Sugeno-type model, adjusting the parameters through a hybrid learning algorithm, which has demonstrated the stability of modeled electrical generation systems for small signals. In [7], the authors apply Genetic Algorithms to a SISO system model adjusting the fuzzy sets supports used in a Mamdani controller. The results shows an automatic adjustment faster and more efficient than the manual, these are compared with a PID controller adjusted with Genetic Algorithms, allowing solutions with few generations, regardless of the number of parameters established. Al-Darraji et al. [8], present a robotic finger, with a Fuzzy MIMO controller, whose inputs are from the force sensors on phalanges. The controller fuzzy parameters are adjusted using a Genetic Algorithm as an optimization technique. The Genetic Algorithm's objective function is to avoid the imbalance pair in the individual joints and reduce the difference between the values of the supplied VSA pairs. In [9], a fuzzy logic controller was developed for tracking the routes of a rescue robot. In order to adjust the membership functions, (to do the minimum deviation from the desired path) the Genetic Algorithm and Differential Evolution were used. In this trajectory tracking application, the fitness function evaluated the robot trajectory, considering the distance and the orientation error of the desired route. The genetic algorithm and the differential evolution algorithm had almost the same results, except for a slightly lower error and fewer control parameters for the DE method. Another use of GA-optimized fuzzy controllers as mentioned in [10–12], is to prevent the arrows of direct current motors from being damaged by controlling their speed since in the Control outputs can be generated over impulses. Ashu et al. [13], made a comparison of three techniques (genetic algorithm (GA), particle swarm optimization (PSO), and differential evolution (DE)) to adjust a speed controller PID and FOPID. In this work, the FOPID driver optimized with GA showed better performance than the other drivers. In [14], are discussed a design of an optimized cascade fuzzy controller for the rotary inverted pendulum system and ball & beam system by using an optimization vehicle of differential evolution (DE) and genetic algorithm (GA). By optimizing the fuzzy control a better response with differential evolution was obtained.

Fuzzy controllers can generate optimal results combined with heuristic methods, for this reason, in this article we present the comparison of a PID, fuzzy, trial and error position controller and after optimized with Genetic Algorithms and Differential Evolution, applied in a direct current motor that generates the simulated virtual ankle prosthesis movement in Adams View to show the computing resources consumption, the position error and the numerical results it presents an optimized controller.

2   Development

The direct current (DC) motor that is used to give movement to the ankle prosthesis is described by the transfer function shown in Eq. (1) in the research of Nguyen H. T. [15].

$$G(S) = \frac{0.5}{S^3 + 13.6667S^2 + 23.48S} \qquad (1)$$

The rotor position is controlled to match a proposal, from the error defining two linguistic variables: the position error and the speed, necessary to get the voltage at the output, where the error is the difference between the desired position minus the actual position. The rotor rotation is controlled with the voltage polarity and it is possible to go from a clockwise to counterclockwise rotation due to its dynamics. Furthermore, the rotor rotation speed is controlled while reaching the desired position. In case of having a negative error (the actual position is greater than the desired one), a negative voltage is sent to the motor so that it reaches the reference.

2.1   Case Study: Ankle Mechanism

Due to its anatomical configuration, the ankle joint is formed by the talar trochlea and the tibiofibular mortise and can do flexion and extension movements shown in Fig. 1 [16]. The foot has a set of joints that allow movement in the 3 planes of space. These are: inversion/eversion, abduction/adduction and dorsiflexion/plantar-flexion [17], which are shown in Fig. 2.

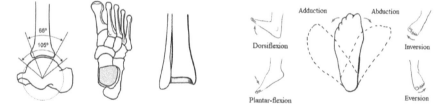

Fig. 1. Ankle bony anatomy [16].   **Fig. 2.** Ankle movements [17].

The restricted motion ranges of ankle joints are shown in Table 1 [18].

Table 1. Ankle motion ranges [18].

Movement	Maximum allowable movement
Plantar-flexion	37.6° to 45.8°
Dorsiflexion	20.3° to 29.8°
Inversion	14.5° to 22°
Eversion	10.0° to 17.0°
Abduction	15.4° to 25.9°
Adduction	22.0° to 36.0°

The model used for the implementation of the fuzzy control is shown in Fig. 3. The dorsiflexion/plantar-flexion movement is performed in the sagittal plane and the eversion/inversion in the frontal plane. This prosthesis is based on a 27-year-old man with a height of 1.70 m. With the following characteristics: foot length of 26.5 cm, ankle circumference of 22 cm, ankle height of 7.5 cm, and tibia length of 20 cm. The movements are performed under the ankle restraints, which are shown in Table 1.

Fig. 3. Ankle prosthesis in Adams View.

2.2   Control System

The trajectory proposed to simulate the human gait, generated by the ankle in the sagittal plane of young people follows, is represented by the darkest line in Fig. 4. The second path is in the frontal plane, it generates the inversion movement and follows a line that depends on time until it reaches 10° as shown in Eq. (2). This angle is to simulate the foot on an irregular surface.

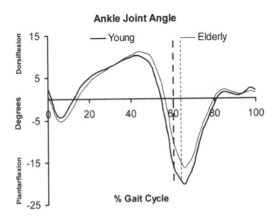

Fig. 4. Human ankle trajectory in the sagittal plane of young and old people [19].

$$x(t) = t \tag{2}$$

To make fuzzy position control, the following characteristics are established:

1. Input variables. The trajectory generated by MatLab.
2. Output variables. The virtual model position in Adams View.

Furthermore, three linguistic variables are proposed for each motor of the prosthesis virtual model, the error (e) in the reference signal position with that obtained by AdamsView, the derivative of the error or change (c), and the output voltage (v). The variables range are set shows that Eqs. (3), (4), and (5).

$$e = [-\frac{\pi}{2}, \frac{\pi}{2}] \tag{3}$$

$$c = [-\frac{\pi}{6}, \frac{\pi}{6}] \tag{4}$$

$$v = [-6.76, 6.76] \tag{5}$$

For each variable, exist 3 linguistic terms:

1. Error: PE: Positive error, ZE: Zero error, and NE: Negative error.
2. Derivative of the error or change: PC: Positive change, ZC: Zero change and NC: Negative change.

The error in the simulation indicates how closely the prosthesis follows the generated trajectory. From the error and the change, the outputs are set: PV: Positive voltage, ZV: Zero voltage, and NV: Negative voltage. This establishes the control rules: a) If NE and NC, then NV, b) if NE and ZC, then NV, c) if NE and PC, then NV, d) if ZE and NC, then NV, e) if ZE and ZC, then ZV, f) if ZE and PC, then PV, g) if PE and NC, then PV, h) if PE and ZC, then PV and i) if PE and PC, then PV.

2.3   Trial and Error Control

The membership functions are proposed for the inputs shown in Fig. 5 and 6, and for the output shown in Fig. 7, they were modified to 'trial and error' until having an error of 0.86°.

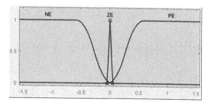

Fig. 5. Error membership features.

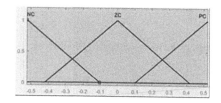

Fig. 6. Change membership features.

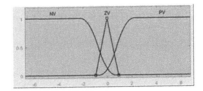

Fig. 7. Voltage membership features.

The discussion universe used for the error 5 is $\pm 90°$ or ± 1.5708 rad because the dorsiflexion and inversion movements are in this range (see Table 1). In the case of the change or variation of the error with respect to time, the universe of discussion is $\pm 30°$ or ± 0.5235 rad, with this it is assumed that the prosthesis will not move at more than $30°/s$. For the voltage, a discussion universe of ± 6.76 is used, as it is that of the DC motor operation.

2.4 Control Optimization with Genetic Algorithms

GA is based on the genetic process of living things and is an adaptive method used to solve search and optimization problems. The parameters that are considered are: chromosome, objective function, reproduction, crossing, and mutation [20]. The membership functions are formed by a Z signal, a triangular signal, and an S type. From 9 parameters, it is possible to optimize the fuzzy control, considering the center's variation and the signal's amplitude. Z and S, and only the amplitude for the triangular signal, leaving the center fixed at zero [21]. The chromosome is made up of the 9 parameters a_1, b_1, c_1, a_2, b_2, c_2, a_3, b_3, and c_3. The a_1 represent the amplitude of the triangular, the b_i the amplitude and c_i the center of the functions Z and S. The parameters b_i and c_i are considered symmetric as in [21] and the subscripts 1, 2 and 3 are for the variables error, error change, and voltage respectively. The membership functions for the inputs shown in Fig. 8 and 9, and for the output shown in Fig. 10.

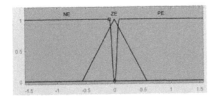

Fig. 8. Error membership features.

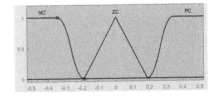

Fig. 9. Change membership features

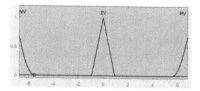

Fig. 10. Voltage membership features.

2.5   Control Optimization by Differential Evolution

The Differential Evolution algorithm is population-based, with a direct and simple search, which is capable of reaching the global optimum in multimodal, non-differentiable, and non-linear functions. This algorithm solves the first point of a problem using the objective function sampling at multiple randomly selected points [22]. The parameters considered are variables number, objective function, scaling, problem dimension, crossing, and mutation, which were proposed with the following values population: 60 individuals, generations: 50, scaling: 0.8, problem dimension: 9, selection: randperm, crossing: 0.7, and mutation: 0.3.

The problem dimension has 9 parameters a_1, b_1, c_1, a_2, b_2, c_2, a_3, b_3, and c_3 which are sent to the objective function in order to evaluate them. The a_i represent the triangular amplitude, the b_i the amplitude and the c_i the centers of the functions Z and S, as in the case of GA optimization. After optimizing with DE, the membership functions for the inputs shown in Fig. 11 and 12, and for the output shown in Fig. 13.

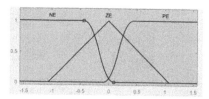

Fig. 11. Error membership features.

Fig. 12. Change membership features.

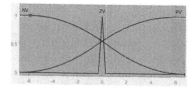

Fig. 13. Voltage membership features.

2.6   PID Control

The PID (proportional, integral, and derivative) controller can be easily performed and visualized in the time domain [23]. The parameters considered for PID controller are: $P = 100$, $I = 6$, $D = 3$, and were used in the Simulink PID block in MatLab, where a maximum trajectory tracking error of $6,867°$ was obtained how we can see in Fig. 14. The PID block controller in Simulink follows the trajectory with an error, (Fig. 15), where the desired trajectory is the dotted line and the real trajectory is the solid line provided by the Adams View plant.

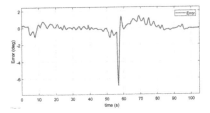
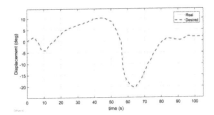

Fig. 14. Error between desired and real position.

Fig. 15. Comparison between actual and desired position.

For the controller's simulation, a co-simulation was accomplishing between the MatLab and Adams programs (Fig. 16), where the mechanism follows the proposed trajectory (Fig. 4).

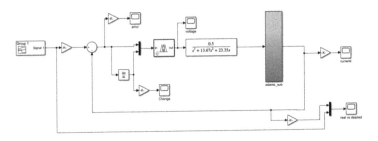

Fig. 16. MatLab-Adams co-simulation in Simulink.

In co-simulation with Simulink exist an input signal in radians fuzzy control, the transfer function of the DC motor, and the plant generated in Adams View. The plant output signal is subtracted from the reference signal to get the error, which is derived and these two signals are sent to fuzzy control.

2.7   Fuzzy Position Control

It is done by trial and error, the error membership functions, the change, and the voltage are modified, to have an error less than $1°$ to the desired signal.

When simulating Eqs. (1) and (2) and the trajectory of Fig. 4, the control follows the trajectory with an error of 0.9° (Fig. 17), where the actual and desired signals overlap. The desired trajectory (dotted line) is generated by Eq. (2), while the actual trajectory (solid line) is provided by the Adams View plant. In Fig. 18, the error between the desired and the real signal is 0.9°. The mistake is big because the membership functions were made by 'trial and error'.

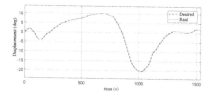

Fig. 17. Comparison between actual and desired position.

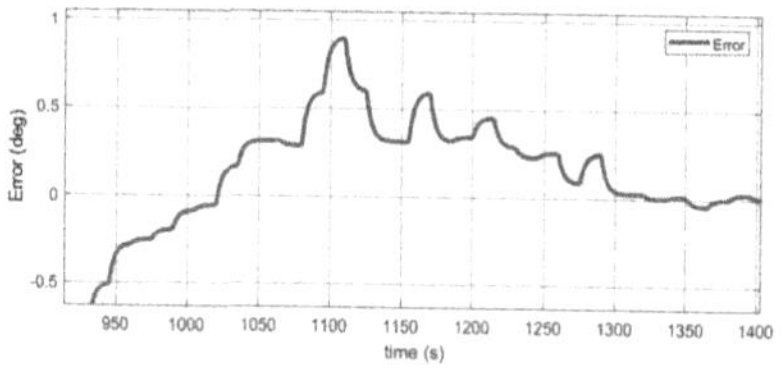

Fig. 18. Error between desired and actual position.

2.8 Fuzzy Control Optimized with Genetic Algorithms

The fuzzy position control is optimized using Genetic Algorithms, considering the parameters with the following values: population of 200 individuals, generations 900, selection of Roulette, crossover 0.8, and mutation 0.05.

The results obtained are shown in Fig. 19 (the real trajectory (solid line) and the desired one (dotted line)), however, the position control approaches the reference because the input signal is faster in comparison with the prosthesis result in Simulink. The error between the graphs shown in Fig. 20 is 0.626°. This error is not significant for human gait purposes, as precision is not needed when the wearer's tibia and prosthesis must be aligned.

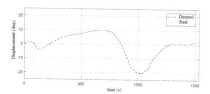

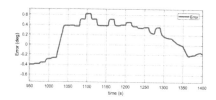

Fig. 19. Comparison between actual and desired position.

Fig. 20. Error between desired and actual position.

2.9 Optimized Fuzzy Control with Differential Evolution

The results are shown in Fig. 21, the real trajectory (dotted line) is close to the desired one (solid line). In the superposition that the error between the desired signal and the real one is less than the controls made at 'trial and error' and optimized with GA. The error between the graphs shown in Fig. 22 is 0.317° and it is the best response. An improvement in the trajectory tracking is observed by 63.13% compared to the control carried out by 'trial and error'.

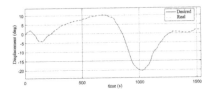

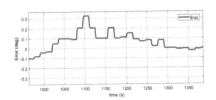

Fig. 21. Comparison between actual and desired position.

Fig. 22. Error between desired and actual position.

3   Results Analysis

The control designed by 'trial and error' presents an error of 0.86°, while the error of the optimized control with GA is 0.618°, with DE is 0.317° and with PID is 6.867°. The results obtained from the optimized control with GA and DE show an improvement in the follow-up of the proposed trajectory, shows that Table 2. The system approaches the reference faster, which provides a better response in the follow-up of gait trajectory.

Table 2. Comparison between the different methods used.

	Plantar-flexion	Without optimizing	Optimized with GA	Optimized with DE	PID
Elevation angle ankle	−0.5°	−0.05°	−0.02°	−0.32°	−0.948°
Decline angle ankle	−12°	−11.2°	−11.4°	−11.7°	−5.13°
Elevation angle ankle	−20.2°	−20.11°	−19.91°	−20.16°	−20.64°
Elevation angle ankle	−12°	−12.9°	−12.62°	−12.33°	−12.79°

4   Conclusions

Based on the results and making a comparison between the PID controller, the fuzzy control by 'trial and error', the fuzzy control optimized with GA, and the fuzzy control optimized with DE; the fuzzy control optimized with GA shown a better result in the follow-up of the trajectory compared with 'trial and error'. It is optimized, having a decrease in the error of 28.13% and the third shown a better result having a decrease in the error of 63.13%, which represents greater precision in the trajectories tracking than other optimization controllers and in the reduction of overshoots in the movement rotor of actuators, as well as energy consumption. Controls optimized with GA and DE were selected after changing parameters such as mutation and selection, thus having the best response for following the proposed trajectory. This type of optimized control is beneficial for a robotic ankle prosthesis since good tracking of the proposed trajectory is obtained and very high precision is not required as required by a medical robot. Comparing the results obtained from the optimized controllers with GA and DE with the PID controller, better results were obtained with DE, although the PID has a faster response, the error is greater ($6.867°$) than error with DE ($0.317°$), which is the best response for trajectory tracking.

References

1. Kwak, H., Kim, D., Park, G.: A new fuzzy inference technique for singleton type-2 fuzzy logic systems. Int. J. Adv. Robot. Syst. **9**, 1–7 (2012)
2. Farfán-Martínez, R., Ruz-Hernández, J., Rullán-Lara, J.: Control Difuso Tipo 2 en el Enfoque de Lyapunov Aplicado a un Servomecanismo. In: Sexto Coloq. Interdiscip. Dr. - Univ. Pop. Autónoma del Estado Puebla, pp. 1–9 (2013)
3. Mamdani, E., Assilian, S.: An experiment in linguistic synthesis with a fuzzy logic controller. Int. J. Man Mach. Stud. **7**(1), 1–13 (1975)
4. Takagi, T., Sugeno, M.: Fuzzy identification of systems and its applications to modeling and control. Readings Fuzzy Sets Intell. Syst. **1**, 387–403 (1993)
5. Fernandez, C., Pantano, N., Godoy, S., Serrano, E., Scaglia, G.: Optimización de parámetros utilizando los métodos de Monte Carlo y Algoritmos Evolutivos. Aplicación a un controlador de seguimiento de trayectoria en sistemas no lineales. Revista Iberoamericana de Automática e Informática industrial **16**, 89–99 (2019)
6. Mitra, S., Maulik, P., Chowdhury, S., Chowdhory, S.P.: ANFIS based automatic voltage regulator with hybrid learning algorithm. In: 2007 42nd International Universities Power Engineering Conference, vol. 1, pp. 397–401 (2007)
7. Mazzucco, M.M., Bolzan, A., Barcia, R.M., Machado, R.A.: Application of genetic algorithms to the adjustment of the supports of fuzzy sets in a mamdani controller. Braz. J. Chem. Eng. **17**, 625–638 (2000)
8. A-Darraji, I., Kılıç, A., Kapucu, S.: Mechatronic design and genetic algorithm based MIMO fuzzy control of adjustable stiffness tendon driven finger. Mech. Sci. **9**, 277–296 (2018)
9. Pishkenari, H.N., Mahboobi, S.H., Alasty, A.: Optimum synthesis of fuzzy logic controller for trajectory tracking by differential evolution. Sci. Iran. Trans. B Mech. Eng. **18**, 261–267 (2011)
10. Xia, C., Guo, P., Shi, T., Wan, M.: Speed control of brushless DC motor using genetic algorithm based fuzzy controller. In: Proceedings of the 2004 International Conference on Intelligent Mechatronics and Automation, pp. 460–464 (2004)
11. Orlowska-Kowalska, T., Szabat, K.: Optimization of fuzzy-logic speed controller for DC drive system with elastic joints. IEEE Trans. Ind. Appl. **40**(4), 1138–1144 (2004)
12. Ö-ztürk, N., Çelik, E.: Speed control of permanent magnet synchronous motors using fuzzy controller based on genetic algorithms. Elsevier Electr. Power Energy Syst. **43**, 889–898 (2012)
13. Ashu, A., Sanjeev, K.A.: Design of fractional order PID controller for DC motor using evolutionary optimization techniques. WSEAS Trans. Syst. Control **9**, 171–182 (2014)

14. Sung-Kwun, O., Wook-Dong, K., Witold, P.: Design of optimized cascade fuzzy controller based on differential evolution: simulation studies and practical insights. ELSEVIER Eng. Appl. Artif. Intell. **25**, 520–532 (2012)
15. Nguyen, H.T.: A First Course in Fuzzy and Neural Control, vol. 1. Chapman & Hall/CRC, Boca Raton (2003)
16. Viladot Voegeli, A.: Anatomía funcional y biomecánica del tobillo y el pie. Rev. Española Reumatol. **30**(9), 469–477 (2003)
17. Lippert, L.S.: Ankle Joint and Foot. Clinical kinesiology and Anatomy, vol. 5. F. A. Davis Co., Philadelphia (2011)
18. Jie, C., Sorin, S., Schneck, C.: The three-dimensional kinematics and flexibility characteristics of the human ankle and subtalar joints-part I: kinematics. Engineering **110**(2), 364–373 (1988)
19. Begg, R.K., Sparrow, W.A.: Ageing effects on knee and ankle joint angles at key events. J. Med. Eng. Technol. **30**(6), 382–389 (2006)
20. Parkinson, A., Balling, R., Hedengren, J.: Optimization Methods for Engineering Design. Applications and Theory, pp. 2–3. Brigham Young University, Provo (2013)
21. Téllez-Velázquez, A., et al.: A feasible genetic optimization strategy for parametric interval type-2 fuzzy logic systems. Int. J. Fuzzy Syst. **20**, 1–23 (2017)
22. Cuevas Jiménez, E., Usuna Enciso, J., Olivia Navarro, D., Díaz Córtes, M.: OPTIMIZACIÓN Algoritmos programados con MATLAB. Alfaomega (2016)
23. Ogata, K.: Modern Control Engineering, 4th edn. Prentice Hall, Upper Saddle River (2002)

Approximate the Clique-Width of a Graph Using Shortest Paths

J. Leonardo González-Ruiz[1]([✉]) [iD], J. Raymundo Marcial-Romero[1] [iD],
J. A. Hernández[1] [iD], and Guillermo De-Ita[2] [iD]

[1] Facultad de Ingeniería, Universidad Autónoma del Estado de México,
Cerro de Coatepec s/n, Ciudad Universitaria, 50100 Toluca, Mexico
{jlgonzalezru,jrmarcialr,xoseahernandez}@uaemex.mx
[2] Benemérita Universidad Autónoma de Puebla, 4 Sur 104 Centro Histórico C.P.,
72000 Puebla, Mexico
deita@cs.buap.mx

Abstract. In this paper, we present an algorithm to approximate the clique-width of a graph. The proposed approach is based on computing the shortest paths between pairs of vertices. We experimentally show that our proposal approximates the clique-width of simple graphs in polynomial time, while other methods that calculate it in an exact way, transform the problem to SAT, that is well-known as NP-Complete.

Keywords: Graph theory · Clique-width · Algorithm complexity

1 Introduction

The clique-width has been recently studied as an invariant that maintains its properties under graph isomorphism, belonging to the theory of parameterized complexity [1], which is a branch of computational complexity theory that classifies the difficulty of problems according to multiple input or output parameters, specifically in graph theory it measures the difficulty of decomposing a graph into a tree-like structure. Computing the clique-width of a graph consists of construct a finite term which represents the graph.

Courcelle et al. [2] presents a set of four operations to construct such term: 1) the creation of labels for vertices, 2) the disjoint union of graphs, 3) the creation of edges and 4) the re-labeling of vertices. The number of labels used to construct the finite term is commonly denoted by k. The minimum k number used to construct the term, also called k-expression, defines the clique-width. Finding the best combination which minimizes the k-expression is a NP-complete problem [3], furthermore, there is no constant error in the approximation algorithms for the calculation of the clique-width [3]. As the clique-width increases, the complexity of the problem in graphs also increases, in the same way the difficulty to achieve the decomposition of the graph increases, in fact, for some automata

---

Supported by CONACYT.

I. Batyrshin et al. (Eds.): MICAI 2021, LNAI 13068, pp. 337–347, 2021.
https://doi.org/10.1007/978-3-030-89820-5_27

that represent certain problems in graphs (according to the main Courcelle's theorem), its computation rapidly consumes memory.

In recent years, the clique-width has been studied in different classes of graphs showing the behavior of this invariant under certain operations. For example, Golumbic et al. [4] showed that for every graph with hereditary distance (a graph in which the distances between all connected induced subgraphs is the same as in the original graph), the clique-width (*cwd* for short) is smaller or equal to 3, so the following problems have a linear solution in this type of graph: minimum dominant set, minimum connected dominant set, minimum Steiner tree, maximum weight clique, domestic number for a fixed k, vertices cover and colorability for a fixed k. Examples can also be found in [5] for graphs with *cwd* 3 or 4.

The importance of classifying these types of graphs according to their *cwd* allows us to have a set of problems in graph theory that allow solutions in polynomial time, which indicates that they are into the tractable problems category. A variant of the problem, which also belongs to the NP-complete class, is to decide whether a graph has *cwd* of size k, for a fixed k number. For graphs with *cwd* bounded, in [6] is shown that there is an algorithm in polynomial time ($O(n^2m)$) that recognizes graphs of *cwd* less than or equal to 3. However, the authors refer that the problem remains open for $k \geq 4$. In the other hand, there is a classification for the graphs of $cwd \leq 2$, since the graphs of $cwd = 2$ are precisely the cographs (graphs that can be generated by a graph K_1 by complementation or disjoint union).

Similarly, the same result holds for the other invariant in graphs, the *treewidth* [7], however, the *cwd* is more general in the sense that graphs with a small *tree-width* also have small *cwd*. Algorithms used to calculate the *cwd* in these graphs require a previous certificate that indicates that they have small *cwd*, however, calculating this certificate or deciding if the *cwd* is bounded by a given number is also a complicated problem in the combinatorial sense. In other hand, the *cwd* of a graph with n vertices of degree greater than 2 cannot be approximated by a polynomial algorithm with an absolute error of n^ϵ unless $P = NP$ [3].

Recently, González-Ruiz et al. [8] showed that the *cwd* for Cactus graphs is less or equal to 4 and a polynomial time algorithm was presented that calculates exactly the $4 - expression$. Furthermore, in [9] they studied graphs called Polygonal Trees, which consist of simple cycles joined by at most one edge, showing that the *cwd* of this type of graph is less or equal to 5 and a polynomial time algorithm was presented that calculates the $5 - expression$.

Additionally Heule et al. [10] present a procedure to transform the *cwd* problem to the SAT problem. Its conversion algorithm is polynomial, however, as is well known, the Propositional Satisfaction problem (SAT) remains NP-complete. They calculate the *cwd* of relevant graphs in the literature for which the exact *cwd* was not known, using SAT solvers. The graphs considered have known topologies such as Brinkmann, Dodecahedron, Frutch, Kittell, McGee, Desargues, among others.

In this article we present a polynomial algorithm that approximates the cwd of simple graphs based on induced paths and show a comparison with the exact results of Heule et al.

2   Preliminares

All the graphs in this article are simple, that is, finite, without loops or multiple edges, and without direction. A graph is a pair $G = (V, E)$, where V is a set of elements called vertices and E an unordered set of pairs of vertices called edges. An edge e is denoted as uv where u and v are vertices. As we know $|A|$ is used to denote the cardinality of a set A. The degree of a v vertex in a graph G is the number of edges of G incident at v. Also the maximum degree of the vertices of G is denoted by $\Delta(G)$. In other hand a graph is connected if for every partition of its set of vertices into two non-empty sets X and Y, there is at least one edge with an end in X and another end in Y. Additionally a graph G', whose set of vertices and edges build a subset of vertices and edges of a given graph G, is called a subgraph of G. An abstract graph represents a class of isomorphic graphs.

Let G be a graph and v, w vertices of G, a path from v to w, denoted by $path(v, w)$, is a sequence of edges: $v_0 v_1, v_1 v_2, \ldots, v_{(n-1)}, v_n$ such that $v = v_0$, $v_n = w$ and v_k is adjacent to $v_{(k+1)}$, for $0 \leq k \leq n$. The length of the path is n. In other way, a simple path is a path where $v_0, v_1, \ldots, v_{(n-1)}, v_n$ are all different. A cycle is a nonempty path such that the first and last vertex are identical, and a simple cycle is a cycle in which there is no repeated vertex, except for the first and last. P_n and C_n denote a path and a simple loop respectively, where n denotes the number of vertices.

Dijkstra's algorithm called minimum paths algorithm determines the shortest path given a starting vertex to the rest of the vertices of a given graph [7], the complexity of this algorithm is $O(n^2)$. In the Algorithm 1 we present the pseudo-code of the procedure of E. Dijkstra (1959) to find the shortest path between a pair of vertices.

In other hand, a spanning tree of a connected graph of n vertices is a subset of $n - 1$ edges that forms a tree. Given a graph $G = (V, E)$, let T_G be one of its spanning trees. The edges in T_G are called tree edges, while the edges $E(G) \setminus E(T_G)$ are called fronds. Let $e \in E(G) \setminus E(T_G)$ be a frond edge, the union of the path in T_G between the end points of e with the same edge e form a simple cycle, such a cycle it is called the fundamental of G with respect to T_G. Each frond $e = vw$ fulfills the maximum path contained in the fundamental cycle of which it is part. The set of fundamental cycles of G will be denoted by C. Let L be a countable set of labels. A labeled graph is a (G, γ) pair where γ is a function that maps $V(G)$ to the set L. A labeled graph can also be defined by a triplet $G = (V, E, \gamma)$ and its labeling function is denoted by $\gamma(G)$. We can say that G is D -labelled if D is finite and $\gamma(G) \subseteq D$.

We now introduce the notion of cwd (cwd, for short). Let $\mathscr{C}$ be a countable set of labels. A *labeled* graph is a pair (G, γ) where γ maps each element of $V(G)$

Algorithm 1. Dijkstra. Procedure that calculates the shortest path between two vertices given a graph G and two origin and destination vertices.

1: **procedure** SHORTEST PATH
2: **let** (v_{ini} an origin vertex and v_{fin} a destination vertex of G)
3: Assign each vertex of $V(G)$ a distance value, zero to the vertices between which the path is sought and infinity to the remaining vertices.
4: The source vertex v_{ini} is identified as the current vertex and the other $v_i \in V(G)$ as unvisited vertices.
5: A set of unvisited vertices is created denoted by B
6: **while** $v_{fin} \in B$ **do**
7:     For the current vertex its neighbors are considered and the different routes are saved as P^i.
8:     The vertices used are removed from the set B of unvisited vertices.
9: **end while**
10: **return** The shortest path P^i with v_{ini} and v_{fin} as endpoints

---

into $\mathscr{C}$. A labeled graph can also be defined as a triple $G = (V(G), E(G), \gamma(G))$ and its labeling function is denoted by $\gamma(G)$. We say that G is C-labeled if C is finite and $\gamma(G)(V) \subseteq C$. We denote by $\mathscr{G}(C)$ the set of undirected C-labeled graphs. A vertex with label a will be called an a-port.

We introduce the following symbols:

- a nullary symbol $a(v)$ for every $a \in \mathscr{C}$ and $v \in V$;
- a unary symbol $\rho_{a \to b}$ for all $a, b \in \mathscr{C}$, with $a \neq b$;
- a unary symbol $\eta_{a,b}$ for all $a, b \in \mathscr{C}$, with $a \neq b$;
- a binary symbol $\oplus$.

These symbols are used to denote operations on graphs as follows: $a(v)$ creates a vertex with label a corresponding to the vertex v, $\rho_{a \to b}$ renames the vertex a by b, $\eta_{a,b}$ creates an edge between a and b, and $\oplus$ is a disjoint union of graphs.

For $C \subseteq \mathscr{C}$ we denote by $T(C)$ the set of finite well-formed terms written with the symbols $\oplus, a, \rho_{a \to b}, \eta_{a,b}$ for all $a, b \in C$, where $a \neq b$. Each term in $T(C)$ denotes a set of labeled undirected graphs. Since any two graphs denoted by the same term t are isomorphic, one can also consider that t defines a unique abstract graph.

The following definitions are given by induction on the structure of t. We let $val(t)$ be the set of graphs denoted by t.

If $t \in T(C)$ we have the following cases:

1. $t = a \in C$: $val(t)$ is the set of graphs with a single vertex labeled by a;
2. $t = t_1 \oplus t_2$: $val(t)$ is the set of graphs $G = G_1 \cup G_2$ where G_1 and G_2 are disjoint and $G_1 \in val(t_1)$, $G_2 \in val(t_2)$;
3. $t = \rho_{a \to b}(t')$: $val(t) = \{\rho_{a \to b}(G) | G \in val(t')\}$ where for every graph G in $val(t')$, the graph $\rho_{a \to b}(G)$ is obtained by replacing every vertex label a by b in G;
4. $t = \eta_{a,b}(t')$: $val(t) = \{\eta_{a,b}(G) | G \in val(t')\}$ where for every undirected labeled graph $G = (V, E, \gamma)$ in $val(t')$, we let $\eta_{a,b}(G) = (V, E', \gamma)$ such that

$E' = E \cup \{\{x,y\}|x,y \in V, x \neq y, \gamma(x) = a, \gamma(y) = b\}$, e.g. $\eta_{a,b}(G)$ adds an edge between each pair of vertices a and b in G.

For every labeled graph G we let:

$cwd(G) = min\{|C| \| G \in val(t), t \in T(C)\}$.

A term $t \in T(C)$ such that $|C| = cwd(G)$ and $G = val(t)$ is called optimal *expression* of G [11] and written as $|C|$-expression.

In other words, the cwd of a graph G is the minimum number of different labels needed to construct a vertex-labeled graph isomorphic to G using the four mentioned operations.

As an example we show the computing of cwd for a simple graph Fig. 1 that consists of a cycle of size 4. Firstable in Fig. 2 shows the creation of vertices 3 and 2 of the original graph by the expression $a(3) \oplus a(2)$, next in Fig. 3 the labels $b(1)$ and $b(4)$ are created. Then, in Fig. 4 the disjoint union of the vertices created in steps 1 and 2 is made using the expression $(b(1) \oplus b(4)) \oplus (a(3) \oplus a(2))$. Finally, in Fig. 5 the edges between the labeled vertices are created, resulting in an abstract graph isomorphic to the original by the expression $\eta_{(a,b)}((b(1) \oplus b(4)) \oplus (a(3) \oplus a(2)))$.

As we can see, 2 labels were used to build the cycle of size 4. It is obvious that a single label cannot be used to build the cycle of 4, since edges cannot be created between the same vertices. Therefore, the cwd of a cycle with size 4 is 2.

3   Shortest Path Procedure

In this section we show a procedure based on shortest paths, which allows, throughout the construction, to use a smaller number of labels, thus optimizing the cwd computation.

Let $G = (V,E)$ be a simple graph and $\mathcal{C}$ be the set of fundamental cycles of G. If $C_i, C_j \in \mathcal{C}$ and $E(C_i) \cap E(C_j) \neq 0$ then $C_i \triangle C_j = (E(C_i) \cup E(C_j)) - (E(C_i) \cap E(C_j))$ forms a compound loop, where $\triangle$ denotes the symmetric difference operation between the set of edges in both loops.

Let $G = (V,E)$ be a simple graph and C_1 the smallest fundamental cycle, the result of the decomposition of the graph by a spanning tree and its co-tree.

Looking to find an optimal way to construct a graph from the minimum, element of G, i.e. the smallest fundamental cycle, we have proposed the following inductive construction of subgraphs representing together G:

$G'_1 = C_1$.

$G'_n = G'_{(n-1)} \cup min\{Dijkstra((V(G), E(G) \setminus \bigcup_{i=1}^{n-1} E(G'_i)), v_i, v_j)|v_i, v_j \in G'_{n-1}, v_i \neq v_j\}$.

Each graph G'_i is induced from the original graph and is contained as shown by the proposition 1.

Proposition 1. $G'_1 \subset G'_2 \ldots \subset G'_n = G$.

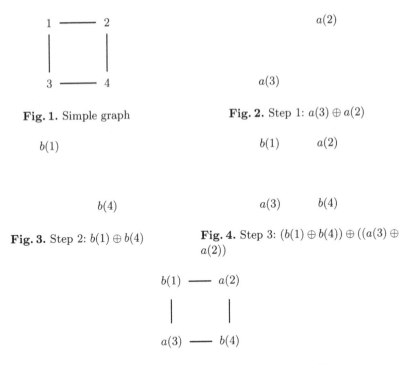

Fig. 1. Simple graph

Fig. 2. Step 1: $a(3) \oplus a(2)$

Fig. 3. Step 2: $b(1) \oplus b(4)$

Fig. 4. Step 3: $(b(1) \oplus b(4)) \oplus ((a(3) \oplus a(2))$

Fig. 5. Step 4: $(\eta_{a,b}(b(1) \oplus b(4)) \oplus ((a(3) \oplus a(2)))$

Proof. $V(G'_i) \subseteq V(G'_{i+1})$ y $E(G'_i) \subseteq E(G'_{i+1}), \forall i, 1 \le i < n.$ □

Now, to simplify the notation we use:

$$P^i_{v_{ini}, v_{fin}} = min\{Dijkstra((V(G), E(G) \bigcup_{i=1}^{n-1} E(G'_i)), v_i, v_j) | v_i, v_j \in G'_{n-1}, v_i \ne v_j\}$$

where v_{ini}, v_{fin} are the initial and final vertex respectively of the shortest path found by Dijkstra's method. Therefore, we can establish the following theorem.

Theorem 1. *Let G a simple graph, and $G'_1 \subset G'_2 \ldots \subset G'_n = G$, we can build each $k_{G'_n}{}^n_1$-expression to calculate the cwd(G), inductively represented by:*
$$G'_1 = C_1.$$
$$G'_n = G'_{n-1} \cup P^{n-1}_{v_{ini}, v_{fin}}.$$

Proof. The proof will be carried out detailing the procedure:

Let L be a set of labels. We construct the k-expression of each induced subgraph G'_i as follows:

- For all $v_i \in G'_1$, take a new $a_i \in L$ and create $a_i(v_i)$.
- The k-expression of the graph G'_1 is: $k(G'_1) = \eta_{a_1, a_l}(\eta_{a_{i-1}, a_i}(a_1(v_1) \oplus \ldots \oplus a_l(v_l))$ where $l = |V(G'_1)|, 1 < i \le l.$

- Let $K = \{a_i | 1 \le i \le l\}$, that is, the labels that have been used to construct the k-expression of the graph G'_{j-1}. The set of labels that can be reused in the construction of the $k_{G'_j}$-expression starting from the expression $k_{G'_{j-1}}$ are defined as:

$$R = \{a_i \in K | a_i(v_k) \in k_{G'_{j-1}}, \delta(v_k) \in G \setminus E(G'_{j-1}) = 0\}.$$

- Let $a_s \in R$ the label that will be used to rename all other R in the G'_{j-1} graph. The resulting expression after relabeling is: $\rho_{a_t \to a_s}(k_{G'_{j-1}}) \forall a_t \in R, a_t \ne a_s$.
- For each $v \in P^{n-1}_{v_{ini}, v_{fin}}, v \ne v_{ini} \ne v_{fin}$, take a $a_i \in R$ with $a_i \ne a_s$ if exists, if not, take a new $a_i \in L$ and create $a_i(v_i)$.
- As $P^{j-1}_{v_{ini}, v_{fin}} \setminus \{v_{ini}, v_{fin}\}$ is a path that can be associated with each vertex, considering its adjacency, an index of the sequence $\{1, \cdots, r\}$ where r is the number of vertices of the path. With this arrangement create the k-expression: $k_{P^{j-1}} = \eta_{a_{i-1}, a_i}(a_1(v_1) \oplus \cdots \oplus a_r(v_r))$ where $1 < i \le r$.
- Thus $k_{G'_j} = \eta_{a_r, v_{fin}}(\eta_{a_1, v_{ini}}(k_{G'_{j-1}} \oplus k_{P^{j-1}}))$, where $a_1, a_r \in P^{j-1}$ are the two labeled vertices of the ends of P^{j-1}. □

Now for a better understanding, we present the algorithm 2 that constructs the k-expression given a simple graph. As input, the algorithm receives a graph and its decomposition into fundamental cycles. It starts using the smallest size cycle and calculating its k-expression, later the vertices already used in the construction are stored in the set A, using these vertices the shortest path between them is searched, when finding it, compute its k-expression and add the vertices of the path to the set A. This method is repeated until the original graph is built, creating edges between already labeled vertices and releasing labels already covered.

Each step of the 2 algorithm is described as follows. From lines 1 to 2 the algorithm starts with G as input and C_1 is the smallest fundamental cycle of G. In line 3 each vertex of C_1 is added to the set of vertices A. In line 4 the vertices involved in the cycle C_1 are deleted from the original graph G. In line 5 we begin to build the k-expression using different labels for each vertex in C_1. From lines 6 to 23 we have the main procedure as long as the number of edges in the resulting G is different from 0. In this procedure, in line 7, the shortest path P is found between each vertex of A on the G graph using the well known Dijkstra algorithm, if you have more than one path with the same cardinality then you can choose the last one found. In line 8 the new k-expression of the path P from step 7 is constructed, at this moment we already have the first and last label of P since it is an element of A, each vertex between the first and last on the way must be different. In line 9 the edges involved in the path P mentioned above are deleted from the current G. In line 10 each vertex of the path P found (except the extremes) is added to A.

Now the following condition allows to release labels to be able to reuse them, from 11 to 14 it is compared if the degree of each vertex in A is 0, if it is true, the corresponding labels are released and the vertex of the A set is deleted since has been covered in its entirety. The above is useful to do less operations. The next condition from 15 to 22 is to verify if the elements of A are connected in the current G, if so, an edge is created using the η operation, which will join the different k-expressions that have already been built. After that, on line 17 the edges found in the last step of the current G are deleted. Finally the same condition is repeated from 18 to 21 as it was done in lines 11 to 14. The *while* instructions will be repeated until all edges are deleted from the graph G.

Furthermore, the complexity of the method presented in this paper is given by two main methods, the first is the well-known Dijkstra Algorithm for simple graphs which is of order $O(n^2)$. In other hand, the proposed method is in the worst case $O(n-3)$, removing the first minimum cycle of size 3. Therefore, the complexity of these methods is $O(n^3)$.

4   Example

This section shows how our algorithm works when considering the 8-cubic graph, which is illustrated in Fig. 6 also called a trivalent graph whose vertices have degree 3. This graph contains 8 vertices and 12 edges. In Fig. 7 we start with the cycle $C_1 = [4, 6, 5]$ so 3 labels are used and the set $A = \{4, 6, 5\}$. In Fig. 8 the computing of the shortest path is shown with the following steps: the shortest

---

Algorithm 2. Procedure that calculates a k-expression (G) when G is decomposed into fundamental cycles.

1: **procedure** k-EXPRESSION(G)
2: **let** $(C_i$ a subgraph of G which is the smallest fundamental cycle of $G)$
3:    3. Add each vertex of $V[C_i]$ in A
4:    Delete the edges $E[C_i]$ from G
5:    Build the $k-expression$ of C_i
6: **while** $|E[G]| \neq 0$ **do**
7:      Find the shortest path P using Dijkstra's algorithm between each vertex of A in the graph G {If you have more than one path of the same size, the last one found is taken}
8:      Build the $k-expression$ of P
9:      Delete from G the edges of P
10:     Add to each vertex of $V[P]$ in A
11:     **if** For each $a_i \in A$, the degree of a_i in G is 0 **then**
12:        Free a label
13:        Delete vertex a_i of A
14:     **end if**
15:     **if** the actual elements of A are connected in G **then**
16:        Build the k-expression using η operator
17:        Delete the previous created edges from G
18:        **if** for each $a_i \in A$, the degree of a_i in G is 0 **then**
19:           Free the label
20:           Delete the vertex a_i of A
21:        **end if**
22:     **end if**
23: **end while**

path between the vertices of A is calculated, the resulting path is $P = [5, 1, 7, 6]$ and 2 more labels are used, as a result $A = \{4, 5, 6, 1, 7\}$, now 2 labels can be released, the ones corresponding to vertex 6 and 5, one of them will be left as a residual label for the entire graph and we have a free one, as a result $A = \{4, 1, 7\}$, 5 labels have been used and 1 remains free to use. Later in Fig. 9 the following algorithm computing is shown, the shortest path is found $P = [7, 8, 2, 1]$, the free label is used and a new one, and the vertices are added to the set A, so far $A = \{4, 1, 7, 8, 2\}$, at this moment labels 7 and 1 can be released, so there are 2 free labels left and the set would be $A = \{4, 8, 2\}$. In Fig. 10 the following path found is shown $P = [8, 3, 2]$, one of the two available labels is used and the set is as follows: $A = \{4, 8, 2, 3\}$, labels 8 and 2 can be released, the resulting set would be: $A = \{4, 3\}$. Finally, in Fig. 11 an edge is created between 4 and 3, to later release these two vertices leaving the set as $A = \{\}$, ending the algorithm and resulting in the $cwd\,(8\;cubic\;graph\;2) \le 6$.

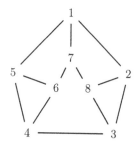

Fig. 6. *8 cubic graph 2*

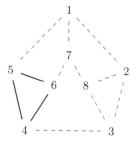

Fig. 7. $C_1 = [4, 6, 5]$

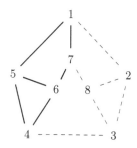

Fig. 8. $P = [5, 1, 7, 6]$

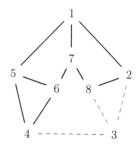

Fig. 9. $P = [7, 8, 2, 1]$

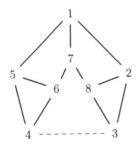
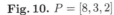

Fig. 10. $P = [8, 3, 2]$

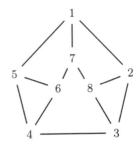

Fig. 11. $\eta_{(4,3)}$

5 Conclusions

This article presents a proposal to approximate the *cwd* of simple graphs. The proposed algorithm is based on the classic Dijkstra algorithm together with the calculation of the shortest paths of induced graphs. To get a conclusion about the efficiency of our algorithm, the results reported by Heule [10] were considered and compared with those generated by our proposal. In Table 1, is shown the name of the graph with its number of vertices and edges, followed by the exact result of Heule et al. and the result of our proposal.

On the other hand, the error between an exact method and an approximation method is given by an equation in [3] as follows: $|A(G) - cwd(G)| \leq n^\epsilon$, where $A(G)$ is the result of the *cwd* using an approximation algorithm (which is our case), the $cwd(G)$ is the exact result, n is the number of vertices and finally ϵ is

Table 1. Comparison between approach algorithm and exact CWD

Graph	$|V|$	$|E|$	Heule	Our proposal	Error
Brinkmann	21	42	10	10	0%
Desargues	20	30	8	10	23.13%
Dodecahedron	20	30	8	8	0%
Errera	17	45	8	8	0%
Frutch	12	18	5	7	27.8%
Kittell	23	63	8	9	≈0%
McGee	24	36	8	10	21.8%
Paley13	13	39	9	10	≈0%
Pappus	18	27	8	9	≈0%
Petersen	10	15	5	7	30.1%
Poussin	15	39	7	8	≈0%
Robertson	19	38	9	10	≈0%
Shirkhande	16	48	9	11	25%

the error, clearing ϵ gives the error of the last column. As can be seen in Table 1, in 8 of the 13 cases the cwd with an $\approx 0\%$ of error was obtained, having in the worst case an error of 30.1% and in the average case an error of 9.8%.

The advantage of this algorithm is that its execution time is polynomial so the approximation has a complexity of the order $O(n^3)$ where n is the number of vertices of the input graph.

References

1. Downey, R.G., Fellows, M.R.: Parameterized Complexity. Monographs in Computer Science. Springer, NewYork (1999)
2. Courcelle, B., Engelfriet, J., Rozenberg, G.: Handle-rewriting hypergraph grammars. J. Comput. Sys. Sci. **46**(2), 218–270 (1993)
3. Fellows, M.R., Rosamond, F.A., Rotics, U., Szeider, S.: Clique-width is np-complete. SIAM J. Discrete Mathe. **23**(2), 909–939 (2009)
4. Golumbic, M.C., Rotics, U.: Graph-theoretic concepts in computer science. In: 25th Proceedings of the International Workshop on Clique-Width of Perfect Graph Classes (WG1999) Ascona, Switzerland, June 17–19, 1999, pp. 135–147. Springer, Berlin (1999). https://doi.org/10.1007/978-3-642-11409-0
5. Langer, Alexander, Reidl, Felix, Rossmanith, Peter, Sikdar, Somnath: Practical algorithms for MSO model-checking on tree-decomposable graphs. Comput. Sci. Rev. **1314**, 39–74 (2014)
6. Derek, G. Corneil, M.H., Lanlignel, J.-M., Reed, B., Rotics, U.: Polynomial-time recognition of clique-width ≤ 3 graphs. Discrete Appl. Math. **160**(6), 834–865 (2012)
7. Bondy, J.-A., Murty, U.S.R.: Graph Theory. Graduate Texts in Mathematics. Springer, New York, London (2007)
8. Leonardo González-Ruiz, J., Raymundo Marcial-Romero, J., Hernández-Servín, J.A..: Computing the clique-width of cactus graphs. Electronic Notes in Theoretical Computer Science. In: Tenth Latin American Workshop on Logic/Languages, Algorithms and New Methods of Reasoning (LANMR), vol. 8, pp. 47–57 (2016)
9. Leonardo González-Ruiz, J., Raymundo Marcial-Romero, J., Hernández, J.A., De Ita. C.: Computing the clique-width of polygonal tree graphs. In: Pichardo-Lagunas, O., Miranda-Jiménez, S. (eds.) Advances in Soft Computing, pp. 449–459, Springer International Publishing, Cham (2017)
10. Marijn, J., Heule, H., Szeider, S.: A SAT Approach to clique-width. In: ACM Transactions on Computational Logic pp. 318–334. Springer, Berlin (2013)
11. Courcelle, B., Olariu, S.: Upper bounds to the clique width of graphs. Discrete Appl. Math. **101**, 77–114 (2000)

Nonlinear Control of a Two-Wheeled Self-balancing Autonomous Mobile Robot

J. Díaz-Téllez[✉], V. Gutierrez-Vicente, J. Estevez-Carreon,
O. D. Ramírez-Cárdenas, and R. S. García-Ramirez

Departamento de Ingeniería Eléctrica y Electrónica, Tecnológico Nacional de
México/Instituto Tecnológico de Puebla, Av. del Tecnológico #420. Col. Maravillas,
Puebla, Puebla, Mexico
juan.diaz@puebla.tecnm.mx

Abstract. This paper presents the non-linear control of an inverted pendulum type two-wheel self-balancing robot. Unlike most of the works in the literature, we propose a robust orientation control without resorting to linearizations around the equilibrium points or assumptions of small angles. The control algorithm has the property of being lightweight for possible implementation in embedded systems with low processing power. To validate the design of the control law, three parameters have been taken into account: settlement time, angles away from equilibrium position and ability to reject external disturbances.

1 Introduction

In recent years, autonomous mobile robots have experienced tremendous growth both in the academic and industrial spheres. This rapid growth is largely due to the development of small-scale embedded systems, microelectromechanical MEMS sensor systems, real-time-based operating systems, and high-energy storage devices. To a large extent, the use of autonomous mobile robots in the industrial area is what has prompted the design of new robots for different tasks. For example, exploration of remote areas, lifting objects, moving units of loads, identification, selection and packaging of merchandise to name a few. Advantages such as precision, speed, load capacity, route scheduling flexibility, connectivity, repeatability and autonomy make this type of robot enter the industrial sector more and more every day. The simplest case of mobile robots are the wheeled robots. Wheeled robots comprise one or more driven wheels and have optional passive or caster wheels and possibly steered wheels. The arrangement of the driven, passive and steered wheels give different configurations of land mobile robots. The Fig. 1 show the most commonly configurations used, nevertheless the list is not exhaustive, synchro-drive, omni-directional, balancing mobile, driving robot, inverted pendulum type robots, etc.

Today, self-balancing robots have gained popularity with the introduction of the Segway commercial vehicle. These robots have the ability to balance on their two wheels making for excellent personal electric transport. Due to their great

© Springer Nature Switzerland AG 2021
I. Batyrshin et al. (Eds.): MICAI 2021, LNAI 13068, pp. 348–359, 2021.
https://doi.org/10.1007/978-3-030-89820-5_28

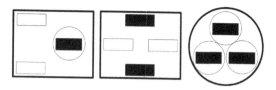

Fig. 1. Commonly wheeled robot configuration.

maneuverability, these robots allow to transport people in short distances with a moderate speed, navigate through confined spaces indoors and outdoors, contain two independently driven motors, to allow balance, as well as driving in a straight line, turning on their axis y in tight curves, in addition to crossing small slopes. This type of self-balancing robot can be classified as inverted pendulum-type robots, which are highly non-linear, under-actuated and with holonomic constraints. So it makes the design of control algorithms a great challenge. Most of the works reported in the literature are based on the design of controls which are derived from the linearization of the model around its equilibrium points, furthermore they are only reasonable under the assumption of small angles. For example, Proportional-Derivative controller in [1]. Proportional-Integral-Derivative (PID) in [2] where ensures almost global locally exponential stability of the upright motion of the two-wheeled self-balancing robot. Similarly in [3] a PID is propoded to regulate the robot's orientation. In [4] the PID is designed for path tracking. Another widely used control strategy is Quadratic linear regulator LQR [5]. In this approach the mathematical model is linearized to its equilibrium point, the gains are found by minimizing a cost function [6]. In [7], the LQR control algorithm is implemented in an embedded system based on FPGA, indoor tests show the effectiveness of the control. The work is extended to follow the trajectory parameterized by waypoint in [8]. A robust control against external disturbances is presented in [9]. Lyapunov-based control are covered in [10] and [11]. Learning approaches are proposed in [12–14]. Recently in [15,16] the system is linearized around its equilibrium point based on the property of differential flatness. Once the flat output of the system has been calculated, an active disturbance rejection control is used. In [17] a simulate approach is used, in addition, a distributed control with communication activated by events is proposed to solve the leader-follower consensus problem. However, in most of the works cited above they do not present a robustness analysis of the control algorithm, they present high oscillations and error in steady state. This type of linear controls (LTI) is limited to a small region of the state space, in such a way that initial conditions far from the equilibrium position, external disturbances or parametric uncertainties can unstable the system. This work focuses on the design of a light, efficient and robust non-linear control against external disturbances to stabilize the orientation of the robot, that is, to keep the inverted pendulum vertical. The present work is structured as follows. Section 2 presents some mathematical preliminaries used throughout the document, as well as the mathematical model of the two-wheeled self-balancing robot. Section 3 presents the mechanical and electronic design of the low-cost mobile robot. In Sect. 4 the design of the control law based on the exact linearization of the non-linear system is presented. Section 5 presents the results obtained in simulation under three scenarios, conditions far from the equilibrium position, regulation and rejection of external disturbances. In this last scenario it is compared with a PD control. Some conclusions and future work are presented in Sect. 6.

2   Two-Wheeled Self-balancing System Model

The mathematical model of the two-wheeled self-balancing mobile robot presented in this work is based on the inverted pendulum principle. Inverted pendulum dynamics has been the basis for bipedal robots, mobile robots, and attitude control on small satellites.

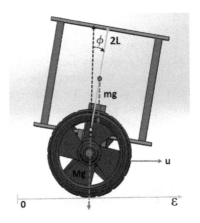

Fig. 2. Two-wheeled self-balancing.

The basic movements of the robot, driving forward-backward movement, and rotate on its own axis. The forward-backward movement is achieved when the speed of both motors are increased or decreased by the same amount. The rotate on its own axis is achieved when the speed of both motors are increased in the opposite direction. The system model is inspired by the work of [18,19]. For the mathematical control model, some restrictions have been considered:

- The center of gravity of the bar is at its geometric center.
- The coefficients of friction of the rotary movement of the pendulum and the linear movement of the base are negligible.
- The wind force is also neglected.

Selecting the following variables (ξ, ϕ) and using the Euler-Lagrange formalism, the dynamics that describe the physics of the vehicle is obtained.

$$\begin{bmatrix} ml\cos\phi - (J + ml^2) \\ M + m \quad ml\cos\phi \end{bmatrix} \begin{bmatrix} \ddot{\xi} \\ \ddot{\phi} \end{bmatrix} = \begin{bmatrix} mlg\sin\phi \\ ml\dot{\phi}^2\sin\phi + u \end{bmatrix} \tag{1}$$

where ξ represents the robot's displacement from a fixed point, ϕ represents the angular displacement of the bar. The input u represents the input torque with which the system is pushed, mainly due to the DC motors. The constants J is the moment of inertia with respect to the center of gravity of the pendulum, l represents the length of the bar to the center of mass, M is the mass of the base of the robot, m is the mass of the bar and the human, and g represents gravity, see the Fig. 2. The Eq. 1 can be represented with respect to the higher-order derivatives as shown below:

$$\ddot{\xi} = \frac{(m^2 l^2 g \sin 2\phi)/2 - (J + ml^2)(ml \sin \phi)\dot{\phi}^2 - (J + ml^2)u}{\Delta} \tag{2}$$

$$\ddot{\phi} = \frac{-(M+m)(mlg \sin \phi) + (m^2 l^2 \dot{\phi}^2 \sin 2\phi)/2 + (ml \cos \phi)u}{\Delta} \tag{3}$$

From Eqs. 2 and 3 we can decouple the system of rotation of the bar from the system of translation of the robot. In such a way that we can address the problem of stabilizing only the angular position of the bar. Defining the following state variables $x_1 = \phi$, and $x_2 = \dot{\phi}$, the Eqs. 4 and 5 are defined,

$$\dot{x}_1 = x_2 \tag{4}$$

$$\dot{x}_2 = \frac{-g \sin x_1 + amlx_2^2 \sin 2x_1/2 + a \cos x_1 u}{aml \cos^2 x_1 - 4l/3} \tag{5}$$

where $a = 1/(M+m)$.

Since the input torque u is provided by the DC direct current motors, the dynamics of DC motors are taken into account. Performing a mesh analysis to the electrical system and using Newton's second law to the mechanical system of the DC motors, the following second-order transfer function is obtained that relates the angular velocity with the input voltage to the motor:

$$\frac{\omega(s)}{v(s)} = \frac{K_m}{LIs^2 + (RI + LB)s + RB + K_m K_a} \tag{6}$$

where I represents the rotor's moment of inertia, R the electrical resistance, L the electrical inductance, B represents the motor's viscous friction constant, K_a represents the electromotive force constant, K_m represents the motor torque constant.

Mechanical and Electronic Design

To test the proposed control algorithm, a low-cost prototype has been designed which consists of four elements: the mechanical structure, the embedded system, the power stage and the actuation. The Fig. 3 shows the low-cost prototype of the mini mobile robot.

The structure of the mobile mini robot consists of a 3 mm caliber acrylic with the following dimensions: 15.5 cm × 6 cm × 10 cm. The actuation system is made up of two 5V permanent magnet direct current motors. The power system

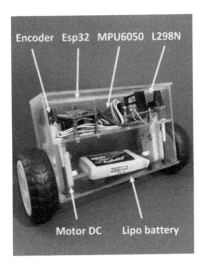

Fig. 3. Low-cost prototype of the mini inverted pendulum robot.

has a 1000 mah 2 s Zippy Lipo Battery and a L298N H-bridge as the power stage. The embedded system is composed of an MPU-6050 inertial unit, a 32 bit dual core ESP32 microcontroller DEVKIT V1 model, with a 240 MHz clock frequency and 16 independent channels to generate PWM signals with a 16 bit resolutions. This chip contains wireless communication modules such as WiFi and Bluethooth.

4 Nonlinear Control Algorithm

The main objective of this work is to design a non-linear control that stabilizes the orientation of the robot subject to external disturbances and conditions far from the equilibrium point without falling into instability. The control objective is to stabilize at the desired reference ϕ_δ with a angular velocity $\dot{\phi}$ equal to zero expressed mathematically:

$$\phi(t) \to \phi_\delta, \ \dot{\phi}(t) \to \mathbf{0}, \ \text{according} \quad t \to \infty. \tag{7}$$

The Fig. 4 shows the proposed control algorithm for the mobile robot. The system is made up of three blocks, the non-linear control, the allocated control and a PID control for each DC motor. First, the data given by the MPU6050 IMU (gyroscope and accelerometer) are processed through a kalman filter to obtain the Euler angles. Both the angular velocity $\dot{\phi}(t)$ and the angular position $\phi(t)$ of the bar are feedback to the non-linear control block. Subsequently, the allocation control block calculates the angular speeds for both motors ($\omega_{L\delta}$, $\omega_{L\delta}$). Finally, a PID control for a rapid stabilization of the angular speed of DC motors. The PID output is parameterized by a PWM pulse width signal ($\sigma_{L\delta}, \sigma_{L\delta}$).

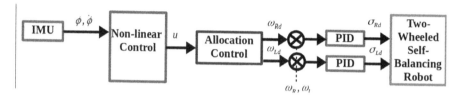

Fig. 4. Block diagram of the two-wheeled self-balancing robot control system.

Consider the mathematical model of the mobile robot, see Eqs. 4 and 5, then defining a transformation of the control coordinate u in a new input γ. By means of this new transformation it is possible to eliminate the non-linearities present in the system. Let's define the auxiliary input γ as:

$$\gamma = \frac{-g \sin x_1 + aml x_2^2 \sin 2x_1/2 + a \cos x_1 u}{aml \cos^2 x_1 - 4l/3} \tag{8}$$

With this new transformation, the system has been reduced to two integrators in cascade, that is, it is in the canonical form of Brunovsky. In this way, the auxiliary variable γ can be synthesized with the following Hurwitz polynomial:

$$\gamma = -2\zeta \omega_n x_2 - \omega_n^2 (x_1 - X_d) \tag{9}$$

where ω_n represents the natural frequency and ζ represents the damping factor. The original control u is obtained from (8, 9).

$$u = \frac{1}{a \cos x_1} \left[\gamma \left(aml \cos^2 x_1 - 4l/3 \right) + g \sin x_1 - aml x_2^2 \sin 2x_1/2 \right] \tag{10}$$

The control law is defined locally, the lack of definition of the control action is found in the following singularities: $\frac{\pi}{2} + k\pi$ where k is any integer.

Efficient DC motor speed control is required for the two-wheeled self-balancing robot. A quick and smooth response will produce high performance in position and orientation control. Defining the angular speed of the DC motor as ω and using the Eq. 6 that describes the dynamics of the DC motor, a PID control is proposed to stabilize at the desired angular speed. The control objective is to design each motor a PWM signal command, such that $lim_{t \to \infty} |\omega_\delta(t) - \omega(t)| = 0$. The angular speed of the motors ω can be obtained from the encoder. The Table 1 summarizes all the parameters found experimentally for the Rantec brand DC motor.

Substituting these values in Eq. 6 the following transfer function is obtained.

$$\frac{\omega(s)}{v(s)} = \frac{1185000}{s^2 + 2405\, s + 107700} \tag{11}$$

354   J. Díaz-Téllez et al.

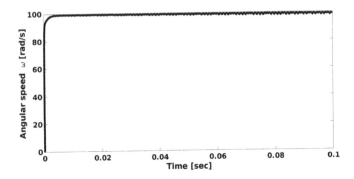

Fig. 5. Response curve of DC motor and PID control, fine tuning of gains.

Table 1. Parameters

Symbol	Description	Value	Units
I	Moment of inertia	0.000031	kg·m^2
R	Armature Resistance	0.425	Ω
L	Electrical inductance	0.00018	H
B	Viscous Friction Constant	0.00028	N·m· s
K_a	Electromotive Force Constant	0.0292	N ·m/A
K_m	Motor Torque Constant	0.0281	N ·m/A
M	Mobile robot base mass	0.48	Kg
m	Pendulum mass	0.16	Kg
l	Pendulum length	0.25	m
J	Moment of inertia of the mobile robot	0.0043	kg m^2
g	Gravity	9.81	m/s^2

So for the design of the PID controller, the Zeigler-Nichols tuning rule is applied, specifically the second method. The values obtained are $K_p = 12.7$, $T_i = 48$ and $T_d = 0.001$, Therefore the transfer function of the PID controller results as

$$PID(s) = \frac{0.61\,s^2 + 600s + 12.7}{48\,s} \qquad (12)$$

The response of the DC motor is examined together with the closed-loop PID at a desired angular velocity of 100 rad/sec is shown in the Fig. 5.

5 Simulation

As the Fig. 4 shows the system has two main sensors, an inertial measurement unit MPU-6050 and an encoder that allows estimating the angular speed of the motors ω(t). The MPU-6050 sensor estimates the angle ϕ(t) using a kalman filter, the angular velocity $\dot{\phi}$(t) is obtained from the Gyros. Angular velocity can be used to propose a position control on the x-axis. The two state variables $\phi(t)$, $\dot{\phi}(t)$ feedback to the control algorithm to calculate the force u. The control assignment block allows to convert the control signal into the required angular velocity $\omega_{L\delta}$ and $\omega_{L\delta}$ for the motors. Lastly, the PID ensures that the DC motor reaches the desired angular speed. The parameters for the simulation of the system is in Table 1.

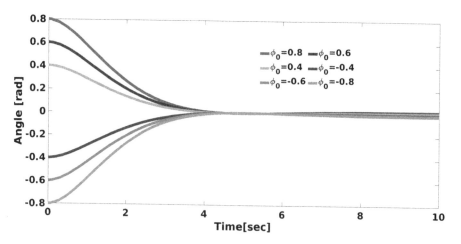

Fig. 6. First scenario, stabilization at the origin. Initial conditions far from the equilibrium position. (Angular position $\phi(t)$)

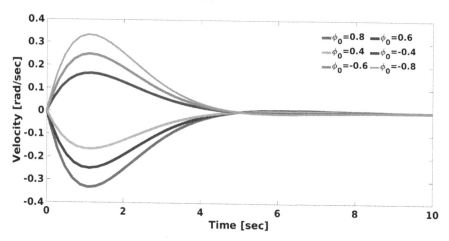

Fig. 7. First scenario, stabilization at the origin. Initial conditions far from the equilibrium position. (Angular velocity $\dot{\phi}(t)$)

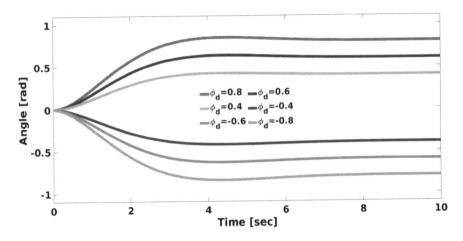

Fig. 8. Second scenario: adjustment to the desired angular position ϕ_s (Angular position $\phi(t)$). https://youtu.be/MTgbZ3cntlU

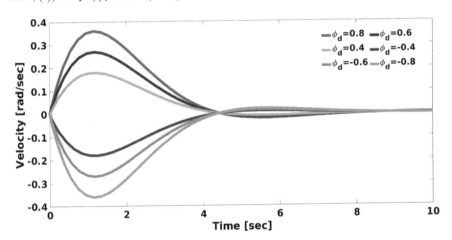

Fig. 9. Second scenario: adjustment to the desired angular position ϕ_s (Angular velocity $\dot{\phi}(t)$)

Three scenarios have been established. The first scenario is to test the ability to stabilize the system at the origin with initial conditions far from the equilibrium position. The Fig. 6 and Fig. 7 show the evolution of the state variables under the initial conditions: $0.8, 0.6, 0.4, -0.4, -0.6, -0.8$ radians. A settling time of 4 seconds is achieved. The second scenario is the regulation of the desired angular position. In the same way, desired references ϕ_d are proposed as $0.8, 0.6, 0.4, -0.4, -0.6, -0.8$ radians. The Fig. 8 and Fig. 9 show the evolution of the state variables, a settling time of 4 seconds is achieved. When tilting the bar by an angle ϕ_d, the base tries to compensate the bar to its vertical position, therefore its movement is towards forward. The reader is invited to

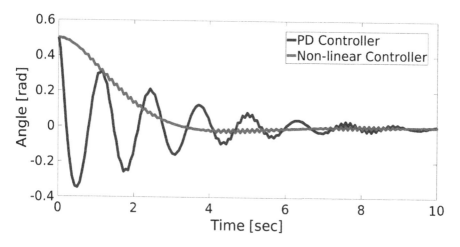

Fig. 10. Third scenario: disturbance rejection. PD vs Non-linear control (Angular position $\phi(t)$)

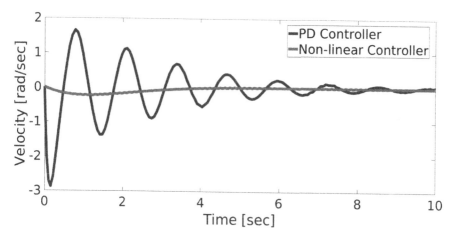

Fig. 11. Third scenario: disturbance. PD vs Non-linear control (Angular velocity $\dot{\phi}(t)$)

view a simulation of the second scenario in the following link https://youtu.be/ MTgbZ3cntlU. In the third scenario make a comparison between the proposed non-lineal controller and a PD controller. The PD design is parameterized by the Eq. 9. For the calculation of the controller gains, we use the pole placement method, a saturation has been used to avoid generating high control torques. A disturbance has been added to the model of the two-wheeled self-balancing robot. The disturbance is modeled as $0.3 \cos 50 * t * \sin t$, this disturbance represents an endogenous and exogenous disturbance, possibly due to the force of the wind, type of surface, joint friction in the actuators and mechanical transmissions. As can be seen in the Fig. 10 and Fig. 11 the proposed control is robust to disturbance and dynamics not modeled, it presents a smooth response without over-elongation with a favorable settling time and has no error in steady state contrary to PD control, where it presents a greater oscillation and produces a high angular velocity.

6   Conclusions

It should be emphasized that the proposed non-linear control algorithm shows the stabilization of the robot with angles far from the equilibrium position. It is robust against endogenous perturbations and unmodeled dynamics, presents a smooth response without over-elongation with a favorable settling time and has no error in steady state. The algorithm is relatively simple to implement in embedded systems with low computing power. The system will be implemented under the ROS midleware using the exchange of asynchronous messages through nodes.

References

1. Lin, S.C., Tsai, C.C.: Development of a self-balancing human transportation vehicle for the teaching of feedback control. IEEE Trans. Educ. **52**, 157–168 (2009)
2. Basnayake, I.D., Madhushani, T.W.U., Maithripala, D.H.S.: Intrinsic PID controller for a segway type mobile robot. In: 2017 IEEE International Conference on Industrial and Information Systems (ICIIS), pp. 1–6 (2017)
3. Ali, M.I., Hossen, M.M.: A two-wheeled self-balancing robot with dynamics model. In: 2017 4th International Conference on Advances in Electrical Engineering (ICAEE), pp. 271–275 (2017)
4. Lee, H., Lee, J.: Driving control of mobile inverted pendulum. In: 2012 9th International Conference on Ubiquitous Robots and Ambient Intelligence (URAI), pp. 449–453 (2012)
5. Shilpa, B., Indu, V., Rajasree, S.R.: Design of an underactuated self balancing robot using linear quadratic regulator and integral sliding mode controller. In: 2017 International Conference on Circuit, Power and Computing Technologies (ICCPCT), pp. 1–6 (2017)
6. Babazadeh, R., Khiabani, A.G., Azmi, H.: Optimal control of segway personal transporter. In: 2016 4th International Conference on Control, Instrumentation, and Automation (ICCIA), pp. 18–22 (2016)
7. Pinto, L.J., Kim, D.H., Lee, J.Y., Han, C.S.: Development of a segway robot for an intelligent transport system. In: 2012 IEEE/SICE International Symposium on System Integration (SII), pp. 710–715 (2012)
8. Muralidharan, V., Mahindrakar, A.D.: Position stabilization and waypoint tracking control of mobile inverted pendulum robot. IEEE Trans. Control Syst. Technol. **22**, 2360–2367 (2014)
9. Huang, J., Ri, S., Liu, L., Wang, Y., Kim, J., Pak, G.: Nonlinear disturbance observer-based dynamic surface control of mobile wheeled inverted pendulum. IEEE Trans. Control Syst. Technol. **23**, 2400–2407 (2015)
10. Uddin, N.: Lyapunov-based control system design of two-wheeled robot. In: 2017 International Conference on Computer, Control, Informatics and its Applications (IC3INA), pp. 121–125 (2017)

11. Yu, Z., Tong, T., Wong, S.F.: Experiment and controller design for two-wheeled robot with nonlinear damping and road disturbance. In: 2018 Chinese Control And Decision Conference (CCDC), pp. 1983–1987 (2018)

12. Fleischer, J., et al.: A neurally controlled robot competes and cooperates with humans in segway soccer. In: Proceedings 2006 IEEE International Conference on Robotics and Automation, ICRA 2006, pp. 3673–3678 (2006)

13. Ahmed, A.A., Saleh Alshandoli, A.: On replacing a PID controller with neural network controller for segway. In: 2020 International Conference on Electrical Engineering (ICEE), pp. 1–4 (2020)

14. Argall, B.D., Browning, B., Veloso, M.: Learning robot motion control with demonstration and advice-operators. In: 2008 IEEE/RSJ International Conference on Intelligent Robots and Systems, pp. 399–404 (2008)

15. Curiel-Olivares, G., Linares-Flores, J., Hernández-Méndez, A., Guerrero-Castellanos, J.F., Mino-Aguilar, G., García-Rodríguez, C.: Two-in-wheeled self-balancing electric vehicle based on active disturbance rejection controller. In: 2019 IEEE International Conference on Mechatronics (ICM), vol. 1, pp. 608–613 (2019)

16. Curiel-Olivares, G., Linares-Flores, J., Guerrero-Castellanos, J., Hernández-Méndez, A.: Self-balancing based on active disturbance rejection controller for the two-in-wheeled electric vehicle, experimental results. Mechatronics **76**, 102552 (2021)

17. Ramírez-Cárdenas, O., Guerrero-Castellanos, J., Linares Flores, J., Durand, S., Guerrero-Sánchez, W.: Control descentralizado basado en eventos para el consenso de múltiples robots tipo péndulo invertido en el esquema líder-seguidor. Revista Iberoamericana de Automática e Informática Industrial **16**, 435 (2019)

18. Sira-Ramirez, H., Marquez, R., Rivas, F., Santiago, O.: Control de Sistemas No Lineales: Linealización aproximada, extendida, exacta (2018)

19. Zhijun Li, C.Y., Fan, L.: Advanced Control of Wheeled Inverted Pendulum Systems (2013)

Author Index

Printed in the United States
by Baker & Taylor Publisher Services